Pastoral Reflections on Global Citizenship

Emerging Perspectives in Pastoral Theology and Care

Series Editor: Kirk Bingaman, Fordham University

The field of pastoral care and counseling, and by extension pastoral theology, is presently at a crossroads, in urgent need of redefining itself for the age of postmodernity or even post-postmodernity. While there is, to be sure, a rich historical foundation upon which the field can build, it remains for contemporary scholars, educators, and practitioners to chart new directions for the present day and age. Emerging Perspectives in Pastoral Theology and Care seeks to meet this pressing need by inviting researchers in the field to address timely issues, such as the findings of contemplative neuroscience, the impact of technology on human development and wellness, mindfulness meditation practice for reducing anxiety, trauma viewed through the lens of positive psychology and resilience theory, clergy health and wellness, postmodern and multicultural pastoral care and counseling, and issues of race and class. The series will therefore serve as an important and foundational resource for years to come, guiding scholars and educators in the field in developing more contemporary models of theory and practice.

Titles in the Series

Pastoral and Spiritual Care in a Digital Age: The Future is Now, by Kirk Bingaman
Women Leaving Prison: Justice-Seeking Spiritual Support for Female Returning Citizens, by Jill L. Snodgrass
The Chaplain's Presence and Medical Power: Rethinking Loss in the Hospital System, by Richard Coble
Neuroplasticity, Performativity, and Clergy Wellness: Neighbor Love as Self Care, by William D. Roozeboom

Pastoral Reflections on Global Citizenship

Framing the Political in Terms of Care, Faith, and Community

Ryan LaMothe

LEXINGTON BOOKS
Lanham • Boulder • New York • London

Published by Lexington Books
An imprint of The Rowman & Littlefield Publishing Group, Inc.
4501 Forbes Boulevard, Suite 200, Lanham, Maryland 20706
www.rowman.com

6th Tinworth Street, London SE11 5AL, United Kingdom

British Library Cataloguing in Publication Information Available

Library of Congress Cataloging-in-Publication Data

Names: LaMothe, Ryan, 1955- author.
Title: Pastoral reflections on global citizenship : framing the political in terms of care, faith, and community / Ryan LaMothe.
Description: Lanham : Lexington Books, 2018. | Series: Emerging perspectives in pastoral theology and care | Includes bibliographical references and index.
Identifiers: LCCN 2018040681 (print) | LCCN 2018046049 (ebook) | ISBN 9781498551373 (electronic) | ISBN 9781498551366 (cloth : alk. paper)
Subjects: LCSH: Pastoral theology. | Pastoral care. | Christianity and politics. | Church and the world. | Citizenship—Religious aspects—Christianity.
Classification: LCC BV4011.3 (ebook) | LCC BV4011.3 .L36 2018 (print) | DDC 261.7—dc23
LC record available at https://lccn.loc.gov/2018040681

♾️ ™ The paper used in this publication meets the minimum requirements of American National Standard for Information Sciences—Permanence of Paper for Printed Library Materials, ANSI/NISO Z39.48-1992.

Printed in the United States of America

To Cyn
and
To all those whose spirits of love and
hope for a better world resist and defy the
darkness of powers and principalities

Contents

Acknowledgments

Research and writing are often solitary activities, though I have learned over the years that there are surprising intellectual and social benefits. I have worked with inspiring people, learned from brilliant interlocutors, corresponded with creative thinkers, and had serendipitous encounters with scholars who became friends. Two years ago, Dr. Kirk Bingham unexpectedly reached out and asked if I would be interested in writing about pastoral theology and politics for Lexington Press. This led to meeting Sarah Craig who, at that time, was an editor for Lexington Press. I deeply appreciated Kirk's invitation and Sarah's support during the process of writing this book. When Sarah moved on for other opportunities in the publishing world, she handed me off to the capable hands of Dr. Judith Lakamper, whose expertise and grace completed the journey toward publication. To Kirk, Sarah, and Judith my deepest appreciation.

I also wish to recognize the scholars who participate in New Directions of Pastoral Theology. Princeton Seminary professors Donald Capps and Robert Dykstra started this group. After Don's tragic death a few years ago, Bob Dykstra insured the group would continue. Over the years this group has been a forum for testing out innovative ideas and exploring different paths. Better, it has been a place for finding new friends. Special thank you to Bob Dykstra and Nathan Carlin for your friendship and support over the years. Another group I have benefited from is the Society for Pastoral Theology's Postcolonial Study Group. I wish to thank Dr. Bruce Rogers Vaughn who has participated in this study group and from whom I have learned a great deal. Every conversation with him, I go away enriched. It is important to thank Saint Meinrad Seminary and School of Theology for providing sabbaticals and grant money. Their generosity is central to having time and support for research and writing. Special thanks to Mary Jeanne Schumacher and Rev. Cindy Geisen for their editorial acumen. They read various drafts of all the chapters with graceful criticism and affirmation. Finally, I offer my deep gratitude for Cyn—friend, lover, truthteller, activist, and all-around good soul.

Introduction

The World Is Our Home

Imagine human beings living in small groups 15,000 years ago. The land they roamed, the forests they hunted, the streams they fished, and the other clans they encountered were their home, their world. It is unlikely that these groups of people could have imagined how vast and varied the African continent was. If we move up the time to 3,000 to 5,000 years ago, we find cities, small vessels plying the waters for trade, the rise of imperial regimes seeking new territories and peoples to exploit (Harman 2017). The sense of the world grew, yet could people living in Greece have imagined the presence of other continents? The sense of how vast the world is gradually emerged as people began to sail to, explore, and colonize the Americas, Africa, and the Pacific. Human imagination, infected by imperialism, could now see and chart the world, yet human beings continued to view their section of the world as their home. NASA's Apollo Program brought with it iconic photographs of a bright blue-green earth against the backdrop of infinite blackness. The sense of the earth's vastness is juxtaposed with the limitless and coldness of space, evoking, for some, a sense of fragility. The term "planet-ship earth" was coined, with the recognition that we are all traveling through the cosmos on this sphere. Not long after the Apollo missions, scientists began to observe signs of global warming and the depletion of the ozone layer, which they hypothesized, were the result of human activity. Over the years the evidence mounted, becoming indisputable, except to self-interested, narrow-minded politicians and constituents who refuse to face facts. Unlike our kin from 10,000 years ago, we now know the world is our home—our only home. My actual home may be in Chicago, but Chicago is inextricably joined to Nairobi and its citizens. The earth is not limitless and the pollution from the United States impacts not simply U.S. residents, it impacts people all over the world. We have one habitat, even though it is varied.

The foundational premise of this book is that the world is our home—home to all human beings and living creatures. Naturally, "home" is a metaphor, but it is also a fact. Metaphors have implications with regard to how we think, perceive, and feel. Metaphors might alter attitudes and behaviors. When we think of home, many of us might have a positive sense, a feeling of warmth, security, nurturance, family, and so on. We care for and about people in our immediate and extended family. We might think of our hometown, city, hamlet, or even state. My home is in Kentucky. My home is the United States. After returning from overseas, I recall a customs agent saying, "Welcome home." Home implies family and families exist within communities, societies, geographical areas. All of this suggests that "home" is connected to political realities. My literal home is my house, where my wife and I can invite whomever we wish, though there are limits placed on this by the state (e.g., one cannot knowingly welcome and harbor a fugitive or terrorist). In our home we share responsibilities and certain "rights" (e.g., right to retreat for a time to a man cave). Also, in our home we share a concern about our common welfare or well-being, recognizing that the well-being of one is contingent on the other. My more metaphorical home is Louisville, Kentucky. I am a resident of Louisville, a citizen of the state of Kentucky, and a citizen of the Unites States. My literal home is inseparable from the political realities of my city, state, and nation. Indeed, to aver that one is a citizen of Louisville (Kentucky, the United S) means that political realities are invoked. Who then are legitimate members of my home and family, whether that is the city or state or nation? People may reside in my home state, but if they are not citizens can they call Kentucky home, can they be Kentuckians? Ideally, home includes some idea of the common good or the common well-being of those living under one roof. Also, if I say my home is Kentucky and the United States, then I am placing myself within a particular polis and with it come duties and responsibilities to Others[1] and the state, as well as legal and social privileges and rights. In other words, I live and I am engaged in the political realities of my home, whether I am conscious of this or not. The point I wish to stress is that the metaphor "home," whether applied to my neighborhood, city, state, or nation, is inextricably entwined with the political.

If we extend the metaphor to the world, then the political is not simply local or national, it is international. If the world is indeed our home, then every human being is not only a resident, but a citizen, though there are no current political realities that enshrine this idea. If the world is our collective home, then the idea of the common good extends to all human beings in light of their particular and unique contexts. If the world is our home, we have responsibilities toward our fellow residents and the habitat we share; we have rights with regard to our individual survival and flourishing. If the world is our home, then we inhabit and share the same air, seas, earth, and skies. If the world is our home, we either cooperate toward maintaining our home or we will perish along with many other species whose home is also the earth.

The metaphor "home," when extended to the world does not negate, but rather includes the local, whether that is understood to be a neighborhood, city, state, or nation. Given this we might wonder what ties these varied realities together. Are there conceptual tools that are applicable in analyzing relations, practices, and visions/goals? What we do know is that in good-enough "homes" there is sufficient care so that members of the family survive and flourish. Caring relations depend on interpersonal trust and fidelity, as well as shared hope—in short, people living in a home embody and live out mutual-personal faith that undergirds cooperation. This cooperation involves people speaking and acting together, ideally, toward the good of the people in the home. In other words, care, faith, and power are concepts that pertain to a home, whether this is the home I live in on my city block, the home as it is understood in terms of the state or nation, and the home as understood as the world. The metaphor of home, then, is inextricably a part of the political realities of human life and can be assessed and understood in terms of the concepts of care, faith, and power.

Of course, we also know that home is a place of contestation. We disagree, discuss, and struggle to work together at times. To live under one roof means finding ways to have difficult conversations, when expectations, ideas, beliefs, and values differ. To live a life in common also means being able to repair relational disruptions. To fail to engage in these conflicts, in difficult conversations, and repair is to insure residents of the home will not find ways to speak and act together toward a common well-being. Homes, as we know, can be dysfunctional or even fall apart. When this happens, people can find new homes, but if the world is our home, there is no other home to escape to if and when this one becomes uninhabitable, because of our dysfunctional refusal to work cooperatively toward caring for the earth and its residents. This makes it all the more important to find ways to speak and act together, even though the discourse is difficult and complex.

The world as our home is also a matter of fact. The earth, as Terry Eagleton (2011) notes, "the earth is the first condition of our existence" (p. 228). Even in creating space labs where astronauts live free from the earth, the conditions of living in space or on the moon means we have to recreate, as best as possible, the conditions of the earth. We can create habitable conditions in space and perhaps on Mars, but these are artificial habitats that cannot sustain humanity. As the first condition of our existence, we are also learning, in ways we have not before, is that failing to care for the earth leads to human suffering and death. An earth that is increasingly uninhabitable will mean that human beings and other creatures are headed for extinction (Klein 2014;

Kolbert 2014). The world is our home and all human beings have a stake in caring for it and its inhabitants. There is no other planet-ship earth.

In this book, our common home is a political reality that I consider in light of the concepts of care, faith, power, and community—concepts that are key in pastoral theological discourses (Graham 2002; Helsel 2015; Mercer 2012; Poling 2002; Ramsay 2018; Smith 1982). It is important to lay some ground-work here with regard to what is meant by "political" or politics and associated notions such as state, the common good, and what political philosopher Hannah Arendt called space of appearances, since these ideas undergird the following chapters. Let me quickly point out the obvious; these concepts are contested and could take up more print than offered here. Yet, I believe some clarity is necessary for the perspectives provided in subsequent chapters.

Let me begin with Plato's brief definition of politics.[2] He argued that politics was the art of caring for souls (in Appiah 2005, p. 155). This ancient notion of politics seems a far cry from the way politics is lived out today, but it is, nevertheless, worth lingering over. The idea of "art" connotes practices, skills, or virtues that have a definitive aim, which is the care of souls. We might also wonder who practices this art. Aristocracies, plutocracies, oligarchies, monarchies, and democracies, as Aristotle (Barker 1971) noted, are different polities that indicate who is charged with exercising this art and who are the beneficiaries. As for "care of souls," two thoughts come to mind. To care implies actions that facilitate the survival and flourishing of citizens. What and who will enhance the lives of citizens of the polis? Those exercising the art, which include political institutions, have a duty to ensure that residents of the polis have what they need to care for themselves and others. Terry Eagleton (1996) echoes Plato's view. Eagleton writes "The sustaining of the political institutions which allow the good life, in a personal sense, to flourish, is also part of the good life, the form part of the content. Politics is not just instrumental in creating the conditions for person well-being, but a major instance of it" (p. 85).

The notion of "souls" or personal well-being connotes something beyond mere materiality. Positively stated, the term suggests inviolableness and uniqueness of the residents of the polis, which implies that the art of politics is fundamentally about human survival and flourishing. Survival includes the basics, such as physical security, a home, food, water, and so on. Flourishing includes access to quality education, access to the arts, leisure, as well as resources and opportunities to find and live out meaningful and purposeful lives. Negatively stated, the art of politics should not involve deprivation, exploitation, or mistreatment of souls (Margalit 1996; Rumscheidt 1998). Plato's notion of politics concerned the city-state, though I contend politics today must also include the world as our common home—for it is the earth that is the very condition for our existence and flourishing of the souls of all folks.

To move to the related notion of "political," not surprisingly, we note its roots in the Greek concept of polis. The polis or city-state, broadly speaking, comprises particular created institutions, rules, regulations, and laws necessary for living a life in common. The political, in other words, refers to the communicative activity of citizens wherein public-political institutions (and attending policies, programs, laws, etc.) are created to address the various needs and concerns of citizens (Arendt 1952, p. 198). This communicative activity is inextricably yoked to collectively shared narratives and rituals that contain people's beliefs, meanings, expectations, and hopes or visions (Honneth 2007a, pp. 21–39). In general, these shared narratives and practices reveal how residents of the polis understand and live out the common good or how the group understands and works toward the survival and flourishing of its members. Coming from another angle, the political entails social rituals, structures, narratives, disciplines, and discourses that inform citizens (and noncitizens) about whom to trust and where their loyalties ought to lie; the political refers to a shared identity that is crucial to making ethical decisions or assigning standards to social practices (Nealon 1998); it signifies and makes licit, for good or ill, the kinds of authority, power, privilege, and prestige that are meted out in diverse public-political contexts (Foucault 1979, 1980); it represents the good aims citizens are to pursue and the sanctions that result when one fails (e.g., justice, Young 1990); it determines distribution of various social goods; it shapes who we care for and how we care in the public sphere.[3] The intricate economic, social, and cultural web serves as the political milieu that gives rise to and shapes citizens' experiences and identity.

In brief, "political" refers to socially held and publicly expressed symbols, narratives, and rituals that are embodied in a polis' institutions and social-symbolic spaces that function to:

a. organize a person's experiences and legitimate an individual's actions in the public realm (Arendt 1952).
b. facilitate collective discourse and action in the public realm (D'Entreves 1994).
c. distribute power and resources (Ransom 1997).
d. legitimate authority and governance.
e. adjudicate claims and discipline and repair breaches of both social order and the laws governing social arrangements and the distribution of resources.
f. provide an overarching social-political identity that supports collective action and discourse, as well as provides for a shared sense of continuity and cohesion.
g. facilitate mutual care of citizens (and noncitizens) for the sake of survival and flourishing.

A less functional notion of the political refers to groups of people, not neces- sarily are always citizens, who are engaged in shared action and discourse pertaining to the common good and decisions being made with regard to (a) who is allowed to participate in public-political discourse (citizenship and identity), (b) who should govern, (c) what type of institution(s) should be the instrument of governing, (d) the kinds of policies and programs that adminis- ter and regulate economic and social affairs, (e) care of citizens and strangers, and (f) the enactment and adjudication of laws that order society and repair social disruptions.

This view of the political may seem to be confined to the geographical boundaries of a nation, but this would be, in part, a mistake. International relations embody the political and its functions, though the governing aspects of the political are associated with particular nation-states. For instance, the United Nations is not a governing body in the sense that it has a territory and a people. It does, however, provide a space for nation-state representatives to engage in creation of shared narratives, policies, guidelines, and so on for the sake of collective interaction vis-à-vis the good of human beings (e.g., UN Charter, UN-sponsored climate talks). The UN also, at times, facilitates and coordinates the distribution of resources to aid countries suffering from natural and human-made disasters. In addition, there are other international institutions that reflect the political realities of nations cooperating in some shared goal (NATO, OAS, G7), but these international institutions are not governing bodies. They are not states or state institutions. While the idea of the political takes on a different hue, when it comes to international relations, it is nevertheless applicable and becomes increasingly so when we consider the earth as our collective home, which I address in greater detail in chapter 7.

The political is most powerfully experienced and lived out in local, state, and national contexts. In these contexts, there are political institutions that are created and responsible for governing. These institutions we associate with the state. Leo Strauss and Joseph Cropsey (1987) indicate that modern people tend to view the state "in contradistinction to 'society'" (p. 6). This distinction is inconceivable, they argue, for classical political philosophers like Plato and Aristotle. Aristotle, for instance, viewed the city-state as "a kind of partnership, association, or community, that is, a group of persons who share or hold certain things in common" (Lord 1987, p. 134), which necessarily comprises governing structures. These governing structures, Macmurray (1991) notes, are human creations and, as such, can be altered or overthrown (p. 137). He also argues that "the State has no rights, no authority, for it is an instrument, not an agent; a network of organization, not a person" (Macmurray 2004, p. 106). As created instrument, the state "exists to make society possible, to provide mechanisms through which the sharing of human experience may be achieved" (p. 106). Put another way, while the "State is merely a mechanism, and therefore a means to an end, [it has] no value in itself" (p. 106). The state's value as a mechanism is its ability to facilitate the sharing of human experience, citizens speaking and acting together, and, of course, the survival and flourishing of the nation's residents. Ideally speaking, the state is created for the people, for the polis, and not the people for the state, though human beings often make the mistake of placing the survival of state before the survival and flourishing of the people.

The state and its institutions are what we typically associate with the political, but this would be a mistake. To be sure the state is the most visible expression of the political and what Plato called the art of politics. Yet, Macmurray and Arendt stress that the political necessarily includes the public engagement of citizens/residents. In instances of brutal totalitarian regimes, the political is restricted to the few, which reflects a distortion of politics and the political. In one sense, this is why totalitarian regimes eventually collapse. The state and the political can also be distorted in democratic polities, as Sheldon Wolin (2008) has demonstrated. He uses the term "inverted totalitarianism" to depict how political power has shifted from democratic state institutions to nodes of nondemocratic economic-political institutions. In this situation, the demos, which is the proper location of the political, is more illusion than fact (Brown 2015). The state, which ideally is created by the people for the people, now serves the economic-political interests of the capitalist-political class.

As indicated above, the idea of the state as comprising governing institutions does not fit well with the idea that the world is our home. We do not have a worldwide governing body representing the diverse peoples of the world. While I will say more about this in chapter 7, for now let me point out that the 20th century ushered into world history something unique. Nations gathered to create the League of Nations and later the United Nations (UN). The UN is not, as I said, a governing institution, yet it does represent an institution that provides a political space for individual nations and their representatives to begin to attempt to work through differences and find ways to cooperate toward common goals—ideally for the well-being of their respective citizens. Perhaps a future generation will have the imagination and will to create global political institutions that will enable shared governance similar to the way the United States' fifty states govern their respective citizens, while ceding some of their sovereignty to federal institutions.

Any discussion of the state necessarily implies the notion of citizen—a legal resident of a bounded geographical territory (e.g., nation). Sheldon Wolin (2016a) argues that "A political being is not to be defined as the citizen has been, as an abstract, disconnected bearer of rights, privileges, and immunities, but as a person who existence is located in a particular place and draws its sustenance from circumscribed relationships: family, friends, church, neighborhood, workplace, community, town, city" (p. 371). He continues, "These relationships are the sources from which political being draws power—symbolic, material, and psychological—and that enables them to act together" (p. 377). Wolin, following Hannah Arendt, ascribes power to citizens speaking and acting together, rather than simply locating power in the state. While I will say more about power in chapter 3, for the moment I stress the relationship between the state and citizens and I wish to briefly problematize this.

As Macmurray argues, citizens create and sustain the state and its institutions, and, in turn, the state provides legitimacy to the title citizen. As a citizen I have rights, privileges, and duties with regard to fellow citizens and the state. At the same time, the state has responsibilities to its citizens, broadly and ideally speaking regarding their survival and flourishing. Yet, in many countries there are residents who are not citizens. They may not have obtained full citizenship or they may have partial legal status, which means they obtain some rights and privileges. There are also residents who have not obtained legal status. In this book, I will tend to view persons as residents or citizens of the world, because I argue every state and its citizens have a responsibility to care for and be just to all residents within their borders, regardless of status. Put another way, to be a person is to enjoin Others and the state to respect concretely the needs and experiences of all individuals. States (and their citizens), in short, are responsible for the survival and flourishing of whoever is present within their geographical territory. This maxim is joined to the idea that the world is our home—all human beings are residents of the earth and, therefore, citizens. While we have diverse states and no overarching world-state, each and every human being is dependent on the earth. While we have fictional borders and nations, while we have diverse customs and cultures, we have one home and we are one people. This view, this belief has a corollary—we are all responsible to and for each other.

Another related concept that helps to tie in the notions of politics, the political, and the state is Hannah Arendt's term "space of appearances." Arendt writes that the polis is "the public-political realm in which [human beings] attain their full humanity, not only because they are (as in the privacy of the household) but also because they appear" (Arendt 2005, p. 21). Axel Honneth (2007a) points out that Arendt "claims that human subjects are naturally dependent on being perceived and affirmed in a public sphere, for it is only in this way that they can acquire the measure of psychic stability and self-confidence needed to cope with their existential problems and risks" (pp. 30–31). The public-political space of appearances means that the humanity or personhood of individual citizens is recognized and affirmed, which bolsters their confidence vis-à-vis participating in the polis. Added to this is Honneth's view that "individual subjects are only capable of experiencing themselves as free beings if they have learned to be actively engaged in public discussion of political affairs" (p. 30). To "appear" in the political space means that the humanity of individuals is recognized, which in turn means they participate as free beings in their own and Others survival and flourishing.

To "appear" in political space requires that people are recognized and treated as persons, which will be discussed in greater detail in chapter 1. For now, let me say that "appearing" in the political space is associated with the political milieu's representational system (collective narratives, rituals/practices) that ideally affirms the personhood or humanity of residents of the polis. Positively, the space of appearances provides individuals the self-confidence, self-respect, and self-esteem to communicate and engage with Others in the public-political realm (Honneth 1995, p. 129). The space of appearances shrinks or becomes nonexistent in cases of totalitarianism or in situations where racism, sexism and other forms of oppression and marginalization exist. For instance, in the United States—a putative democratic nation—African Americans have been oppressed and marginalized in many ways, which means they have appeared in the political space as less than human, less than persons. Even after being emancipated, African Americans have been restricted or denied from communicating and participating in the political realm. Another example is seen in the history of women's suffrage. We are approaching the hundredth year anniversary of women's right to vote. Prior to attaining this right, women vis-à-vis the space of appearances were not recognized or treated as full and free human beings vis-à-vis the public-political realm. They continue to be underrepresented in political offices today. The space of appearances, which depends on the representational systems of a polis and its accompanying institutions, waxes and wanes in accordance with who and to what degree individuals are recognized and treated as persons.

Naturally, the idea of the space of appearances as a political concept refers mainly to adults. Children, who have no legal right to vote, are nevertheless a part of this space (Bunge 2001; Miller-McLemore 2006). White, upper-class children have more social-political-economic privileges, resources, and freedom to flourish than poor, children of color. We may say publicly that all children are persons, but we need to consider the social-political-economic context and institutions to see whether this is mere lip service or propaganda. One can be quite certain that when parents are being excluded or restricted vis-à-vis the space of appearances, their children are negatively impacted. Put another way, recognition vis-à-vis the space of appearances impacts not simply individuals' participation in the public-political sphere, it also impacts them in material ways (lack of education, lack of or poor housing, food deserts, etc.; Fraser and Honneth 2003; Mercer 2012). Children may not be able to participate in the political sphere to the same degree as adults, but they are fundamentally impacted by the polis' space of appearances.

Arendt's notion is typically confined to a state or nation. But, one can certainly imagine the possibility of recognizing and treating all human beings as persons. Many pastoral theologians invoke the Judeo-Christian ideas of *imago dei* and children of God to suggest, at the very least, that all human beings carry the imprint of God and thus we are all obliged to recognize and embody this when we encounter strangers. Naturally, human beings often fail miserably in this, but the idea nevertheless remains—a burr under the saddle of our more parochial, narrow-minded types of recognition. While we fail often, we can also point to numerous occasions when differences have been accepted and human beings recognized and treated strangers as brothers and sisters. There are many gracious and openhearted people who welcome immigrants into their countries. Groups such as Doctors without Borders provide medical care for poor people regardless of color or polis. The UN Charter reflects ideas that all human beings have rights that are to be respected. If one agrees that the world is our home, we necessarily must create narratives, institutions, and practices that make possible the space of appearances for all people and likewise affirm parity of participation in public-political spaces. At the same time, we must actively discourage local, state, national, and international individuals, groups, and institutions from undermining the space of appearances through acts of political humiliation, intimidation, marginalization, violence, and terror. Because of human finitude and sin, there will always be individuals and groups who seek to undermine the space of appearances. Vigilance is required.

Having provided a cursory depiction of these concepts, which will be further developed throughout the book, I now turn to questions of why I have written this book and who my intended audience is. As a pastoral theologian I have worked with individuals, couples, and families who are struggling with various challenges. My work demands an understanding of human flourishing and the various social, political, and economic obstacles to human survival and flourishing. At first, I understood the sufferings of individuals from psychoanalytic and theological perspectives. This quickly changed when, for example, I began to realize that the sources of suffering are not simply rooted in childhood, the family, or the unconscious. There are other key macro sources of suffering that impinge on the psyches and bodies of individuals, sources that undermine family ties, and sources that disrupt individuals from reaching for a good. In time my field of analysis broadened. I ended up agreeing with Franz Fanon (2008–1952), who sought (a) "to '*consciousnessize*' [the patient's] unconscious, to no longer be tempted by a hallucinatory lactification," and (b) "to enable [the patient] to choose an action with respect to the *real source of the conflict*, i.e., the social structure" (p. 80; emphasis mine). Considering the relation between economic-political structures and psychological distress was one step. The other was my growing concern about climate change and its consequences—consequences that impact persons' daily lives and psyches, especially members of the most vulnerable populations (e.g., effects of environmental racism/classism). As will be apparent, the issue of climate change is inextricably a part of the scourge of global neoliberal capitalism, which is a subject I take up in this book. In short, as a pastoral theologian I am interested in understanding human suffering and flourishing in light of the macro political, economic, and cultural forces and institutions that contribute to both.

When it comes to my imaginary readers, I have in mind members of my guild, but more importantly a wider audience interested in political-economic issues and their impact on human survival and flourishing. Of course, this larger audience will realize that my perspective is informed by Christian anthropology and theological ideas, such as *imago dei*, ecclesia, and incarnation. Put another way, a Christian anthropology serves as one interpretive lens for assessing and critiquing macro structures and systems, which pastoral theologians have been doing for decades (Ashby 2000; Poling 2002; Smith 1982).[4] In addition, I rely on philosophers like John Macmurray, Hannah Arendt, Wendy Brown, and Axel Honneth, as well as political scientists such as Sheldon Wolin and other experts vis-à-vis economics and class. This cross-disciplinary approach is common for pastoral theologians (LaMothe 2016; Ramsay 2004), which is often a scandal to our systematic colleagues.[5] Nevertheless, this approach emerges from my belief that we must engage in conversation across disciplines (and across cultures) given the global challenges that face all of us. A cross-disciplinary approach, then, is fundamentally connected to my interest in reaching and conversing with readers outside my discipline. We must find ways to converse, to exchange ideas, to formulate new possibilities, new institutions if our world is to become a habitable home for all. I expect disagreement, contestation, yet I also believe and hope that we can learn from each other and consider together how we might move forward. Stated differently, the space of appearances must be expanded and in so doing friction will arise. It is respectful interpersonal contestation or friction that can create sparks to light fires of change that benefit residents of our world.

Let me shift here to articulating a brief outline of the book. I consider the first four chapters of the book as addressing key, interrelated ideas that form a lens for assessing political matters, which are the focus of the last three chapters. In chapter 1, I argue that care is a foundational political concept. This requires explaining what is meant by care, which then serves as a hermeneutical lens for critiquing political-economic realities. The notion of care is not simply a critical lens, however. It also provides a political vision. In brief, care is a necessary political concept for addressing questions regarding sovereignty, the role of the state, political power, social justice, the common good, political discourse, international relations, and social-political struggles such as racism, sexism, and classism. In chapter 2, I address the notion of faith, which is a corollary of care. From a pastoral theological perspective, these two concepts are inextricably intertwined and as such are seen to be foundational to living a life in common. While faith is often thought of in religious terms, I argue that it is an existential human reality necessary for the survival and flourishing of individuals living a life in common. Like the notion of care, faith can be used as a hermeneutical lens for evaluating the polis.

Any philosophical or theological reflection on politics must confront the reality of power. Chapter 3 addresses political power as speaking and acting together, as well as its relation to care and faith. In chapter 4 I turn to the idea of community as key for a well-functioning society. The notion of community has been of interest, at times, to various philosophers, but it is a core idea of Christian anthropology and, likewise, central to pastoral theology (Harris 1991; Holton 2011). As Richard Horsely (2009) points out, the term *ekklesia* "referred to the assembly of citizens in a self-governing city state" (p. 14). To understand the idea of community as a political concept I discuss distinct types of associations that found both community and society. This helps in being able to differentiate between community and society, as well as the relation between these and the state.

Chapter 5 signals a shift to analyzing complex political-economic realities in terms of care, faith, power, and community. In particular, this chapter addresses the rise and proliferation of neoliberal capitalism and its impact on shaping our understanding of care, faith, and power. I argue that care, faith, and power (speaking and acting together), in their manifold expressions, are informed, supported, and legitimized by semiotic or representational systems, which, in turn, are reproduced and enforced by the group's justificatory and disciplinary regimes or institutions. Our present market society, then, possesses representational systems associated with neoliberal capitalism, which not only shapes (distorts) subjectivity (*homo oeconomus*), but also care, faith, and power such that community is undermined.

The rise and global proliferation of neoliberal capitalism accompany incredible disparities in income and wealth throughout the world (Piketty 2014). These disparities accompany obstacles in gaining access to education, health care, food, clean water, and habitable spaces. These realities fall under the headings of class and classism. In chapter 6, I define and discuss class and classism that exists in market societies, like the United States. While class has seemingly been a part of societies prior to the rise of capitalism, it (and classism) is an indelible feature of market societies. One could argue that throughout history societies had markets, which means markets were subordinate to the state and society's political organizations. In the 21st century many societies are dominated by capitalist narratives, institutions, and practices, insuring that class and classism proliferate. In brief, this chapter defines and examines class and classism from the perspectives of care, faith, and power.

The last chapter turns to international relations. Admittedly this is a difficult topic to address in one chapter, let alone consider it from the perspective of care, faith, and power. Obviously, I do not have the expertise or space to offer an exhaustive excursus on international relations. I simply offer some thoughts about how we as citizens of the world can think, converse, and work together toward the common well-being of all peoples with all of their attending particularities, which includes caring about their habitats and the overall habitat of the earth. My modest aim is to invite readers to imagine the possibilities of founding international institutions that can facilitate local, state, and national institutions to cooperate in a common goal of caring for our home.

I end this introduction by recalling Einstein's prescient words: "For without that greater community no single country will long endure."[6] He likely was thinking of the two world wars and other imperial conflicts. His capacious mind could envisage a common world, but also the very real possibility of humanity's self-immolation in nuclear war. Did he also see the possibility of the demise of humanity by way of climate change? In either case, human beings have the capacity to alter their habitat, but not change the conditions of their existence. We need clean air, food, moderate temperatures, and so on to survive and flourish. I believe Einstein recognized that our greatest hope lay in cooperation, which can only happen when we see, when we believe, when we act toward all human beings as children of God sharing a common home.

NOTES

1. I frequently use "Other" not simply because it is gender neutral, but also because for me it suggests an otherness even in our close relationships and in ourselves.

2. Plato and Aristotle have had a considerable influence on theologians and philosophers in the West and it is because of this and the fact I have been educated in the Western philosophical and theological traditions that I begin with Plato.

3. It is helpful to make a distinction between the notion of "public" and the notion of the "political." "Public" is broader than the concept "political." For Arendt (1952), the public sphere comprises the space of appearances or the space of political freedom, which I have associated with the political, *and* the *common world*—"a shared and public world of human artifacts, institutions, and settings" (p. 76). The public square, this common space, is where people can raise and discuss issues and concerns, as well as participate in other shared activities. This common world certainly includes political realities, but it is broader, including cultural and religious artifacts and activities. There are many examples of the public realm. The mall, dining at restaurants,

attending sports venues, going to movies and plays, camping, hiking, visiting the zoo, are just some examples. To be sure, each of these has political tendrils in the sense that laws and regulations are associated with the market (mall), safe food, care of animals, and so on, but these are not in the foreground of public engagements. This distinction is important when we come to differences between political and public theologies. Public theologians may address the political, but they may also focus on theological analyses of common world realities related to culture such as music (theological analysis of bluegrass music), media (theology of "The Simpsons"), and so on. While the ideas of public and political are distinct, they also overlap. I add here that the distinction becomes very important when we discuss, in later chapters, the rise of neoliberal capitalism and its tendency to privatize public spaces.

4. It is important to point out a distinction between pastoral theologians who consider the impact of macro forces on the particular needs and sufferings of individuals, families, and communities (e.g., Graham 1992; Miller-McLemore 1995) and my perspective and direction. Like pastoral caregivers, many pastoral theologians typically focus on a specific issue, for example, domestic violence (Poling 2002), and then consider how systemic forces and structures contribute to the problem. As a pastoral theologian I am interested in considering the macro forces, institutions (e.g., the state), and systems themselves in terms of the concepts of care, faith, power, and community.

5. Pastoral theologian Valerie DeMarinis overheard a systematic theologian characterize pastoral theology: "One said to the other, 'They are just like scavengers. They have no real theory, just hunting and pecking, grabbing and applying. There is no order for them. And they can never explain what they do or why they do it, only that something works or not. . . . It is a very sad state of affairs'" (in Carlin 2014, p. 120). Of course, I disagree, arguing that pastoral theological engagement with and use of other disciplines enriches the field, though it does make for more uncertainty regarding a clear body of knowledge.

6. http://spartacus-educational.com/USAeinstein.htm accessed February 27, 2018.

Chapter 1

Care and Society

David Milch's celebrated television series, *Deadwood*, depicts a town in the Dakota Territory during the 1870s. Relying on newspaper and diary accounts of that period, Milch's fictional account portrayed a Hobbesian, or better, near-dystopian polis that had the thin façades of law and civilization. Greed, lust, and pride fueled violence, coercion, exploitation, and intimidation, which seemingly operated as the organizing principles of daily life. Watching the show, one may wonder why this town, this polis on the edge of civilization's law and order, does not descend into a frenzy of chaotic violence. A closer look reveals that the vicious and ruthless characters of the town are more complicated. There are surprising moments of care and affection, of trust and loyalty. Al Swearengen, the merciless and violent owner of Gem Saloon and a major figure of the town, shows care in unexpected ways. Seth Bullock, the town's elected marshal, and Sol Stern are friends who hope and work for law and order, all the while demonstrating care for and loyalty to Trixie, a prostitute, and Calamity Jane, a disruptive alcoholic. Many other instances of care and affection appear amid the town's daily violence and coercion, leaving viewers to conclude that the town's survival and growth are not necessarily simply and solely dependent on greed and violence as the polis' organizing principles. Indeed, a thread that keeps the town together is reminiscent of Hardt and Negri's (2005) comment that "love serves as the basis for our political projects in common and the construction of a new society" (p. 352).

It may seem odd for a political pastoral theologian to begin with a dystopian town—a city located in one of the circles of hell—instead of a utopian town—a City of God. To be sure, one can examine towns like Deadwood to construct a political pastoral theology on what not to do, but that is not my aim here. While Deadwood is dystopian, I believe that it does not descend

1

into an orgy of corruption and chaotic violence precisely because of the presence, albeit insufficient, of care and faith. Put another way, this town survives as a polis because of "the shared concerns of human beings to take care of themselves and the part of the world they claim as their lot" (Wolin 2016, p. 248). The absence of care and faith would mean that Deadwood would indeed be dead—a political corpse incapable of providing survival for its inhabitants. Care and faith animate and keep a polis alive, though the more care and faith are diminished, the unhealthier a polis is.

In this chapter, I argue that care (and faith—discussed in chapter 2), while constitutive for subjectivity and intersubjectivity, is necessary for living a life in common—even in a dystopian polis. More positively, care—existentially and theologically understood—is a political concept because it is foundational for the survival and flourishing of a city and a society. As a political concept, it serves as a hermeneutical lens for assessing and critiquing a polis and its structures and practices. At the same time, this concept points to a political vision where citizens, living a life in common, survive and flourish. In brief, whether as a hermeneutical lens for critique or a political vision, care is a necessary political concept for addressing questions regarding sovereignty, the role of the state, political power, social justice, the common good, political discourse, international relations, and social-political struggles such as racism, sexism, and classism.

A reason for beginning with care is my belief in taking seriously Aristotle's claim that human beings are political animals. If this premise is true, and I think it is, then we must begin with the fundamental attributes of this political creature as we move toward questions of power, sovereignty, and other political questions and matters. Here, then, we begin with anthropology and its basic questions about what it means to be human and what is needed for human survival and flourishing. More precisely, by defining and describing the attributes of care, I contend that care (and faith) is a foundational feature of this political animal. Considering care as a political concept provides an opportunity to reenvision political philosophy and political theology, the urgency of which is evident in the specters of the myopic greed and sociopathy of global capitalism and its deleterious impact on global warming, where we see clearly that the polis is no longer simply bound to the personal and the local, but global.

Given these remarks, let me turn to how this chapter is organized. I begin by defining care before describing the attributes of care from existential and theological perspectives, while locating the notion of care squarely in the polis and its space of appearances. An aim here is to argue that while care is an anthropological concept—hence universal[1]—it takes on particular hues of meanings, aims, and practices given one's religion, culture, community, and polis. A pastoral theological perspective, then, will ground this existential concept in the Judeo-Christian tradition, though not positing that this perspective is universal or timeless.

CARE: A FOUNDATION OF THE POLIS

The notion of care is central to pastoral theology. Pastoral theologians are concerned about the foundations and practices of pastoral care (Clebsch and Jaekle 1994; Doehring 2015; Dykstra 2005; Gerkin 1997; Patton 1993; Scheib 2016), care of children (Flesberg 2008; Lester 1985), care of older women (Scheib 2004), care for the traumatized (Poling 2002; van Deusen Hunsinger 2015), care for ostracized persons (Marshall 1997; Sanders 2017), care for the grieving (Kelley 2010; White 1998), and innumerable other issues of human suffering and need. While pastoral theologians seek to understand and address diverse instantiations of human suffering, they also recognize that care is inextricably connected to political realities (Helsel 2015; Rogers-Vaughn 2016; Smith 1982). Yet, the notion of care vis-à-vis the polis and political forces and structures is under-theorized. For this reason, I wish to take time to depict care as a political concept and because I am interested in conversing with a wider audience, I turn to more existential, philosophical renderings of care—renderings that are in concert with a pastoral theological anthropology.

In approaching the concept of care, one notes the term is ubiquitous and dizzyingly plastic in its meanings, aims, and objects. We say "take care" when saying goodbye to friends and strangers. Daily we may remark about and show how we care about music, sports, various kinds of food, politics, art, education, the economy, our country, family, friends, and, on rare occasions, even enemies. At the same time, in speech or action (or inaction), we inevitably reveal the things, persons, and activities that we do not care about or for. The realities of racism, classism, and sexism manifest the ways human beings can be careless in their indifference and without care in their cruel prejudices that are institutionalized in shared narratives, rituals, and social-political-economic structures that serve to oppress and marginalize persons and communities. It appears that to be human necessarily involves our obligations and choices to care and our decisions not to care, while also experiencing the caring and non-caring actions of others.

Relying on an existential viewpoint, liberation theologian Leonardo Boff (2008) contends that Martin Heidegger understood care "as a primordial structural totality" (p. 15), which means that care is "at the very root of being human." For Heidegger, care is "a fountainhead, an original and ontological aspect which it is impossible to totally disregard" (p. 15), though Heidegger could not seem to follow his own philosophical dictum when it came to citizens who were Jews. Framed in complex philosophical discourse, the ontological reality of care simply means that without care human beings cannot survive, let alone flourish. If care was to be existentially absent, human beings would not be human. Heidegger is not the only philosopher to recognize the importance of care—care loosened from its Judeo-Christian roots. Recent care theorists such as Carol Gilligan (1982), Joan Tronto (1993), Diemut Bubeck (1995), Selma Sevenhuijsen (1998), Fiona Robinson (1999, 2011), and Maurice Hammington (2004) argue that care is an existential reality and, therefore, political, because human beings are social—beings living a life in common.

Religious creation myths, which long preceded abstract philosophical theorizing about human beings, demonstrate the ontological, if you will, nature of care. In Jewish scripture, the Genesis stories tell of God's creation of the world and of human beings, to whom God pays particular caring attention to the extent of providing a place to meet their needs for survival and flourishing. Having abused God's Edenic hospitality, the first couple found themselves in a less friendly world, though this banishment did not exclude God's covenant of care. Indeed, Judeo-Christian scripture is rife with examples of human perfidy and deceptions, which does not sway God's steadfast obligation to care for human beings. Another ancient creation story is Roman in origin. The God Cura (Care), out for her morning constitutional, approaches the river's edge. Where the water has receded, she notices some wet clay and, in a burst of creativity, molds a figure. Jupiter happens to stroll by and Cura asks him to breathe spirit into the clay figure, which he readily agrees to do. Cura is delighted it is alive and decides to name the creature, which annoys Jupiter because he believed he had the naming rights. The dispute heightens when the God Tellus jumps into the fray, arguing that since the creature was made of the earth, she should name it. To name the creature is not simply a divine narcissistic endeavor, but one that indicates who would be responsible to care for this new creation. Well past noon, with tempers flaring, it becomes evident that the gods are getting nowhere and they ask Saturn to come up with a solution, which he does:

> Jupiter, since you have given the spirit, take the soul after death: Tellus, since she provided the body, should receive the body. And since Cura first molded him, let Cura possess him as long as he is alive. (in Hamilton 2013, p. 3).

This trinity of gods agrees to the terms, each obliged to care in different ways. Commenting on this fable-myth, Leonardo Boff (2008) notes that "care accompanies the human being while it makes its pilgrimage in time. . . . Care is the fundamental ethos, the deciphering key, of the human being and of its potential" (p. 55).

The Roman myth reveals a very passive human creature in need of the gods' constant attention, while in the Jewish creation story the first couple is more active, agentic. With this difference, we might point out how each is similar and in that the act of creation means God or gods are obliged to care for the finite creation. From these myths, we also note that it is not simply the gods who are obliged to care. Rather, each human being is existentially obliged to care for each other and the earth (Engster 2007), though this care often is understood or depicted in parochial ways. Regardless, the point here is that these and many other creation myths ontologize the reality of care. That is, they indicate that care is foundational in the act of creation and in tending to the creature and created order. In addition, I note that in Judeo-Christian scriptures, human beings, as created in the image and likeness of God, participate in the creation process. Good-enough parents, biologically and psychologically, cooperate in the creation of their child, finding innumerable ways to care for this almost totally dependent and finite being. From a theological perspective, parents, in caring for their children, incarnate God's creative love and thus participate in God's care for human beings.

Creation myths are not simply nice stories shared with one's children so that they have answers to questions about where they come from and to whom they owe loyalty and gratitude for life. The myths are part of the larger symbolic narrative web of a people living a life in common. In this sense, these stories are political in that they affirm the origins and legitimate the existence of a particular people. To be sure, these stories do not refer to specific forms of governance, yet they lend support to particular political arrangements over time. Consider the varied political forms of governance in Jewish scripture (e.g., tribes, judges, monarchy: Walzer 2012). While the political structures change, the polis and its legitimizing creation myths remain foundational for securing a sense of shared recognition and identity necessary for living a life in common.[2] Given this, one can draw a conclusion that care and the polis are inextricably yoked. In God's act of creation, human beings are meant to live together, to care for each other as God cares for them. Put another way, the act of creating human beings also entails the creation of the polis so that human beings may survive and thrive. Aristotle's notion of human beings as political animals parallels the ideas of *imago dei* and the kingdom of God—we are meant to live a life in common. Shifting from a Greek philosopher to Roman political philosopher Cicero, we see the necessity of care in the polis and, for Cicero, the responsibility of political leaders vis-à-vis care. He argued that care is the first aim of political leaders, insuring that "everyone shall have what belongs to him" (in Wolin 2016, p. 19). Care, in short, makes possible life lived in common wherein residents[3] are able to survive and thrive.

Scripture stories make manifest the quotidian necessity of care in daily life in the polis, paralleling philosophers' anthropological premise—care is a foundational feature of being human. Yet we are left with questions of what care means and what its attributes are. Acknowledging that there are no definitive answers to these questions of care will not, of course, serve as an obstacle to defining care and depicting its attributes. Indeed, contestation is needed, because care, like love, is not simply an abstract concept that is universally the same. Both terms are rooted in the embodied, relational, and historic particularities of daily life and, therefore, infinitely and wonderfully complex, diverse, and dynamic. Given this, Boff (2008) provides a starting point that offers further evidence of the existential necessity of care. Care, he notes, is derived from the Latin "cura" and "in its most ancient form . . . was used within the context of relations of love and friendship. It expressed the attitude of care, of devotion, of concern, and of worry for the loved one or favorite object" (p. 58). Here we see the close connection between care and love,[4] which can muddy the waters even more in our journey to a definition.

If care is a central feature of being human and living a life in common, we need to arrive at some definition. Milton Mayeroff's (1971) definition is a small step in gaining greater clarity regarding care. He offered a terse, general definition of caring, writing that caring is helping the other person to grow (p. 7), which requires accurately assessing the experiences and needs of the other person. This definition focuses on the individual and the notion of growth and, is, therefore, limiting and vague. For instance, while we can acknowledge the value in helping people grow, it is not entirely clear what growth means. Also, some caring situations have nothing to do with growth, such as caring for a dying patient. Finally, caring acts can be directed toward families, communities, and societies—not simply individuals—which raises the question about what growth means in these contexts. Care theorist Joan Tronto's (1993) definition, while similarly broad, moves away from a simple dyadic view of care and includes other important aims beyond growing. Caring, she argues, "is a species of activity that includes anything we do to maintain, continue, and repair our 'world' so that we can live in it as well as possible. That world includes our bodies, ourselves, and our environment" (p. 103). Like any general characterization, this covers a large swath of human activity, ranging from an environmentalist caring for the earth to human rights activists protesting the torture of prisoners, to a school teacher tending to the needs of his students. Philosopher Daniel Engster (2007), who critiques Tronto's definition, can bring us a bit closer. He posits that care is "everything we do to help individuals meet their vital biological needs, develop or maintain their basic capabilities, and avoid or alleviate unnecessary or unwanted pain and suffering, so that they can survive, develop, and function in society" (p. 28).

Let me pause here to clarify and critique a few key features of this definition. Tronto's definition highlights the necessity of caring for our world if we are to care for each other—a point of view Engster agrees with. The intersection of caring for human beings and caring for the earth is not necessarily new. We see this in Jewish scriptures and the injunction to leave sections of the field to lie fallow for a time so that the earth can rejuvenate itself. Yet, in the Anthropocene Era (Kolbert 2014), we are becoming increasingly aware that care for the earth, seas, and air is vital for our collective survival, with the implication that every polis and its members are obliged to care for the earth. All politics may be local, but in the face of climate change, the local is inextricably yoked to and dependent on the universal. Second, many definitions of care tend to focus on individuals and their biological and psychological survival and development. Individual human beings, though, exist in families, communities, and societies. In my Roman Catholic tradition, the family is considered the cell or basis of community and society (John Paul II's *Familaris Consortio* 1981; Francis's *Amoris Letitia* 2016). Pastoral ministers are to care for families and communities of faith. This is not merely an obligation for religious leaders. Political leaders, Roman Catholic documents claim, are tasked with promoting social policies and structures that make it possible for communities and families to care for their members (see O'Brien and Shannon 1977). So, a definition of care means expanding our understanding of care vis-à-vis the individual to that of caring for families', communities', and societies' survival and flourishing. Third, I am not entirely comfortable with Engster's aim of functioning in society. The Roman Catholic social documents often critique societies that create obstacles to caring for segments of the populace. One would not wish to advocate helping people "function" in a society where political, economic, and social structures lead to massive inequalities, oppression, and marginalization. There are numerous examples of people (e.g., Nelson Mandela, Emma Goldman, Dorothy Day, Frantz Fanon, Rosa Parks, Martin Luther King, Malcolm X, Nelson Mandela, Eugene Debs, to name only a few) who did not seek to "function" in societies that were oppressive—where care and the aim of flourishing are offered to the privileged few. Some of these individuals were deemed dysfunctional and labeled by political authorities as traitors, pathological, and so on. At times, they are/were imprisoned and killed. Sometimes, then, care means not functioning in societies that oppress and marginalize politically powerless groups. Not functioning or not adapting to the polis may itself be an act of care as long as the intention is to decry and undermine individuals, groups, and systems that harm persons and communities. Finally, while I agree with the ideas of development, growth, and so on, I prefer the notion of human flourishing, whether that is understood in terms of an individual, family, community, or society. Yes, it is admittedly vague, like the other concepts, but it connotes excellence and points to self-realization and freedom,[5] which go well beyond mere surviving. This vagueness means we can leave the particularities and meanings of human flourishing to the specific social-political contexts and eras in which human beings live.

Given this, I offer an amended definition of care. Care is everything we do to help individuals, families, communities, and societies to (1) meet vital biological, psychosocial, and existential or spiritual needs of individuals, families, and communities, (2) develop or maintain basic capabilities with the aim of human flourishing, (3) facilitate participation in the polis' space of appearances, and (4) maintain a habitable environment for all. I add to this definition that care as a political concept involves shared critical[6] and constructive reflection on how the structures (and their accompanying narratives and practices) of the state, governing authorities, and non-state organizations (e.g., businesses, labor unions, and religious and secular communities) and actors meet or fail to meet the four features of this definition of care.

Political philosopher Sheldon Wolin (2016) echoes this view and articulates the link between care, the political, and the common good or well-being. He writes, "It is the nature of the state that, insofar as it claims to be political, it will govern for the good of the entire community and not serve primarily the interests of a particular class or group" (p. 247). "The political," he continues, "means the common well-being is the end and the definition of what is authentic political action." The definition of care above delineates the meaning of well-being, both in terms of survival and flourishing. In other words, this "common life resides in cooperation and reciprocity that human beings develop in order to survive, meet their needs, and begin to explore their capacities and the remarkable world into which they have been cast. The political emerges as the shared concerns of human beings to take care of themselves and their part of the world they claim as their lot. The political emerges, in the literal sense, as a 'culture,' that is cultivating, a tending, a taking care of beings and things" (p. 248). For Wolin, the political, which includes the state and the people, is not simply framed in terms of notions of justice, but also in the concept of care that is inseparably joined to the notion of the common good.

A few illustrations of each of these aims will provide further clarity regarding this definition of care as a political concept. There are obvious biological needs necessary for survival, such as food, clean water, housing, and health care. When we consider the reality of food insecurity or food deserts in the United States, we immediately know that local, state, and national governing structures and authorities have failed to make it possible for individuals and families to care adequately for themselves and others, precisely because they lack access to and the means to afford healthy foods. Another egregious failure of state authorities to care is seen in the suffering of the citizens of Flint,

Michigan. To save money, government-appointed officials shifted Flint's source of water to a polluted river. This failure was compounded by a second grievous failure. Officials not only failed to heed the numerous health concerns and complaints of citizens, they also ridiculed them (Bosman, Davey, and Smith 2016). Basic biological needs, like clean water, are closely aligned with psychosocial needs, though these needs are sometimes more difficult to obtain clarity and consensus. People who live in poverty (lacking the meeting of basic biological needs) and those who struggle to make ends meet are more likely to struggle with anxiety and depression (Desmond 2016; Ehrenreich 2011; Mander 2012; Marris 1996). More positively, when governments provide programs and policies that enable access to good-enough childcare (healthy food and clean water), we can say that psychosocial needs of children are being met as well as the psychological needs of their parents. Parents who know their children are receiving good care have lower psychological stress. Spiritual[7] needs are even more challenging to delineate with precision, yet for individuals and for people to survive and flourish, individual persons and a community or society need ultimate, transcendent, or vital meanings and purposes that ground their lives. A negative illustration of this is provided by Jonathan Lear (2006), who described the cultural devastation of the Crow people by the United States government and their citizens. Attempts to deny the Crow people land, language, and rituals had terrible effects on the spiritual, psychological, and physical health of the Crow people. To be sure, they survived, but, to use Agamben's (1998) term, "bare-life," they did so despite the woeful lack of care and concern demonstrated by U.S. political leaders and white residents. To undermine a people's core narratives and rituals negatively impacts their spiritual and psychological needs.

The second category of developing basic capabilities refers to things such as language, education, agency, and creativity. Good-enough parents, for instance, are motivated to teach their children language and social skills so that they assert themselves as they live a life in common—in the polis. In a complex, technological society, a viable state is also interested in the education of its citizens/residents. It is not simply a matter of justice when we discover that poor children of color receive fewer resources for their education, thus creating more obstacles for them to develop their agency and creativity in the larger polis; it is a matter of callous carelessness by the political leaders and associated systems that deny basic rights to these children and their families. These failures to care reflect tragic shortsightedness, because failure to meet the needs of poor and working-class children leads only to more problems for the entire polis—a less well-functioning and healthy polis. Of course, politicians of all stripes tout the importance of education, but the reality of huge disparities in access to quality education give the lie to their proclamations and confirm their lack of political integrity, courage, and will. The presence of structural racism, sexism, and classism, which from a pastoral theological perspective are examples of sin, are also symptoms of carelessness vis-à-vis a polis and its political and economic structures. These social sins clearly impact the education of many people of color and, in turn, create obstacles to individuals' development of basic capabilities.

Racism, classism, and other forms of oppression and marginalization segue into the third feature of the definition of care, namely, participation in the space of appearances. While I will say more about this below in terms of knowledge and recognition, I note that care, as a political concept, means that people in the polis participate in public-political spaces to the degree that they are able. Political philosopher Nancy Fraser (Fraser and Honneth 2003) uses the notion of parity of participation as a criterion for analyzing issues of political recognition (identity politics) and redistribution. "According to this norm," Fraser writes, "justice requires social arrangements that permit all (adult) members of society to interact with one another as peers" (p. 36). I would add care to the notion of justice (LaMothe 2017).[8] An important feature of Fraser's criterion is parity, which for her means equivalence in acting in a democratic society. If we turn to Aristotle's notion of human beings as political animals, parity in his political realm and era would refer to men of property, thus excluding women, property-less men, and slaves. The exclusion of some adults inevitably raises issues of both justice and care. Excluding women from the polis' space of appearances likely leads not only to the lack of political voice in raising their concerns, but also restrictions in meeting their basic capabilities and needs. Of course, women who are excluded continue to participate in the polis, but clearly their participation does not come close to the criterion of parity. This said, even when a constitution enshrines inclusion and the principle of all adult citizens possessing the right to vote, parity still can be lacking. After seventy years of agitating for the right to vote in the United States, women achieved this right in 1920. One would be hard-pressed to say that women achieved parity in 1920 or in the decades that followed, given that women's representation in government positions is considerably less than the percentage of women voting (Shepard 2012). Jim Crow laws (and subsequent laws after Jim Crow: see Alexander 2010; Anderson 2016) are also examples of attempts to keep political parity at bay vis-à-vis African Americans. Jim Crow laws emerged after Reconstruction and enabled southern states to suppress violently black participation in the political realm, which had significant poisonous effects on their access to resources that could be used to care for themselves and others. Not surprisingly, then, restricting participation in the space of appearances negatively impacts the survival and flourishing of individuals and groups (e.g., African Americans, Native Americans, Hispanics). More recently, voter suppression laws and the Supreme Court's ruling, *Citizens United*, are clear illustrations of undermining the principle of parity of participation. I wish to stress here that these are not simply issues of justice. When individuals and groups are inhibited from parity of participation in the polis' space of appearances, one can be sure that there is a corresponding reduction in resources in meeting needs and developing capacities.[9]

The fourth feature of care as a political concept involves habitation. At its most basic level, care in the polis means providing places for people to live. Sociologist Matthew Desmond (2016) researched the lives of people living in impoverished areas of Milwaukee. For a variety of complex political and economic reasons, many people in these areas had been evicted or were under threat of eviction. These evictions were "legal" and one could weakly argue just (in that they were legal evictions), but in terms of the notion of care these evictions and the threat of evictions clearly evidence the lack of care by political and economic leaders as well as the political-economic structures that supported and gave legitimacy to the evictions. To care for oneself and others requires adequate food, money, and safe, affordable *housing*. A Rice University (2015) study demonstrates that evictions have significant negative impacts on persons' psychological and physical well-being—findings found in other studies done in various Western countries. A state that cares more for the well-being of the propertied classes and ignores or gives scant attention to the basic needs and capabilities of the society's least powerful residents is failing not only with regard to justice, but also care. As Wolin (2016) notes, "Democracy, or rather democracy-in-bad-faith, is reshaped to serve as accessory to inequalities" (p. 447) and the lack of affordable housing is a symptom of political carelessness associated with pervasive economic and political inequalities.

While having a home is necessary for people to care for themselves and others, we also need to consider more systemically what a habitable environment means. This can be understood in two related ways. First, a habitable environment can be undermined, so to speak, by the state's complicity in privileging mining corporations over the habitable needs of local citizens and communities. For instance, mountain top removal (MTR) has had poisonous health effects on local populations (Hedges and Sacco 2012, pp. 116–175). Jason Howard (2012) writes that MTR is a "radical form of strip mining that has left over 2,000 miles of streams buried and over 500 mountains destroyed. According to several recent studies people living near surface mining sites have a 50 percent greater risk of fatal cancer and a 42 percent greater risk of birth defects than the general population." Environmental racism (and classism) is another systemic example of political failures to care for the habitation of its citizens, leading to adverse health effects. The U.S. General Accounting Office (GAO), for instance, found that poor African Americans and other minorities were more likely to live closer to hazardous waste sites, resulting in health issues and lower lifespans (Skelton and Miller 2016). Again, this is not simply an issue of justice, but one of care. Second and relatedly, we are now in the Anthropocene Era, where climate change is already altering the habitats of millions of people (Kolbert 2014), resulting in diverse negative psychological and physical health effects (Parenti 2011; Sassen 2014). Citizens and political leaders not only need to care about their local, regional, and national environment (air, water, land), but also the larger world, as pastoral theologian Larry Graham (1992) argued decades ago. We can no longer simply care for our piece of the earth, sky, and sea. All political communities are tied to one habitat and therefore the notion of care as a political concept demands that everyone and every polis participate in caring for the earth.

Roman philosopher and jurist Cicero believed that those tasked with administrating society have as their duty to first care for citizens and their property so that they might survive and thrive (Wolin 2016, p. 79). The idea that care is a political concept is not often in the foreground of political philosophy or theology, though it is never completely absent. Pastoral theologians can contribute to political discourse and planning by affirming the utility of the concept of care in evaluating social, economic, and political realities. Defining care as a political concept moves us to raise questions about its attributes.

THE ATTRIBUTES OF CARE FROM
A POLITICAL PERSPECTIVE

With a definition of care, we can begin to examine more closely the attributes of care, using a political lens. Caring activities, I argue, entail three interrelated features, namely, knowledge, dispositions, and equal regard, which can be seen in prepolitical and political activities.[10] I start with Maurice Hamington (2004), who writes that knowledge "is a *necessary condition* of care" (p. 44). To understand this further, I turn to two political philosophers, John Macmurray (1991/1961) and Alex Honneth (1995).[11] Macmurray, a neo-Kantian, divided human knowing into object and personal knowing. Object knowing involves recognizing objects in space, which can include instrumental and calculative forms of knowing. This form of knowing is present from birth, though rudimentary, as the infant learns to locate and categorize objects using his/her various senses. As the child grows, object knowing becomes increasingly sophisticated in terms of categorizing objects and becomes the foundation of instrumental and calculative types of reasoning, which are necessary for acts of care. The sophistication of object knowing is connected to the symbol systems the child is thrown into and learns to make use of in categorizing objects and organizing experience. A simple example is the emergency room physician whose instrumental, calculative reason or object knowing is based largely on a complex system comprised of medical symbols and practices, which aid him/her in diagnosing the patient's condition so that healthcare practitioners can adequately treat the patient. From a more abstract political perspective, instrumental and calculative forms of object knowing are used in the construction of policies and programs, which ideally have as their aims justice and/or care. The congresswoman who writes a bill that reduces the taxes of poor and working-class people may be said to use object knowing to diagnose the political-economic reality with the aim of enabling persons to care for themselves and their families. The calculative and instrumental reasoning she uses to develop the legislation is dependent on a complex array of collectively held narratives and other culturally and politically contingent semiotic forms (e.g., political documents, research papers).

While object knowing, for Macmurray, appears first in human development, personal knowing develops later and is foundational for living a life in common and in that the goals of personal knowing are individual and collective survival and flourishing. In brief, personal knowing is fundamentally contingent on the recognition[12] of the Other as a person—unique,[13] valued,[14] inviolable,[15] responsive, or agentic.[16] This type of knowing is, for Macmurray (1991/1961), the basis for all human knowing (p. 169). More specifically, personal recognition not only grounds knowledge necessary to care, but is foundational to a functioning and thriving polis. As Fiona Robinson (1999) writes, "Responding with care towards others emerges out of an ability to see the other as a concrete, particular person who exists not as 'other' in an absolute, objective sense, but as another whose uniqueness and particularity emerges through her relations with others" (p. 102).

Personal recognition/knowledge is important, especially when we consider political philosophers like Thomas Hobbes, whose depiction of society is grounded in the "primal act of recognition as enmity" (Wolin 2016, p. 418). This Hobbesian primal act of recognition constructs the Other "as a collection of usable powers" to meet one's self-interests (p. 418—instrumental reasoning) and, while this view might sustain a dystopian society bent on mere survival, it is hardly one that can envision and enact a flourishing polis. By contrast, in Macmurray's philosophy of personal knowing, the primal act of recognition is personal and is foundational for living a life in common, whether that is a family, a community, or a society.[17] In a polis, the Other as person-resident is not a mere collection of usable powers—waiting to be exploited or to exploit—but a unique, valued, inviolable, responsive subject. In a decent or good-enough society, recognition of Others as persons is to intend their survival, self-realization (Honneth 1995, pp. 172–178), and freedom (Margalit 1996, pp. 200–201). In short, mutual-personal recognition founds the polis and in that it is a civil-moral act that regards the Other's needs and creates space and resources for his/her self-realization (Honneth 2007, pp. 337–338).

I will say more about the political act of personal recognition and care below. Now, however, it is important to delve more deeply into Macmurray's premise that personhood is both an existential fact—which from a pastoral theological perspective might fall under the ontological category of *imago dei*—and a matter of intention. Macmurray acknowledges that human beings are relatively free and thus can choose to ignore the existential fact of personhood—intending to recognize and treat human beings as objects. When people are primarily recognized as objects, one can be assured that personal care is absent. Perhaps we can think of intentions and acts of recognizing other individuals as person as participating in God's ongoing acts of creation—incarnating God means, in part, creating human beings as persons—unique, valued, inviolable, agentic subjects. We are obliged to acknowledge this ontological fact,[18] but we are also free to reject it. When we choose not to, there is the inevitable misrecognition or nonrecognition, which reflects the reality of sin and thus attending forms of alienation—exploitation, marginalization, and oppression. Theologically, grace restores the relationship through a recovery of the intention to recognize the Other as a person. The City of God, then, would involve a life lived in common wherein all intend to recognize and treat each other as persons and, when this fails, there are rituals to restore mutual-personal recognition and treatment. Whether understood philosophically or theologically, human beings have the agency to construct the Other as a person, leaving object knowing subordinate to personal knowing.

Alex Honneth (Fraser and Honneth 2003) holds a similar perspective to Macmurray's, though he frames this largely in terms of distributive justice and offers a way to parse out recognition vis-à-vis the polis. He argues that in a just (and caring society) "social recognition is always substantively shaped by the normative principles determined by the elementary structures of mutual recognition" (p. 175). This, he argues, enables "the personal identity-formation of all members of society" (p. 177). Interestingly, he anchors this personal-identity formation to "affective care" (p. 181). Mutual-personal recognition is not simply a matter of justice, but one that is integral to mutual care. Relying and building on the works of Hegel and Mead, Honneth (1995) parses recognition and care (and justice) into love (e.g., family, friends), law (legislative, judicial, and executive), and the social (society or public realm), with each area possessing complex narratives and practices that support personal recognition.[19] When personal recognition occurs in these realms or spaces of appearances, an individual obtains basic self-confidence, self-respect, and self-esteem (p. 129). Implicit here is that mutual-personal recognition/knowing in a polis means that one's psychological, social, and physical needs are being met so that persons not only survive, but also thrive (self-realization for Honneth). Put differently, mutual-personal recognition means that a society's distribution of resources is provided to members whereby they can care for each other's needs. By contrast, Honneth notes that failures in mutual-personal recognition in the polis has material effects and in that resources needed to survive and thrive are denied or restricted vis-à-vis individuals who are misrecognized or not recognized as persons. He writes, "Even material inequalities . . . must be interpretable as expressing the violation of well-founded claims to recognition" (Fraser and Honneth 2004, p. 134). Put differently, misrecognition of individuals in the polis, which depends on narratives and practices, means that knowledge of these misrecognized Others is distorted, leading to an attenuation of the space of appearances, maldistribution of resources needed to care, and losses in self-confidence, esteem, and respect (see Ritterman 2017; Sayer 2005). Simply stated, recognition for Honneth (Fraser and Honneth 2003) has very clear political, psychosocial, and material consequences.

To expand on and further clarify the idea of personal recognition/knowledge and its relation to care and the polis requires saying a bit more about Macmurray's epistemology and, in particular, the relation between personal knowing and object knowing. Personal knowing necessarily includes object knowing. We must be able to locate and categorize objects, even as we recognize the Other as a person. A parent, in responding to the cries of his/her infant, locates the infant as an object in space, diagnosing or analyzing (instrumental reasoning) the meanings and purposes of the infant's cries, all the while recognizing the infant as a person. Physicians, therapists, and others in helping professions diagnose patients, which necessarily involves object knowing and this is necessary to care for the person. A problem arises when object knowing remains in the foreground and personal knowing is secondary. This would entail a kind of objectification or reification of the Other, raising questions about care (and justice). That is, the patient is seen and treated as a category—patient—and secondarily as a person. For Macmurray (1961), this is *only* ethical if it is time limited and clearly for the benefit of the patient. Physicians, for instance, who, after treating the patient, continue to recognize and treat the patient in instrumental or diagnostic ways are doing so not for the sake of the patient but for their own sake. There are, of course, numerous occasions in human life in the polis where there is an eclipse of personal knowing and the overwhelming dominance of object knowing—slavery, racism, sexism, anti-Semitism, and so on. In these instances, the Other appears in the space of appearances as an objectified negative construction and not (or less than) as a person. Even occasions where care is provided in the public realm to a negatively constructed Other, the Other is seen as less than a person (distorted knowledge) and adequacy of care (and justice) is called into question.

The autobiography of Malcom X (Haley 1964) provides a tragic illustration. Months after his father was murdered, his mother was having a very difficult time trying to keep the family together. As a black woman during the depression, she encountered numerous obstacles that prevented her from having the necessary resources needed to care for her children. She slowly succumbed to the pressure, eventually having a psychological collapse. During her struggle to care for her children, the family relied on the government for food, and social workers often checked on Malcolm's family and, in particular, monitored his mother. After this experience, Malcolm X concluded, "I truly believe that if ever a state social agency destroyed a family, it destroyed ours. We wanted and tried to stay together. Our home didn't have to be destroyed. But the Welfare, the courts, and their doctor, gave us a one-two-three punch. And ours was not the only case of this kind" (p. 22). This case illustrates problems of care that were rooted in recognition inflected by racism (and classism)—misrecognition—that had material and psychological effects. When individuals are not recognized and treated as persons in the space of appearances, one can be assured that knowledge of the Other is distorted and this distortion leads to injustice and acts of carelessness, giving rise, in Honneth's view, to problems in distribution of resources and correspondingly to diminution of self-confidence, self-respect, and self-esteem. Put another way, political misrecognition or nonrecognition, which is supported by collectively held narratives and institutional practices (disciplinary regimes), eventuates in the attenuation of the space of appearances and disruptions in the distribution of resources needed to care (Fraser and Honneth 2003, p. 134).

Malcolm X's story, then, represents situations in the polis when misrecognition vis-à-vis the Other as less than a person is derived from the ongoing presence of object knowing and the subordination of personal knowing, leading to distorted knowledge, an attenuation in the space of appearances, and distortions of care. This means that the misrecognized Other is not permitted to exercise his/her agency in participating fully in the polis' space of appearances and, whenever this occurs, one can be sure care is distorted or eclipsed. Forms of misrecognition in the polis, then, accompany disrespect, conflict, and reduced resources for the misrecognized Other to care for his/her needs and the needs of others. Honneth (2017) similarly points out that misrecognition or nonrecognition leads to forms of sociopolitical exclusion and this "isolation always entails an internal loss of freedom, a stagnation of prosperity and growth" (p. 61). Put differently, misrecognition reduces the individual's (or group's) sociopolitical agency to assert him/herself in the space of appearances, which has very real consequences in terms of obtaining the resources needed to care for him/herself and others. By contrast, Alex Honneth (1995) notes that only "when all members of society mutually respect their legitimate claims can they relate to each other socially in the conflict-free manner necessary for the cooperative completion of societal tasks" (p. 50).

There are three other notable features of personal knowing and recognition to address, namely, immeasurability, un-representability, and identification, which highlight the paradoxical and complex reality of knowing. When we recognize the Other as a person, we acknowledge that s/he is valued and unique. By this, I mean that s/he is beyond all human attempts to assess or calculate her/his value, which are aspects of object knowing. Of course, there are times when the resources needed to care are limited and there may be necessary political calculations regarding the costs of caring for a person or community. Yet, the limitation of resources does not erase the existential or theological (*imago dei*) fact of the immeasurable value of the individual as a person or the immeasurable value of groups of persons. Unfortunately, in daily life we encounter many examples where individuals and groups are objectified, reified, and commodified. In these instances, there is an eclipse of recognizing the Other as a person of inestimable value and the dominant presence of instrumental object knowing that assigns measurable value vis-à-vis the Other and the relationship. A few years ago, I happened to overhear two businessmen calculating the costs associated with hiring new employees vis-à-vis profits for their shareholders. While the logic of this kind of thinking in a neoliberal capitalist era makes sense to many people, it nevertheless involves recognizing the Other in terms of circumscribed value—Others as usable powers. This calculation serves to rationalize and justify decisions that are aimed solely at the survival and flourishing of the company—an entity and not a person.[20] Michael Sandel (2012) offers another egregious case where personal knowing is absent, while acquisitive, calculative reason is dominant. A Walmart employee died while working and Walmart received $300,000, because it had taken out life insurance policies on some of its workers. A spokesperson for Walmart rejected the idea that the company profited from the death of this worker. "We had considerable investment in these employees," the spokesperson said (pp. 131–133). The man's value as a worker was determined by the market, which for most people is quite chilling, precisely because it contradicts the value and uniqueness of the person. The insurance, in other words, is for a "cog" (apparently worth $300,000) in the machine, rather than for the person. The man's survivors, who clearly needed the money to care for family members, received nothing, which is further evidence of Walmart's business leaders' cruel refusal to recognize any obligation to recognize and care for persons.[21]

Closely connected with immeasurableness is the un-representable reality of person. To be sure, each of us possesses many representations of people we care about, yet these representations cannot fully capture or define the individual as a person, which means there is psychic and relational space for the Other to appear as his/herself. Ideally, caring acts necessarily involve representations of the Other, but there is an unstated or unconscious realization that the individual as person is beyond any and all representations. No diagnosis, no single or group of representations can capture the Other as a person or capture a people. Emmanuel Levinas (1969, 1998) employs the metaphor face in his philosophy, which points to the un-representable nature of the other as person. From a theological perspective, Levinas' notion of the face of the Other is seen in the metaphor *imago dei*. We have representations of the un-representable God and this un-representable God creates human beings in God's image. Tragically, there are numerous routine examples in the polis when human beings take a representation of an Other(s) and believe it fully defines him/her—a totalizing representation. Racism is a form of recognition (knowing that is not-knowing because it is based on an ontological illusion—white superiority) wherein the Other is represented and treated in negative and totalizing ways, which denies both the immeasurableness and un-representableness of the Other as a person. Occasions of racism (or sexism, classism, ableism, etc.) involve representations of the Other that are contingent and associated with objectification and instrumental, calculative reasoning. It involves a relational demand that the Other accept and live out of this imposed representation, instead of the Other expressing agentically his/her own representations associated with being a person—unique, valued, and inviolable. In these moments, then, we are not surprised that racists do not know the Other as a person because s/he totalizes the black person. When this occurs, there is an eclipse of care (and justice) for the Other.

Immeasurability and un-representability of personal knowing, while quite abstract, are linked to the particularities of individuals and their families, communities and cultures. While persons are immeasurably valued and un-representable in the sense that personhood cannot be confined or limited to representation, they have particular (understandings of these) needs, experiences, traits (physical, psychological), beliefs, and so on. This is true when we think about the knowledge (object and personal) needed to care for another individual. From birth, good-enough parents recognize their baby as a person, which entails learning her unique and particular traits and needs from her various assertions. This particular knowledge and associated representations are necessary if parents are to care effectively for their child. At a more macro and ambiguous political level, William Easterly (2013) researched the work of organizations that provide care to groups of people who are in need (e.g., rural communities in Ethiopia). These experts, having good intentions, tended to diagnose (knowledge and recognition) the needs of these people and develop programs to care for them without listening to them and getting to know them in all of their uniqueness.[22] To be sure, the results were not all bad, but they were deeply flawed because staff members did not know the people personally and they did not obtain their input with regard to the problem and solutions. One might say that the experts[23] recognize rural people as persons, but in a very abstract or intellectual way, which results in a lack of necessary concrete personal knowledge for effective caring interventions.

One of the tragic realities of human life in the polis is the tendency to believe that one's particular representations of personhood, alongside the immeasurability and un-representability of life, are reserved for those in one's group or community. Members of one's group are recognized and treated as persons, while those who are not are deemed to be less than persons. Racism and classism are examples of this tragic aspect of life in a polis. For instance, whites treat each other with respect, believing each other to be persons, while blacks are considered less than persons, which means their value can be measured and the representations assigned to them are *the* truth. Naturally, this leads to a distortion of knowledge and, correspondingly, an attenuation of the space of appearances and care. On these occasions, we note the presence of idolatry (elevation of one's group's representations) and a denial of the scriptural truth that all human beings are created in the image and likeness of God—all are immeasurable and, like God, unmeasurable.

The third aspect of the recognition of Others as persons is identification. Psychoanalyst Roy Schafer (1990) notes that "identification refers to another kind of internalization" (p. 16), which involves "modifying the subjective self or behavior, or both, in order to increase one's resemblance to an object taken as a model" (p. 16).[24] This means that an individual finds traits and representations of the Other to be like him/herself—the Other is like me. In terms of recognizing the Other as a person, identification is on a continuum. On one end, there are individuals of my family, community, or society who share a common identity. This common identity includes myriad representations— rooted in shared narratives and rituals—connected to my identity, which, in turn, is connected to my seeing them as persons. This kind of particular, contextual personal identification is central to obtaining a society that coheres and is relatively stable. At the other end of the continuum is the stranger— the one with whom I do not share any representations. Personal recognition, in this case, means that there is a rudimentary, existential identification by which I mean that I identify the Other as a human being—a person like me.

Let me complicate this a bit further to highlight the necessary paradoxical reality of personal recognition, care, and the space of appearances. The parent who cares for his/her infant tends to have numerous identifications. "Doesn't she look like daddy?" "He has the same traits as his mother." This is necessary to form an affective bond, but identification must accompany healthy disidentification—the baby is not me. This disidentification creates a prepolitical space for the child to assert his/her unique personality in the parent-child space of appearances. When a parent overidentifies with the child, it reduces this space, forcing the child to comply with the parent's projected representations. A good-enough parent holds the paradoxical tension of identification and disidentification—likeness in difference and difference in likeness (Benjamin 1995)—and, in so doing, creates a space for the child to assert his/her agency and live out of his/her own representations. Similarly, in a polis there must be a paradoxical tension between identification and disidentification if the space of appearances is to be inclusive of difference, while affirming likeness. If the polis bends toward the pole of identification, then we can expect to see people excluded—people who do not hold or live out dominant representations. These people, these Others, will be disidentified, which can take the forms of physical exclusion, exploitation, marginalization, and oppression. When the paradoxical tension declines, moving toward disidentification, there will inevitably be failures in care (and justice). Examples abound. Gays and lesbians in the United States (and Britain) hid in the shadows of the polis for decades. If they were exposed, public humiliation, imprisonment (e.g., Oscar Wilde), and other social and political sanctions occurred—all signifying strong disidentification, exclusion from claiming agency in the polis' space of appearances, and eclipse of care from the general public. Since the 1969 Stone Uprising in New York City, LGBTQI persons have made significant gains in being recognized and treated as persons, which indicates that disidentification (for many heterosexual citizens) has moved toward identification and this accompanies caring acknowledgment in living a life in common.

The challenge of identification-disidentification vis-à-vis the personal recognition of Others in the polis is a perennial struggle, which Honneth (1995), relying on Mead, argued has a particular historical trajectory. The development of societies, Honneth notes, is a "process in which the meaning of legal recognition (as persons) is gradually broadened" (p. 84). "Like Hegel," Honneth continues, "Mead considers the motor of those directed changes to be a struggle in which subjects continually strive to expand the range of their intersubjectively guaranteed rights" (p. 84). Put another way, those in a polis who mostly experience the dominant group's disidentification will eventually seek or demand personal recognition, like the growing LGBTQI movement in the 1970s. This pursuit is not to be understood simply in terms of legal or social personal recognition. The demands for personal recognition is the demand to be cared about and to have access to the resources needed to participate in the polis' space of appearances and the resources necessary to care for themselves so that they too might flourish. The long and ongoing struggle for civil rights in the United States by African Americans illustrates this tension of identification-disidentification and its relation to the distribution of political, social, and economic resources needed to care for each other.

Ferguson, Missouri, is a recent example of systemic racism (and classism), white disidentification vis-à-vis black citizens, and the exploitation of poor and working-class African Americans (Balko 2017). Citizens speaking out and protesting this situation are examples of attempts to (1) claim the paradoxical tension between identification-disidentification in personal recognition and (2) repair the space of appearances wherein poor black persons can obtain the necessary resources to survive and thrive.

The issue of recognition's identification-disidentification in the polis also concerns the stranger—the one not in or of the polis. We might immediately think of immigrants as well as enemies. Some countries do well in welcoming and caring for refugees who are fleeing economic and political oppression. In these instances, the notion "refugee" suggests a creative tension between identification and disidentification wherein the refugee, who is not one of us, is like us in that s/he is a person. Refugees, in this situation, may be expected to assimilate into the wider society, while still retaining their unique culture and its concomitant representations. Even in countries where refugees and other immigrants are accepted and provided the care necessary to survive and thrive in the society, there are, more often than not, citizens who are less welcoming. In these cases, there is anger and fear that "immigrants" are a threat to the polis, which reflects strong disidentification (collapse of the paradoxical tension) and, correspondingly, the motivation to deny care and to evict these Others from the polis' space of appearances. There is also the issue of the stranger who is the enemy. This is likely to be the individual (and group) where there is a near-absolute disidentification, which would accompany expulsion from the space of appearances and denial of any care (Guantanamo is a modern example of both expulsion and torture). Near-absolute disidentification is one step toward torturing and killing the Other. During the Nazi regime, Jews were identified as enemies, signifying near complete disidentification, the evidence of which was the extrajudicial murders of 6 million persons. Turning the lens to ourselves, the torture, humiliation, and killing of "Islamic radical jihadists" represents a parallel disidentification. The ethnic cleansing of Native Americans, slavery, Jim Crow, concentration camps for Japanese Americans, and environmental racism are also examples of extreme disidentification, misrecognition, and resulting carelessness.

One might claim that this is the nature of having enemies, but this would be a mistake. The scriptural command to love one's enemies means that one will have enemies, yet we are to care about and for them. It is, then, possible to maintain the tension between identification and disidentification in caring for one's enemies or for strangers.

A foundational attribute of any act of caring in the polis, then, is personal knowing/recognition wherein object knowing is secondary to personal knowing. I have stressed that personal knowing entails recognition of the Other as a person—unique, valued, inviolable, agentic subject—and these acts are an integral part of living a life in common. This recognition includes immeasurableness and un-representableness of persons. Moreover, I argued that recognition of Others as persons, with their own unique particularities, means that they participate in the polis' space of appearances and, in so doing, make possible the reception and giving of care. To be sure, there are always occasions of misrecognition, which demand that a polis has rituals or processes to repair these relations so that care and justice can be restored. All of this may sound idealistic, but I would suggest that we think about this as existing on a continuum, with one end being a Hobbesian polis where primal recognition of enmity (a dystopia) is the order of the day and the other end where the primal recognition is that of personhood (the City of God). A good-enough polis is dynamic and falls somewhere between these poles. One other point about personal knowing and the polis I wish to emphasize concerns and unique expressions and attributes of individuals and the polis. As indicated above, each person is unique, having different memories, stories, desires, and so on. The same can be said for each family or group. Personal knowing means understanding and appreciating these group stories and rituals, especially if one seeks to care for and about them. In terms of the polis' space of appearances, this means acknowledging the creative and vital tension between plurality of persons (families, communities) and their stories and collectively held stories. When knowledge of the dominant group is forced onto less powerful groups, the less powerful group's stories (particular representations of being persons) are excluded. This results in the exploitation, marginalization, and oppression of the less powerful individuals and groups. Put another way, misrecognition, which accompanies distorted knowledge of Others, includes the corruption and attenuation of the polis' space of appearances, which correspondingly obstructs care (and justice).

Another key attribute of care to consider is disposition or motivation. While knowledge is necessary for care, it is, according to Hamington (2004), not sufficient (p. 44). I am confident all of us can recall times in our lives when we had the knowledge to care, but were not disposed or motivated to do so. This can be both individual and societal, shaped by collective narratives, constitutions, and institutions. As a nation, we have the knowledge and resources to care for the material, health, and educative needs of poor people. Yet, because of how poor people are represented (e.g., Isenberg 2016), many citizens and political leaders lack the disposition and political will/courage to confront their misrepresentations (knowledge) of persons deemed poor and to redistribute resources so that poor persons can care for themselves and others.[25] One, therefore, must have not only knowledge but also the disposition to care, and this is not simply individual, but collective. This said, what comprises the disposition necessary to care in the polis? There are many possible answers to this question and I am going to briefly identify three, namely, openness to difference, equal regard or respect, and willingness to repair.

The disposition of openness vis-à-vis the polis' space of appearances and care suggests the willingness to recognize and accept the particularities of the Other as a person (including particular groups of persons). Put another way, it is a willingness to be moved by the Other's story. In Judeo-Christian scriptures, it is commanded to welcome the stranger, widow, and orphan. Being hospitable requires both openness and ignorance (stranger as outside one's experience or unacquainted) that create the space for the stranger to appear as s/he is and not what I think s/he should be. This disposition and the willingness to be moved by the Other require the skill of listening. Corradi-Fuimara (1990) believes that "unless we are ready, receptive—and also, possibly, vulnerable—the experience of listening appears to be impossible" (p. 119). To return to Easterly's (2013) criticism of experts, we note that these gifted people wished to help people in places like Ethiopia, yet they failed to listen to and be moved by the stories, needs, and experiences of the very people they wanted to help. Care, in these contexts, is faulty because the disposition to be open to Others is occluded, which results in distortions of the knowledge needed to care adequately. Closer to home, the Black Lives Matter movement is, in part, an attempt to speak to the larger white society and its political leaders regarding the lack of care and justice associated with the ways people of color are treated by the police and the judicial system. In terms of the space of appearances, blacks are trying to be heard in the larger polis that has historically shunted them aside. The question remains whether political leaders and white citizens will have the disposition to be open, to listen to, and be moved by the experiences and needs of people of color. The quick rejoinders such as Blue Lives Matter and All Lives Matter indicate a disposition of refusal—a refusal to be open to and care about the particular stories and experiences of black people, especially poor black persons.

Openness is often a source of anxiety in the polis. How much openness can we tolerate? Does openness mean living without borders? Do we welcome all strangers? Does anything go? Are there no boundaries if we are open? A polis by definition must have boundaries, whether they are understood as political geographical borders or boundaries associated with a collective identity and its concomitant stories and practices. From a system's perspective, a polis seeks some level of stability in its attempts to survive and thrive. The desire for stability can become exacerbated by anxiety and fear vis-à-vis the Other, whether the Other is already in the polis or outside. Real and imagined threats heighten fear and anxiety, which leads to closing borders and minds/hearts. This is seen in the move to elect populist rightwing leaders in Europe and the United States as they play upon and manipulate the fears, hatreds, prejudices, and ignorance of voters. The challenge for political leaders and citizens of the polis is to maintain boundaries and a collective sense of identity while being disposed to those who are different, those who are strangers. One can listen and understand Others without agreeing with them. One can care and be open, while also having expectations, demanding accountability, and maintaining boundaries.

Let's consider a group of people who are "strangers" in their own country, where economic (classism) and racial (racism) apartheid exist. Michelle Alexander (2010) and Mark Taylor (2015) describe how the judicial system has penalized and incarcerated people of color disproportionately. This is a tragic fact, but worse are the numerous punitive obstacles placed in the path of ex-felons who are returning to society. Extrajudicial fees, social-political-economic stigmatization, obstacles to employment and housing, and the denial of having basic voting rights are some of the problems these men and women face. The space of appearances is excessively restricted in these cases, which means that political leaders and citizens refuse to be open to and listen to the experiences and needs of these persons. In the process, these "people" are unknown, forgotten, and not cared about or for.[26] On the one hand, being open to and listening does not negate the need for the rule of law and the consequences for breaking laws. Citizens can do both. On the other hand, listening and openness may lead to the realization that some of these laws and policies are unjust or unjustly applied. Also, being open to those who are Othered, like prisoners, means finding ways to care for them in prison[27] and after they have completed their prison terms. Prisoners are first and foremost persons (theologically, created in the image and likeness of God), which existentially obliges us to care. There is, and will likely always be, a tension in how open or closed a polis will be, how disposed citizens are to care for strangers, but one can be sure that those citizens or noncitizens who are excluded from or marginalized vis-à-vis the space of appearances are more likely to be ignored, more likely to experience carelessness, more likely to be kept from resources needed to care for themselves and others, and more likely to experience exploitation and injustice.

Implicit in the disposition of openness is the notion of equality or equal regard.[28] Equality, in part, involves an attitude and belief that *persons* have a right to participate in political conversations and engage freely in civic life. This attitude and belief necessarily includes respect for the integrity of each participant and respect for the differences inherent in their experiences, needs, and values. Diversity and alterity vis-à-vis a democratic polis rest on the principle of equality that undergirds social respect or equal regard. The importance of respect, Hannah Arendt (1958) notes, is "not unlike the Aristotelean *philia politike*, [which] is a kind of 'friendship' without intimacy and without closeness; it is a regard for the person from the distance which the space of the world puts between us. . . . Thus the modern loss of respect, or rather the conviction that respect is due only where we admire or esteem, constitutes a clear symptom of the increasing depersonalization of public and social life" (p. 243). Sadly, Arendt's observation is noted in the U.S. political-public realm with the election of a celebrity who disparages and bullies those who disagree or challenge him. The depersonalization Arendt refers to reveals the presence of the totalitarian tendency, a tendency that fundamentally eschews equal regard, which is a key feature of the principle of equality. No respect, no equality. Positively stated, the principle of equality and the disposition of equal regard are inherent in civil discourse and action wherein each cares for everyone else and no one for him/herself (Macmurray 1961, p. 159). Care vis-à-vis the polis means that there is sufficient equality and equal regard such that the space of appearances is inclusive. Nancy Fraser (Fraser and Honneth 2004) frames this in a similar way, arguing that "participatory parity *is* the meaning of equal respect for equal autonomy of human beings *qua* social actors" (p. 231). Respect and participatory parity means that individuals' needs, desires, and experiences are recognized and affirmed, which, for Fraser and Honneth (2004, p. 176), is a matter of justice and, in my view, a matter of care. A negative example is racism, wherein people of color are not considered equal and thus not deserving of respect, pointing to an attenuation or collapse of the space of appearances. This belief and attitude are supported by institutions (or disciplinary and justificatory regimes), narratives, citizens, and leaders who believe in and seek to enforce the ontological falsehoods of white superiority and black inferiority. That is, the knowledge of blacks and whites is distorted by these illusions and the distortions privilege white people vis-à-vis equality, while establishing inequality vis-à-vis African Americans. This results in the marginalization of blacks from the space of appearances, which concretely means there is a corresponding lack of care (and justice).

Equal regard and respect do not imply agreement with or acceptance of the Other's position. I may strongly dislike and disagree with a person's economic proposal to reduce taxes for the wealthy, though because I hold to the principle of equal regard, I believe that s/he has a right and obligation to participate in the conversation. I abhor and politically resist the racist views held by another person, but I regard him/her as an equal who has a place in the polis' space of appearances even if he or she is trying to exclude others. I can agree that a person should be sent to prison for political corruption, yet because of equal regard, insure that he is treated fairly and cared for during his time in prison. Equal regard means, in speech and action, respecting the person qua person as being a part of the polis. In theological terms, even one's enemies are deemed children of God and we are commanded to love our enemies. One cannot love or care about one's enemies while not respecting them.

It is important to stress that in the polis, there may be individuals and groups that advocate violence and oppression of some of the polis' residents. Philosopher Avishai Margalit (1996) argued that a decent society can deter or reject immoral groups. Immoral groups are "Forms of life," he writes, "that lack value are those by which humiliation is a constitutive element. Racist groups such as the Ku Klux Klan or skinheads might constitute encompassing groups for their members, but they lack value because their form of life is based essentially on humiliating others" (p. 174). Humiliating other persons necessarily means that openness, equal regard, and respect are absent, which, in turn, means an eclipse of care—care necessary for the vitality of the polis. That said, Margalit does not mean that the state should be involved in humiliating the KKK, but rather find ways to observe and restrict the organization. Put another way, the state (and other citizens) need to continue to respect KKK members as persons—as citizens—but this does not mean respecting their beliefs or practices, which have no civic value. Indeed, the state can find ways to discourage, limit, and restrict humiliating ideologies precisely because they have no civic value (no equal regard). The danger here is that the dominant group of a society can determine what encompassing group is morally legitimate and illegitimate. The anxiety and fear of Christians resulting from terrorist attacks can lead some political and religious leaders to suggest that Islam is not a morally legitimate religion because it putatively gives rise to terrorists. Since some political leaders cannot sequester or expel Muslims they find ways to increase surveillance or restrict entry. If we rely on Margalit's view, we detect an irony here. Those who consider Islam to be morally illegitimate are advocating a form of political humiliation, calling into question their own legitimacy.

One might press this further raising a question about the limits of the principle of equality in the polis. In other words, should we allow the participation in societal discourse of neo-Nazi groups, Al Qaeda, and so on? The principle of equality suggests a very wide interpretation of participation, but the limits, in my view, are drawn by the presence or advocacy of harm or violence toward others, which is a symptom of the loss of the principle of equality, an attenuation or collapse of the space of appearances, and, correspondingly, the rise of carelessness and injustice. Persons who advocate violence, who exploit others, who oppress and marginalize individuals and groups, eschew any notion of equality and equal regard that undergird justice and care in the polis. Indeed, a polis, like Deadwood, cannot thrive, though it can survive, in the presence of violence, hatred, and excessive fear. Individuals, who show no interest in the common good and parity of participation in the polis' space of appearances, must be restrained legally. This includes undermining institutions that advocate for and support inequality.

Of course, we have the problematic issue of social, political, and economic institutions that enforce practices that clearly contribute to a lack of disrespect and support structural inequalities that impede the distribution of goods needed for despised individuals and groups to care for themselves and others. In these instances, justice (and care) is "but a vain word" (Hobbes, in Wolin 2016, p. 241). Honneth (1995) believes that the trajectory of history demonstrates that individuals and groups who are treated unequally eventually speak out and demand parity of participation. Women's suffrage, the civil rights movement, and LBGTQI groups' demand for civil rights illustrate the desire for equality and equal regard. Perhaps the challenge for marginalized and oppressed groups in a polis is choosing the means to effect political change while maintaining equality and equal regard in the face of resistance. Martin Luther King Jr. and many others in the civil rights movement embodied equality and equal regard in the face of hatred and violence.[29] A polis thrives when there is equal regard, because people recognize the needs and experiences of persons and groups who are different from themselves, which makes it more likely that care (and justice) will be mostly realized.

The ideals of being disposed to openness and equal regard are exactly that—ideals. This suggests that, as human beings, we frequently fail to live up to and embody these ideals in the polis. We often do not have the necessary knowledge to care because we are not disposed to be open to the Other, and we may not be disposed to care because we do not possess the attitude and belief of equal regard. These situations lead to societal disruptions, alienation, enmity, and divisions (e.g., class). From the perspective of care, these situations reflect varied degrees of failure in care (and justice) between persons and groups. Examples abound, ranging from the horrific treatment of Native Americans to conflicts and divisions between political-corporate leaders and workers who are denied a living wage. These sociopolitical disruptions of care require a willingness to repair social disruptions so that some level of care and cooperation can be restored. The refusal to do so does not mean a polis will necessarily fail, but, wherever this failure is experienced, that part of the polis will not thrive. Naturally, citizens can refuse to do the work of repairing or reconciling and that becomes a decision to maintain divisions and associated carelessness and injustice.

The willingness to do the work of repair is not simply an individual decision, but a collective one, and it is crucial for a thriving polis. Moreover, the decision to repair is connected to narratives and institutions that facilitate the decision and enable the process through which some level of repair can take place. In the Catholic tradition, the Church is considered to be a society or, we could say, polis. The Church has long recognized the importance of the sacrament of reconciliation vis-à-vis the spiritual health of individuals and communities. This example points to an existential reality or truth. Human relationships, whether seen in marriage, families, communities, and societies, need to have (1) narratives that uphold the demand or command to repair and thus the hope for reconciliation and (2) institutions and processes to do the hard work of repair so that care can replace enmity and division. Consider a secular example of this existential political truth—the South Africa's Truth and Reconciliation Commission. Archbishop Desmond Tutu's (1999) book, *No Future without Forgiveness*, portrays the deep emotional struggles of South Africans. Understandably, many black South Africans wanted revenge for the decades of cruel apartheid policies and the corresponding state-sanctioned white oppression and violence enforcing these policies. Black South Africans knew that most white South Africans had supported political, economic, and social policies of exclusion, resulting in profound poverty, violence, and exclusion from the polis' space of appearances (in the sense of having no power or voice). The lack of equal regard and respect accompanied a collapse of the space of appearances and correspondingly a loss of public self-respect, esteem. All of this was felt materially, in the restricted distribution of resources (e.g., poor housing, lack of healthcare, poor education, economic exploitation), which made it very difficult for black South Africans to care for each other. Archbishop Tutu and many other religious and secular leaders realized that, without the demanding work of forgiveness, the future of South Africa would be determined by a hopeless cycle of carelessness, violence, hatred, and injustice. The institution and process of the Truth and Reconciliation Commission were aimed at doing the challenging work of forgiveness, reconciliation, and repair so that South Africa as a polis could not only continue to survive, but to thrive in new ways.

The fact that the United States has never instituted a Truth and Reconciliation Commission regarding Native Americans and African Americans means this will result, in my view, in more division and alienation between groups. When a dominant group in a society refuses to face the sins of its past, it means the group does not really believe in equality and equal regard vis-à-vis the Other. What the dominant group believes in is its own superiority and innocence, which leads not only to willed amnesia with regard to one's political sins, but also the continuation of strife and alienation. Put differently, denial and rationalization of one's sins ensures that the shadow side of the polis is alive and well, undermining care and giving rise to ongoing injustice. Certainly, individual citizens can decide to become aware of the long history of failures to care, failures to know and treat blacks and Native Americans as equals. But the polis as a whole has not addressed this history or attempted to work through past and present failures to care adequately. As long as the United States exists without facing this history and doing the work of repair, there will be no post-racial America.

CONCLUSION

In this all-too-brief overview, I have argued that care is a political concept. As a political concept, the notion of care comprises various attributes such as knowledge, disposition, equal regard, and a willingness to repair. As human beings living in society, we know that no society possesses enough knowledge, openness, and equal regard to care for all its citizens. There are always political failures to care, some of which are repeated because of the collectively held narratives, rituals, and institutions that make these failures possible. Failures to care, whether in the prepolitical space of parent-child interactions or in the larger political space of the larger polis, require practices of repair, if the polis is to survive. Even the dystopian town of Deadwood, where violence and the threat of violence were ever-present, had attempts at repair. That there is no City of God on earth only tells us of the continual need for both justice and care in the polis, not simply for the sake of the polis' survival, but for the flourishing of its residents. Thus care, as a political concept, is as necessary as the notion of justice when examining a society and in considering political actions, especially as we face grim realities such as racism, classism, sexism, and the looming threat of global warming. As Fiona Robinson (2011) remarks, "Caring practices and labor must be recognized as a vital activity of citizenship and as the most fundamental feature of well-functioning communities and states" (p. 119).

NOTES

1. I can understand and appreciate the skepticism about discourse that uses universal principles or notions of a generalized Other, especially when this has served to eclipse the particularities of a culture and the needs and experiences of the oppressed group. Yet, in my view, we should not abandon discourse that involves universal ideas, principles, rights, and so on, not only because human beings, while diverse in language and culture, are alike in many ways, but also because we are facing global challenges due to climate change—challenges that give rise to injustice, non-justice, carelessness, and non-care. With regard to care and faith, we need to face and engage the diverse particularities of people, as well as the similarities we all share. Toward this end, I agree with Seyla Benhabib (1992), who argues for an interactive universalism that "acknowledges the plurality of modes of being human, and differences among humans, without endorsing all the pluralities and differences as morally or politically valid. . . . Interactive universalism regards difference as a starting point for reflection and action. In this sense, 'universality' is a regulative ideal that does not deny embodied and embedded identity, but aims at developing moral attitudes and encouraging political transformation that can yield a point of view acceptable to all" (p. 153). She is careful to note that interactive universalism "is not the ideal of

consensus of fictitiously defined selves, but a concrete *process* in politics and morals of the struggle of concrete, embodied selves" (p. 153).

2. One realizes that a shared identity while necessary for living a life in common, can also be exclusive, nativist, and dangerous. Yet, a shared identity can also be open, welcoming, and inclusive of Others who are different. Moreover, shared identity can be expansive in the sense that a people recognize that Others are human beings and thus part of our common heritage.

3. I have deliberately avoided the term "citizens" and have chosen the more inclusive notion of "residents." A cursory glance over Western society reveals that nations have laws about who is a citizen and who is not, usually resulting in some residents being marginalized from the polis' space of appearances. So-called "illegal immigrants" are present day examples of this. My view is that the polis should be concerned about the survival and flourishing of all residents. And today I would go further and say that given the realities of global warming, we should be concerned about the survival and flourishing of all human beings (and other life forms).

4. I view love and care as related but distinct concepts. Love includes care, but to care does not necessarily include love. I can care about people I have never met, while sending them aid. The Samaritan cared for the injured man, but I do not think he loved him. Some might try to make the case that he did love him, but this is love in the abstract. A physician or nurse can care for someone who she thinks is despicable. There is care, but no love. Care, then, from my perspective, is more a fundamental human reality and a more fundamental political concept. I believe, then, that developing and maintaining caring attitudes and behaviors in society are more realistic goals than love. Care for others, for neighbors, is more likely and more common than love.

5. Arendt (1958), Honneth (1995, 2007a), and Margalit (1996) are three recent political philosophers who indicate that the aims of a well-functioning polis are self-realization and freedom, which depends, for Margalit (and Honneth), on recognition of others as persons (p. 117). They do not see these as merely individual aims whereby individuals compete to achieve both—a Hobbesian polis. Rather, these are aims that are achieved in concert with others. One other point, because of the uniqueness of each person and polis, citizens engage in political and public discourse that gives specifics to these aims.

6. Horkheimer commented that "The future of humanity depends on the existence today of the critical attitude" (in Wolin 2016, p. 231). Giroux (2012) and Dufour (2008), arguing from different perspectives, contend that with the rise of neoliberal capitalism there has been an increase in the formation of subjects or citizens who are acritical of the systems that contribute to their suffering and the suffering of others.

7. I am using this term in a very broad sense, which includes humanist perspectives. That is, I would regard a person(s), who is agnostic or atheist, to have "spiritual" needs in that s/he expresses and lives out a need for ultimate or vital concern—meaning and purpose. Put differently, spiritual means seeking the good (see Doehring 2012).

8. Axel Honneth (2007a) argues the postmodern philosophical perspectives have complexified the realm of the moral by including the concept of care. He writes, "What has been said so far . . . must also be accompanied by the conclusion that care be awarded that place in the domain of the moral which it has all too frequently been

denied in the Kantian tradition of moral philosophy. Just as solidarity constitutes a necessary counterpoint to the principle of justice inasmuch it furnishes the affective impulses of reciprocal recognition in a particularistic manner, care represents its equally necessary counterpoint, because it supplements this principle of justice" (p. 135).

9. It is dispiriting to realize that 46 million people in the United States are in poverty (see U.S. Census Bureau 2018). Daniel Weeks (2014) explores some of the reasons why poor people are marginalized from the political process. There clearly is not a parity of participation in the space of appearances.

10. Care theorists like Nell Noddings (1984) and Virginia Held (2006) claim that skills are a crucial feature of care. Noddings (1984) suggests that one's motivation to care "pushes me to acquire skills in caretaking. But it is important to recognize that they *are* skills" (pp. 122–123). The intern, for instance, is motivated to develop his/her skills, as well as to deepen his/her knowledge so that s/he can be effective in caring for patients. Virginia Held brings up another point. She argues that care "is a practice involving the work of care-giving and the standards by which the practices of care can be evaluated. Care must concern itself with the effectiveness of its efforts to meet needs, but also with the motives with which care is provided" (p. 37). While I agree that skills are an important attribute of care, a discussion of skills vis-à-vis care as a political concept will require more space than allotted for a chapter. In addition, the discussion of care in terms of knowledge and dispositions will, in my view, implicitly point to skills.

11. Macmurray's and Honneth's theories of personal knowing and recognition reveal the essentially relational, interdependent, and contextual nature of human life lived in common. Their philosophies/anthropologies respect the Enlightenment's regard for the individual without succumbing to the social-political-economic perils of individualism—especially the type of individualism that is wedded to and fuels neoliberal capitalism.

12. Scholars from various disciplines have followed the Hegelian emphasis on recognition and its relation to politics (Benjamin 1995; Benhabib 1992; Taylor 1989). While I find myself in their camp, I believe there is a lack of clarity about the notion of recognition in their work. For instance, Fraser (Fraser and Honneth 2003) argues that recognition is a matter of justice and that misrecognition is a violation of justice. We could replace the notion of justice with care, but I would still not have much clarity about what recognition means and why it is a matter of justice. A parent, for instance, may misrecognize the infant's assertion, resulting in a failure attune. This occurs often and is hardly a matter of justice, though it is a moment of a lack of care. The parent's misrecognition, then, is not a failure of identity or one that means the child is depersonalized. I think this is why Macmurray's epistemology is helpful and more nuanced. To recognize the Other as a person is the basis for just and caring acts. Misrecognition can take different forms, ranging from ambiguous moments of care and justice to egregious forms of carelessness and injustice. An example of an ambiguous form of misrecognition would be political leaders who recognize and believe that the "homeless" are persons, yet do not provide enough programs to address their particular needs. In these situations, care and justice are present, but inadequate.

13. We may consider an object unique because of its recognized characteristics and its rarity. If the object were to lose some or all of its characteristics and/or become common, it would no longer be considered unique. This is not the case when the Other is omnipotently constructed as a person. In the omnipotent construction of the baby as a person, for instance, uniqueness is primarily an ontological attribution and secondarily refers to the baby's specific traits (see, Mounier 1952; Levinas 1969, 1981; Zizioulas 1985, 2006). Uniqueness is not contingent on the attributes, skills, or achievements/productivity of the individual.

14. The valuation associated with objects concerns the object's capacities and qualities vis-à-vis the needs and desires of the individual who assigns the value. An object is valuable because it is rendered so by the individual(s). The valuer constructs the object as being valuable because of its qualities and functions. If the object were to lose some or all of its qualities or uses, while remaining what it is, the valuer might alter or withdraw his/her valuation. This said, when it comes to constructing the individual as a person, valuation takes on a different character. The individual as person is of value in him/herself. The valuation of the individual is not simply or solely based on his/her specific qualities, characteristics, or uses/functions, though these are certainly part of the mix. The individual qua person is existentially valuable in him/herself (Raz 2001).

15. Philosopher Joseph Raz (2001) remarked that when we "equate being an end in oneself with being of value in oneself, and take that condition as a ground for a certain treatment, that is, respect" (p. 155). Respect means security from being infringed upon or breached vis-à-vis one's embodied subjectivity—inviolableness. Political philosopher Rawls contends that "Each person possesses an inviolability founded on justice that even the welfare of the society as a whole cannot override" (Wolin 2016a, p. 3).

16. Niebuhr's (1963) anthropology contains the premise that human beings are responsive creatures—agentic. Even an infant has a rudimentary agency as s/he accepts or resists the parent's ministrations. The parent's agency includes (a) the omnipotent construction of the baby as person and (b) corresponding actions that communicate to the infant his/her singularity, inherent value, inviolability, and ability to act in the world. This omnipotent construction of the baby as person includes the belief or necessary illusion (and corresponding behavior) that the infant is an agent—an actor who possesses a will and mind of his/her own. This means that a good-enough parent accepts and affirms the baby's resistance—assertions—precisely because it is the baby's resistance that contributes to the parent's knowledge of the baby, as well as confirms the baby's self-experience as an existent—a self (Levin and Trevarthen 2000; Trevarthen 1993).

17. Simon Weil (1952) held a remarkably similar philosophical perspective vis-à-vis recognition and the polis. Using a different term, she wrote, "The object of any obligation, in the realm of human affairs, is always the human being as such. There exists an obligation towards every human being for the sole reason he or she is a human being, without any other condition requiring to be fulfilled, and even without any recognition of such obligation on the part of the individual concerned" (p. 5). The nature of this obligation is respect—effectively expressed (p. 6). Of course, this

obligation is, for varied reasons, often ignored in society, but without some respect, which is the basis of care and personal recognition, a society hardly seems viable.

18. One of the core features of French philosopher Emmanuel Levinas's (1969, 1981) philosophical work is the idea of the "face," which places an infinite obligation on the Other to respond. Levinas's philosophy is, in my view, inextricably joined to Jewish theology and I would a Christian pastoral theological anthropology that holds a view that each individual is a child of God—*imago dei*—an ontological fact.

19. Honneth's delineation does not mean that these three realms of personal recognition are disconnected. He views these as distinct realms, but interrelated. So, for instance, the illustration below on Malcolm X reveals how racism involves the misrecognition of African Americans in the realms of law and society, which in turn negatively impacts African Americans.

20. A reader will note that the concept of person is also a legal matter, which means that an institution like the Supreme Court of the United States can rule that corporations are persons in the sense of free speech and being able to participate in the space of appearances. From a philosophical and theological perspective, this ruling is ludicrous, though it does provide evidence for Macmurray's claim that "person" is a matter of intention. In other words, human beings have an incredible ability to recognize something as a person, as well as to refuse to recognize other human beings as persons.

21. This critique is not meant to suggest that business people ought to get rid of calculative rationality based on the contingent value of workers' labors. Indeed, these calculations (cost/benefit) analyses can take place in contexts of care, such as hospitals where physicians make decisions about treatment costs and benefit to the patient. There are, then, going to be instances when care takes place in the context of limited resources. I would echo Macmurray here and argue that this kind of analysis should not subordinate or eschew the recognition and treatment of the Other as a person.

22. Alex Honneth (2017) remarks that "The more those who are affected by a problem are involved in the search for the solution to that problem, the more historical-social experiments will lead to better and more stable solutions" (p. 62). Easterly's research confirms the necessity of inclusion of those who are most affected and this inclusion means a recognition of them as persons who possess the agency to participate fully in the space of appearances.

23. We can distinguish between direct and indirect care. Direct care involves people in face-to-face relations, which can involve errors in overlooking the particular beliefs, experiences of the person—errors that lead to problems in the effectiveness of care. Indirect care involves individuals, like Easterly's experts, who are not in direct contact with the people who are the recipients of aid. These experts are likely good-intentioned people who recognize the personhood of the people who are in need, but indirect care is often more likely to miss the target precisely because the particularities of the people are overlooked or simply not understood.

24. In psychoanalytic literature, identification can be healthy or unhealthy and it can also be viewed as a defense (McWilliams 1994, pp. 135–138). For my purposes, I focus more on identification in light of the recognition of Others as persons, which indicates the existential and political nature of identification. Moreover, I am less

concerned with the "unhealthy" forms of identification and disidentification, which are legion, than with the paradoxical reality of both vis-à-vis personal recognition.

25. Someone might point out that the way the poor are represented suggests that they are not recognized as persons or recognized as less than persons, which means that knowledge is not present or distorted. I agree, in part, but would add two things. First, one's disposition toward the Other can certainly result in a distortion of knowledge and hence care in the polis. In this scenario, the Other is constructed as less than a person and hence not meriting care. Second, one can have the personal knowledge of the Other, but not be disposed to care. We can collectively agree that poor citizens are persons, but not be disposed to care or care adequately because our collectively held neoliberal belief in individual economic responsibility leads to seeing them as responsible for their plight.

26. An egregious example of not only the refusal to listen, but the sadistic cruelty of white people in positions of political power, in this case Republicans, is described in Gilligan's book. Gilligan (2011) researched the effectiveness of college education for people who were in prison, reducing the recidivism rate to zero for those who had obtained a college degree (pp. 90–91). In publicizing their research, several state legislatures and the U.S. Congress decided to cut funding for these programs, arguing that prisoners should not receive these benefits—an example of a punishing state and political leaders and citizens who are not only care-less, but sadistically cruel. Gilligan considered these to be irrational and self-defeating policies, but they are rational if one recognizes that, in so doing, they insured private prison companies would have a more secure supply of "product" to exploit (p. 92).

27. There are all kinds of cruelty that go on in prisons, such as extended periods of solitary confinement, prison guards who rape, and so on. See Taylor (2015, pp. 101–110). It is easier to engage in cruel practices when prisoners are demeaned by the wider public and prisons remain out of the public spotlight (or space of appearances) and thus not held accountable.

28. One of the first modern political philosophers, Thomas Hobbes, notwithstanding his view that enmity is the first relation, argued that "when each individual consented to becoming a member of a system of rules, he was guaranteed a basic equality with every other member" (Wolin 2016, p. 241). This equality must be enforced by the sovereign with regard to justice and taxing if social stability is to take place. Wolin highlights a complication in Hobbes' approach, which is that Hobbes never dealt with the reality of inequalities that are "produced by unhampered pursuit of interest" (p. 241).

29. I would include Malcolm X, especially toward the end of his life. Unlike King, Malcolm X did not advocate nonviolent resistance, but he did recognize the need for equality and equal regard for all persons after his pilgrimages to Mecca (Haley 1964, p. 382).

Chapter 2

Faith and Care

The Foundations of a Polis

Faith, so common in daily discourse, is a term that has never been captive to scholarly delineations. Like other commonly used terms, faith takes on different meanings and has different references. In Catholic circles, "faith" is often restricted to the dogma of Catholic faith. Does he share the faith? We (Catholics) are the faithful. Of course, Catholics are by no means the only ones to do this. Many people who call themselves Christians may use "the faith" in reference to belief in Jesus Christ. People who are not religious may consider faith to be a category reserved for people who call themselves Christians, Jews, Muslims, and so on. Atheists and agnostics, for instance, may deny that they have faith at all because they believe that faith refers only to religion or spirituality. In the United States, we often hear about the separation of church and state, which can provide further impetus to restrict faith to religion. In one sense this is unfortunate, because it presupposes that the state is or should be somehow free of faith, while religious faith requires protections and fences or that the state needs to be wary of religion. Any cursory glance of even atheistic forms of government, like the former Soviet Union, reveals that faith is necessary for the state to survive. In my own country, the term "civil religion" refers to a kind of humanistic faith that is tied to values and beliefs associated with the U.S. Constitution and this humanistic faith is not tied to theological traditions and their associated religious communities. While I appreciate the use of the term "civil religion," I think it would be better to acknowledge that every polis possesses a political faith, which is necessary for civil cooperation vis-à-vis survival and flourishing.

In his discussion on the political philosophy of Thomas Hobbes, Sheldon Wolin (2016) notes that "the identity of the political was in large measure a product of beliefs, almost an act of faith" (p. 259). Hobbes, Wolin continues, considered every political order to be "artificial" (p. 260), in the sense that it is the creation of human beings, which political philosopher John Macmurray (1961) echoed centuries later in his discussion of the state (p. 203). Wolin remarks that "it remains true that however crude or sophisticated our notion on these matters, our beliefs exert an appreciable effect on the way we perceive political happenings and how we react in political settings" (p. 260). So, the action of creating a polis and acting in it is not "almost an act of faith," it is faith—a civic faith.

To understand this claim, we must move out of the realm of political philosophers, primarily because they are not experts on the subject of faith, often equating faith with religion. Prominent theologians, by contrast, do not confine the notion of faith to religion. Roman Catholic theologian Karl Rahner (1984) once stated that faith is "an abiding feature of man's mode of existence as a person" (p. 496). Indeed, it is faith, Paul Tillich argued (1952, 1957), that is constitutive for the very existence and development of selfhood and personality. Tillich (1963) went further, contending that "faith is actual in all life processes" (p. 134). Human faith, as an anthropological concept, is thus understood as "primarily and properly not a relation of man to things, propositions, or formulas, but a *relation* to persons" (Fries 1984, p. 520; emphasis mine). This human fact is noted in that "questions of faith arise in every area of human existence" (Niebuhr 1989, p. 1), which, of course, includes the polis and its space of appearances.

That H. Richard Niebuhr believed faith to be integral to living a life in common is evident in his concern with the forces that undermine faith. Writing in the shadows of World War II, Niebuhr considered that it was possible that "human history will come to its end neither in the brotherhood of man nor in universal death under the blows of natural or man-made catastrophe, but in the gangrenous corruption of a social life in which every promise, contract, treaty and 'word of honor' is given and accepted in deception and distrust" (p. 1). This bleak assessment, seemingly more true today, ends with a question: "If men no longer have faith in each other, can they exist as men?" (p. 1). Niebuhr rightly points out that faith is constitutive to social relations, to society, and thus to the polis. Aristotle's political animal is one whose survival and flourishing depends on existential faith—a faith that is inextricably yoked to care. The corruption of this impacts the survival and flourishing of the polis. Indeed, as Wolin and Macmurray indicate, the very creation of the state is an act of faith. One could rephrase the question: If human beings no longer have faith, is care for each other possible and can they exist as human beings living a life in common? For pastoral theologians the answer is an obvious and resounding no.

The premise that faith and care are interrelated and foundational to human existence and flourishing vis-à-vis the polis is evident throughout scripture. God makes a covenant with Abraham and this covenant is an expression of faith in God's care for the chosen people—the covenant is both a political act of care and faith because the covenant embraces not just Abraham but the whole people of God. To be sure, the covenant is broken many times, giving rise to alienation from God that leads to struggles of the community, both with regard to their survival and flourishing (e.g., Babylonian exile). The disruption of religious-political faith, then, accompanies a disruption of care, and when this breach of faith is repaired, care is restored and the community of faith flourishes.[1] While the notions of faith and care in Jewish scripture are theologically grounded, they nevertheless reveal an anthropological reality, namely that faith and care are foundational for the survival and flourishing of the polis.

The intersection of faith and care is also seen in the Christian scriptures. In Acts, we read that in this new community of believers in Jesus Christ "no one claimed private ownership of any possessions, but everything they owned was held in common. . . . There was not a needy person among them, for as many as owned lands or houses sold them" (Acts 4:3–4). Faith in Jesus Christ founded this kind of faithful cooperation and mutual care, wherein everyone cared for Others and no one simply for him/herself. Interestingly, these verses are immediately followed by the deceit of Ananias and Sapphira regarding the selling of their land and withholding resources from the community—a deceit that breaks the promise or covenant of this early Christian community. Ananias and Sapphira may have held back for fear (lack of trust) that there would not be enough to care for themselves: "Maybe this new community is not going to make it. So, let's hold something back." One possible interpretation of this stark passage is that deceit and the breaking of a vow, which emerge out of distrust, undermine not simply faith in God, but social faith in the polis. Deceit, distrust, and betrayal, in turn, undermine the resources marshaled to ensure that members of the community receive care. Put differently, faith and care in this early Christian polis involved mutual-personal recognition and participation in the fair redistribution of resources so that community members could care for themselves and each other—faith impacts the distribution of resources. I add here that this scriptural passage reveals not only the intersection between care and faith vis-à-vis the polis, but also the perennial human challenges of living out of faith and concern in the polis. In other words, to care for others means mutual-personal recognition and living out one's obligation to meet their needs—a sacrifice that we often fail to make because of anxiety and fear—theologically, sin. As much as care and faith are integral to the polis' survival and flourishing, so too it is undermined by our fears of vulnerability, loss, burden, lack, and so on.

Add to this the struggle of the early Christian polis in relation to the Roman Empire. Sheldon Wolin (2016) argues that the "significance of Christian thought for the Western political tradition lies not so much in what it had to say about the political order, but primarily about the religious order" or the community of faith (p. 87). Wolin, citing Henry Newman, claims the early church offered a "counter-kingdom" (p. 90) or counter-polis, given the overarching political realities of the Roman Empire. While religious leaders told their congregants to obey secular laws, they also proclaimed that they were citizens of a New Jerusalem (p. 90). Here we see a clear depiction of faith in the context of a religious polis—a polis distinct from and deemed superior to the obligations, promises, loyalties, and hopes of the larger Roman society. This juxtaposition and tension between civic faith and religious faith, between a secular polis and religious polis continues throughout the centuries to this day.

In this chapter, I provide an emended definition of H. R. Niebuhr's view of faith, before discussing briefly how faith and care are essential features of the polis. I am claiming that existential-civic faith[2] and care are political concepts and, while not often seen in political theologies or philosophies, these concepts operate as interpretive frameworks to understand and assess a polis. To begin, I define faith by depicting its dynamics. This sets the stage for addressing other central features of faith vis-à-vis the polis, namely (1) subjectivity and intersubjectivity, (2) social cooperation and the polis' space of appearances, (3) repair of breaches in civic faith, and (4) sovereignty or political rule.

THE DYNAMICS OF FAITH AND THE POLIS

Niebuhr (1989) argues that faith comprises three interrelated, dynamic pairs that operate on a continuum—belief-disbelief, trust-distrust, and loyalty-disloyalty (pp. 43–62). I add a fourth pair, hope-hopelessness. Very simply put, I believe in someone because s/he is trustworthy, and s/he is trustworthy because s/he has demonstrated his/her loyalty or fidelity to me.[3] This experience of trust can also be understood in relation to the ongoing recognition and treatment of the Other as a person—that the Other is for me (see Honneth 1995, pp. 36–37), which is foundational for relationships and living a life in common. In terms of hope, I have a belief and confidence in our relationship with regard to future actions, precisely because I have experienced trust and fidelity. For instance, a child learns to believe in Jesus Christ (or Buddha or Mohammed or humanism) because she trusts what her parents have told her about Jesus Christ. This trust is anchored in her many experiences of the parents' caring actions, which reflect their personal loyalty to her. The child's religious faith is connected to her social faith with her parents (see Rizzuto 1979). By contrast, all human beings are familiar with the more painful side of failures in faith. A wife discovers that her husband is having an affair. She no longer believes him when he tells her he has to work late.

Her disbelief is directly joined with her distrust, which, in turn, is part of her experience of his infidelity—his breaking of a vow. All of this gives rise to a sense of hopelessness about the marriage.

At the level of politics, Sheldon Wolin (2016), commenting on the works of Plato, argues that any political system is "the direct product of the beliefs held by its members" (p. 35). We might add disbelief as well, because it undermines the polis (p. 260). Citizens, in other words, may lose trust in their leaders because they have failed to live up to shared political promises, beliefs, and obligations. Richard Nixon's violation of numerous laws and betraying the oath of his office is an example of someone who lost the trust of citizens. Resigning from office was a public acknowledgemnt of not only wrongdoing, but the loss of trust and heightened disbelief. Distrust also can be associated with political institutions. A Gallup (2011) poll indicates that Congress' job approval rate was 15 percent, while citizens' trust or confidence in Congress was around 6 percent. This elevated level of distrust is, in part, explained by an extensive Princeton study by Martin Gilens and Benjamin Page (2014). Examining the years from 1981 to 2002, they found that when "the preferences of economic elites and the stands of organized interest groups are controlled for, the preferences of the average American appear to have only a minuscule, near-zero, statistically non-significant impact on public policy" (p. 575). They note further that "The preferences of economic elites have far more independent impact upon policy change than the preferences of average citizens do" (p. 576). Indeed, whenever "the majority of citizens disagrees with economic elites or with organized interests, they generally lose" (p. 576). Their study, in my view, highlights not simply the failure of political-economic elites to recognize and care about the needs, voices, and parity in participation of ordinary citizens, it also signals the decline of trust that has resulted from political leaders who have expressed fidelity to business elites (plutocracy) and infidelity to democratic principles and the common good (see Brown 2015).

That the dynamics of existential-civic faith are evident in the polis also is seen in the forms of group resistance that develop as a result of rising disbelief, distrust, and feelings of betrayal. Bert van den Brink (2007) contends that "people rebel because they truly sense the estranged state they are in" (pp. 90–91). This experience of betrayal points to the principle that "most political theorists from antiquity to the present have accepted . . . the principle that the political defines a distinct kind of association that aims at the good of all, depends on the contributions, sacrifices, and loyalties of all" (Wolin 2016a, p. 247). When this principle is betrayed by political leaders, civic trust declines and resistance rises.

Of course, persons' sense of estrangement and betrayal do not necessarily mean that people are oppressed. The mainly white Tea Party, while having other determinants, rose, in part, as a result of people who believed that the Republican establishment had betrayed what members felt were core conservative values. The Occupy Wall Street protests emerged in response to the growing inequalities between the 1 percent and the 99 percent and the attending betrayal of a neoliberal government that has promoted policies leading to the redistribution of wealth to the top 5 percent, while, at the same time, abandoning the notion of the common good. This group of activists distrusts economic and political elites because elites fail to care about the interests of the common citizens. The main point here is that political resistance and rebellion can be understood in light of the dynamics of faith vis-à-vis the polis.

Before moving to discuss further the intersection of care and faith in the polis, it is important to linger here so we might understand the complexities of existential faith and its dynamics or what can be termed prepolitical faith. Child psychoanalyst Erik Erikson (1952) posited that the first stage of life involves the parent and child navigating trust and mistrust. While the child has only a nascent cognitive life and subjectivity, s/he experiences repeated parental attunements to his/her needs and assertions, which form the basis of preverbal, procedural or pre-symbolic organizations of trust (see Stern 1985; Sroufe 1995). Put another way, the parent's consistent mirroring (care) is the foundation of a preverbal, global sense that the world is trustworthy and loyal—a global or undifferentiated form of existential faith. An infant's cry is the expression of this relational trust and loyalty in that s/he hopes the world will recognize his/her cry and respond accordingly. All of this is organized pre-symbolically, outside of conscious awareness. Naturally, there are moments when the parent fails in some fashion to care, which evokes anxiety and distrust. Repairing these failures restores and deepens trust, assuring the child of the parent's loyalty despite failures, and instills a pre-representational hope that future mistakes will be repaired (see Tronick and Gianino 1986; Tronick and Cohn 1989).

In time, these preverbal faith organizations become organized symbolically, which means that they are connected to and informed by the parents' and their group's larger narratives and practices.[4] Niebuhr's (1989) excursus on faith suggests this when he notes that a group's core narratives and rituals reveal to the members who is to be trusted (and not) and to whom members owe loyalty (and not). For example, imagine a child who is born into a patriotic family. As he develops, the child's pre-symbolic organizations of faith become joined to the parents' patriotic beliefs and their accompanying narratives (e.g., stories of the American Revolution) and practices (e.g., standing and singing the national anthem at games). These narratives and practices inform the child about whom and what to care for and about, whom and what to trust, and to whom one owes loyalty. The parents are the first teachers of the polis' narratives and practices of faith.

I stress here that the child's experiences of the parents' caring ministrations are inextricably a part of his/her experiences of trust, fidelity, and hope. The child is not only learning about care, but also about faith in this family, wherein good-enough care and faith create a space for the child to appear. This space of appearances is prepolitical. It is prepolitical in the sense that the child is not yet participating in the public-political realm, though s/he is a part of it. It is also prepolitical in that aspects of the macro-political realm are evident in family life and in the way parents may care for their children, even though the children are organizing their experiences of care and faith pre-symbolically. For instance, the social-political narratives that contain beliefs about gender will shape parental care and faith vis-à-vis the gender of their child. In this prepolitical space of appearances the child's assertions and construction of experience are shaped, but not determined, by social-political narratives and practices. Erikson (1952) noted this in his study of the parenting of Sioux and Yurok peoples. He observed how care for their children was clearly informed by the collective narratives and concomitant visions of the people. As Erik Erikson (1952) said once, all parents aim their children and, in my view, the aim is informed by political realities and social-political faith.

The prepolitical dynamics of faith vis-à-vis the parent-infant relationship segues into the dynamics of faith in any viable polis. The examples are limitless, but let me start with two founding documents for the United States— the Declaration of Independence and the Constitution. These are complex political documents, yet I briefly consider them in terms of the dynamics of faith. Both documents represent the shared beliefs and values of those who contributed to their creation. They both are faith statements, creeds, if you will. The Declaration of Independence delineates a long list of reasons for citizens' distrust and sense of betrayal by their sovereign and these reasons preface their resistance and rebellion.[5] Put another way, King George's failure to recognize and heed the voices of the people reflects a lack of care and fidelity to his subjects in the colonies, which gave rise to their experiences of betrayal and distrust. The document also proclaims the political belief that all "men" are created equal and, therefore, have the right to speak, but also a corresponding belief that the sovereign has a duty to listen and to care about citizens' needs—the common good. The Constitution is also a political document that attempts to establish shared beliefs, values, institutions, and practices for the organization of a viable polis. Acceptance of the Constitution by individuals and states means we agree to trust (in spite of contestations) this document in organizing our lives for the common good. That is, the shared agreement reflects some degree of shared fidelity and some degree of fellow care among citizens. This is what I would call civil or political faith.

Of course, any casual student of history will immediately note that the Constitution excluded women, Native Americans, and African Americans.

We could say that the Constitution, the creation of which is an act of political faith, established a framework that spelled out recognition with regard to participation in the space of appearances, which impacts political faith of citizens. There is no parity of participation with regard to African Americans, Native peoples, and women in the original Constitution and this suggests that the dynamics of faith were attenuated in all kinds of ways. For instance, exclusion from the space of appearances means one's voice is not recognized or it is dismissed, which in turn means that the common good is meant for those who have parity of participation. When this is the case, one can be assured that the distribution of resources necessary to care for oneself and others is weighted toward those who have a voice and how are allowed to participate in the political process. This breeds distrust and hopelessness that the political realm has anything good to offer. African American writers like Frederick Douglas, W. E. B. Dubois, Zora Neale Hurston, Richard Wright, James Baldwin, Alice Walker, Amiri Baraka, and Ta-Nehisi Coates understandably express a deep distrust of the political-juridical system, even as they express and live out resistant forms of political faith. Regardless of its significant limitations, the Constitution represents the organization of a particular polis and assenting to it signifies a shared civic faith.

ATTRIBUTES OF POLITICAL FAITH

Faith as Constitutive of Subjectivity and Intersubjectivity in the Polis

So far, I have addressed the dynamics of faith in general terms vis-à-vis the political. To more fully understand the complexity of faith and the polis, I turn to depicting its various attributes. When Niebuhr raised the question about the connection between faith and what it means to be human, he was, I believe, pointing out that faith is constitutive for subjectivity and intersubjectivity. To return to the infant-parent couple care, the dynamics of faith are inextricably intertwined with the child's emerging subjectivity and parent-infant intersubjectivity (Trevarthen 1998, 1999). The infant's subjectivity, then, emerges, survives, and develops in relation to the parent's reliable attunement (and repair) to the infant's assertions (Beebe, Lachmann, and Jaffe 1997). This infant-parent potential space is a precursor to the polis' space of appearances (LaMothe 2014).

To add to this, the interactions between the child and parent exemplify a complex intersubjectivity that the infant pre-symbolically organizes, or what Stern (1985) calls representations of interactions that have been generalized (RIGs). In my view, these RIGs, which are early subjective and intersubjective organizations of experience, also represent interhuman faith and care. The child attaches these RIGs to his/her first transitional objects, which s/he uses for emotional self-regulation (Winnicott 1971). I have argued elsewhere that transitional objects are faith objects under the child's omnipotent control (LaMothe 2010). The child uses them, in part, to negotiate the dynamics of faith in relation to other objects under her omnipotent control. Later, as the child develops the capacity for symbolization, subjective and intersubjective organizations become more complex and, as stated above, linked to the collective narratives and rituals held by the family and, later, the larger culture.

That care and faith are constitutive to subjectivity and intersubjectivity can be seen in negative examples where care is lacking and distrust, betrayal, and hopelessness abound. In these instances, subjectivity and intersubjectivity are fractured and diminished. Children who are physically or sexually abused by their parents or parent figures not only struggle to trust others, but their subjectivity is damaged and their intersubjective relations marred. I recall a woman who, after having been sexually abused by her father, believed herself to be dirty, damaged, and different, which points to an attenuated subjectivity and intersubjectivity, in that she feared sharing with and trusting others. Not surprisingly, she had difficulty believing that another person would be loyal to her or care about her, which reduced her experiences of self, Others, and the world.

Care and faith in infancy and childhood clearly have a foundational impact on subjectivity and intersubjectivity. Yet, we can see this claim manifested in adulthood in relation to the polis. I turn to two negative examples to highlight the relation between faith, care, and subjectivity. In his essay, "Torture," French journalist Jean Amery describes his experience of having been tortured by the Gestapo.

> But with the first blow from a policeman's fist, against which there can be no defense and which no helping hand will ward off, a part of our life ends and it can never be revived. . . . If from the experience of torture any knowledge at all remains that goes beyond the plain nightmarish, it is that of great amazement and a foreignness in the world that cannot be compensated by any sort of human communication. . . . Whoever has succumbed to torture can no longer feel at home in the world. (1995, pp. 127, 135, 136)

Amery continues: "The expectation of help is as much a constitutional psychic element as is the struggle for existence. . . . If no help can be expected, this physical overwhelming by the other then becomes an existential consummation of destruction" (p. 127). The policeman's fist is not only the antithesis of care; it represents a violation of existential trust and fidelity that undermines both subjectivity and intersubjectivity. Amery's earlier expectation or belief that he could cry out and someone would respond was shattered. One cannot help but read in this and other passages how Amery's subjectivity was damaged in his experience of being tortured. Indeed, torture is an exemplar of human perfidy and reflects the absence of care, obliterating any possibility of intersubjectivity. A polis that advocates torture is filled with fear and distrust, restricting care to those recognized as "like us" and consequently narrowing citizens' subjectivity and intersubjectivity. In these moments, care, faith, and equal regard are tossed aside in favor of denying the Other any voice or agency vis-à-vis the polis' space of appearances.

Another example of the impact of political faith (and care) vis-à-vis subjectivity and intersubjectivity in the polis is seen in the works of African American writers like Richard Wright. Abdul JanMohamed (2005) examines Richard Wright's novels. In Wright's first novel, *Native Son*, JanMohamed claims the book "illustrates the process whereby fear cements the subject in place" (p. 162). What "Wright implies," JanMohamed notes, "is that the subject is 'death-bound' by being more or less squeezed between the 'external' threat of death and the 'internal' fear of death" (p. 162). In a Jim Crow society, Wright and other black citizens are admitted "as a member only if he succumbs to the status of a socially dead subject" (p. 159). The socially dead subject of the polis has no voice, is not recognized as a person, and therefore is owed no care. The socially dead subject is trusted to the extent s/he is obliged to believe in his/her own inferiority and to be subjugated to white illusory belief in their superiority, which I will address in greater detail in chapter 6. For now, I note that in a racist polis, blacks' subjectivity and intersubjectivity are precarious, forced, by disciplinary regimes, to submit to a bare-life. The constant threat of violence from whites (and political institutions that serve as disciplinary regimes enforcing white superiority and violence toward blacks) is a symptom of pervasive, profound political faithlessness and carelessness.

Negative illustrations of distorted civic faith, like racism, are often countered by positive movements toward civic faith that are inclusive. For instance, for decades in the 19th and early 20th centuries, women (and some men) in the United States advocated for women's right to vote and hold political office (Zinn 1998, pp. 340–347), finally succeeding in 1920. Women's parity of participation in the polis' space of appearances included political recognition of women (ideally) as persons. To be sure, a century later, women have not achieved parity in many social and political arenas, but this does not negate the achievements of the suffragettes and their faithful civic resistance and advocacy. Similarly, the long and ongoing history of African Americans in their desire and hope for equal recognition and treatment reflects the resilient political faith nurtured in African American churches and other groups. By way of example, Martin Luther King Jr.'s (1998) religious faith community offered a space of mutual care where, as a child, he was recognized and treated as a person, providing him social trust, subjective confidence/esteem (somebodiness), and hope in the face of racism. The positive examples of achieving civil rights—where political subjectivity and intersubjectivity are recognized and affirmed and where the space of appearances and trust and fidelity are expanded—often arise out of political misrecognition, distrust, and infidelity. Forms of resistance and revolution are, in some instances, attempts to recover or construct civic faith that founds a more viable subjectivity and intersubjectivity for citizens.

Types of Faith and Cooperation in the Polis

A second and related aspect of faith as a political concept is seen in social cooperation and the space of appearances. Let me return to the parent-infant interaction to unpack this idea before linking it to the polis. A good-enough parent's recognition of the infant as a person and his/her resulting caring actions provide the infant with sufficient experiences of trust and fidelity to engage in cooperative interactions (e.g., nursing, cleaning, putting to bed). This cooperation necessarily accompanies the space of appearances in that the infant experiences enough trust and fidelity to risk asserting his/her nascent self. I say risk because in the womb, where every need is met before it can become conscious, there is no risk because there are no failures in meeting needs. Once a child is birthed into the world, her assertions of her needs and desires may not be met, be met partially, or be delayed. One reason the child learns to cooperate (no need of cooperation in the womb) is so that her needs are met. Put another way, after birth, the child must do the work of asserting his/her needs for the parent to recognize and attune to the child's psychobiological needs.[6] This complex child-parent cooperation is linked to and dependent on sufficient experiences of trust, loyalty, and hope.

As the child develops, s/he learns to recognize (eventually as a person) the parent and accept the parent's assertions. Here mutual-personal cooperation develops into being able to tolerate, accept, and share differences vis-à-vis the individual's appearances in this dyadic space. For example, the cooperation between infant and parent is significantly different from the cooperation between teenager and parent, suggesting that developmental stages or phases invite participants to adapt to psychobiological changes and form new cooperative faith interactions, which extend to other family members and to trusted persons outside the family. This, of course, means that cooperation will be accompanied by moments of contestation and disruption, which, when worked through successfully, deepen faith, care, and the cooperation necessary for the family to survive and thrive.

All of this is complicated enough in the context of family life. It becomes even more complicated in the polis. Generally speaking, for a polis to survive and thrive, mutual recognition, vis-à-vis the space of appearances, must accompany sufficient trust and loyalty needed to make cooperation possible. Yet, when we consider the complexity of social relations in the polis, we realize there are different types, degrees, and levels of cooperation, suggesting variances in faith and care. To understand this further, I depict four types of cooperative faith that exist in the polis, namely, contractual, organic-functional, mutual-personal, and transcendent. While I contend that these types of cooperative faith exist in the polis, the prevalence of one or another indicates whether a polis is merely surviving or whether it is thriving. In addition, identifying four types of cooperative faith does not exhaust the possibilities for what I call civil (or political) faith.

The first type of political faith is contractual. Contractual faith involves an exchange between two or more people and exists on a continuum, with one end being a Hobbesian society where the "primal act of recognition [is] enmity" (Wolin 2016 p. 418) and the other end mutual agreements among self-interested individuals. In a Hobbesian society, human beings "endeavor to destroy, or subdue one another" (Hobbes in Kirkpatrick 1986, p. 20). Each individual (or group) is bent on pursuing his/her interests and only enters into cooperative relations to pursue his/her ends. One can imagine that trust and loyalty in this society are low, bordering on nonexistent, which raises the question about cooperation. To insure cooperation, as Hobbes envisioned, there must be contracts between individuals (and groups) and these contracts "must be backed by the sanctions of force" that the state provides (p. 20). The enforcement of rules, regulations, and laws provides participants with enough trust to work cooperatively toward agreed upon goals. At least this is the case when the terms of the contract are jointly agreed upon. Alternatively, some societies have small or large segments where enmity exists between persons/groups and cooperation is forced by the more powerful person or group. Again, this forced or coerced cooperation exists on a continuum. For instance, slavery, which was supported and enforced by social, religious, and political institutions, involved an objectifying recognition, an eclipse of the space of appearances, and a contractual cooperation enforced through violence and terror. Slaves, constructed and seen as less than human, cooperated to survive. Those who cooperated night have received "care," in the sense of the master having provided the very basic of human needs necessary for survival and for the performance of a slave's function.[7] Moving along this continuum is the contractual arrangement between low paid workers and the company's boss. Economic laws and regulations provide the boss with the power to enforce cooperation, at times, by exploiting the labor of the worker. The worker feels compelled to cooperate because she cannot find other work and has to care for her family. Trust and loyalty are established through economic and political coercion. As long as the worker contributes her low-wage labor to achieve the company's aims of productivity and profit, she is trusted. If she fails, the boss owes no loyalty toward her. Willy Loman, in Arthur Miller's *Death of a Salesman*, realized this when his boss let him go after decades of work because Willy was no longer contributing to the bottom line. Since Willy was not fulfilling his side of the contract, the company owed him no loyalty because of his failure to cooperate with the company's goals.

There are, of course, all kinds of social contracts that are not based on enmity, conflict, or exploitation and are not necessarily enforced by the state. When I buy a plane ticket, I trust that the pilot is well trained and wishes to live. A financial contract exists here that is supported by state regulations and laws regarding plane safety, pilot training, and so on. There is also the contract between the pilot who commands the plane and the passenger—a cooperative faith whereby I agree to pay money and obey the rules and the pilot and crew will do everything possible to ensure safe travel to my destination. There are more informal and less regulated contracts in the social-political realm. For instance, a neighborhood teenager negotiates with me to cut my lawn for $30. Or parents make a contract with their son whereby he can go to summer camp if he obtains good grades. What makes these informal contracts viable is mutual trust in people fulfilling their roles in the exchange. These and thousands of other examples of contractual faith are part of the functioning of any society.

This type of faith cooperation, however, links trust, loyalty, and hope to the contractual relationship and, therefore, *faith and care are conditional*, except in those situations (friendship, family) where mutual-personal faith founds the relationship. The conditional aspect of contractual relationships rest largely on each party's rational calculation of his/her self-interest, except in the draconian examples when coercion and violence force cooperation. As indicated above, philosopher Thomas Hobbes is perhaps best known for a kind of contractual society wherein individuals' cooperation involve mutual calculation of their self-interests. Kirkpatrick (1986) quotes Hobbes: "For no man giveth, but with the intention of good to himself . . . if men see they shall be frustrated, there will be no beginning of benevolence, or trust; nor consequently of mutual help; nor of reconciliation of one man to another" (p. 22). "Trust," Kirkpatrick writes regarding a contractual society, "is essentially defined by the terms of the contract" (p. 22). It is also important to highlight that Hobbes indicates that breaches of trust will lead to the loss of care and foreclose the possibility of reconciliation. Here we are a far cry from the polis of the early Christian community of Acts, but it is clear that societal cooperation is, partially, comprised of contractual faith that, in many instances, is enforced by the state.

While this type of faith is a significant part of the polis, we know that some contracts are based in depersonalization wherein cooperation is enforced through forms of terror, violence, and other forms of anxiety evoking coercion. There is a kind of trust here, but it is a depersonalized trust, much like I trust the cog to work in my car. When it fails, I can easily discard it. A polis that is dominated by this kind of contractual faith is truly a Hobbesian society, where the polis as a whole is merely surviving, while a few individuals and their families flourish. It is not a sustainable society, because it is based primarily on achieving individual self-interests, which is the soil for injustice and carelessness. A present-day example of a society dominated by contractual cooperative faith is a neoliberal capitalistic or market society—a society rife with objectification or reification (Brown 2001; Lukács 1968), enormous economic and political inequalities (Piketty 2014; Sayer 2005; Stiglitz 2012), and significant negative consequences on the physical and mental health of many citizens who are unable to obtain the resources necessary to meet their needs and the needs of others (Mander 2012).[8] A contractual polis may survive, but in terms of flourishing it is unstable, because the common good is, at best, secondary to contractual self-interests of the elites. Stated differently, it is unstable, because it leads to small segments of the polis flourishing at the expense of others.

Moving from the overemphasis of individual self-interest evident in contractual faith is the organic-functional model, which, in his survey of philosophers and sociologists, Kirkpatrick (1986) describes. Hegel's philosophy, Kirkpatrick contends, embodies this model. For Hegel, the state or the community "has a moral and metaphysical supremacy which the individual in isolation lacks" (p. 68). This does not mean that the state is against the individual, but rather the "state is the 'substance' of individuals, their very essence, their telos or final end" (p. 69). In this view of society, "no member is end and none means" (Hegel in Kirkpatrick, p. 69). In Hegel's model, the individual's self-interest and self-realization can be conceived of and achieved only by participating in the whole and its ends (p. 69).[9] One might say that, for Hegel, a flourishing society results from the shared obligation of mutual recognition of the needs of each other, rather than the Hobbesian "rational" calculation of individual self-interests. Indeed, in many ways, Hegel's political philosophy is a response to and critique of the sterile, dark, and dystopian political philosophy of Thomas Hobbes.

Karl Marx, who was well versed in and critical of Hegel's philosophy, also advocated for this model, though he strongly emphasized the importance of interconnected individual members with regard to the survival and flourishing of the whole (pp. 91–86). This view is connected to Marx's anthropological premise that an individual's "existence is a social activity, and therefore that which I make of myself, I make of myself for society and with the consciousness of myself as a social being" (Marx in Kirkpatrick, p. 87). In Marx's organic-functional model, the individual does not merely function or cooperate to achieve the ends of the society, thus subsuming his/her interests for the sake of the interests of the larger group. Sociality "rests on the necessity of cooperation in the pursuit of individual ends" (p. 89). Kirkpatrick states that "the social nature of human persons resides primarily in the fact that if they are wise they will choose their ends so as to maximize social cooperation" (p. 90). However, a limitation of this view is that mutual "functional cooperation between individuals is not the same as their living for each other in mutual love" (p. 90).

There are additional limitations to this model, but my interest here is to suggest that this model reflects a type of civic faith and cooperation present in societies. Indeed, for societies to survive and thrive there must be some level of cooperation determined by functional faith. If we turn to scripture, we see this type of cooperative faith in the emphasis on the chosen people and the people of the early ecclesia—an "assembly of citizens in a self-governing state city" (Horsely 2009, p. 14). The community or group, not the individual, is the focus. In other words, the covenant was not simply an agreement between God and Abraham or Moses, but a covenant with the Jewish people. What is good for the survival and flourishing of the people of God, one presumes, is good for its individual members. We also see this in entities like businesses, churches, sports teams, and other groups wherein the mission and goals of the social entity are, more often than not, placed at a higher level than the individual's beliefs, intentions, and goals. Indeed, individuals within the system function and cooperate such that the group's goals can be achieved, while hopefully or ideally meeting the interests and needs of its members. In terms of the dynamics of faith, the individual's cooperation emerges out of his/her trust in and loyalty to the group's ethos, goals, and so on. A good employee or church member is someone who functions in such a way as to express and help achieve the group's mission and s/he is trusted by the state, leaders, and so on to the extent that s/he cooperates with others toward the group's ends. These individuals manifest a kind of cooperative faith that is shaped by caring about and for the values and goals of the larger group. In this sense, individual self-interests are shaped by and aligned with the interests of the group.

By contrast, anyone who is seen to disagree or act against the community's or society's ends is deemed untrustworthy, disloyal and, often, denied care vis-à-vis other individuals who share the group's goals. Heretics, traitors, rebels, and non-team players are labels for those who disbelieve the cherished beliefs and practices of the group or who are seen as not cooperating with group goals. As a result, these persons are often denied the same care that trustworthy members receive. Jesus, for instance, was seen to challenge both the Roman Empire and Jewish establishment and their collective ends (Crossan 1995, 2007; Horsely 2003, 2011). Crucifixion was used both to rid society of those who challenged Roman rule and to terrorize others into cooperating with the aims of imperial Rome. The crucified individual, deemed to be politically untrustworthy and disloyal, was both violently expelled from the polis' space of appearances and deprived of care. Lynching African Americans was the modern version of Roman "justice" with regard to blacks deemed to resist, deny, or undermine the goals and practices of a white supremacist polis (Cone 2011). Another modern example was the House Un-American Activities Committee (HUAC) during the 1950s. People who were thought to be communists and were constructed as (faithless) traitors by powerful political leaders were publicly excoriated, often losing their jobs.

Any cursory reading of history reveals the obvious downsides to the organic-functional model of social cooperative faith. There was a significant amount of trust in, loyalty to, and cooperation among German citizens vis-à-vis the Nazi state and communists in the Soviet Union. On our side of the Atlantic, white European settlers who believed and trusted the U.S. ideals and aims of Manifest Destiny, cooperated in the brutal exploitation of Native Americans and others. Eugene Debs, Emma Goldman, Martin Luther King Jr., and many others who questioned, critiqued, and protested were often viewed as traitors—people who did not cooperate with the dominant group's goals. We see the same attitude reflected on something as banal as car bumper stickers—Love America or Leave It. If you do not ascribe to the dominant patriotic view of American exceptionalism, one is considered un-American, for having betrayed the values and aims of the group. From a different angle, distrust and disbelief in church leaders who covered up pervasive sexual abuse led some Catholics to leave, refusing to cooperate because the leaders had not lived up (betrayed) to Christian communal values.

While there are tragic examples of this type of faith gone wrong, numerous other illustrations reveal the importance and value of this type of civic faith vis-à-vis the survival and flourishing of the group. Many Black churches and their members, believing in the values of equality and freedom enshrined in the U.S. Constitution, worked tirelessly to achieve their civil rights, as well as civil rights for all people. During the 1980s, various churches and their members cooperated in the Sanctuary Movement, providing shelter to people fleeing violence in Central America—violence fueled by the U.S. government. The caring responses of individual citizens and groups toward people suffering from the earthquake in Haiti or the devastating tsunami in Asia signified people working together because of the group's shared beliefs in caring for people who suffer natural disasters. Despite negative examples of this type of faith, we need to recognize that, for any polis to survive and flourish, an organic-functional faith is necessary for shared cooperation in living out the values of the polis and meeting its aims. Nevertheless, we need to be cognizant of how individuals can be sacrificed (versus individuals choosing to sacrifice for the group) for group ends and how sometimes the values and ends of the group are immoral in that they lead to individuals and groups not surviving and not flourishing (e.g., the nuclear attacks on Hiroshima and Nagasaki).[10]

The third type of faith related to care and cooperation is mutual-personal faith. For Kirkpatrick, philosophers John Macmurray and Martin Buber—I would add Axel Honneth (1995) as a more recent philosopher who advocates this view—reflect this type of faith wherein there is a mutual recognition of Others as persons—unique, valued, inviolable, and agentic subjects. As indicated in chapter 1, the intention to recognize and treat the Other as person obliges one to respond to the Other's needs. In mutual-personal relations there exists a reciprocal and cooperative recognition and meeting of needs. This type of faith founds families and communities wherein cooperation is aimed at addressing individuals' needs and working toward the achievement of the common good—the survival and flourishing of the group. Unlike functional faith, mutual-personal faith includes the self-realization of individual persons (Honneth 1995, pp. 172–178). In other words, an individual's needs and desires are not simply subordinate to the group's goals and aims. A society or community that comprises this type of faith relations is one where "each cares for all the others and no one for himself" (Macmurray 1935, p. 159). A mutual-personal faith establishes a kind of cooperation among members of the society that is based on personal, noncontractual trust and loyalty shaped by the needs of individuals and the group/community. Put another way, civil trust and loyalty are not conditioned by a contract or function vis-à-vis the group's ends, but rather by unconditional personal recognition. Of course, contracts and functions remain, but are secondary.

This type of faith is more readily seen in vibrant families and communities where individuals engage in mutual-personal cooperation, caring for each other. Indeed, it is difficult to imagine a thriving family and community that did not have this type of faith. Churches, temples, and mosques whose members are active, who provide materially and emotional support to each other, who express devotion and fidelity to each other, and who manifest meaningfulness have a mutual-personal type of faith. Ideally, cooperation among group members is done and experienced without condition. For example, a Lutheran congregation's members trust each other and respond to each other's needs. Ideally, mutual-personal faith's recognition is not determined by the condition of being Lutheran—one's identity/subjectivity—or by the individual's function vis-à-vis the group's goals. To be sure, each member recognizes each other as Lutherans, but mutual care, trust, and cooperation, while shaped by this particular recognition, are not contingent on it. Moreover, their personal recognition and care can be extended to those who are not deemed to be Lutheran, which I will address more fully below.

Some self-help groups may likewise possess this type of faith as they cooperate to address their particular life struggles, though there may be some conditions in these groups that can shape faith and care. We also see, in the larger polis, glimpses and moments of this type of faith and cooperation, for example, when there are natural disasters. Individuals and groups work together in rushing to meet the manifold needs of people who have experienced the disaster. A city, such as Louisville, Kentucky, can aspire to live out mutual-personal faith by claiming the ideal of being a compassionate city. A flourishing polis, in my view, must nurture and possess, to some degree, cooperative faith shaped by mutual-personal recognition.

The early Christian experiments in communal life exemplify this kind of faith and also point out the challenges of living this out. To return to Ananias and Sapphira, their actions could be understood as violating this mutual-personal type of civic faith, wherein their needs and self-realization took precedence over the needs of others in the group, which struck at the very foundations of this Christian community's mutual-personal faith. Greed, fear of Others, anxiety about scarcity, preoccupation with one's self-interests undermine the trust and loyalty of mutual-personal faith, and stifles unconditional cooperation. While this may suggest that this type of faith is utopian when it comes to the polis, I argue that any thriving polis, while having contractual and functional types of faith, must have a critical mass of civil mutual-personal faith. Moreover, this polis must possess narratives, practices, rituals, and institutions that encourage this kind of political faith relations and subjectivity/intersubjectivity. So, when we consider the polis, we may assess whether and to what degree the polis facilitates and/or undermines mutual-personal faith relation. Consider, for instance, a negative example. Numerous scholars from various fields (e.g., Harvey 2005; Giroux 2012a; Jones 2012; Mander 2012; Mann 2013) have depicted the rise and consequences of neoliberal capitalism as the dominant social imaginary structuring U.S. society. This has accompanied, if not fueled by, ideas regarding individualism and achieving one's self-interests, which, in my view, corresponds to the dominance of contractual and functional types of faith and the decline of mutual-personal faith. A neoliberal culture does not and cannot produce mutual-personal faith relations. Indeed, mutual-personal faith relations (e.g., friendships) actually undermine the aims of capitalism, because capitalism is fundamentally based on exploitative relations—capitalist class garnering as much surplus value as possible. People like Ananias and Sapphira, perhaps fearful of scarcity and distrustful of others, are the norm in this kind of society. This does not mean that mutual-personal faith and cooperation are absent in a neoliberal Hobbesian society, because it would be hard to imagine family life and friendships without this type of faith. However, the values, expectations, and beliefs of neoliberal capitalism are geared for a polis that survives primarily by contractual and functional faith relations and cooperation. I purposely refuse to say thrive, because of the near absence of the notion of common good, the considerable amount of poverty in the United States, rising rates of anxiety and depression, and increasing economic and class inequalities.

Mutual-personal faith, while seemingly a desired form of faith and cooperation, can also be inherently problematic in a polis. This occurs when individuals confuse the particular shared representations associated with "persons" with their particular identity, their shared personhood. This is typical of human beings and frequently tragic. We tend to associate the personal with our clan, family, or polis. So, mutual-personal faith may exist within a group and this group survives and thrives. The problem arises in that faith, cooperation, and care are parochial and, worse, exclusive. By this, I mean that cooperation and care for Others may be diminished, nonexistent, or contingent on meeting certain conditions. For instance, a local Christian community expresses mutual-personal faith among its members, but not with Others in the larger polis. Another religious community may offer care for nonmembers, but make it contingent upon accepting their beliefs and practices. For example, a Christian community provides care for the homeless as long as the homeless pray before meals or as a condition of receiving food and a bed. At the extreme end are racist groups that may demonstrate mutual-personal recognition and faith among members, but not toward Others who disagree or who are constructed as the despised race. In these instances, we see that the personal is restricted to those who fall under the parochial representations of the group—group identity/subjectivity. From a psychological perspective, this is a problem of differentiation in that one is unable or unwilling to acknowledge the likeness between one's particular representations one associates with the notion of person and the Other's representations of personhood. All one acknowledges is difference, which results in attempts to overcome this difference through sameness, wherein disidentification and identification are split off from each other. It is also an epistemological difficulty because it involves confusion of the subject with the object—confusion of the particular with the universal. By this I mean, the individual confuses his/her representations of personhood/subjectivity with the personhood itself, leaving in question the personhood of all Others. And it is a theological problem (i.e., idolatry) in that it restricts the notion of *imago dei* to my group. Cooperation, then, becomes narrow, confined to this particular group's mutual-personal faith relations.

The problems of mutual-personal faith fade with transcendent faith. By transcendent, I am not referring to a supreme, infinite, otherworldly divinity. Instead, transcendent refers to something quite human, which is the capacity for and ability to (a) recognize Others as persons, (b) trust and express loyalty to these Others, and (c) cooperate with Others. Actually, transcendent faith is a category of mutual-personal faith, but without the parochial tendencies and, at times, without the mutual-personal feature. This is understood as follows: loyalty and trust associated with transcendent faith are not contingent on the group's shared narratives and institutions. Instead, trust and loyalty are contingent on the existential belief and trust that the Other, the stranger or enemy, is a person. To be sure, this belief must be codified in the group's narratives, institutions, and practices, but to be recognized and treated as a person does not depend on the Other being a member of the polis or on a citizen's cooperation with the aims of the polis. The polis' space of appearances, in other words, is open to strangers or noncitizens, both recognizing and responding to their particular experiences and needs. Within a complex cosmopolitan polis, this kind of faith is also critical because of cultural diversity—myriad of Otherness.

The existential belief (personhood of all human beings) of transcendent faith, with its personal trust and obligation, is not contingent on mutual recognition.[11] The story of the Good Samaritan is an example of this kind of transcendent faith. The Samaritan's care for the man, who was not of his tribe or religious faith, was rooted in a transcendent faith—a belief in the personhood of the injured man. By meeting the man's needs, the Samaritan demonstrated fidelity to him. Yet, the Samaritan's actions were not contingent on *mutual* recognition of the injured man's personhood or on the expectation of cooperation. We can easily think of other examples of individuals who manifest this type of faith—persons who are obliged to care for people who are different (e.g., Dorothy Day, Eugene Debs, Martin Luther King Jr., and Mother Theresa). To single out Martin Luther King Jr., he recognized that all human beings are children of God, hence persons. King was willing to treat his enemies as persons (Christian dictum of loving one's enemies), as well as to listen and, if possible, cooperate with them. This did not mean that King was unwillingly to challenge both his supporters and his detractors. In his famous Riverside speech, King's transcendent faith was also evident in his care for the people of Vietnam who were suffering from U.S. aggression. His message was that we are obliged to care for people who are not like us, and to care enough to understand how our actions are hurting them. Many from his own community dissented from King after this speech (Smiley and Ritz 2014), pointing to the difficulty in achieving transcendent faith in a polis.

It is important to stress that while King's transcendent faith was grounded in his theological beliefs, transcendent faith can be linked to and supported by nonreligious stories, practices, and so on. Eugene Debs, a socialist, fought tirelessly for the needs of those at the lower rungs of society. He said, while serving time in prison for protesting the war, "While there is a lower class, I am in it, while there is a criminal element, I am of it, and while there is a soul in prison, I am not free."[12] For him, the driving principle or truth of life was service, especially to the marginalized and oppressed in society (Freeberg 2008, p. 246). In my view, Eugene Debs' life work is an expression of transcendent faith. Where many in society rejected poor, working class, and people in prison, Debs was their advocate. A contemporary of Debs was the firebrand Emma Goldman who, as Salem Brand noted at her funeral, "was a brave soldier in the war of liberation. . . . I fancy no man or woman of her day had a keener sense of justice or a more passionate love of liberty" (Moritz and Moritz 2001, p. 202). While Goldman was an atheist, Brand experienced her as living out the foundational Christian values of love and justice for all. Like Debs, Goldman recognized the needs and aspirations of those who were marginalized and oppressed—those who were restricted from full participation in the polis' space of appearances and who received less care. Both Debs and Goldman exhibited a kind of transcendent faith wherein all human beings are deemed to be persons and to be treated with respect and dignity.

The interesting thing about transcendent faith vis-à-vis the polis is that it invites cooperation, but it usually evokes noncooperation by many people who fear Others and/or who dread the demands of trust and loyalty to Others, because it results in having to give up power, prestige, and privilege. People may also resist this form of civic, cooperative faith because it may demand one to acknowledge and confess one's sins. King and other civil rights leaders who advocated for civic and economic justice for blacks (and others) were not surprised to find "non-cooperation" from white racists who feared equality would mean the loss of cherished beliefs in white supremacy and the loss of political power and social prestige. Similarly, Eugene Debs and Emma Goldman faced noncooperation from government officials who constructed both as subversives. One can expect prophets, who hope to invite civil cooperation, to meet resistance and noncooperation when they point to the sins of the group and when they advocate care and justice for all.

While transcendent faith tends not to be the norm in the polis, it is a necessary faith to challenge citizens to extend the common good and parity of participation to people who are typically not deemed to be or treated as persons. One might even say that whenever there has been progress in extending political rights to previously disenfranchised persons (e.g., blacks, women) and progress in providing justice to people who are oppressed and marginalized (e.g., civil rights), transcendent faith has been the leaven that has given rise to cooperation among enough people to catalyze change in the polis, even as they faced significant forces of noncooperation. When I think of the profound challenges facing all of humanity because of climate change, it is just this kind of cooperative faith that may be the key to the survival of humanity. We know now more than at any time in history that each society's survival and flourishing is tied to the fate of the planet. A transcendent faith can embrace the particularities of one's unique polis and identity, while also recognizing and accepting the particularities and diversity of other individuals in their societies. This transcendent trust and fidelity to all can serve as a foundation for mutual-personal cooperation with the aim of making and maintaining an earth that is habitable for all. If this is to be a realistic possibility, then societies' political, economic, and cultural institutions, narratives, and practices must cultivate this kind of political faith and global civil cooperation.

Disruptions in Faith and the Necessity of Repair in the Polis

Although faith is a constitutive element for living a life in common, inevitable social disruptions lead to distrust, betrayals, and hopelessness that undermine various types of cooperation in the polis. These relational disruptions, whether prepolitical or political, are understood as an attenuation or foreclosure of the space of appearances that result from acts of misrecognition or nonrecognition, heightening experiences of distrust and hopelessness. Naturally, these disruptions exist on a continuum spanning a wide range of emotional pain, self-other alienation, and noncooperation. Ruptures in existential faith reveal not only the reality of human finitude, failure, and sin, but the necessity of repair if a couple, family, community, or polis is to survive and thrive.[13] The work of repairing relational disruptions in the polis falls under the headings of care and justice. The notion of justice is an important category in political theology and philosophy, however, my focus is care and faith. That said, the claim is that care aimed toward repairing relationships that have been marred by distrust and real or imagined betrayals leads to the restoration of the space of appearances and new opportunities for cooperation, whether that is seen in prepolitical relations or in other areas of the polis.

As noted in chapter 1, the routine aspect of repair in human life is evident in the small relational (prepolitical) disruptions between parent and child (Schore 2003; Stern 1985; Sroufe 1995; Stern 1985; Tronick and Gianini 1986; Tronick and Cohn 1989). These repairs are necessary for restoring cooperation; they also can deepen interpersonal trust, loyalty, and hope. That is, in time, the child gains greater relational confidence and hope that the next time there is a relational failure, it can be repaired and mutual-personal faith restored. Naturally, there are also parental failures in repair and, if they recur, the child's ability to cooperate in reparative actions will be damaged, leading to greater distrust, hopelessness, and relational alienation.

Prepolitical disruptions and repair, while connected to the polis, are not identical to it. Yet, one thing we can be certain of is that ruptures in relationships are found in all relationships within every polis. This means that when we examine a society, we would also note the various ways relational disruptions occur and how the society is organized to repair the ruptures, restore the space of appearances, and invite new possibilities for civic faith and cooperation. Let me begin by considering Jewish scripture and the notion of covenant, which is/was central to the Jewish community/polis. Indeed, one could say that scripture is a testament to the history of the disruptions and repairs of the chosen people in their relationship to God. Many stories in scripture describe human distrust in God and breaches of the covenant. When the Israelites or Jewish polis, anxious and afraid, created the golden calf, it signaled their distrust in Yahweh and resulting lack of cooperation. Sin, in this context, was their distrust and turning away from God. God's punishment or discipline can be seen, by the Jewish community of that time, as a method to restore the relationship or covenant and cooperation. Discipline, whether noted in scripture or secular venues, is often used to enforce and restore cooperation and maintain the polis, though it is equally important to note that discipline (political-juridical) can also create and maintain disruptions (e.g., incarcerations of minorities; see Taylor 2015), which I will say more about below. This said, discipline is not the only method used to repair disruptions in Judeo-Christian political communities. For instance, the ritual use of the scapegoat, Yom Kippur or Day of Atonement, God's love incarnate in the life Jesus, the sacrament of reconciliation, and Lenten observances are just some of the ways Jews and Christians have established narratives about and social ritual practices of repair. These practices are not to be considered as simply repairing one's individual relationship to God, but also the relationship of the community to God and the relationships within the community.

Repairs in the polis can be parsed into three basic types, namely state, juridical, and social,[14] which are often interrelated. Here my main focus is on state and juridical expressions of repair. Repairs in terms of the state refer to breaches of trust in the relationship between the people and government leaders/institutions, as well as between states.[15] These can involve informal and formal public acts of confession, which may be accompanied by asking for forgiveness, promising to continue to serve the public trust, resignation, and/or prosecution or impeachment. Presidents Nixon and Clinton come to mind as examples. There are also public admissions of past wrongs, such as the public apology for slavery and Jim Crow laws by the U.S. Congress. While it is debatable how effective these rituals are in restoring trust and repairing the space of appearances, they are illustrations of the existential need to restore faith and cooperation in the polis.

Of course, state reparative actions can include drafting legislation to address a political-social wrong. For example, the 1964 Civil Rights Act ended segregation in public places and curtailed discrimination in employment. The racist disruptions, long practiced and institutionalized, recognized African Americans as inferior and, from this racial logic, they were kept from white public spaces. The state acted to repair practices that excluded African Americans from public spaces by claiming them to be equal citizens (persons) and thus permitted to engage in any public space. A similar and important piece of legislation followed the next year. The Voting Rights Act of 1965 sought to address egregious practices of barring African Americans from participating in the political sphere. One could say the act was aimed at repairing breaches of trust and the attenuation or foreclosure of the space of appearances. As persons, as citizens, equal before the law, they had the right to vote, to be recognized as full citizens (persons), and to have their views represented.

When we look to the state for actions leading to the repair of present and past wrongs, we find it is often ambiguous in its effects. For instance, legislative victories were hugely successful in aiding African Americans in their quest for parity in participation in the political process. As a result, more African Americans held local, regional, state, and national offices (Freeman 2013, pp. 199–218), which suggests greater trust and hope in the state vis-à-vis recognition and participation in the space of appearances—civic cooperation. At the same time, these legislative repairs did little to address the past wounds of racism or the present prevalence of racism in the United States. Since racism, by its nature, is disruptive to the polis—because of its social-political practices of misrecognition and lack of mutual-personal faith (more accurately, depersonalizing faith and relations)—we can expect and predict unrepaired experiences of distrust between African Americans and whites. As long as the political leadership avoids dealing directly with past and present consequences of racism, they are failing to repair the wounds of alienation. Moreover, one can expect a continuation of harm, hurt, and civil discord.

The state's actions toward repair, in the case of the Civil Rights Act and Voting Rights Act, are also ambiguous because of legislation passed in the 1970s and 1980s that sought stricter juridical practices and statutes. To be sure, criminal activity, which is defined by the state, can be seen to create ruptures in the polis. Typical methods of restoring order to the polis are arrest, prosecution, and the imprisonment of offenders, which gives citizens a sense of confidence and trust in the state and judicial system, all of which is necessary for the polis' survival and flourishing. Even a dystopian polis like Deadwood with all of its criminality presented a façade of law and justice. Nevertheless, moving to the specifics of the legislative and juridical system, we generate questions regarding how crimes are identified and categorized, what crimes are prosecuted, and who receives the harsher sentences (Goldberg 2009; Taylor 2015). If laws and the judicial system serve to attend to disruptions in the polis, what groups within the polis benefit and what groups do not? A specific example of the complexity and ambiguity of state and juridical repairs is depicted in Michelle Alexander's (2010) book, *The New Jim Crow*. Not long after winning political and social freedoms for African Americans, the state, ostensibly to get tough on drugs and other crimes, passed legislation resulting in dramatic increases in prison populations. Consider that, in 1980, under two million people were in the judicial system (prison, jail, probation, and parole), with around 200,000 in prison. While the overall numbers of people in the penal system has declined *slightly* since 2009, it is still just under 7 million with over 2.3 million in prison and jail Bureau of Justice Statistics 2016). From 1970 to 2005, the prison population grew by 700 percent (Hedges 2014). It will come as no surprise that a disproportionate percentage of people in the penal system are African Americans and Hispanics.[16]

Get tough policies did not end with imprisonment. As Michelle Alexander (2010) notes, "Nearly every state allows private employers to discriminate on the basis of past criminal conviction" (p. 146). This also extends to housing, making it very difficult for persons who have served their time to find adequate housing (pp. 141–144). Added to this, ex-prisoners who are fortunate enough to obtain a job, quickly discover that fees are owed to various agencies. Alexander reports that some of these pre- and post-conviction fees result in the garnishment of wages, adding yet another punishing obstacle to success (pp. 150–152). These obstacles add to the high recidivism rate. Men and women in the penal system are people of color and, as a group (including their families), they are one of the most socially, politically, and economically marginalized vis-à-vis the polis' space of appearances. Moreover, the state's actions that have led to this represent how reparative state-juridical policies and actions can create more trust and cooperation for one segment of the population, while creating more hopelessness, distrust, and fragmentation for another segment, leaving the larger polis without any real political repair. It is sadly ironic that not long after the Civil Rights and Voting Rights Acts, laws and juridical practices were established to get tough on crime, resulting in the diminution of rights for millions of African Americans. Until the people of the United States and its leaders face the political and socially rupturing reality of racism, enmity, distrust, betrayal, and hopelessness, the polis' thriving will be impeded.

When the state and the juridical aspects of the polis fail to repair breaches, there can still be social-political repairs—or attempts at repair. These are manifold and can take the form of NGOs (nongovernmental organizations) or more informal groups—local, state, or national. To return to the era of civil rights, the National Association for the Advancement of Colored People (NAACP), the Southern Christian Leadership Conference (SCLC), the Student Non-Violent Coordinating Committee (SNCC), and other groups, through political agitation and resistance, sought to gain civil and economic rights, which can be seen not simply as correcting past and present wrongs, but also repairing the social fabric or space of appearances by seeking justice. The recent Occupy Wall Street and Black Lives Matter movements are also illustrations of social groups—formal and informal—seeking to address changes for the sake of repairing disruptions in the polis. Put another way, these groups often represent voices that have been marginalized in the polis' space of appearances. No longer having trust in political and juridical institutions, these organizations resist and disrupt the larger political space in hopes of catalyzing social, political, and economic changes that will contribute to greater equality for those they represent. In my view, their disruptions of the polis are aimed at repair.

One might quickly point out that some of these social groups and institutions are themselves disruptive to the polis and may exhibit questionable intentions and efforts at repair. This view overlooks the disruptions that are hidden until sufficient numbers of people speak out. For instance, the decades of African American struggle for justice came to national prominence in the 1950s and 1960s. In particular, the horrific police brutality on Bloody Sunday (March 7, 1965) shocked the nation, because of the films and pictures that recorded the event. The march was disruptive, but the disruption was a response to decades of perfidious maltreatment of African American citizens, often brutally excluding them from participating in the polis' space of appearances. Civil disobedience, in these instances, represented attempts to repair social injuries and establish a civic faith marked by parity of participation in the polis' space of appearances. There are times, then, when the disruption of the polis reveals long and deep, though hidden, ruptures created and maintained by the dominant group. In religious parlance, acts of civil disobedience are akin to the prophets who disrupt the social-political order to get people to pay attention to the ruptures that already exist, but are not heeded and thus not repaired. So, some social disruptions are aimed at manifesting and repairing the latent breaches of trust and experiences of betrayal in the polis.

There are three points here. First, a state's involvement in repairing the fabric of social-political faith and the space of appearances, while necessary, is often ambiguous in its effects. Second and relatedly, attempts to repair breaches of civic faith are often contested because the breaches involve institutions, laws, programs, and collectively held narratives that privilege one group, while harming another. In other words, attempts at repair may be seen by some citizens as a threat to their political and economic power, privilege, and prestige. Third, social and political attempts at repair may initially be very disruptive to the polis, as people who are marginalized, exploited, and oppressed agitate to obtain recognition, parity of participation, justice, and access to material resources to care for themselves and others.

A question remains about how these repairs of breaches of civic faith can be understood as acts of care. While they properly fall under the category of justice, I suggest that state and juridical repairs begin with some semblance of care for and about those who have experienced exploitation, marginalization, and oppression. The demand for and pursuit of justice emerges out of recognizing the Other as a person who has needs, a voice, and aspirations. True justice emerges out of care and is not separated from it.

Faith, Care, and Sovereignty[17]

It may seem odd to end this chapter with a brief discussion of the relation between sovereignty and faith-care. Yet, any cursory reading of scripture reveals that the very existence of the Jewish polis is founded on this relation. Abraham, Moses, Aaron, and the prophets are called by a sovereign God to lead the people of Israel. Prophets like Isaiah, Jeremiah, and Ezekiel lament the faithlessness and corruption of the people, calling them to return to the covenant. They warn that the failure to do so will result in the withdrawal of God's care and, at times, more active forms of punishment. Prophets like Micah and Amos point to the failures and faithlessness of political leaders who cause the people to suffer. Prophets, chosen and sent by the Sovereign, seek to restore or repair the covenant and, in so doing, the Jewish polis will survive and flourish. In addition, in Jewish scriptures, other forms of sovereignty (e.g., patriarchy, judges, monarchy) are explained and justified in terms of God's sovereignty (Walzer 2012). In Christian scripture, Jesus, the good shepherd, is a descendant of the house of David, sits at the right hand of God, and represents and embodies the kingdom of God. It is pretty clear who has sovereignty in the New Jerusalem. The various versions of human political sovereignty in scripture are justified and/or critiqued in relation to the sovereignty or supreme rule of God. One could say that scripture is the ongoing story of the people of God and the challenges of their covenant of faith with a sovereign God.[18]

We can shift here and understand these scriptural depictions of sovereignty in terms of what they might reveal about an existential truth. By this, I mean that human beings, as social-political creatures, are always trying to figure out how the polis should be organized and led. And we find innumerable ways to explain and justify political organizations and leadership, whether that involves theological or philosophical renderings. Moreover, the diverse constructions of sovereignty reflect the particular dynamics of civic faith in that citizens believe in, trust in, and are loyal to both the particular sovereign and attending political organizations. When disbelief and distrust prevail in a society, vis-à-vis the sovereign, the polis becomes unstable, leading, in some cases, to resistance and revolutions. The Declaration of Independence, for instance, can be understood as a list of reasons explaining why colonists lost faith (trust) in the King and his government and, therefore, no longer felt obliged to be loyal to him. The list of injuries begins with the King's refusal to assent to laws that were for the public good, which means the complaints are not simply about injuries with regard to injustices, but injuries associated with carelessness. The rejection of British sovereignty left open the question of American sovereignty and what it would look like. The United States Constitution, then, sets out to consider how sovereignty will be lived out without a king and parliament, justifying the new political arrangement with a mix of nature and religious ontology. Depictions of sovereignty, in short, point to an existential truth—the connection between faith-care, lived out in the polis, and the particular human reality of rule.

To continue along this line, we can ask further what gives rises to disbelief and distrust in political leaders. Often it has to do with consistent failures to address and meet the needs of citizens. The prophet Micah (3.1-12) railed against the Jewish political leaders who exploited their people and, in so doing, broke faith with God and the covenant. One interpretation here is that legitimate sovereignty requires fulfilling the responsibilities of the covenant to care for the people, since human leaders represent God's sovereignty. In this case, human failings in governance did not lead to a loss of faith in the sovereignty of God, but rather a loss of faith in political leaders who fail to heed the voices of the people. A more secular version of this is Wolin's (2016) discussion of Machiavelli and his notion of sovereignty. Machiavelli, Wolin argues, "held that the political order must insure the equality of treatment of its members," because the polis "could not survive unless the dominant interests were satisfied" (p. 209). Citizens will "support the political order" when their material needs are met and there is protection of their possessions (p. 208). To be sure, there are times when citizens, for all kinds of reasons, will continue to believe in, trust, and be loyal to the sovereign even when there are ongoing failures in care. For Wolin, when this occurs, an "obscuring 'myth'" supplies the emotional trust and loyalty "to cover the fact of economic, social, and political equality have, at best, very limited practical meaning" (p. 209). Patriotism and the myth of U.S. exceptionalism are recent examples that screen vast economic and political inequalities in putative U.S. democracy. In the absence of an obscuring myth, there are always tyrants who retain sovereign power—caring for themselves and their handful of supporters—by way of coercion, intimidation, and terror. However, tyrants breed fear, distrust, and betrayal because people know the tyrant cares only for himself (and sycophants) and maintaining his power. The common good is, at best, secondary. Tyrants manifest a kind of sovereignty that breeds carelessness and faithlessness, eating at the foundations of the polis and giving birth to resistance and revolution.

Faith, care, and sovereignty become more complicated when we turn to the notion of democracy—the demos where the people rule. Of course, in the United States we call ourselves a democracy, but that is a fiction we tell ourselves. It is a fiction in three senses. First, it is a fiction because we are a representative democracy, at least in name. We elect persons to engage in the powers of governing and legislating. Second, representative democracy is also something of an illusion because there are segments of the citizenry (and residents) whose voices and needs are not represented or poorly represented at the level of government (e.g., poor people, socialists, communists). It is also important to mention the long history of the United States, which reveals the exclusion of various groups of people from the machinery of sovereignty (e.g., poor men, women, blacks). Also, the dominance of the two-party system (supported by corporate media) makes it very difficult for citizens who hold different views to gain representation and participate in the governance of the nation (e.g., Green Party candidates). Another aspect of the illusion of representative democracy and the sovereignty of the demos is the reality that most political leaders are more responsive to lobbyists and corporate leaders than to their constituents. Finally, representative democracy is, in part, an illusion because the political power or sovereignty does not simply reside in manifest governmental institutions and leaders, but in the networks of power associated with economic elites and their organizations and businesses. Sheldon Wolin (2008) called this inverted totalitarianism, which is supported by obscuring myths.

It is necessary to linger here to unpack the notion of inverted totalitarianism. First, this concept overturns the facile idea of democratic sovereignty that is held in this society. Second, inverted totalitarianism reveals problems with regard to civic faith and care—framed in terms of the common good. Wolin differentiated between classic state totalitarian systems (e.g., Nazi Germany, Soviet Union) and what he termed inverted totalitarian systems. Inverted totalitarian systems project power inward by "combining with other forms of power, such as evangelical religion, and most notably encouraging a symbiotic relationship between traditional government and the system of 'private' governance represented by the modern corporation" (p. xvi). Wolin argued that inverted totalitarianism makes use of the state to legitimate its dominance, whereas in classic totalitarianism, the state uses business to achieve its aims of projecting power outward. The accumulation of the various forms of power means there is no clear leader or sovereign of the system, as there would be in a state totalitarian system (p. 44). In totalitarian states, there is a dictator or strong man, while in inverted totalitarian societies there are many leaders from different parts of society (e.g., political, economic, religious) who support and shape the totalitarian system. Political-economic power is dispersed between government, corporate leaders, and institutions, which undermines any idea and reality of the sovereignty of the demos.

To add another layer of complexity, neoliberal capitalism functions as a key feature of the inverted totalitarian system wherein the state is used to legitimate and extend the power of the market, through the ostensibly legal privatization of public institutions, de-regulation, austerity measures, and the proliferation of money in the political process. In inverted totalitarianism, non-state institutions such as corporations, think tanks, lobbying groups, and so on, work closely with the state to de-regulate and privatize public spaces and institutions. Because there is no clear, single organization or person involved in using the state, it becomes impossible to locate the leaders who are responsible, heightening a sense of helplessness, distrust, and futility among many citizens, making room for the election of a demagogue. I would add that, while the center of power is difficult to locate, citizens continue to believe that the power resides in the traditional government institutions (obscuring myth), though they may have less trust toward them because their voices are not heard and, therefore, their needs and concerns go unanswered. Many citizens continue to have faith in democratic notions of sovereignty, even though actual sovereignty is played out among a network of economic, social, and political nodes of power. Here we note that fictions or illusions regarding sovereignty may be important factors in stabilizing a society, at least for a time.

A related feature of an inverted totalitarianism regime is that it constructs and "prefers a citizenry that is uncritically complicit rather than involved" (Wolin 2008, p. 65). Giroux (2012) similarly argued that the hegemony of neoliberal symbol systems contributes to the construction of acritical subjects (unquestioning faith) who either rabidly support capitalism or who never think to question it or its link to democratic sovereignty. Neoliberal capitalism, as a central feature of an inverted totalitarian system, becomes unquestionable (Frank 2000; Nelson 2001). Citizens or noncitizens who do question the system become marginalized or attacked as socialists, Marxists, communists, and so on, which serves as a warning to others who might deviate from accepting the system as it is. These "heretics" have broken faith with the "American democratic" system and are deemed disloyal and untrustworthy. Simply stated, inverted totalitarianism holds sovereignty under the façade of democracy and this is possible because of citizens' unquestioning faith in democracy and capitalism.[19]

An acritical and passive citizenry can be achieved in a number of ways. In traditional totalitarian systems, the state uses police and military forces to instill compliance and to brutally repress dissent. Totalitarian states, at the same time, also use patriotism (a type of civic faith) to mobilize the masses and to squelch critique. As Wolin (2008) notes, inverted totalitarian systems do not need the brutal tactics of police and military oppression to keep citizens in line and obtain cooperation. Instead, an inverted totalitarian system establishes itself as an unquestionable and pervasive reality. That is, inverted totalitarian systems involve the use of the state (all three branches of government), nongovernment groups (e.g., think tanks), and other power centers (e.g., media, religious communities and leaders) to legitimate, if not sacralize (Frank 2000; Nelson 2001), the system and faith in it.

To retain the hidden and amorphous sovereignty of inverted totalitarianism, Wolin (2008) notes four categories of tactics used to maintain civic faith—an uncritical and controlled citizenry. First, the dominance of neoliberal capitalism leads to "downsizing, reorganization, bubble bursting, unions busted, quickly outdated skills, and transfer of jobs abroad" (p. 67). This creates "an economy of fear, a system of control whose power feeds uncertainty, yet a system that, according to its analysts, is eminently rational" (p. 67; see also Marris 1996)—a Hobbesian society of contractual faith. Fear for one's economic survival, especially in a society that lauds individualism, keeps citizens focused on how they are going to meet their basic needs of food, housing, health, and so on. When they cannot make ends meet, they often blame themselves (Silva 2013).[20] Workers may fear organizing lest they lose their jobs, and communities may fear advocating for a living wage because corporations threaten to move their jobs to more compliant communities or countries. Anxiety, uncertainty, and fear function as social control, even as many citizens accept the seemingly ineluctable logic of the so-called free market.

Fear is a powerful motivator in persons' compliance and cooperation with the demands of any totalitarian system, yet Wolin (2008) points to another emotional experience that gives rise to a compliant and acritical citizenry. Relying on de Tocqueville, Wolin wrote that the inverted totalitarianism of capitalism "prevents things from being born, it does not tyrannize, it hinders, compromises, enervates, dazes, and finally reduces each nation to nothing more than a herd of industrious animals of which the government is the shepherd" (p. 80). The neoliberal capitalist system, in other words, enervates much of the population. Citizens are weighed down by economic insecurity yet are unable to locate the real sources of their suffering. Moreover, because of the varied powers using the state, many citizens feel helpless and hopeless regarding their political participation. The inverted totalitarianism of neoliberal capitalism does not use the violence of the state to instill fear and helplessness. Instead, the hidden hand of the market accompanies the hidden fist of economic cruelty and violence, creating social control through fear, helplessness, and weariness.

Of course, not all of the compliant citizenry are fearful or helpless. For Wolin (2008), many citizens unwittingly and uncritically combine capitalism with patriotic faith (p. 112), which functions to maintain the hidden power of an inverted totalitarianism system. "Americans," Wolin notes, "are being successfully kneaded into a citizenry less suited to democratic demands and increasingly more accepting and supportive of the dominant forms of power, not out of Nazi enthusiasm, but from fear and misguided patriotism" (p. 113). To be a good, patriotic American means accepting and touting capitalism. Here we see the joining of patriotic-political blind faith with belief and trust in the economic system, which is a major factor in the sovereignty of inverted totalitarianism.

The fourth feature of social control is noted in what Taylor (2007) called disembedded political subjects. The rise of neoliberal capitalism accompanied the collective embrace of the myths of individualism and self-reliance. In glorifying individualism and self-reliance, many citizens see themselves as wholly responsible for the success or failure vis-à-vis their pursuits and achievement of their financial well-being.[21] Citizens are told in countless ways to pursue their "rational" self-interests, desires, and needs, which fosters the tendency to blame economic "losers" and self-proclaim individual merit for economic success, all the while securing civil-economic faith—trust and loyalty to the economic system. In addition, citizens view themselves in competition for scarce resources, fostering the perception of Others as obstacles or allies in pursuing their desires. Social capital becomes more fragile in this inverted totalitarian system (Bellah, et al. 1985; Putnam 2000, 2015) and there is more social fragmentation, making it very difficult to organize against the system—an occult sovereign. As Wolin (2008) argued, "Classical totalitarianism mobilizes its subjects; inverted totalitarianism . . . fragments them" (p. 196). People "are encouraged to distrust their government and politicians; to concentrate upon their own interests; to begrudge their taxes; and to exchange active involvement for symbolic gratification of patriotism, collective self-righteousness, and military prowess" (p. 23). The rule of divide and conquer applies in neoliberal capitalism's dominance as a social imaginary.

The link between faith, care, and sovereignty becomes complicated in a society that possesses and touts democratic ideas and institutions, yet the actual power organizing society and distributing resources is hidden. Many citizens realize their voices are not heard, their needs and concerns are not being met, which gives rise to distrust in manifest institutions of sovereignty. Consider that, in early 2017, the poll numbers regarding approval of Congress was 19 percent, with 76 percent disapproving. Consider further that millions of people cheered and voted for Donald Trump—someone who pledged to drain the political swamp of Washington, D.C., while making it a cesspool. In my view, the distrust and discontent of many citizens regarding the institutions representing the ideas of democratic sovereignty have grown as a result of these institutions' and leaders' failures to listen to and address the needs of millions of Americans. As noted above, the Princeton study by Martin Gilens and Benjamin Page (2014) reveals the harsh realities of an inverted totalitarian system. That is, "the preferences of the average American appear to have only a minuscule, near-zero, statistically non-significant impact on public policy" (p. 575). In inverted totalitarianism, there is no tyrant who overlooks the needs of the people in favor of his own. Instead, it is a network of power and concomitant elites that are primarily concerned with maintaining their political-economic power, prestige, and privilege, while paying scant attention to the common good. This means that traditional democratic institutions and sovereignty are subverted, even though the space of appearances seems undiminished. The reality is that the real space of appearances (where individuals' voices are heard and individuals can act politically to effect change) is comprised of a network of power nodes inhabited by the political elite and the 1 percent. Like a tyrannical government, inverted totalitarianism represents a kind of occult sovereignty that inevitably undermines civic faith vis-à-vis the idea of democracy and its institutions, largely because of the maldistribution of resources such that many people struggle to care for themselves and others. Civic faith withers in a polis where an occult sovereignty of the economic and political elite pursues their own good all the while undermining efforts to work toward the good of all residents.

CONCLUSION

A casual observer will note the close connection between faith and care when watching a loving parent with her/his child. It is more difficult to note this relation when we turn to the larger polis and its institutions. Yet, I have argued that we need to bring these two concepts together when we consider the realities of a particular polis and the forms of cooperation needed to enable a polis to survive and thrive. In short, political realities, I argue, are imbued with faith, which is connected to care and its sibling, justice. Theocracies, oligarchies, plutocracies, democracies, and other forms of political sovereignty all express kinds of civic faith, which in turn reveal how care and the common good are understood and realized, or not.

NOTES

1. A qualification is necessary here. The political faith and care of Jewish scriptures also reveal a parochial side of both. That is, the covenant God makes is to the Jewish people. So care for the Jewish people by leading them to the Promise Land also means the killing, removal, and subjugation of Othered peoples. The exclusionary aspects of care/faith and the theological justification of violence (absence of care) reveal the human tendency to restrict personal recognition to those who share similar

self-representations, which attenuates or obliterates the space of appearances for those who are Othered. This limitation does not undermine the view that care and faith are political concepts.

2. The notion of existential faith is an anthropological category that claims that to be human is to have faith. If one accepts this premise, then there are all kinds and contexts of faith. Civic faith refers to the faith necessary for living a life in common.

3. Wolin (2016), writing about the political philosophy of Thomas Hobbes, notes that justice means "keeping one's promises, especially the promise contained in the original covenant" (p. 241). Later, he remarks that loyalty and the subversion of collectively held beliefs undermine the polis (p. 260). Broken promises (or vows) are political betrayals, giving rise to disbelief and distrust, which reveals a breach in the polis. I am suggesting here that Wolin, without acknowledging it, is using the various aspects of civil-existential faith to address the dynamics of life in the polis. See also Arendt (2005), *The Promise of Politics*.

4. There have been a number of studies on the relation between parents' understanding of gender and how these notions or constructs shape their interactions and care of children (Pomerleau, Bolduc, Malcuit, and Cossette 1990; Witt 1997; Leeb and Rejskind 2004). I make note of this to point out that gender also shapes faith and that these are codified in the group's narratives and rituals.

5. http://www.ushistory.org/Declaration/document/ accessed December 29, 2016.

6. Alex Honneth's (1995) important work, *The Struggle of Recognition*, depicts the challenges of personal recognition in the polis. Nonrecognition and misrecognition, in other words, are aspects of life in the polis. Philosopher Avishai Margalit (1996) also addresses misrecognition, though in the form of political humiliation. Given these two philosophers, we could also say that there is a struggle of faith in the polis, because of the realities of broken promises, real and imagined slights, disillusionment, and forms of misrecognition or nonrecognition. Yet, both the struggle for recognition and faith can also be understood in terms of the moments of pleasure in forms of cooperation wherein personal recognition and faith are mutual. The struggle of recognition, in other words, is evident in moments of noncooperation.

7. When an individual "cares" for a human being who is constructed as an object, this is a distortion of the very notion of care as a political concept.

8. Chapter 4 deals more directly with the impact of neoliberal culture/capitalism on care, faith, and power in society.

9. Kirkpatrick (1986) points out that Hegel also viewed the state as an individual, which, as Kirkpatrick notes, is a problem because when "the state is itself an organic individual, then those individuals who comprise it cannot have the same degree of metaphysical primacy or authenticity" (p. 70). One can immediately see the danger of totalitarianism here, which is a corruption of civic faith in that trust, loyalty, and hope are in relation to an abstract, legal, impersonal entity that is incapable of acts of care. Only persons have faith and care. The state and other constructed institutions are fictions that have no agency, except perhaps in the imaginations of the U.S. Supreme Court in their Citizens United decision.

10. This raises questions about groups like the KKK. We, of course, would not want these groups to survive and thrive. Or someone may raise the question about

defeating the Nazis during World War II. Citizens need to consider the aims and values of groups and assess whether they lead to the survival and flourishing of human beings, not simply one segment of the population or one society versus another (see Margalit 1996). Groups like the KKK must be opposed and the war against the Nazism may have been a just war. We also need to recognize that the just war tradition does not say that our side is innocent. We participate in evil even as we fight the just war (Niebuhr 1942, 1943). There are two points here. First, the cooperation of citizens to achieve group ends may be just, but it does not mean there are not negative consequences for people within the polis and those of other societies. Second, organic-functional faith and cooperation need to be assessed in terms of who benefits and who is harmed in the achievement of societal aims.

11. Honneth (1995) stresses the importance of mutual-personal recognition in a just and caring society. I agree, but transcendent faith sometimes includes situations where recognition is not mutual. The most common example is a parent caring for his/her infant. Yet, there are also occasions when we care for people who cannot or choose not to engage in mutual-personal relations (e.g., people who are sick and incapable of cooperation, sociopaths who commit crimes, and one's enemies).

12. https://www.brainyquote.com/quotes/quotes/e/eugenevde400619.html accessed December 27, 2016.

13. Hannah Arendt (1958) discussed the importance of forgiveness vis-à-vis the health and stability of the polis (pp. 236–243). She noted that to deal with the unpredictability and uncertainty of the future, human beings make promises, which they often break or fail to fulfill. Broken or failed promises heighten distrust and result in breaches in social relations. These breaches necessitate, in her view, forgiveness. While using different terms, Arendt is writing about the importance of repair in the polis. I think her view is correct, though restricted. There are many other types of repair in the polis, not all of them stemming from failed promises and the requirement of forgiveness.

14. I understand social repairs to involve informal and formal actions performed by individuals (friends, acquaintances, parents, and children) and groups (e.g., self-help groups). I have already mentioned parent-infant repairs when there is misattunement. Friends who are estranged can ask and accept each other's forgiveness. A local church that is mainly white can reach out and invite black churches with the aim of establishing new forms of cooperation between relatively estranged groups. A self-help group, like AA, may enable its members to admit their contributions to estrangements in their families and to seek to repair those relationships. These are only a few examples of the innumerable possibilities of social repair vis-à-vis existential faith. To be sure, these repairs are part of the polis, but are not typically or clearly associated with political realities.

15. There are examples of state officials participating in ceremonies with other nations aimed at acknowledging past wrongs and solidifying interstate trust and loyalty. For instance, Prime Minister Shinzo Abe's condolences at the Pearl Harbor ceremony commemorating the attack on Pearl Harbor in 1941 (Schmidt 2016).

16. This is not simply an issue of race, it is also related to class and how state institutions serve as disciplinary regimes (see Soss, Fording, and Sanford 2011; Wacquant 2009).

17. This is a deeply complex topic that numerous political philosophers have tackled (see, Ryan 2012; Strauss and Cropsey 1987; Wolin 2016). I will address this issue further when I discuss political power in chapter 3.

18. Wolin (2016) addresses the challenges Christian theologians faced in the early centuries of the Church navigating political sovereignty with sovereignty of God (pp. 86–126). Once Constantine established the Church as the state religion, differences between secular and religious sovereignty became increasingly blurred.

19. Jamison (2016) noted that "it is easier . . . to imagine the end of the world than to imagine the end of capitalism" (p. 3). This observation points to the collective and blind faith many people have in capitalism. Faith in the hand of God has been replaced by Adam Smith's hidden hand of the market.

20. Here is where the notion of democratic sovereignty and individualism undermine citizens' participation. In the demos of a market society individuals are sovereign and therefore failure to be successful must be the individual's fault. This is what Wendy Brown (2015) calls responsibilization, "forcing the subject to become a responsible self-investor and self-provider" (p. 34). The subject, then, as "human capital . . . is at once in charge of itself, responsible for itself, and yet a potentially dispensable element of the whole" (p. 110).

21. Illouz (2007, 2008) depicts how mental health professionals use therapeutic narratives (self-actualization, family history, self-exploration of memory and desire) to identify successful managers and workers, uncritically adapting to the capitalistic system (see also Cushman 1995; Hochschild 2012). This is most clearly seen in Silva's (2013), recent book, where she notes that working class young people have adopted the therapeutic narrative in trying to understand their failures to be financially successful.

Chapter 3

Power and the Polis

Michael Walzer (2012) writes that "around the year 1000 BCE, the elders of Israel come to Samuel, the established judge and seer, and ask him to 'make us a king to judge us like other nations' (8:5) and to lead Israel into battle" (p. 54). This request was not without precedent. Gideon was asked to rule over the people, and his response was to reject the offer for himself and his sons, reaffirming the covenant of God as sovereign. Nevertheless, the request to be ruled by a monarch marked a significant shift in Israel's history. Prior to this request, kingship was located in God. Richard Horsely (2009) writes, "Having experienced hard labor under an imperial monarchy, the Israelites valued their new-found freedom under God. Their king was now literally to be Yahweh, who had delivered them from that bondage" (p. 51). Samuel's response reflects this past. He warns the people that a king will exploit the people, taking their sons for war, their land for his harvests, their daughters for his household, and so on. In the end, the people will be the king's servants (1 Sam. 8:1-7). Like other warnings in the Bible, it went unheeded and the result was that Samuel's predictions came to fruition. Horsely depicts further the economic exploitation that resulted from changing to a monarchal system of governance. In response, prophets denounced political rulers for their abuses and for their failure to accede to the covenantal principles of mutual care, economic justice, and the common good.

This is a story not simply about sovereignty, but one about the exercise of political power and its ends. The Israelites, perhaps gathering in more complex social associations, were, in asking for a king, seeking to resolve questions about power. Who (or what institutions) will exercise power? Who will have the power to make and enforce laws? Who will possess judicial power? Who will organize the people to provide security? Who will command the armies against our enemies? Who has the power to execute citizens? These questions do not simply concern this period of Israel's history. One could view scripture, in part, as a testament about how people have understood and worked out these questions regarding the use of political power. This includes the New Testament, where there is a distinction between the kingdom of God and imperial Rome. Jesus' understanding of political power was decidedly different from those who used torture and terror. "The kingdom of God is among you" reveals a power of care, reaching out to the poor, the ill, and the disenfranchised, versus the imperial power of violence, terror, coercion, and exploitation. And in Acts, we note that the first Christian communities were trying to figure out how to organize the community (a Christian polis) so that the exercise of power would result in the distribution of goods to meet the needs of all members of the community.

I suspect that political power has been a contentious issue ever since human beings began gathering in groups larger than families. Whether we address questions of power directly or indirectly, they are present in every polis. What is political power? In whom or what does it reside? Is political power possessed? Who and what exercises political power? How is political power arranged within a society? How is political power legitimated in society? What, in other words, are its foundations? What are the ends of the use of political power? What are the types of political power? What is the relation between political power and justice, political power and care, political power and the common good? Who benefits from the exercise of political power? What is the relation between political power and justice or care? Philosophers and theologians have long reflected on these and other questions, while politicians and citizens, living a life in common, have struggled to live out the answers to these questions.

The breadth, depth, and complexity of the idea of and questions/answers about political power are staggering. Any political theology and philosophy will come face to face with this reality. I accept that it is impossible to do justice to the concept of political power and its varied history of complex arrangements in a single book, let alone a single chapter. The impossible paradoxically frees me to write about political power using the two concepts developed in the previous chapters, while relying on the insights of political philosophers such as John Macmurray, Hannah Arendt, Sheldon Wolin, and Alex Honneth, as well as philosopher Michel Foucault. My premise is that any expression and testament regarding political power reflects socially held beliefs, perspectives on trust and loyalty, and visions of hope, which are necessary for some level of cooperation to achieve common aims. Wolin (2016a) notes that "power becomes political when it is based; not when a victor emerged and imposes his will, but when shared and common concerns are discovered through a process of deliberation among civic equals and effected through cooperative action" (p. 403). Of course, political power can also represent distrust, betrayals, and hopelessness, especially for those who are not the beneficiaries of political power and excluded from the common good.[1] In these instances, cooperation in the polis comes about through violence, coercion, and intimidation. Since I have argued that care and faith are inextricably linked, I also consider political power from the perspective of the notion of care. Simply stated, if a polis is to survive and thrive, then the exercise of political power, whether by the demos or governors, must exhibit, to some degree, care vis-à-vis the attainment of the common good. As Joan Tronto (1993) argues care provides a critical hermeneutic "for a critical political analysis . . . to reveal relationships of power" (pp. 172–173). Tyrannies eventually collapse because of the deep sense of distrust and betrayal they produce due to lack of care for the demos and lack of concern for the common good. Correspondingly, the violence and terror used by the regime to enforce cooperation undermines the regime.

The reason for bringing care, faith, and power together is, first of all, to argue that they are key features of any polis, even dystopias. Second, they provide an interpretive lens for assessing other factors of living a life in common, such as how care and faith are represented in the polis and how these representations reflect forms of knowledge and power related to political-economic realities, race, class, and international relations. I begin by describing the prepolitical power relation exemplified in parent-infant interactions. This may seem an odd starting point, given the differences between the kinds of power exercised in the parent-child dyad and the complex configurations of power exercised in the polis. Yet, it is not without precedent. Wendy Brown (2014) states, "From Hobbes to Locke, Rousseau to Rawls, political sovereignty is generated by prepolitical sovereignty of the subject in the state of nature and legitimated by the postcontractual sovereignty of the subject in society" (p. 108).[2] While sovereignty is distinct from power, they are nevertheless intertwined. This said, let me offer three reasons for beginning with the prepolitical. First, this early relationship, I contend, reveals existential truths about power and its relation to care and faith in human relationships.[3] Second, power in life is first experienced and organized in this relationship—power is fundamentally relational, extending to the earliest period of human development. Lest one think there are no links between power experienced in childhood and political power, one need only read scripture to see references to God's sovereignty and power in relation to the people of God. God is the caring and just parent/father. Also, it is not only psychoanalysts like Ana-Marie Rizzuto (1979) who demonstrate the link between a child's experiences of his/her parents and later use of God representations; linguists too—George Lakoff (2008), for instance—note the relation between early childhood schemas and political views of authority. A third reason for beginning with the prepolitical is that it allows me to describe power in terms of knowledge, care, faith, and the space of appearances, and this, in turn, serves as a foundation for developing these in relation to the political. From here, I move to a definition and description of political power. More particularly, in this section I identify and depict some of the (1) attributes of political power, (2) types (e.g., coercion, violence/terror, and governmentality) and arrangements or nodes of political power, and (3) the problems and ambiguities of political power. I end with a brief turn to Foucault's notion of pastoral power and what I call civic power.

Since a key strand of this book is pastoral theology, it is important to offer some clarifications before beginning.[4] In commenting on the political theology of Stanley Hauerwas, R. R. Reno (2007) writes, "The point is not to try to control or direct secular power according to moral principles or theological concepts. A genuine political theology must attend to the ways in which Christian truth takes form as a power in its own right" (p. 303). There are two related issues here. The first is the distinction between secular and religious power, which has deep roots in the Judeo-Christian tradition. That said, there is no historical evidence that theocracies are any more just and caring than secular democracies. In some ways, religious political power may be more susceptible to distortion and abuse, precisely because the foundations are theologically grounded and therefore may be deemed to be unquestionable. This does not imply one should excise theological perspectives on the polis. The distinction between the secular and religious can be helpful in situations where the theologically articulated values of the kingdom of God—love, equality, and justice—are in opposition to the injustice and carelessness of imperial states. That said, rather than argue that a transcendent religious truth is embodied in some particular political forms of power, it would be better, in my view, to argue that religious truths *may* express existential values necessary for living a life in common. This might introduce a little theological humility into the conversation, as well as reduce religious parochialism. Stated positively, this approach can place us in a mutual critical and constructive conversation with our secular or humanist brothers and sisters, who also possess and live out of existential truths.

Second and relatedly, Reno claims that Hauerwas focuses on articulating Christian power and truth and how they practically make "a difference in the world" (p. 304). This suggests that a particular or unique Christian truth is revealed and can be manifested in the exercise of political power, though I suspect it is highly doubtful we would gain much consensus among Christians about either truth or the form of power. The claim seems to indicate some particular kind of power, distinct from secular power. The fact is that political power is articulated and grounded within a group's particular language game. There are philosophies and theologies of power, each depicted within its narratives or representational system. I would put it this way:

Political power is an existential fact that is understood, legitimated, and supported by using one's particular narratives and rituals. I add here that the group's established social institutions serve as justificatory and disciplinary systems vis-à-vis political power. The challenge, it seems to me, is not to get caught up in the language used to understand and ground (or prove) power, but rather to focus on the efficacy of political power vis-à-vis the well-being of residents of the polis. Perhaps Samuel's warning is an example of this. The people of Israel can understand human kingship theologically, which functions to legitimate this particular human expression of power in the polis. Yet, consider the routine practical realities of this kind of political power—taking their sons for war, their land for the king's harvests, their daughters for his household. In brief, there are and have been many ways to articulate and live out the foundations of political power, but the existential truth of each, with its particular geographically and historically oriented perspective, must also be universal in the sense of being relevant to all human beings—such as the existential notions of care and faith. This is especially important today because of the threats of global warming. We must, from our own representational systems and social-political locations, despite contestations, find existential truths regarding the exercise of political power so that the global polis might survive.

PREPOLITICAL POWER

Most people have heard the adage "the hand that rocks the cradle rules the world." Of course, the "hand" here is the mother's and, I suspect, the baby in the cradle is a male child, which might suggest the adage was written, in part, to support women's social-political role in raising children, while men rule the world. Nevertheless, I think there is a common existential truth here. We could imagine the parent's rocking the cradle to soothe the infant, so that s/he might sleep or stay asleep. The child's drifting off to sleep presupposes a relational trust—the world of the cradle is safe enough for me to fall asleep. This trust is dependent on the parent's fidelity of caring actions over time. As the child grows, care provides the background of his/her self-confidence and agency in the public realm, even to the point of governing a people. The parent's caring actions, one could say, are prepolitical expressions of power that have a link to kinds of power existing in the political realm. How might we understand the power manifested in this common existential relationship?

When we are thrown into life, into a particular time and place, into a particular family and its cradle, we are, according to Winnicott (1960, p. 592), absolutely dependent on the caring actions of parents for our psychological and physical survival and flourishing. Absolute dependence refers to the near-absolute power parents have in relation to an infant. The Merriam-Webster's Dictionary defines "power" as "the ability to act or produce, capacity for being acted upon, possession of influence over others." Given this definition it is clearly evident to even the most casual of observers that good-enough parents have an exponentially greater capacity to act than do their infants. Indeed, if we were to consider sovereignty in terms of having the power to decide life and death,[5] parents have this existential power, even if states enact laws prohibiting actions that lead to the harm or death of children. Regardless of the parents' power to act,[6] the infant is not completely powerless. Infants demonstrate some capacity to act (and the capacity for being acted upon or what Ortega y Gasset called openness to the other[7]), and any parent who has woken up in the middle of the night to feed a screaming infant knows the power of a cry to influence a parent to act. In this asymmetrical relationship, the infant has rudimentary power evident in his/her capacity to act and to influence, and not simply the capacity to be acted upon.

To further understand this type of prepolitical power and its relation to care and faith, I address power in terms of knowledge, the space of appearances, and speaking and acting together (forms of cooperation). Francis Bacon commented that "knowledge and human power do really meet in one" (in Wolin 2016, p. 395). Centuries later we find a further elaboration of the intersection of power and knowledge in the work of Michel Foucault. For instance, in one of his works, Foucault (1979) stated, "There is no power relation without the correlative constitution of a field of knowledge, nor any knowledge that does not presuppose and contribute at the same time to power relations" (p. 27).[8] What is this knowledge vis-à-vis the prepolitical power seen in parent-infant relation? In chapter 1, I indicated that the foundational form of knowing in care is personal knowing—the parent's recognition of the infant as a person—a unique, valued, inviolable, and responsive subject-agent. The parent's personal knowledge of the infant includes recognizing and understanding the infant's particular needs and desires represented in the infant's assertions. This knowledge is reflected in caring actions (e.g., attunement), which are understood as power—the capacity to act. The power in caring actions is also revealed in the parent's knowledge associated with repairing moments of relational disruption.

Acts of repair and attunement include both knowledge of ends, namely the particular well-being of the child, and self-knowledge. There is, then, knowledge of what is good for the infant vis-à-vis his/her survival and flourishing. At the same time, the parent's knowledge is not simply about the infant. It also includes the parent's knowledge of him/herself, which is crucial to taking appropriate caring actions toward the infant. Discussing a different context of power, Foucault (2005) makes the link between knowing oneself and caring for oneself. "Ultimately," he writes, "'take care of yourself' will mean 'know yourself'" (p. 419). Self-knowledge and taking care of oneself "makes oneself capable of taking care of others" (p. 175). To add to this, good-enough care/power of the infant requires the parent's self-knowledge associated with regulating his/her emotions and understanding his/her motivations or intentions. A parent who wearily gets up for the third time at night to comfort an infant will need to regulate his/her emotions, such as frustration, and thoughts, such as "let him cry. I am going to shut my door and go back to sleep." Similarly, a good-enough parent possesses sufficient self-knowledge to avoid projecting onto the child representations that are not in tune with the child's assertions. Stated positively, "It is, then," Ortega y Gasset (1957) writes, "within the ambit of living together opened up by the relation 'we' that the 'you'—or unique human individual—appears to me" (p. 110). For the child to appear in his/her uniqueness parental projections must be minimal. In brief, power vis-à-vis good-enough parents requires the use of both knowledge of the child and knowledge of the self in acts of repair and attunement—power/knowledge relatively free of projections or knowledge enough to recognize and set aside projections.

In the Introduction I also indicated that knowledge, which includes recognition of the infant as a person, is foundational for the creation of a space of appearances. Here the question is what is the relation between power/knowledge and the space of appearances? "Power," Arendt (1958) argues, "preserves . . . the space of appearance" (p. 204). Put differently, "the space of appearances comes into being whenever men act together in the manner of speech and action" (p. 199). I frame this a bit differently. The parents' power/knowledge is exhibited through actions (ministrations) that create a space of trust for the infant to assert his/her self. The parent's use of knowledge and power requires refraining from projecting representations onto the child that are discordant with the child's assertions. Of course, parents do project onto their children positive and negative representations. A good-enough parent demonstrates his/her power/knowledge in realizing and stopping the mistaken projections, which restores the vibrancy of the space of appearances wherein the child asserts him/herself. To shift to the child's side of the space of appearances equation, parental personal recognition in concert with the child's assertions provides what Alex Honneth (1995) considered to be key experiences for a child's ongoing engagement in social life, namely, self-confidence, self-respect, and self-esteem.

The relation between power/knowledge and the space of appearances also raises a question regarding the child's knowledge, since s/he has a rudimentary ability to act. The notions of mirroring and attunement illustrate this process, wherein the parent recognizes and responds to the infant's assertions and, in so doing, reflects back to the infant the infant's self. Mirroring, in other words, does not mean the child mirrors the parent, but rather the parent mirrors the child. This contributes to the child's emerging pre-symbolic organization of experience—self-knowledge. As the child develops, she will be able to know more about what her needs are and find ways to meet those needs—care of self and, as Foucault notes, care of self-with-and-for-others. So, while the parent's power/knowledge is vastly larger than the infant, the infant has and slowly develops agency and self-knowledge.

So far, I am framing the parent's care, through acts of personal attunement and repair, as an expression of power/knowledge necessary for the creation of the space of appearances. Put differently, acts of care are contingent on accurate knowledge of the infant's assertions and *care as action is power*. From the infant's side of the equation, his/her power, while nascent, is inextricably joined to the parent's care, whereby the infant is gaining self-knowledge—pre-symbolically-somatically organized, as well as experiences of self-confidence, respect, and esteem. I have added here the term "somatic." Foucault (1979) is helpful here. While writing in terms of adults' exercise of power in the political arena, he argued that "the body itself is invested by power relations" (p. 24), which is accompanied by knowledge of the body (p. 26).[9] I take this to mean that the infant's experiences of self-confidence, respect, and esteem are an embodied, preconscious knowledge (pre-symbolically organized) that is derived from the good-enough parents' power/knowledge manifested in personal recognition and caring acts.

Another feature of power is necessary to address to better understand the relation between power and faith. Arendt and Foucault both view power as something that is exercised. Arendt (1958) writes that "power springs up between men when they act together" (p. 200), which parallels Foucault's (1979) view that "power is exercised rather than possessed" (p. 26). Of course, they are addressing power in adulthood and in the contexts of political realities, but this can be seen in the prepolitical relations between parent and child. The parent does not "possess" power, though s/he does possess knowledge, which is necessary for exercising power. This exercise of power is in connection with the assertions of the infant. Arendt's view of power springing up when people act together is fitting here. The relational interaction between parent and child reveals that power is relational and realized in cooperation.

For the moment, I remain with Arendt's notion of the exercise of power as acting together, though, as will become clear below, this view has some problems. While the parent-child relationship, in terms of power, is notably asymmetrical, there is, nevertheless, a mutual interaction or cooperation is necessary for achieving the aim of the infant's well-being. This cooperation points to the relation between power and faith. The parent's power/knowledge, as represented in acts of care (attunement and repair), provides the infant with self-other sense of trust and loyalty, which is linked to embodied experiences of self-confidence, self-respect, and self-esteem. Relational disruptions are moments of failures in cooperation, which if repaired provide the infant with sufficient trust and hope that future mishaps will be repaired. Negatively stated, consistent failures in attunement and repair represent parental carelessness, mis-knowledge, distortions of power, and an attenuated space of appearances, resulting in heightened anxiety, a decline is self-confidence, and rise in distrust, betrayal, and hopelessness, which together leads to miscooperation. Children who have been abused (severe relational disruptions of faith/care) lack self-confidence, self-respect, and self-esteem, reducing their motivation and capacity to cooperate. Positively stated, self-confidence, respect, and esteem emerge in cooperative relations of care where mutual trust and fidelity are demonstrated in the exercise of prepolitical power.

While the discussion above is mostly a positive perspective of prepolitical power, there are hints of less savory aspects of power/knowledge. Arendt (1958) differentiated between power, which is realized in people working together (p. 201), and force, which is an alternative to power (p. 202). She adds that "while violence can destroy power, it can never be a substitute for it" (p. 202). While I appreciate Arendt's distinctions and her positive view of political power, it seems more realistic to consider force and violence as negative expressions of power, especially when we realize that force and violence in the political realm, including democracies, are often accomplished by people speaking and acting together. Moreover, force and violence can, in some situations, be ambiguous in that persons can aim for the good and be motivated by care. Let me return to our fictional parent and child. There may be occasions when the parent's power/knowledge is expressed by force. For this not to be damaging, it would have to include personal recognition, be of short duration, and clearly used for the sake of the child's well-being. A simple example is a parent who sees that her child is in danger of getting hit by a car and pushes the child to safety. Parental violence, however, is clearly a negative expression of power and has no ethical basis because, in the moment, the child is not recognized as a person. In violence, there is a distortion of knowledge/care, a corresponding foreclosure of the space of appearances, an absence of cooperation, and a resulting decline in trust and experiences of self-confidence, self-respect, and self-esteem. I would include here that corporal forms of punishment are violent and thus are negative expressions of power, though I acknowledge, even if I disagree with its use, that this punishment can be mitigated by moments of love and affection as long as the punishment is neither arbitrary nor severe. African-America writer Ta-Nehisi Coates' (2015) describes a time when he was six. Coates wandered off in a park, getting lost. "When they found me," he writes, "dad did what every parent I knew would have done—he reached for his belt. . . .

I would hear it in my Dad's voice—'Either I can beat him, or the police'" (p. 16). Later in the book, he remarks, "It was a loving house even as it was besieged by its country, but it was hard" (p. 126). The violence in the family emerged against the violence and hatred of vicious white racism. His parents' discipline was an attempt to protect their son from the harsher, uncaring, and cruel realities of racism. His father's violence was accompanied by love and care, which together supported mutual fidelity and cooperation.

In summary, the prepolitical power seen in parent-child relations is seen in good-enough parents' acts of care that are aimed at fostering the child's well-being. These caring actions are dependent on personal knowing/recognition of the child's unique agentic assertions of his/her needs and desires and this knowledge/recognition creates a space wherein the child experiences sufficient trust, fidelity, and hope to act and to be acted upon, which accompanies growing sense of self-confidence, self-respect, and self-esteem. Acts of care, in short, are positive expressions of prepolitical power that depend on parent's personal knowing/attunements in concert with the infant's agentic assertions, which give rise to and depend on trust, fidelity, and hope.

POLITICAL POWER, CARE, AND FAITH

The prepolitical care/power of good-enough parenting is, in my view, a necessary psychosocial foundation that enables an adult to engage constructively in the complex realities of civic life. But my depiction of prepolitical power was less to defend that claim than to begin to address the notion of political power in terms of care and faith. This said, while prepolitical power possesses its own complexity, when we move to the level of power in the polis, we encounter dizzyingly complicated realities. Also, unlike the relational embodied immediacy of prepolitical power, political power has greater abstractions and manifests complex arrangements and imbrications with social, cultural, and economic institutions, narratives/myths,[10] and practices/rituals (Wolin 2016a, pp. 325–326). In addition, when we consider political power from the standpoint of a (democratic) state with its executive, legislative, and judicial branches, another layer of complexity is added. That is, what is the relation between political power exercised by the state and the political power expressed in social, cultural, and economic institutions? As I said in the introduction of this chapter, an entire book could be written about political power. My aim here is to offer a brief depiction of political power and frame this using the concepts of care and faith, which includes notions of knowledge, space of appearances, and cooperation. Also included is a brief discussion differentiating types of power (e.g., coercion/force, violence, and biopower) and a depiction of the nodes or arrangements of political power in modern societies. Obviously political power has been and should be understood in light of other concepts, such as justice, ethics, social order, and so on. But space is limited and it is more important to sketch out a different way of conceptualizing power in the polis.

The polis, I stated in the Introduction, is both an existential reality, in the sense of its necessity for human survival and flourishing, and a human construction, in the sense that human beings create the institutions, narratives, rules/laws, and rituals necessary for living a life in common. Creating together institutions, narratives, and so on signifies a political power, which is the "basis of every political community and is the expression of a potential that is always available to actors" (D'Entreves 1994, p. 79). Every political community entails living and acting together, and, Arendt (1958) notes, this is where political power springs up (p. 199). This power is manifested in shared speaking and acting, which "preserves the public realm and the space of appearances" (p. 204). This said, power does not mean there is agreement or that political space is without contestations. Speaking and acting together in the polis necessarily means dealing with differences, disruptions, and conflicts among equals.[11] As Sheldon Wolin (2016a) remarks, "The necessary condition of a political ground to power has been stated and restated for about 2,500 years: power becomes political when it is based; not when a victor emerges and imposes his will, but when shared and common concerns are discovered through a process of deliberation among civic equals and effected through cooperative action" (p. 404). Alex Honneth (2016) holds a similar view. Members of a society exercise power when people act with each other *and* for each other (p. 19). These deliberations/actions among equals are often contentious as citizens work toward common actions and goals. In my view, the general goals of speaking and acting together or political power are the survival and flourishing of individuals and the polis. These general goals are embedded in the specific shared narratives, practices, and rituals of each polis with its particular expression of power and telos.

Naturally, this view of political power is an ideal, especially when we consider the complexities of modern states and their multiple nodes of power (e.g., corporations, think tanks, administrative organizations).[12] What would speaking and acting together mean when we live in a society where state and national governments include elected and the nonelected officials, as well as various and diverse bureaucracies that regulate speaking and acting together? What persons, in other words, are speaking and acting together and to what ends? Who (or what) is exercising power? Even if we return to the seemingly simpler Greek polis or city-state, we see that human beings band together and create institutions that are tasked with carrying out various functions for the polis. Each created institution contains individuals who are speaking and acting together toward the goals assigned to the institution by a ruling body—goals that may conflict with the common good. And when we look carefully, we might raise questions about what group of people in the polis speak and act together in creating these institutions. So, for example, Jewish men petition God to establish the institution of the monarchy—one-man rule—even though Samuel warned them of the consequences (Horsely 2009). Monarchy was simply another iteration of patriarchy, excluding women from the polis' space of appearances, valuing men's knowledge as superior to women, and reducing care to women's actions. Closer to home, white educated men of property exercised power in creating institutions and policies vis-à-vis the fledgling U.S. representative democracy in the late 18th century. This was a different political arrangement than monarchy, though it remained a patriarchal state based in class. To this, I add the question about what are the aims of those who speak and act together. Speaking and acting together would logically imply that there are stated and unstated ends, which, given human beings' tendency toward self-interest, might be understood generally as survival and flourishing. If we go back as far as Aristotle, we note that the ends of the polis are not simply "mere life, but it exists for the sake of a good life" (Ryan 2012, p. 83). Yet, this brings us back to the question: Whose survival and whose flourishing? *Qui bono?* Those who speak and act together, those who exercise power will likely be biased toward themselves. So, in the Greek and Hebrew polis men of property and education flourished, while women and slaves were excluded from exercising political power. Similarly, the U.S. Constitution, which manifests the creation of institutions to exercise power, originally excluded women, poor white men, African Americans, and native peoples—groups whose knowledge, needs, and experiences were shuffled to the side.

It is important to point out here that power as speaking and acting together is not simply associated with those who run for and hold elected office. A small town may have public gatherings where they deliberate on decisions that will impact the community. People may gather to protest actions taken by elected leaders. Individual citizens may create organizations (e.g., Mothers against Drunk Driving) that invite people to work together to change state and federal laws. Corporations, individually and collectively, are comprised of persons who work for common economic goals that are inextricably tied to the political. They often speak and act together to influence legislation that will further their aims (e.g., American Legislative Exchange Council). Social justice organizations (e.g., ACLU, Southern Poverty Law Center, NAACP) marshal people to work together to protect the rights of residents and citizens.

If we agree with Arendt that political power is speaking and acting together, what other attributes are involved? Briefly, political power, as speaking and acting together, has the shared aims of the survival and flourishing of individuals and the polis. These aims are informed and supported by a group's particular narratives and practices/rituals—those who speak and act together. Indeed, commonly held narratives and attending beliefs serve as the basis for mutual-personal recognition, shared knowledge, and common action toward agreed-upon political aims. Moreover, people speaking and acting together create public institutions that carry out aims that are informed by commonly held narratives and practices. This suggests, then, that political power rests on shared knowledge, not only about the aims, but also about the methods and institutions needed to achieve these aims.[13] Moreover, shared power/knowledge and common action depend on (a) mutual-personal recognition/knowledge and (b) a sufficient amount of trust and loyalty for people to cooperate together to achieve shared aims (vision-hope)—faith.[14] I add that knowledge/recognition and action are understood in terms of the notion of the dynamic space of appearances, which can include vigorous contestations along with rituals of repair. Indeed, because human beings are complex and diverse, the space of acting and speaking together necessarily includes various attempts at repair to reestablish cooperation for the sake of the polis and its residents.

Let me say more about political power and the notions of care and faith. At its most basic level, speaking and acting together in the polis necessarily rests on some level of mutual care rooted in the recognition/knowledge of the Other as person—both like me and different from me. This means there will be shared beliefs, values, needs and experiences, as well as differences in each. Even in contested political environments, there must be a basic level of mutual recognition/knowledge if the polis is to survive (e.g., despite all our differences, American citizens largely cooperate together despite contestation). A Hobbesian society of mutual enmity is empty of care and naturally depends on a Leviathan to survive, because mutual-personal recognition is lacking. Knowledge/recognition in this Hobbesian polis is instrumental, dominated by self-interests, and focused on the Other as obstacle or threat. The Leviathan enforces cooperation, but it cannot enforce care or mutual-personal faith. A Hobbesian society may endure, but it will never thrive. Of course, this kind of society is an extreme case. There are also more common situations where citizens (and other residents) are not recognized as persons (e.g., in racism) and thus are excluded from participating fully in the political realm—leading to a reduction of the space of appearances. The excluded group's needs and experiences are, at best, sidelined and, at worse, denied. For instance, in racism, knowledge/recognition is distorted thereby corrupting care and the ability to speak and act together, which I will say more about in chapter 6. In cases like racism, the polis survives and the dominant group may even thrive, yet at the expense of marginalized Others who "exist" to benefit the more powerful. It often seems that some groups thrive, while others struggle for bare life. I add here that an excluded group may speak and act together, thus exercising some political power. Yet, their power pales in comparison to the power of those who control and have access to the created political institutions, institutions that are given the power and authority to enforce knowledge/recognition and rules/laws that govern the space of appearances, all of which benefits the dominant group.

I would not be surprised if readers were skeptical about the idea of care and political power as speaking and acting together. The current state of political discourse and polarization would seem to be enough evidence to debar the claim. Not much care is evident between polarized groups vying to enact their political agenda and a great deal of suspicion and distrust divides the political left and right in the United States. The knowledge polarized groups have of each other is not rooted in personal knowledge of particular Others, but a kind of adversarial, instrumental object knowing that is conducive to conflict and enmity, rather than deliberation among equals—working and speaking together. Moreover, the present support for the cruelties of neoliberalism by Democrats and Republicans alike would further debunk the claim of care, unless we understand care as benefiting corporations (as persons) and the economic elites. In addition, there are examples of tyrants and dictatorships that not only belie the notion of power as speaking and acting together, but undercut any meaningful attempt to link care to power.

To complicate this further, in the exercise of political power, other motivations can undermine care and justice. People and their politicians may be determined to enact and enforce a particular ideology (knowledge) that will serve their self-interests (e.g., American Legislative Exchange Council), while harming others. Some may be motivated by greed, lust for power/knowledge, privilege, and prestige, or some other vice. Others, feeling the loss of social power and shared identity, may work to reestablish a vision of an earlier time (e.g., "Make America Great Again"). This indicates that care can be confined to the interests and aims of a specific group or what we call interest groups. That is, people within the group care about their shared values, expectations, and knowledge, seeking to benefit themselves and not necessarily the common good. In a polarized society like the United States, this seems common enough, but often some voices are still given to caring for citizens and residents, even if it is mere rhetoric. Neoliberal politicians, for example, claim they are concerned about health-care availability for citizens, even though the legislation they support will never amount to enabling health care for all citizens. Some Republicans and Democrats announce their concern for the poor, though legislation falls short of helping the poor, which highlights the gulf between what is said and what is done and calls into questions both the knowledge/recognition of those deemed poor and the exercise of power.

Let me clarify here that I am not suggesting that the use of political power is limited to those working in elected offices and nonelected offices or means that care is to be understood simply as the state being tasked with meeting the needs of citizens. This is the charge of neoliberal politicians who decry the existence of a so-called nanny state—read a state that embraces humanistic and socialist values. This is too simplistic. Persons acting and speaking together are not simply elected officials. Political power is exercised in numerous ways and not confined to the state, though, of course, the modern state and ancillary institutions (e.g., corporations, lobbyists, think tanks) wield tremendous political-economic power. There is a two-pronged perspective regarding political power vis-à-vis the state and care. First, the state ideally provides for a fair distribution of resources for citizens to be able to care for themselves and others. Second, the state may create entities aimed at providing direct care to its citizens (e.g., single payer health care). Care vis-à-vis the polis and political power, then, does not simply rest with the state and its institutions. In a good-enough polis, there should be some correlation between state care and care manifested in the public and private spaces of citizens speaking and acting together.

As noted earlier, political power as people acting and speaking together entails mutual-personal recognition/knowledge, which is the basis of care. Given this general view, further clarification is necessary. Many kinds of knowledge are associated with and necessary for the exercise of political power. Recall from Chapter 1, Macmurray (1991–1961) addresses object knowing, which is always a necessary part of personal knowing, though ideally subordinate to it. In the exercise of political power, there is object knowing, though hopefully it is subordinate to personal knowledge/recognition. For instance, congressmen and women gather and speak together to establish legislation about health care. In this exercise of political power, all kinds of complex forms of knowledge are needed to construct legislation. Ideally, forms of object knowing, while abstract from personal knowing, will result in care of individual persons. If the resulting legislation fills the coffers of health-care corporations while reducing health care for citizens, then it becomes clear that personal knowledge/care is absent from the political process. In this case, political power/knowledge and actions are corrupt and corrupting with regard to the polis, because knowledge and power are not aimed at the survival and flourishing of citizens qua persons. It may be that the more those who speak and act together are removed from the daily struggles and needs of ordinary citizens, either because of high office or they are part of the economic-political elites, the greater likelihood that their exercise of power will be corrupt and corrupting. From a different angle, Honneth (2016) notes, "The more those who are affected by a problem are involved in the search for solutions to that problem, the more such historical experiments will lead to better more stable solutions" (p. 62)—a point also made clear by William Easterly (2013). In these cases, power is less likely to be corrupt as people deliberate and work together toward shared knowledge and concrete goals aimed at survival and flourishing of persons (not corporations). In short, the lack of personal knowledge vis-à-vis the consequences of speaking and acting together is a recipe for corruption.

Unfortunately, there are numerous examples of people speaking and acting together (mutual-personal recognition and knowledge) whereby the exercise of political power entails knowledge that harms citizens, while benefiting themselves. The American Legislative Exchange Council (ALEC) website indicates that ALEC "is America's largest nonpartisan, voluntary member-ship organization of state legislators dedicated to the principles of limited government, free markets and federalism."[15] It goes on to say that it com-prises nearly one-quarter of the country's state legislators and is sponsored by numerous corporations. It touts having been instrumental in creating millions of jobs. People and corporations, they argue, speak and act together to ben-efit the citizens. All this sounds quite wonderful, as most propaganda does. The Center for Media and Democracy has investigated ALEC and the con-sequences of their use of political power. The state legislation ALEC wrote and had legislators pass undermines workers and consumer rights, leading to lower wages, loss of economic protections, and lower benefits. In my view, the corruption of political power in the polis is evident when personal know-ing/recognition is either absent or suborned in favor of kinds of object know-ing that benefits some people and groups while harming others. One could argue that most modern societies do this to some degree, which does not deny my claim that when it is present political power is corrupt—the degree and breadth to which it is may be the question.

Before moving on, a positive illustration is helpful. Mutual recognition that founds this speaking and acting together reveals a shared knowledge vis-à-vis this particular group of persons. Let's imagine a group of persons and its political representative are concerned about the health of people in their community, because they live near a city landfill that has been identified as a superfund site. Citizens want their representative and others at state and national offices to provide the resources to clean up the site and deal with the health effects associated with the pollution. The exercise of political power in this situation is clearly aimed at caring about and for people whose health is negatively impacted by the landfill. This requires knowledge about (1) the source of negative health effects, (2) the specific personal experiences of citi-zens, and (3) the workings of the political system. In this case, the exercise of political power is not corrupt, because care is integral to the forms of knowing associated with speaking and acting together.

Above, I touched on the relation between care and faith as aspects of political power. Chapter 2 argued that care and faith are integral features of human existence and, therefore, political concepts. That chapter included a discussion regarding types of cooperation—contractual, organic-functional, mutual-personal, and transcendent—which depend on faith. Cooperation is another way of talking about speaking and acting together. Each of these types of cooperation reflects differing configurations and deployments of care and faith. At its most basic, any exercise of political power as speaking and acting together requires some degree of trust and loyalty, which are necessary for acting cooperatively. In a good-enough polis, mutual recognition/knowledge undergirds and accompanies the mutual trust and loyalty necessary to speak and act together toward the goals of survival and the flourishing of individuals and the polis. On the other end of the continuum is a Hobbesian society wherein cooperation is enforced by the Leviathan—that political institution that demands submission to a rule of law so order may prevail. This said, in terms of realpolitik, I would argue that most political power vis-à-vis the state and ancillary political institutions is exercised in terms of contractual cooperation. In these contexts, trust and fidelity are contractual and functional, which are dependent on laws and ethical codes. On the other hand, local town hall meetings might exhibit more mutual-personal kinds of cooperation, in addition to contractual and organic-functional types of speaking and acting together. It is rarer to see political power in relation to transcendent forms of cooperation, though we might see this in the religious ideal of the kingdom of God and in the attempts by the early Christian communities to be inclusive and to act together to share resources so that the needs of all in the polis were met, as we see in Acts. Here mutual-personal trust and loyalty were exhibited in speaking and acting together aimed at caring for the needs of everyone in the community. While we know these early communities fell short of their aims, this kind of political community has, throughout history, long interested many people (Boer 2014, pp. 86–93). It may be that these political communities have difficulty surviving because of the reality of selfishness or sin, the lack of institutions that facilitate mutual-personal trust and care (and associated forms of knowledge), and, as communities grow, increasing complexities and abstractions can make mutual-personal speaking and acting together more difficult. That said, I would argue that, in some ways, this kind of cooperation and faith were exhibited in the principles seen in Martin Luther King's idea of the beloved community (rooted in the Gospel of John) and his critique not only of U.S.'s exercise of political-military power in Vietnam, but also of capitalism, which negatively impacts the poor. There were, in King's view, enough riches and knowledge to share with all citizens. So, while contractual-functional faith is prevalent in the exercise of power, there are glimmers of mutual-personal faith, which is more likely to occur in communities where there are more face-to-face interactions.

In summary, political power is exercised in people speaking and acting together toward the shared goals of survival and flourishing of individuals and the polis—goals that take on a particular hue given the group's shared narratives, practices, and rituals. I argued further that to speak and act together requires mutual-personal recognition/knowledge for a dynamic space of appearances. Because the space of appearances—as speaking and acting together—involves complex and diverse human beings, knowledge must include acts of repair so the space of appearances remains dynamic. Knowledge/care and cooperative action depend on faith—trust, loyalty and hope. The corruption of political power is evident in the reduction of the space of appearances, wherein a small group of citizens speak and act together for the sake of their own benefit and not the good of the larger polis. This corruption depends on the restriction of personal knowledge/recognition to the few, which is seen concretely in the redistribution of resources away from some citizens, making it more difficult for them to care for themselves and each other. Whenever political power is corrupt, we see the attenuation of the space of appearances accompanied by diminishing trust in and loyalty to political leaders and institutions.

TYPES OF POWER AND ITS AMBIGUITIES

Arendt (1958) differentiated between power as speaking and acting together and notions of force, strength, and violence (pp. 201–207). While I appreciate these distinctions, there are numerous examples of people speaking and working in the polis for the sake of their survival and flourishing, while at the same time coercing or even terrorizing other segments of the population or persons from other countries. The long history of racism in the United States reveals countless occasions of whites enacting legislation aimed at coercing, controlling, and restricting African Americans' individual and collective actions (Anderson 2016). At the same time, whites speaking and acting together used various forms of terror (e.g., lynching, rape, beatings) to keep African Americans from participating as equal citizens (McGuire 2011), which highlights the connection between and corruption of power, equality, care, and faith. In this one illustration alone, an individual could argue that force, violence, and terror undermine the polis, yet when we consider that slavery lasted centuries and that, even after emancipation, many white citizens used forms of political power to disenfranchise African Americans for over a century, the polis seems quite stable. To complicate this further, whites exercising power demonstrate care, faith (trust/loyalty), and cooperation within the confines of their group and distrust/disloyalty and lack of cooperation toward African Americans. The agreed-upon use of political power as coercion, violence, and terror vis-à-vis African American citizens reveals the absence of care, the corruption of knowledge, and the presence of faithlessness toward black citizens. Restricted from the polis' space of appearances, African Americans continued to speak and act together, demonstrating a political power of mutual care, faith, and cooperation that remained outside the formal political institutions of power. To be sure, the exercise of political power by African American citizens after emancipation was, and in cases still is, decidedly less than the power exercised by white citizens, yet speaking and acting together in public reveals political power that defies the corrupt knowledge of racism. This brief example illustrates my disagreement with Arendt. There are types of political power, types of speaking and acting together, that in one context benefits one group while at the same time force and violence are used to undermine other groups.

In this section, I identify several negative and often ambiguous types of political power usually, but not always, associated with state institutions, namely coercion/force[16] and violence/terror. I add to this list a type of power in modern states that Foucault identifies and describes—governmentality. I will, in chapter 5, address in greater detail a recent configuration of governmentality, which appeared with the rise of neoliberal capitalism. Neoliberal governmentality represents the corruption of the political power of the polis or what Wolin (2008) termed inverted totalitarianism. The discussion of types of power also leads to issues of equality or what Fraser (Fraser and Honneth 2003) calls parity of participation, which I consider from the perspective of care/faith and what I call civic power.

States enact legislation, establish penalties, and create institutions to enforce laws and penalties. Coercion or force is a type of political power that is, at times, ambiguous in its effects. State and local elected officials, for instance, establish traffic laws and regulations for the sake of maintaining order on the roads, reducing accidents, and saving lives and property. Police officers enforce the laws and, for those who break them, various kinds of penalties may be adjudicated by administrative offices or the court system. The laws/penalties, police, and administrative/courts fall under the heading of disciplinary regimes, exercising political power as coercion, ideally for the political aims of citizen cooperation, individual well-being, and a well-functioning polis. In other words, power as coercion is, more often than not, a good thing that citizens accept as part of providing order and stability in the polis. It is important to recognize that citizens speaking and acting together hand over political power as force/coercion to elected leaders who enact laws that police agencies and state judicial organizations enforce, all in the name of the survival and flourishing of the polis. This means the exercise of political power as coercion by the state rests not simply with the state but with the people who consent to it.

It is also important to point out that political power as coercion does not necessarily have to be enacted to have its effects. Simply stated, laws and penalties function as a deterrent. I follow the speed limits and traffic laws not merely for my own safety and the safety of others, but because I do not want to get in trouble with the state, which will take time, money, and likely cause my insurance rates to go up. So, coercion as an expression of political power can subtly or overtly establish and maintain cooperation.

Political power as coercion can also be necessary when one state entity is corrupt, using power as intimidation, coercion, and violence against some citizens/residents. For instance, several police departments in the United States have been found to systematically violate persons' constitutional rights. The Justice Department can investigate and, where there are problems, demand changes (Grinberg 2016; Meisner, Sweeney, Hinkel, and Gorner 2017; USDOJ 2015). That is, one organization of the state can exercise its coercive power to demand that police departments fulfill their constitutional obligations. In these situations, the goal of justice is achieved through the exercise of political power as coercion. Other illustrations of power as coercion aimed at correcting injustices are boycotts and protests. Labor leader Cesar Chavez helped lead the grape boycott, which aimed at improving pay and working conditions (Zinn 1998, pp. 614–615). Occupy Wall Street and Black Lives Matter protests represent people speaking and acting together to address economic and political injustices.[17] These examples represent political power as coercion in line with Frederick Douglass' view that power concedes nothing without a demand—a coercive demand.

There are also laws and disciplinary regimes that are more ambiguous forms of political coercion. Laws, for example, are enacted to protect owners and their rental properties from renters who fail to pay rent. There are some protections for renters, but by and large these laws, regulations, and those who enforce them are weighted toward the property owner. In many cases, there are few problems. However, as Matthew Desmond (2016) points out, poor people are often evicted and then find it increasingly difficult to find a habitable home. Moreover, he documents how landowners profit from this system, which punishes people who have little political-economic power to enact legislation that protects them. To evict people, political power as coercion/force must be available for use, whether through the local law enforcement official who evicts or a court system that adjudicates the eviction. From the perspective of care, these kinds of laws and regulations manifest a political power/knowledge that demonstrates care toward the needs and concerns of landowners at the expense of the needs and experiences of poor renters. Put another way, landowners, legislators, police, and administrative organizations cooperate together to insure economic advantage to property owners. Moreover, the laws reveal a kind of trust and fidelity to property rights and their owners and a perfidy toward poor people and their need for habitable, stable housing.

A reader might respond by asking how owners handle people who will not pay. What about the owner's rights? Are we to simply let people continue not paying, thus taking advantage and exploiting the owner? In this example, there are layers of complexity with regard to political-economic power as coercion and class (and in many cases, race), as well as questions about the very complicated historical issue of property ownership, which I will not take up here. Poor people are, in general, not organized and, as a result, exercise less political-economic power because they are not speaking and acting together. They are on the fringes of the polis space of appearances and knowledge of their needs and experiences barely register in the mind of the broader public. On the one hand, as citizens they are legally deemed to be equal. On the other hand, the reality of their situation reveals there is little in terms of the parity of participation in the political realm. They are equal in name only. This means concretely that poor people have little leverage in having political leaders enact legislation that will address their needs and experiences. Property owners, however, have political-economic associations (e.g., local, state, and national Chambers of Commerce) they can join with the aim of advancing their political-economic interests, which includes the use of state power/knowledge to coerce the eviction of poor people—disregarding their needs and concerns. While there are some protections for poor people, the weight of the state's power favors property owners.

This is not an argument either against political power as coercion or property owners. Rather, it is to highlight the complexity of political power as coercion and that power as coercion often reveals problems in knowledge, care, and inequalities with regard to political-economic power as speaking and acting together. Moreover, the presence of political power as coercion often indicates that care is leveraged toward one group and not the other, which accompanies distrust (owners may not trust poor people and poor people do not trust the system because it is weighted in the owner's favor) and raises questions about loyalty. This is not to say that property owners are unconstrained by regulations and laws that protect renters—rules and regulations that coerce owners not to exceed acceptable levels of exploitation. These protections are enacted because of organizations acting on behalf of renters and persons of lower classes. The point here is that competing groups use political power to advance their interests, though to reemphasize that, historically, property owners in the United States have exerted political power/ knowledge as coercion to advance their interests (profit), while poor persons have had considerably less political-economic power.

There are also less formal examples of political coercion. Imagine going to a sporting event and refusing to stand while the national anthem plays. There is no law that says one must stand. There is no police enforcement. Yet, the public acting and speaking together exercise political power as coercion, not simply by taking part, but by humiliating those who do not. Even the threat of possible public ridicule and rejection coerces some people to stand.

Political power as coercion should immediately raise questions about what is taking place in the polis that gives rise to the need for coercive laws and their disciplinary regimes or coercive public actions. Who or what group is the target? Who benefits from these laws and who does not? What knowledge is being deployed and where is knowledge lacking? Does coercion reveal and support political and economic inequalities? What are the aims of political coercion? Is coercion for the common good, for the sake of the survival and flourishing of the polis and the residents within its borders? Is political power as coercion coming from the motivation to care, for justice, to strengthen interpersonal trust and fidelity?

Violence is another form of political power, not simply used by the state.[18] Two clear examples of state power as violence is the sanctioning of killing, whether that is the execution of citizens or violence directed toward other countries. Like coercion vis-à-vis the state, citizens speaking and acting together cede the power of violence to the state, which suggests that individual citizens hand over any right (except self-defense) to use deadly violence. The state, in other words, cannot legitimately execute a criminal without elected legislators enacting laws and the judiciary that sanction and enforce state-sponsored violence.[19] Of course, many people and groups can oppose this expression of state violence, though, as yet, they do not have the political power to alter the laws that make state executions possible. Similarly, in a representative democracy, the state is allowed to declare and wage war ostensibly to protect the polis. This is true even though almost all the wars (or more broadly military actions) the United States has engaged in have not been to protect this country, but rather to advance its own political and economic interests (Zinn 2005). This does not deny the fact that this kind of state-sanctioned violence depends on citizens' support. When citizens turn against a war—acting and speaking together (e.g., Vietnam)—elected leaders realize the political legitimacy of the war is lacking and, therefore, they must act or face the possibility of losing in the next election.

The use of violence, while legal, is a form of political power/knowledge that is deeply problematic and only sometimes ambiguous. By problematic, I mean the exercise of state-sanctioned violence within the state's borders represents systemic failures within the polis and, more often than not, distorted knowledge, profound inequalities, and the concomitant eclipse of care and faith. Let's return to egregious examples of state-sanctioned and permitted violence against African Americans. The list is long, but we can narrow it to forms of physical and psychological violence during slavery and Jim Crow (beatings, rape, nonjudicial and judicial murders, stealing of wages, denial of health care, medical experiments, etc.). These forms of state violence/terror were aimed at maintaining white supremacy (a corruption of knowledge)[20] and the continuing exploitation of African Americans for the sake of white economic, social, and political privileges (Anderson 2016). Clearly, violence in these contexts represented an absence of care/knowledge of black people and lack of trust and loyalty toward them. This violence sought to ensure that blacks were ejected from the space of appearances (not recognized as citizens or human beings) and, consequently, from exercising political power as speaking and acting together in the public realm. These political inequalities accompanied systemic economic inequalities. Of course, the presence of political power as violence did not mean that care/faith in the polis itself was absent. It was present, but it was a corrupt form of care/knowledge, because care among whites was based on the shared illusion of white supremacy (black inferiority) and the use of coercion, intimidation, and violence to insure the "reality" of this illusion.

As noted above, the lack of political-economic[21] power of African Americans did not mean they had no power/knowledge vis-à-vis speaking and acting together. During the political violence of the Jim Crow Era, many African Americans participated in their churches, which in my view, was an expression of power that was permitted by whites (Hendricks 2011). Moreover, many African American churches, especially before and during the civil rights movement, mobilized members to protest, resist, and overturn racist laws (King 1998; Smiley and Ritz 2014; Zinn 1998), signifying political power as resistance. Churches, in other words, were not simply religious communities; they were also political communities.

Let's consider a more ambiguous form of state violence. Various police organizations (city, state, FBI, ICE, DEA, etc.) are charged with insuring that residents are obeying the laws for the sake of public order and stability. They are permitted to use violence to subdue people who are considered dangerous and they have the right to use appropriate force/violence to protect themselves and others. This seems reasonable. I suspect that most nations have police who are given these kinds of powers and safeguards. Yet, if we consider issues of race and class, the actual exercise of violence disproportionately impacts people of color and the poor. The Black Lives Matter Movement emerged in response to police killings of African Americans—police who were protected by the political-judicial system. Distrust of the police is high among African Americans because the police are seen as persons who are not protecting their communities, but rather controlling them. Another way of saying this is that the police, from the perspective of Black Lives Matter activists, do not really care about blacks. On the other hand, police in many municipalities likewise lack trust, and we see that cooperation between the groups is diminished. The exercise of political power vis-à-vis state-sanctioned violence is, more often than not, deeply ambiguous, raising questions that need to be answered.

Who is given the right to exercise this kind of political power? What knowledge attends this power? How is knowledge corrupted?[22] Is care the goal and if so who are the recipients? Who, in other words, benefits from the exercise of political power as violence?

Most of the time, when we think of political power as violence, physical harm and killing come immediately to mind. There are other forms of violence that are occult, though the consequences are not. The Merriam-Webster's Dictionary defines "violence" as the use of force to harm, injure, or abuse. The related verb "violate" means to break, infringe, offend, or transgress. When the exercise of political power, whether by the state or corporations, injures the health of citizens (or causes deaths), then we are in the territory of political violence, even though it may not be seen as such. For instance, Hedges and Sacco (2012) identify sacrifice zones throughout the United States where people and their lands are devastated by exploitive corporations that receive the blessings of political and business leaders. One such place is West Virginia, which was exploited by coal mining companies, leaving polluted waterways, toxic coal dams, devastated landscapes, and pervasive negative health effects. The violent expropriation of resources has had devastating psychological and physical consequences on these residents—physical illnesses and premature deaths. Other examples of occult political violence are environmental racism and environmental classism (Bullard 2004)—a violence that reveals profound political-economic inequalities resulting from the exercise of political and economic power by elites speaking and acting together. In other words, because poor people of color have little political power and influence, corporations in concert with political leaders can enact laws and regulations that enable them to pollute, causing all kinds of health issues for poor communities. I add here the current administration's intention to undo environmental regulations is a form of occult violence, because to do so transgresses the future health of U.S. residents and residents of the earth—the poor feel the effects sooner. The failure of political and corporate leaders to provide health care for all residents represents another form of violence toward those who cannot afford health care and those who seek bankruptcy because of medical bills (see Alderman and Newman 2002). When states and non-state institutions act or fail to act such that residents suffer physically or mentally, then likely a form of political power such as occult violence is present, signaling a lack of care about and fidelity to citizens and their well-being.

Political coercion and violence are evident in most, if not all societies, likely stemming from the first gathering of families into clans. Socrates, for instance, was tried and given a death sentence. In Jewish scriptures, God is often seen as giving permission to the people of Israel to kill and subdue other peoples. There are also laws governing the killing of recalcitrant youth. Occult forms of violence also exist in any polis where there is neglect and indifference toward persons, which results in some harm. To return to scripture, I think the injunction to care for widows and orphans was an attempt to address the occult exercise of patriarchal power, though not to change it. In other words, in a patriarchal system, women are not part of the space of appearances and must rely on the protection of males. When this protection is lost, as in the case of death of a husband/father, then the surviving woman's health may be transgressed because of the system itself. An injunction, like caring for widows and orphans, is an attempt to remedy this, without calling into question the very system that gives rise to the need for this injunction.

A critic may object to my claim that the use of violence is always ambiguous and, more often than not, problematic, arguing that there may be some occasions when violence is needed to insure security and stability of the polis, whether it is executing people who have committed heinous crimes or engaging in war to protect the country. I am not opposed to the use of violence and would agree that there are times when it may be necessary for survival vis-à-vis the polis. Yet this does not mean it is not problematic. With regard to the execution of citizens, the very act of execution is a symptom of problems within the polis. Any cursory glance at the history of executions in the United States reveals systemic issues of race and class, profound inequalities in the justice system, and the collective refusal to face all of this. Moreover, to cede this power to the state reinforces citizens' lack of knowledge/care for and about people who have committed crimes. Also, it reinforces citizens' not taking responsibility—the state executes, citizens do not.[23] Executions, as representing state power, are symptoms of much deeper problems of care, faith, and equality in the polis, which we often fail to address. As for violence in terms of war, the long tradition of just war theory is used to justify this kind of political power. I grant that there are instances when a state and its people may need to engage in violence for protection. Let's presume that there is a clear unambiguous situation where a country was unjustly attacked another country. This does not mean that defensive violence is not problematic or unambiguous. The violence of war is fraught with depersonalizing forms of knowledge, an eclipse of care, and profound distrust vis-à-vis the enemy. That a war may be just (and I believe very few wars in history are) does not mean one is innocent (see Niebuhr 1942, 1943).

While traditional types of power continue to exist, there is another type of power that Foucault identified as a modern form of power, namely governmentality or biopower.[24] Foucault, Wendy Brown (2015) argues, identified an important historical shift in the exercise of state power from "'do this or die' to what Foucault calls governing through 'the conduct of conduct'—'this is how you live'" (p. 117). This modern form of power, Brown (2006) contends, "involves the subjugation of bodies and control of population through the regulation of life rather than the threat of death" (p. 26). Put another way,

since the 18th century, state power has been comprised of "institutions, procedures, analyses and reflection . . . calculations and tactics . . . which has as
its target population, as its principal form of knowledge, political economy,
and as its essential technical means apparatuses of security" (Foucault, in
Dean 2009, pp. 124–115). The historical shift, for Foucault, centered on the
movement from power in terms of the sovereign to power that "would no longer be dealing simply with legal subjects over whom the ultimate dominion
was death, but with living beings, and the mastery it would be able to exercise
over them would be applied at the level of life itself" (in Ransom 1997, p. 61).
Biopower, in other words, "brought life and its mechanisms into the realm of
explicit calculations and made power-knowledge an agent of transformation
of human life" (p. 61).

Biopower or governmentality, Brown (2006) points out, encompasses
several aspects.

> First, governing involves the harnessing and organizing of energies in any
> body—individual, mass, international—that might otherwise be anarchic,
> self-destructive, or simply unproductive. And not only energies but needs,
> capacities, and desires are harnessed, ordered, managed, and directed by govern-
> mentality. . . . Second, as the conduct of conduct, governmentality has multiple
> points of operation and application, from individuals to mass populations, and
> from particular parts of the body and psyche to appetites and ethics, work and
> citizenship practices. Third, far from being restricted to rule, law, or other vis-
> ible and accountable power, governmentality works through a range of invisible
> and nonaccountable social powers. (p. 81)

Ransom (1997) echoes this last point, arguing that this kind of power involves
"operations [that] are much dispersed and anonymous" and thus are "resistant
to analysis and focused opposition" (pp. 18–19).

Traditionally, citizens view the organs of the state as bearing political
power, but governmentality suggests that political power is not centralized,
but diffused over government and nongovernmental organizations that shape
human behavior and perception, not necessarily through threats, but through
the formation of subjects' desires and perceptions. Governmentality, in other
words, "represents power in terms of the diverse ways of regulating human
life, which in turn involves the formation of subjects" (Brown 2006, p. 83).
This formation is "less about power as coercion or violence in terms of instill-
ing cooperation than it is about establishing laws and employing tactics" (p.
79). While I will say more about this in chapter 4, consider the formation of
citizens as *homo oeconomicus* or entrepreneurial subjects. Numerous scholars
have noted that the rise of a neoliberal culture has resulted in forming citizens into entrepreneurial (and consumer) subjects who are fitted for a market
society (Dardot and Laval 2013; Harvey 2005). Sandel (2012) provides

numerous illustrations of this to include how persons have commodified their bodies, using their bodies, for instance, as advertisements. To say that this formation has occurred as a result of the exercise of the power of the state (governmentality) would be partially correct. To be sure the state makes laws that shape the market and society. Yet, corporations, the media, schools, and so on shape desires (Sung 2007), perceptions, values, and beliefs associated with entrepreneurial subjects who unwittingly cooperate with the market and its goals (rather than the goals of the common good). Citizens, in other words, are formed by a variety of governmental and nongovernmental organizations, becoming consumers and entrepreneurs, pursuing their individual self-interests (self-knowledge/care). Power, Foucault (1980) argues, "is not localized in the state apparatus" (p. 60), but is diffused over a broad network of intersecting organizations, making it difficult to identify who or what institution exercises political power. Take, for example, National Public Radio (NPR).[25] One might find it difficult to consider that NPR operates as a disciplinary regime for a market society and is thus a node of power in the diffusion of power in governmentality. NPR's news programs largely present neoliberal capitalism without critique (or offering alternatives), thus serving as a node of governmentality—reproducing a neoliberal culture. At most, they might feature economist Paul Krugman on the show, but usually they bring in a conservative and progressive economist, neither of whom critiques the market itself. This quietly lends credence to the market—as if it is an unquestionable reality. It is a safe bet that the good people who work for NPR would not see themselves this way, which means they are unwitting in their participation in governmentality.

Governmentality as political power vis-à-vis a market society forms citizens into entrepreneurial subjects and, in so doing, I argue, undermines and distorts care, faith, and the space of appearances. I will address this in greater detail in chapter 5, but for now let me say that care is distorted because of a preoccupation with individuals pursuing their self-interests instead of considering the needs of others. That is, it undermines the exercise of power wherein people act *with* each other and *for* each other (Honneth 2017, p. 19). Faith is corrupted by placing trust in and fostering fidelity to the values and aims of the market instead of the common good. In addition, faith is undermined because, in a market society, mutual-personal recognition is subordinate to constructing the Other as an object that either will or will not cooperate in fulfilling my self-interests. Trust and loyalty become contingent, conditional, and contractual. All of this accompanies an attenuation of the space of appearances because political agency is transformed into entrepreneurial and consumer agency/freedom. Put differently, political power as speaking and acting together morphs into economic exchange—civic space is transformed into a market space. Similarly, equality as parity of participation is deformed in that it shifts from political participation/equality to economic participation.[26]

It is important to stress that governmentality as a type of political power does not mean that coercion and violence do not remain potent political tools. In terms of a market society, for instance, poor people are disciplined and punished because they are not apparently submitting to governmentality's formation (Wacquant 2009; Soss, Fording, and Schram 2011). Also, any attempt to offer an alternative to capitalism is met with corporate media's and politicians' dismissal or rejection. While political power as coercion also forms subjects in a market society, motivating them to cooperate to achieve the aims of the state, governmentality is subtler than coercion and more influential in obtaining persons' cooperation. As noted above, it is a type of political power that quietly regulates and shapes desires, values, and beliefs. We do not even know, in most instances, that formation has taken place; that we are entrepreneurial subjects cooperating with the aims of a market society, having trust in and fidelity to the market. In some ways, this type of political power is more powerful than the threat of death—political violence. At least with power as political violence, one knows who is exercising the power and can take steps to resist, even if that is a passive resistance. When people do not realize they are oppressed, when they attribute their self and other alienation to themselves, when they consider themselves responsible for a bare life, then they cannot exercise their political agency and power—as speaking and acting together—toward the real sources of suffering.

Types of political power, whether that is coercion, violence, or governmentality, shape care and faith in the polis. These types of power, I have argued, are, at times, ambiguous and problematic. There are times when coercion as political power leads to positive results and other times when it does not. Violence, which I find fundamentally problematic, may be on a rare occasion necessary. And governmentality, in terms of a market society, contributes to the creation of wealth, while undermining the demos by increasing economic inequality. A reader might wonder if there is a positive type of speaking and acting together—a type of political power that aims for the common good. I think the discussion above points to it, and here I will be explicit about it, though briefly.

Foucault used the notion of pastoral power to differentiate it from governmentality. Pastoral power, John Ransom (1997) writes, "is directly concerned with the welfare of the individual. In its ecclesiastical form, this care centered on the physical well-being of the individual and on the group—as well as the state of the soul of each individual" (p. 64). In short, "Pastoral power is a power of care" (Foucault in Helsel 2015, p. 160). As indicated in the discussions on prepolitical power and political power above, the knowledge vis-à-vis care is founded on personal recognition, which means specific knowledge about the needs of the other and how to meet these needs. Thus, pastoral power, as speaking and acting together, is founded by personal recognition and aimed at cooperating for the sake of the well-being of Others in the polis. This power also cannot exist without mutual trust and fidelity, as well as the intention and desire to repair moments of disruption.

Understandably, Foucault associates pastoral power with the Judeo-Christian tradition. We could point to God's care for the people of Israel, the command to care for widows and children, jubilee laws, Jesus' care of the sick and hungry, the early community of Acts and mutual care of its members, and the numerous other stories in Christian traditions of care. Of course, this history is also filled with coercion and violence. I would argue that pastoral power simply points to an existential, not simply, a religious reality of power. Parents acting and speaking together in meeting the needs of their child can be understood theologically, but it is, first and foremost, an existential expression of the power as care. Likewise, individuals acting and speaking together to welcome immigrants, to educate prisoners, to provide health care for the poor, to insure people have access to healthy foods, to provide habitable housing for the poor are just some examples of what Foucault would call pastoral power, but I would call power as civic service. Pastoral power has religious roots, while the notion of civic power is understood existentially (and secondarily theologically). Civic power entails mutual interpersonal recognition that founds residents of the polis acting and speaking together for the sake of the well-being of individuals, families, and the polis.

Power as coercion, violence, and governmentality help us understand how people act and speak together in the polis with the aim of the survival of the polis. I might even add flourishing as a goal with the proviso that it is almost always confined to a group(s) within the polis and the common good. Civic power, like Foucault's pastoral power, may not be as obvious or even as influential as the other types of power, but it is foundational in the daily lives of a polis that is flourishing. In thousands of seemingly small routines, daily mutual interpersonal actions are aimed at caring for fellow residents. Civic power is the glue of a decent or good-enough polis.

CONCLUSION

When we turn our gaze to the functioning of a polis, its leaders and institutions, it seems obvious that the exercise of political power is based on coercion, threat, intimidation, and violence. There are seemingly countless examples we could point to in the present and throughout history. That there are all manner of political acts that reflect carelessness, self-interest/greed, and perfidy does not exclude understanding political power, not in terms of human vice, but in terms of care and faith. Perhaps if we move toward analyzing the exercise of power in terms of care and faith, we might begin to move toward evaluating political leaders, government institutions, and citizenship in terms of how we might act and speak together for the sake of the survival and flourishing of all the polis' residents—civic power/service. In the face of global warming, the importance of understanding political power in terms of care and faith becomes even more urgent if we are to find ways for all of the residents of the global polis to survive.

NOTES

1. Wolin (2016a) writes that Roman leaders "who governed were exhorted and pressed to promote the common good as the *suprema lex*, and the legitimacy of their power was declared to depend on it" (p. 430). In some sense, this is true of the covenant in that leaders of the people of God exercised power legitimately by promoting the common good.

2. Philosopher Axel Honneth (2014) uses developmental theorists in his discussion on social freedom and John Macmurray (1991–1961) reflects on infant-parent relations in his philosophy of the person.

3. Wolin (2016), in his discussion on Marx's theory of power, notes that Marx viewed power as emerging naturally (p. 419), and what is more natural than the prepolitical power exhibited between parents and children.

4. Pastoral theologians are, in general, very interested in the notion of power, whether that is because of asymmetrical relations in ministry, the abuse of power in communities of faith, distortions of power exhibited in various isms, and so on (Dillen 2014; Doehring 2015; Helsel 2015; Lartey 2013; Lee, McGarrah Sharp, and Shepherd 2017; Ramsay 2017). My focus differs not because I am focusing on political power, other pastoral theologians have done so (e.g., Helsel 2015), but because I consider power in terms of faith, care, and the common good.

5. This is in reference to Carl Schmitt's political theology, wherein he argues that the state of exception is what marks the boundaries of sovereignty and the sovereign's political power (see De Wilde 2006, pp. 192–198). The state of exception, in part, means having the power to decide life or death. By analogy, parents clearly have this ability, though it is curtailed by the state.

6. Arendt (1958), while referring to political power, indicated that the limit of power "is the existence of other people" (p. 201). The limit of the parent's near-absolute power is the infant. I understand this limit to be the infant's own nascent agency, which serves as a limit to the parent's projections. Of course, this limit can be denied, overlooked, and so on by the parent who has exponentially greater ability to act—power.

7. Ortega y Gasset (1957) argued that human beings are born "open to the other, to the alien being; or, in other words: before each one of us becomes aware of himself, he had already had the basic experience that there are others who are not 'I'" (p. 106). This openness can be understood as the capacity to be acted upon.

8. For an analysis and critique of Foucault's view of power, see Alex Honneth (1991) *Critique of Power.*

9. Foucault's view that the body is invested by power relation is important when it comes to addressing political power, which we see clearly in the state's power to execute and incarcerate. One could easily spend an entire chapter on this idea alone, but unfortunately I do not have the space and time to address this here.

10. Wolin (2016a) stated that "myths embody mankind's first attempt to envision power systematically" (p. 322). He goes on to argue that the modern state "destroyed the myth-ritual conception of power as repair of the world and replaced it by a conception of power as domination over both nature and man" (p. 328). I think that the remnant of the earlier view of power is evident in some religious communities and theologies, which can take the form of secular practices, such as truth and reconciliation commissions. What I am arguing, in part, in this chapter is that power as repair continues to be a latent feature of the modern state.

11. For a discussion of power and the liberal notion of tolerance see Brown (2006), *Regulating Aversion.*

12. See Wolin (2016, pp. 315–385) for a discussion on the rise of organizations in modern states and their relation to the exercise of power.

13. There are three important points I wish to emphasize here. First, in Aristotle's view, the polis is a "sphere of conscious creation" (Barker 1971, p. xlix). This indicates that the polis and its institutions are human creations. Echoing Aristotle, Scottish philosopher John Macmurray (1991) argued that governments are human creations and, as such, can be altered or overthrown (p. 137). Put another way, for Macmurray (2004), "the State has no rights, no authority, for it is an instrument, not an agent; a network of organization, not a person" (p. 106). The state, Macmurray noted, "exists to make society possible, to provide mechanisms through which the sharing of human experience may be achieved" (p. 106). Macmurray's views parallel John Dewey, who said the "state is pure myth" (in Wolin 2016, p. 510). More particularly, he viewed the state as an organization for the public—"for the protection of the members" (p. 510). So, we could say that *citizens, acting and speaking together, create the state, which functions to carry out the various aims of survival and flourishing.* This sounds reminiscent of the modern version of constructivism, where there is a dialectical tension between the given and the made. The second point is that while an individual is, according to Aristotle, intended by nature to live and thrive in the polis, "the polis is prior to the individual" (Ryan 2012, p. 78). This is perhaps why many citizens tend to overlook the fact that the polis and its institutions are created and as such can be changed or even destroyed in favor of creating other political institutions. Third, and relatedly, Carl Schmitt's notion of sovereignty as the rule of exception and the idea that the state has the power to take life can exist only if people in the polis agree. The sovereign can act only by virtue of sufficient numbers of people in the polis in agreement with this. Of course, the exercise of power by the sovereign can be enforced through violence and force, whereby the population submits. But even in these situations, if the people rise up, as they did in the French Revolution, the sovereign's power (rule of exception) is taken away.

14. Wolin's (2016a) comment about the modern state supports the view of faith and power. He wrote that the modern "state has even more important consequences

for ordinary citizens. It represents not only the greatest concentration of coercive power in history, and it not only demands obedience, but it asks for loyalty, even affection, from its subjects" (p. 242). While I will comment about coercive power later, I highlight here that Wolin's perspective indicates there must be some degree of faith in the polis, even where the exercise of power is coercive vis-à-vis insuring cooperation.

15. https://www.alec.org/about/ accessed March 20, 2017.

16. Philosopher John Rawls, Wolin argues (2016, p. 547), believes that political power is coercive. Rawls' view is similar to Max Weber, who viewed the nature of the state as a physical force (in Wolin 2016a, p. 321). While I agree that a great deal of political power can be coercive, it is not coercive in all cases, as I argue below.

17. Corporations can exert, positively or negatively, significant coercive power to get state legislatures to enact or rescind legislation. For instance, North Carolina instituted a law regarding the use of bathrooms by transgender persons. Numerous corporate and sporting events were canceled in the attempt to coerce state leaders to get rid of the law. The economic costs, according to *The Washington Post*, are currently about $3.7 billion (Berman 2017).

18. Carl Schmitt, a central figure in political theology in the 20th century, viewed sovereignty as the state of exception, which means that there is "no legal limit whatsoever to the sovereign's emergency powers" (De Wilde 2009, p. 193). This includes, then, the use of violence by the state to insure order and stability. Schmitt's viewpoint has been roundly criticized (e.g., Brown 2014; Hollerich 2007), but the point I want to make is that the use of violence by the state is a type of political power that has long been justified by political philosophers. In addition, citizens generally agree to abdicate their use of violence in favor of the state, though not in the cases of self-defense.

19. Since 9/11, there have been questions about the legality of extrajudicial killings vis-à-vis American citizens who are allied with terrorist groups. Again, this is reminiscent of Carl Schmitt's notion of political power/sovereignty as the state of exception (Hollerich 2007). Does a president have the legal right to order an execution of a citizen who has been found to work with U.S. enemies overseas, without recourse to the courts? The issue remains contested.

20. I will address this in greater detail in chapter 6. In the meantime, let me state that beliefs in white supremacy and black inferiority represents a kind of knowing based on shared illusions—illusions that distort self-knowledge and knowledge of the other. This distorted knowledge is inextricably tied to public-political institutions and practices that attempt to make these beliefs "reality" through the exercise of political power as coercion and violence/terror. Since this knowledge is based on an existential (and theological) lies, the power as violence and terror must be continually used to enforce the "truth" of these lies.

21. The economic power of African Americans in U.S. history is significant, though they could not exercise this power during slavery and Jim Crow because laws insured it was handed over to whites (Baptist 2014).

22. Political scholars have long debated the use of violence by the state and many, for example, have supported occasions of justifiable violence (e.g., Just War Theory). I think there are times when violence is justifiable, but I would argue that even in

those cases knowledge, care, and faith are distorted. I think Niebuhr (1942, 1943) was, in part, establishing this when he challenged Americans during World War II. While he agreed that it was just a war, this did not mean Americans were innocent in their use of violence.

23. I am not against just punishment (and reform, when possible) of residents who have committed serious crimes. I am arguing that executions as an example of state violence are fundamentally flawed. The state is a created entity and for this entity to have the power to take a citizen's life obscures the fact, from a theological perspective, that no one has the right to execute a person. Yet, we have come to believe that a created institution has this power, which makes the state a theological entity in that it has the power to take life. See Taylor 2015.

24. Biopower and governmentality are often, in the literature, used interchangeably, though there are some scholars that indicate that Foucault differentiated between the two (Lemm and Vatter 2014). Since I am not a scholar of Foucault, I will follow those scholars who indicate that these two terms are closely allied in Foucault.

25. Wolin (2016a) writes that the state "represents not only the greatest concentration of coercive power in history, and it not only demands obedience, but it asks for loyalty, even affection, from its subjects" (p. 242). In another work, Wolin (2008) describes what he calls inverted totalitarianism, which seems to undercut the comment about the state's power, because in inverted totalitarianism the state is only one of the nodes of power in a complex, diffused network of power. I do not see these as contradictory. The state continues to have a great deal of power, yet nongovernmental organizations also influence the state, especially in a neoliberal culture.

26. I have deliberately left off economic equality because neoliberal capitalism is based in economic inequality and thus conflicts with the notion of political equality.

Chapter 4

Community and the Polis

In the 19th century, a Crow child had a disturbing vision, which he took to the elders for interpretation. In one part of the dream, there was "a tremendous storm in which the Four Winds begin a war against the forest. All the trees are knocked down but one" (in Lear 2006, p. 70). The guide in the dream says to Plenty Coup, the young child, "In that tree is the lodge of the Chickadee. He is least in strength but strongest in mind among his kind. He is willing to work for wisdom. The Chickadee-person is a good listener . . . never misses a chance to learn from others" (p. 70). The elders believed the Four Winds foretold the coming devastation of native peoples by the influx of white settlers, the fallen trees were the destruction of other Native peoples, and the Chickadee, a new Crow totem, represented the way the Crow people were to survive—a survival dependent on learning and wisdom. Plenty Coup, who later became the chief of the Crow people, led his people in an era when the United States actively undermined their culture and marginalized and oppressed Native peoples and their communities.

There are several interrelated aspects to Plenty Coup's story. First, it is not simply individuals who seek political recognition and parity of participation in society. Communities, like the Crow, as well as other groups, seek to be recognized by the larger society; and this political recognition is necessary if the community is to survive and thrive. Negatively stated, forms of misrecognition or nonrecognition (e.g., racism, anti-Semitism) are accompanied by social, political, and economic institutions and practices that hamper a community's ability to survive and thrive. As Simon Critchley (2007) observes, "in symbolically impoverished societies" forms of community disappear (p. 70). The U.S. deprived the Crow of their core symbols and rituals. Second, it is not only individuals who must find ways to cooperate in a complex society, communities must as well. Plenty Coup's totem animal represents a collective ego-ideal aimed not at fighting against white people, but at seeking to learn and find ways to live with the power of the Four Winds—the power of the white world. In other words, the Chickadee's strength lay not in military or economic power, but in intelligence and wisdom—virtues necessary for the Crow people to survive in a white Eurocentric society that consistently sought to marginalize them and, at the same time, worked to subvert their traditions and language. Third, the power of the state (and related institutions) vis-à-vis recognition can be used to facilitate the vitality of communities, ignore communities, or, in the case of Native peoples and other communities, intimidate, coerce, and violently discipline and subjugate communities.

When it comes to political theory, the notion of community is not a key term, except for communitarians (e.g., Taylor, Macmurray, McIntyre). Generally, political philosophers in the West are accustomed to addressing the relation between the individual and the state vis-à-vis political rights, responsibilities, freedom, distribution of goods, and so on. This is all well and good, but it can lead to overlooking a central insight of theological anthropologies, which is that human beings are not only social-political creatures, they are communal-political creatures as well. "Community," Jean-Luc Nancy (1992) writes, "is simply the real position of existence" (p. 2). This view is echoed in the Judeo-Christian scriptures and traditions. We discover that community was a key feature of the chosen people and how they organized themselves. Each tribe of Israel represented a group comprised of communities sharing an identity and customs necessary for living a life in common—what I would call thick relations.[1] The twelve tribes, as one people, signify a more complex confederation or polity of communities with the aim of mutual protection and survival. These are thin social relations in the sense that the identification is not as strong as one's own tribe/community; there is less day-to-day interaction and greater loyalty to one's tribe. Nevertheless, the centrality of the community is part and parcel of Jewish tradition, which Simone Weil (1952) recognized. "To be rooted in a community," she wrote, "is perhaps the most important and least recognized need of the human soul. It is one of the hardest to define. A human being has roots by virtue of his real, active and natural participation in the life of a community" (p. 43).

In moving to Christian scriptures, Richard Horsely (2009) notes that the term *ekklesia* "referred to the assembly of citizens in a self-governing state city" (p. 14). The assembly of believers was, he argues, an alternative political and religious body or community. To jump from scripture to my own religious tradition, the family is viewed as the "primary vital cell of society" (Flannery 1980, p. 779).[2] If we take this metaphor a bit further, the cells make up various organs (communities) of the body (society), each organ is distinct in terms of identity and function, yet the organs operate together as one body.[3] The polis, then, is comprised of families that subsist in communities. These somatic metaphors are not used simply to portray a poetic anthropology. They have clear implications for political theorizing by Roman Catholic theologians regarding the nature and responsibilities of the state vis-à-vis families and communities (and vice-versa). In other words, the state enacts legislation aimed at the common good, which includes not simply individuals, but also families and communities in which individuals have their being (Appiah 2005, p. 156).[4] Finally, it is my contention that pastoral theologians, in particular, can contribute to political philosophy and theology, because of their sustained study of care and faith as rooted in and contingent on community, in the *ecclesia*. In other words, for pastoral theologians (e.g., Chinula 1997; Doehring 2015; LaMothe 2014a), community is a central anthropological category and "is ultimately that through which all life must be considered" (Baker 2009, p. 15).

In this chapter, I explore the notion of community within the context of the polis, differentiating community from the idea of society. My argument, in brief, is that community is a foundational element of the polis, because it provides the context of thick relations for acting and speaking together, out of which care and faith emerge, develop, and thrive in all their particularities. As such, the survival and flourishing of the polis depend on the viability of communities and their cooperation with each other. Put differently, Sheldon Wolin's (2016) question regarding how to create a common rule in a context of differences (p. 56) is understood not simply in terms of different individuals finding ways to work together, but different communities cooperating to achieve the common good for the larger society. How are the organs of the body, with all of their unique identities and functions, going to cooperate for the sake of the survival and flourishing of the body—society? When communities are deeply polarized, when the state does not facilitate intercommunal cooperation, the polis suffers. When communities are undermined, the polis suffers. Positively stated, when the state recognizes communities, facilitates cooperation among diverse communities, and assists in providing resources for communities to survive and thrive, then a modern complex and diverse polis flourishes (Mignolo 2011, pp. 31–20).

To argue that community is foundational for the polis, I begin with a depiction of types of association in the polis and their relation to care, faith, and power. This sets the foundation for differentiating between community and society—two distinct yet related concepts. In this section, I also address the particular attributes of community, which will be important in chapter 5's analysis of neoliberal culture/capitalism and its undermining of community. All of this leads to a discussion about the relation between community and the state from the perspective of recognition, responsibilities, rights, and the space of appearances.

Because of the complexity of this topic, it is necessary to provide a number of clarifications before embarking on this journey. First, I wish to make clear I am not idealizing community, as if it is *the* answer to political-social problems. Indeed, communities are often part of the problem in the polis. In my view, communities, like families, exist on a continuum from dysfunctional to healthy.[5] That said, the fact that there are dysfunctional families wherein individuals experience deprivation or other harms does not lead to the conclusion that the family as a social institution should be abolished, as if that is possible.[6] The same can be said for communities. Both families and communities are necessary to the life of the polis. When we encounter struggling families and communities, the aim is not to lament these institutions, but to consider and address the various sources that undermine the vitality of each, and to construct interventions to facilitate their healing and liberation. Second, communitarians, liberal critics argue, emphasize community at the expense of individual self-interest and freedom. These critics, with good reason, fear that communities restrict freedom and eschew diversity for the sake of identity and adherence to customs. On their side is ample historical evidence of communities marginalizing and oppressing (or worse) individuals who are different, individuals who question cherished traditions, and individuals who rebel. Communitarians, on the other hand, argue that liberalism fosters hyper-individualism that undermines community by advocating freedom as the exclusive pursuit of one's self-interest. Moreover, communitarians contend that liberal critiques of community naively equate community with obstacles to individual freedom, rather than seeing good-enough communities as vehicles for freedom and self-realization. I think John Macmurray's political philosophy offers a bridge between these positions.[7] His notion of person as a unique, valued, inviolable, and responsive subject is rooted in the interpersonal recognitions of family and communal life. For Macmurray, a good-enough community is the milieu for the possibility of individual self-realization and freedom.[8] When individuals are oppressed, marginalized, and prevented from self-realization by a community, this community falls short of the ideal of a good-enough community. A good-enough community entails narratives and practices that support and protect interpersonal recognition, which necessarily means this community not only protects and tolerates individuals and their differences, but supports and appreciates differences.[9]

I also want to take a moment to indicate further why the notion of community should be addressed in political philosophies and theologies. As noted above, the notion of community for theologians is a central anthropological claim. The community of believers, the people of God, the beloved community, the ecclesia are terms that refer to the political reality of community and, to the degree these communities express and live out love, compassion, and mercy, they reveal, if partially, the kingdom of God—a political metaphor.

This religious anthropology claims that the individual's survival and thriving depends on a good-enough community, which, in turn, depends on political, economic, and social institutions of the larger society. The Crow community's marginalization and oppression at the hands of the larger Anglo society and its political institutions meant that individual Crow persons struggled to survive. The interconnections between and intersection of individual persons and the sociopolitical realm are the reasons for placing the notion of community squarely in political discourse, but there are more urgent reasons, which Chapter 5 makes clear. For the moment, though, let me briefly say that it is urgent because of various forces (e.g., neoliberalism and capitalism) and challenges (e.g., global warming) that undermine both community and society. I contend, then, that it is unimaginable that a society can thrive without viable and strong communities, though perhaps, as we seem to be finding out, a polis can survive with ersatz communities (i.e., organizations) that provide people with the illusion of community (Anderson 1983). From a different angle, in novels or movies that depict dystopian societies one will find the near absence of any vibrant communal life.

Finally, let me acknowledge at the outset that the notion of community is elastic in terms of meaning and context. It has been used to refer to nations, large cities, organizations, and even businesses. In the discussion that follows, I identify the attributes and contours of community, differentiating its thick relations from society and groups/organizations. I am not claiming this view is definitive or comprehensive. I am, however, saying it is an important concept to address and engage when addressing diverse political matters in a society.

TYPES OF ASSOCIATION IN THE POLIS

The term "community" appears often in social discourse, suggesting its emotional and social significance and appeal. I suspect that for many people community has positive associations, conjuring up images of intimacy, fellowship, or communion. Yet, when we ask people what community means or we try to define it, things get murky. They may point to a specific group, town, professional association, organization, state, group of nations or to experiences of communion. The concept of community is indeed protean, varying in meaning, for instance, from one philosopher to another (see Kegley 1980; McDermott 1980; Rucker 1980; Steeves 1996). As in previous chapters, I rely principally on the work of John Macmurray in explicating the concept of community. Macmurray is a particularly relevant source precisely because he returned repeatedly, over the course of his professional life, to the idea of community, its relation to society and other forms of association, its importance vis-à-vis human freedom, its connection to reality, knowledge, and truth, and its relation to human consciousness and the self. To clarify the concept of community and its distinctions from society, I begin by briefly discussing Macmurrian scholar Frank Kirkpatrick's (1986) three types of association that comprise society and community. I consider these associations in relation to the dynamics of faith, cooperation, care, and power. Greater attention will be spent on the attributes of mutual-personal associations, because these thick associations found community.

Macmurray (1993–1949) recognized that, in a society, "associations of human beings are of various types . . . and rest upon *different principles of unity*" (p. 35; emphasis mine). Kirkpatrick (1986) identified three models of human association represented in various philosophies—atomistic/contractual (e.g., Hobbes, Locke), organic/functional (e.g., Hegel, Marx, Whitehead), and mutual/personal (e.g., Buber, Macmurray). All three types of association represent different aspects of faith and care. The first two associations, which are reminiscent of Aristotle's (1947) view of relationships that are formed in terms of utility and pleasure, are similar in that they are conditional—determined by either contract or function (Macmurray 1993/1949, p. 35). Conditional means that the association and cooperation depend on shared agreement with regard to expectations and/or function. The principles of unity in these associations, then, are contractual and functional, indicating that once the contract is fulfilled or the function is met, the association ends.

While Kirkpatrick noted differences between contractual and functional associations, Macmurray (1992–1935) argued that all "associations of people which are not personal are functional. I mean by this that the place of the individual is determined by his function in the group, by a particular service he renders to the general purpose of the whole" (p. 59). Using the example of economic organizations, Macmurray argued that, in functional associations, "people are not primarily persons but individuals performing an economic function" (p. 59). Each individual in this economic association (e.g., business) has a particular function and, in cooperating together, the group moves toward or achieves its aims (profit). If the purpose of the relationship has been achieved or has failed, then the unity of group is in question. A business that cannot remain profitable will cease to exist. With regard to functional and contractual associations, when individual members no longer function in relation to the group's aims or conclude their contractual obligations, then they are no longer deemed to be part of the association. To return to the example of economic associations, when the salesperson is unable to meet his/her quotas, s/he is fired.

Contractual and functional associations reflect a particular kind of dynamics of faith. Trust (and distrust) and fidelity (and infidelity) are defined primarily in terms of the particular ends spelled out by the contract or by the function(s), which points to the conditional aspect of faith. Let's consider a couple of examples. A group of individuals gather once a month to read and discuss a book. Members have agreed to meet at a particular time and to have read the book prior to that meeting. Moreover, they have selected two people who will take turns facilitating the discussion. Imagine that several members continue to show up not having read the book. Other book club members may experience frustration, losing their trust that these individuals will fulfill their part of the contract. Put another way, the three members are not functioning vis-à-vis the group's aims, signaling to other members' noncooperation. Imagine also that the two selected leaders turn out to be terrible facilitators. One leader clearly has an agenda, interrupting and controlling the conversation, while the other just lets everyone talk, offering no guidance. Group members will lose confidence in these leaders because they do not contribute to the overall functioning of the group. In time, members leave because the reasons for meeting (i.e., reading and discussing books) are absent.

Another common association in society involves individuals who seek help from professionals. A person with mental illness, for instance, enlists the aid of a therapist and psychiatrist. The shared contract is for these two professionals to offer their expertise and for the patient to follow the proposed treatment plan. Each participant has a function and role. The patient has confidence in the therapist and psychiatrist because both display knowledge and skills and trusts them because they have demonstrated their care for and fidelity to the patient's well-being. When the patient has been cured or achieved his/her goals, the association ends, revealing its conditional nature.

Contractual and functional relationships range from impersonal to personal, which also points to the level of care manifested in these associations. In a complex society, individuals contract with individuals and companies for all kinds of reasons (e.g., utilities, home repairs, landscaping, etc.). Many of these associations are impersonal, which does not mean that we do not recognize those we contract with as persons. I am friendly to the Orkin man who comes to my home to spray for pests. I clearly recognize him as a person, but it is impersonal because the relationship and dynamics of faith are determined by function/role and contract—a very thin relation. I chat with the friendly cashier at the deli. Of course, I see the cashier as a person and have a basic level of care for him as a person, but the relationship is impersonal in the sense that it is conditional, lacking shared interpersonal knowledge and lacking personal obligation beyond the terms of the contract. Of course, there are also functional associations that are impersonal in the sense that they reflect little or no care for the other person. Prostitution, forms of slavery, and other objectifying relations are egregious examples of impersonal functional associations in that there is no personal recognition/knowledge and no care for the Other except to the degree "it" performs the function. Less extreme examples of these impersonal contractual associations are seen in business, wherein the CFO calculates the cost of company workers and decides to fire individuals to bolster company profits. Workers in these situations are mere cogs. On the other end of the spectrum are contractual/functional relationships that are highly personal, but nevertheless conditional. To return to the example of a patient-therapist association: Therapists often possess a great deal of personal knowledge regarding the patient and, while the relationship is asymmetrical, the patient has some personal knowledge about the therapist. Often there develops a deep sense of care about the patient's well-being and, correspondingly, a deep sense of trust in and loyalty to the therapist. There is, in short, an intimacy, a thickness in relating, that develops in some of these helping relationships. That said, these associations are still conditional in that once the aims have been achieved, the relationship ends. Moreover, the patient and therapist do not live a life in common.

There is, then, not only a wide variety of conditional contractual and functional relationships in society, but also various levels of personal trust, fidelity, and care. Added to this complexity and diversity is the reality of power exercised in these associations. Let me begin on the positive side. Visualize individuals forming an association to protest injustices and to seek change. The Women's March in Washington after the 2017 Presidential Inauguration involved the gathering of women (and men) to promote women's rights. The association was contractual, for the short-term purpose of advocating for women, and once the march was over, the group disbanded. This association represents what I called civic power in chapter 3. That is, the association of people acting and speaking together was founded on the shared aim of advocating for the well-being both of persons and the polis. There are other examples of civic power vis-à-vis contractual/functional associations that are of longer duration, because the aims will never be fully achieved or will take generations (e.g., American Civil Liberties Union, National Association for the Advancement of Colored People).[10]

Negative examples of the use of power in contractual/functional associations in society involve the exercise of power as coercion, intimidation, and even terror to enforce cooperation among its members, as well as the use of coercion and intimidation toward nonmembers for the sake of achieving the group's ends. This likewise can be seen on a continuum. A business enforces cooperation among its employees in disciplinary ways (evaluations, pay, etc.). Of course, negative inducements to function cooperatively can occur alongside positive ones, such as promotions and bonuses for excellent performance, but even these positive examples have an underlying coercive side—failure to perform equals no bonus and possibly job loss. A labor union may use coercion by threatening to strike. One might argue that this is a positive example of the exercise of power because it is aimed at benefiting workers. In that sense, yes, but coercion is nevertheless negative because it signals and perpetuates problems in interpersonal trust and fidelity. Labor and management are at odds, each using coercive power to achieve their respective ends. At the extreme end, contractual/functional associations may use violence or the threat of violence to ensure cooperation. Criminal associations can resort to this exercise of power both in relation to its members and to those with whom it contracts. Government-sanctioned associations may also use this form of power. For instance, police departments can, in a poor black section of the city, use violence and intimidation to insure cooperation, while the very same association will use other tactics or forms of power in white wealthy sections of the city. Of course, power as violence or threat of violence, whether directed toward the association's members or at others in the polis, undermines political faith and does not, in the end, contribute to the well-being of the polis and its residents. A Hobbesian society with its dependence on coercion and the threat of violence can certainly survive in the short term, but it never thrives.

The third association found in society is mutual-personal relations. The principle of unity in these associations is the personal, by which I mean that the association is founded on mutual-personal recognition. Friendship is perhaps the more obvious example, but we would also include marriage, family, and communal relations (Macmurray 1993–1949, p. 60), which I will address in greater detail below. For now, I emphasize that mutual-personal associations are not conditional, because they are founded on personal recognition. This does not mean that these associations are devoid of contractual and functional elements, but these are secondary to the principle of unity. My friend, for instance, may agree to take care of my yard while I am away on vacation and, in return, I will do the same for him when he takes a trip. This contract is not what defines the relationship. Even if he fails, I may be disappointed and frustrated, but he remains my friend. The principle of unity is personal and not functional, though function and contract are part of this relationship. I may also have a friend who performs certain functions for me because I am ill. These functions emerge out of the friendship, but they do not define it. We are friends whether he performs these functions or not. This means that mutual-personal relations are not conditional—they are *not determined* by function or contract. This said, mutual-personal associations can be considered conditional in the sense that there may be occasions when personal recognition and treatment become absent. A wife, for instance, discovers that her husband has been having an affair for several months. To have an affair is not to take into consideration the wife's psychological well-being, which suggests something other than personal recognition and care. This does not mean that, when they were married, they made a "contract" to recognize and treat each other as persons. However, the very foundation of marriage is mutual-personal relations. The husband's extramarital affair simply means he is no longer treating her as a person and the mutual-personal association that had previously existed dies. In other words, the husband has moved from the unconditional association of mutual-personal relations to the conditional realities of functional associations (e.g., his wife not "functioning" in some way for him).

This last example segues into addressing mutual-personal relations in light of the dynamics of faith and care. As noted in chapter 2, the principle of unity here is personal, which means that trust and fidelity are founded on this form of recognition. My trust, fidelity, and care for my friend are not dependent on contracts or functions, but on him/her being a person, which suggests that the association is a thick relation in that knowledge of the Other is personal, extensive, and deep. Even when my dear friend fails to take care of my yard, I retain trust and loyalty toward him despite my disappointment. A parent cares for and is loyal to her child qua person. The father of the prodigal son continued to be faithful despite his son's departure. Nevertheless, there are limits, like the case of the husband's affair. His affair represents a breach in mutual-personal recognition and faith. That is, he has not broken a contract but a covenant, wherein they agreed to love/care and be devoted to each other's personal well-being and the well-being of their relationship. The affair is a betrayal of and rupture in mutual-personal relations, evoking profound distrust and likely hopelessness in his wife.

Power vis-à-vis mutual-personal associations in society is often overlooked, because we are more familiar with power as coercion, violence, or civic power, as in groups that organize to effect political changes. We do not, in other words, tend to see friendships, families, and communities as asserting or representing power (speaking and acting together) in the public-political realm. I would suggest, however, that there is significant social power evident in mutual-personal relations—a power that we take note of in its resistance to coercive and violent forms of power. The fellowship of the disciples after the brutal political torture and crucifixion of Jesus is an example of the power of mutual-personal relations to resist the coercion and terror of imperial Rome. Mutual-personal associations in African-American churches (e.g., King's beloved community) helped and help members to resist, survive, and protest social, political, and economic forms of racism. Of course, mutual-personal relations can have elements, at times, of coercion. Parents, for instance, discipline their children. But coercion as a form of power to enforce cooperation must be occasional and clearly for the sake of the other's well-being; otherwise it eventually corrupts the mutual-personal power that founds these associations. While mutual-personal associations may exhibit coercion, at times, power as violence indicates the loss of mutual-personal relations. In other words, mutual-personal associations by definition cannot express power as violence in the social-political realm without destroying the association.

In summary, Kirkpatrick identified three types of association in society, each representing different principles of unity. Each of these associations manifests distinct aspects of care, faith, and power. While we all engage in these associations, mutual-personal relations are foundational for the thick relations one finds in friendships, marriages, families, and communities.

SOCIETY AND COMMUNITY

A society and community comprise contractual, functional, and mutual-personal associations. To differentiate between society and community and gain greater clarity about community, I first turn to Macmurray's views on social and personal life. Social life, for Macmurray (1999–1935, involves entering into associations where there is a shared purpose and function. In a social group there are customs and traditions "in which we are enmeshed and which, by more subtle pressure, cuts across individual tendencies and compels us to conform to ways of living which are conventional" (p. 54). Some degree of conformity is necessary if one is to participate in a social group. "We have to co-operate with one another," Macmurray wrote, "very often with numbers of people whom we do not know or do not like, for common purposes" (p. 54). A viable social life, where cooperation is necessary to achieve the aims of the group, "depends upon entering into relationship with other people, not with the whole of ourselves but only part of ourselves. It depends on suppressing, for a time at least, the fullness and wholeness of our natures" (p. 55). One might hear echoes of Rousseau's or Freud's negative view of society/civilization in this formulation, but this would be incorrect. Social life, for Macmurray, is necessary for living in society. The fact that we might suppress a part of ourselves is not, in and of itself, damaging or an obstacle to achieving self-realization. Put differently, in a social group, shared loyalty and trust are founded on a common purpose that individuals assent to. A reason why individuals might withhold "the fullness of [their] natures" is because trust and loyalty are contingent on this purpose and function. That is, consciously or unconsciously, individuals recognize that trust and loyalty are conditional and that, once the purpose has been achieved, the existence of the group is in question.

A couple of examples will illustrate this view. In U.S. society, most residents willingly agree to follow traffic laws established for the purpose of safety and orderly traffic flow. On the twenty-mile stretch of highway that has little traffic, I suppress my desire to go hundred miles per hour, because I have assented to these rules and laws. These common laws are not obstacles to achieving self-realization, but they may, at times, serve as limits to my self-interests and desires. Another example is the law requiring all 18-year-olds to serve two years in military service. For some citizens, this law requires the suppression of parts of themselves, which they may willingly do for the sake of protecting the larger society. The suppression of a part of oneself for a limited time is ideally for the sake of cooperating with others toward attaining the common good. On the other hand, laws, rules, and customs that require citizens to continually suppress their desires, needs, and talents (racism, sexism) so that another segment of society can obtain social, political, and economic privileges reflect a society that undermines the social life of certain individual residents and thus falls quite short of the ideal of a good enough or decent society. Laws and customs that oppress people for the sake of the privileged group are unjust and, as Augustine stated, unjust laws are no laws at all.

The social life we engage in is distinct from the personal life. The personal life "demands a relationship with one another in which we can be our whole selves and have complete freedom to express everything that makes us what we are. It demands a relationship in which suppression and inhibition are unnecessary" (Macmurray 1999–1935, p. 56). This relationship has many names, he noted, but "what is common to them all is the idea of a relationship between us which has no purpose beyond itself" (p. 56). Indeed, the "personal life is not 'other-then-functional' but 'more-then-functional'" (2004–1941, p. 145). These kind of mutual-personal relationships instantiate communal life—life lived in common wherein "the enjoyment of a unity [is] created by affection" (p. 146). I call these thick relations. Ideally, communal life, then, is personal life. A reason why individuals can express and be themselves in these relationships is that loyalty and trust are unconditional. Loyalty and trust are not dependent on purpose or function, but on synchronic and diachronic recognition and treatment of the Other as person. While there are purposes and functions in personal relationships, these are secondary and subordinate to recognizing and being with the Other as person. Ideally, in mutual-personal relationships (friendships, family, and community), there is shared cooperation toward mutual self-realization while living a life in common.

Macmurray's position, then, is that a personal life is necessarily social, but distinct from social life; the personal life is communal. Human beings must find ways to cooperate with other individuals in society to achieve shared purposes, such as survival. However, in personal living, social life is subordinate. This said, while personal life is always social, social life is not necessarily personal. Self-help groups, for instance, are social and accidentally personal in that friendships may form, which is not the focus of the group. Book clubs, professional associations, and corporations are groups that have shared purposes and members have various functions in relation to common aims. They are not communities. The personal is present, but subordinate to the aims of the group. By contrast, friendships, families, marriages, and so on are associations that ideally represent the personal life. In short, what constitutes the social life of the group is a purpose, while a personal life, which is social, is for its own sake.[11]

Society is a cognate term of the social. A society, Macmurray (1993–1949) argued, "is a group of persons cooperating in the pursuit of a common purpose. The common purpose creates the association; for if the purpose should disappear, the society will go into dissolution. It also dictates the association; since members must cooperate in the way which secure the common end" (p. 35). Members function in relation to the shared purpose and aim (1991–1961, p. 157). While the relation is functional, the members are persons, "but only in virtue of the specific functions they perform in relation to the purpose which constitutes the group" (1993–1949, p. 36). Macmurray understood society to be "an organic unity, not a personal one" (p. 36). This said, society, while an organic unity, *exists for the life of personal relationship. Personal life does not exist for society*" (1999–1935, p. 59; emphasis added).[12]

The idea of society, then, is distinct from, yet related to the notion of community. A community, Macmurray wrote:

> rests upon a different principle of unity. It is not *constituted* by a common purpose. No doubt its members will share common purposes and cooperate for their realization. But their common purposes merely express, they do not constitute, the unity of the association; for they can be changed freely without any effect upon the unity of the group. Indeed, it is characteristic of communities that they create common purposes for the sake of cooperation instead of creating cooperation for the sake of common purposes. (1991–1961, p. 36)[13]

As indicated above, the principle of unity for community is neither functional nor organic, but rather personal (Macmurray 1993–1949, p. 27). Clearly, a community possesses functions and purposes, but these are secondary and subordinate to the principle of unity, which is the recognition and treatment of Others as persons and the motivation to live a life in common with these Others. Baker (2009) wrote that in "communities individuals stay together in spite of everything that divides them, while in society, individuals remain divided in spite of everything that might unite them" (p. 108).

In short, a community "is a group which acts together; but, unlike a mere society, its members are in communion with one another; they constitute a fellowship. A society whose members act together without forming a fellowship can only be constituted by a common purpose. They cooperate to achieve a purpose that each of them, in his own interest, desires to achieve, and which can only be achieved by cooperation. The relation of its members are functional" (1991–1961, p. 157). From Macmurray's perspective, "Every community is then a society; but not every society is a community" (p. 146). This said, a society and the forms of association that constitute it are necessary in that they ideally exist "for the life of personal relationships" (1991a–1957, p. 59). In brief, community "is prior to society" (1993–1949, p. 37), because *"it is communal life that fulfills and completes the life of that self who, without community, would be alienated, isolated, lonely, and valueless. . . . The individual can only become fully real within the mutuality of community"* (1991–1961, p. xvii, emphasis added). For Macmurray and others (e.g., Bataille in Baker 2009, p. 22; Feuerbach in Kirkpatrick 1986, p. 140), an authentic self, a vital self, is realized only in mutual-personal associations—community—associations that subordinate the social to the personal.[14]

There are several points to be highlighted here. First, Macmurray was not an idealist. Having fought in World War I, seen the ravages of racism in South Africa, and experienced struggles in his marriage, Macmurray was well aware of problems and failures of social and personal life in society and community. That there are conflicts, crises, and failures in societies and communities do not negate the necessity of both for human survival and flourishing. Instead, these features of human life simply reinforce the necessity of relational-faith repairs. Second, there may be some concern about the implied conservative nature of Macmurray's focus on community or other communitarian perspectives (see Robinson 1999). Macmurray, well aware of the oppression and marginalization of women and black South Africans, was also critical of communities (and societies) that inhibited the freedom and dignity of certain members, while privileging others. A good-enough community respects and nurtures diversity, freedom, and dignity—personal lives.[15] Societies and communities that do not foster these fall short of the ideal. Third and relatedly, for Macmurray self-realization is most likely to be found in communities where mutual-personal relations exhibit unconditional trust and loyalty. Contra the critics of communitarians, the premise here is that good-enough communities do not inhibit self-realization, flourishing, or freedom. When they do, they are failing or dysfunctional. Freedom in these relationships is not *freedom from* the demands and obligations of love and care, but the *freedom to* love and care. Yes, the Other can be experienced as a burden and limits one's options/choices, but because I recognize and care for her as a person, I freely choose to take up those burdens. He ain't heavy, he's my brother.

Before turning to the role of the state vis-à-vis community, there is one more important characteristic of community to be discussed, namely deep symbols. All human associations, whether functional, contractual, or mutual-personal, have various symbolic or representational forms (e.g., myths, narratives, rituals) that organize interactions, shape conscious and unconscious perceptions and experiences, and provide an individual and a shared sense of identity. Susan Langer's (1951) notion of life symbols and Edward Farley's (1996) view of deep symbols help further understand community and its relation to society. Deep symbols, Farley argued, "are the values by which a community understands itself, from which it takes its aims, and to which it appeals as canons of cultural criticism. To grow up in a community is to have one's consciousness shaped by these symbols. Thus, they empower both individuals who live from them and the community that embodies them in narrative and ritual acts" (p. 3). These symbols also "arise within and express the historical determinacy of a community" (p. 3) and sustain a community's thick relations of care and faith. Farley calls these symbols deep symbols "because they reside in perduring linguistic structures that maintain the community's very existence" (p. 3). Macmurray's (1991a–1957) view furthers Farley's point. Macmurray wrote, "[T]here is from the beginning an element of symbolic activity involved which has no organic or utilitarian purpose, and which makes the relationship, as it were, an end in itself" (p. 58). *A community's deep or core symbols express, maintain, and order how individuals within the community are recognized and treated as persons and live out, in particular ways, their commitments to live a life in common—a shared personal life.* The life symbols of community, in other words, reveal particular expressions of interpersonal care, faith, and cooperation/power—forms of living a life together.

An important feature of deep symbols is that they are both synchronic and diachronic. Merriam-Webster's dictionary defines synchronic as "concerned with events existing in a limited time period and ignoring historical antecedents." A community's deep symbols are synchronic inasmuch as personal identity and faith/care relations are lived out in the immediate present. Put differently, living a life in common in the present moment is supported and shaped by the community's deep symbols. The term "diachronic" refers to a period of time or changes that take place over time. Living a life in common means not only living in the present, but over time. The diachronic nature of deep symbols, then, means that a community recognizes and treats each other as persons in the present, which is inextricably yoked to the past and future. That is, the diachronic nature of deep symbols means that previous generations are included as members of the present community and the community of tomorrow. The Christian notion of the communion of saints, burying members on church grounds (symbolizing the Christian cosmology—Kingdom of God), and Asian cultural, ritual practices of venerating the dead members of families and religious communities are illustrations of the diachronic nature of deep symbols—symbols that found personal relations. Put another way, the statement "these are my people" is synchronic in the sense that I recognize and treat these individuals as persons living a common life. The statement is diachronic in the sense that previous generations are still considered part of the community in the present, if only in individual and collective memory.

Of course, other social groups memorialize the dead—groups that are not communities. As a society, we remember and venerate past leaders such as George Washington, Abraham Lincoln, Susan B. Anthony, Frederick Douglass, Rosa Parks, and others. Professional societies and academic institutions elevate celebrated members long deceased. These groups, however, are not communities, though fellowship and friendship within the group may occur. In other words, these individuals may represent a movement, a society, a scientific theory and practice, but they do not represent a particular community, because relationships are founded on purpose and function and members do not live a life in common. Moreover, only certain members of a society or group are memorialized because of some elevated (or notorious) trait or contribution. Communities recall celebrated figures as well, but communities remember past members simply because they were persons of this community. To be remembered in a community is not necessarily or primarily a function of achievement. Memory is personal. We remember our fellow community members because they are persons we care about and that we shared a common faith and life together.

Another feature of deep symbols vis-à-vis community is power. Farley (1996) briefly notes three features of the power of deep symbols or what he calls words of power, namely, enchanted, normative, and transcendent or rooted in a master narrative (pp. 4–8). The words or symbols, in my view, are not necessarily powerful. The power is seen in people depending on and using deep symbols to speak and act together. *Deep symbols are living symbols in that they are used by members of the community to speak and act together (space of appearances) toward shared life and toward goals and purposes.* By way of illustration, let's return to the Crow people. Their deep symbols formed a complex web, linking narratives, myths, and rituals that expressed their shared personal faith, care, life, and identity—thick relations. For instance, they had various rituals (e.g., sun dance, counting coup) that defined what it meant to be and live as Crow persons. Their deep symbols expressed and maintained *a unique common life as Crow persons*—unique life expression, a common faith, and shared identity. As Jonathan Lear (2006) points out, the threatened loss of these narratives and rituals as a result of U.S. interventions undermined the very existence of the Crow people and their way of life. It undermined their power of speaking and acting together—a power rooted in and dependent on their deep symbols. Take away or undermine a people's deep symbols and you thwart their ability to speak and act together, you disrupt their mutual-personal care, you erode their shared identity and undermine their faith. Plenty Coup's leadership and partial reframing of core Crow symbols enabled the Crow people to hold onto their culture and traditions (life expressions) despite efforts of the U.S. government and society to assimilate the Crows. That is, Plenty Coup's leadership enabled his community to speak and act together as Crow people—a civic and communal power that enabled them to resist U.S. efforts to marginalize and destroy (assimilate) them as a people.

It is important to mention that the particularity of deep symbols does not necessarily mean that the personal is restricted simply and solely to a specific group of people. A deep symbol that synchronically and diachronically particularizes personhood-in-community can also be universal. For instance, a core or deep symbol, common to both Jewish and Christian communities, is *imago dei*—human beings are created in the image and likeness of God. This symbol, which is part of a theological web of symbols, has the paradoxical function of being both particular and universal. That is, in my specific Jewish or Christian community, *imago dei* means that I recognize and treat community members as persons. Indeed, the Other's personhood is rooted in the transcendent and, therefore, has an ontological character and demand. As a member of the community, one realizes that this deep symbol obliges one to not only recognize people within my particular community as persons, but those outside it as well.[16] The stranger, the alien is not of my community, but I am obliged to recognize and treat him/her as a person. Deep symbols, then, can be both particular and universal, yet the universal meaning of the personal does not necessarily include living a life in common. It simply means recognizing and treating the Other, the stranger, as a person with his/her own identity and community.

In sum, community, which is also a society, comprises interpersonal, social relationships wherein Others are recognized and treated as persons and there is a shared motivation and commitment to live a common life. This common life, which is the personal life, is rooted in deep symbols, which comprise particular language, narratives, and rituals that support and maintain synchronic and diachronic unconditional, personal obligations, loyalty, and trust—faith—as well as thick relations of mutual care. Naturally, conditional obligations, loyalties, and trusts are necessarily part of a community as a society, but these are subordinate to and conditioned by the unconditional obligation to recognize and treat members as persons and to care for them. This shared personal recognition possesses its own particularity given the community's unique narratives, language, and rituals, all of which shape individual and collective identity, as well as personal, shared memories and hopes for the future life lived in common. This living a life in common, which depends on deep symbols, reflects the power of speaking and acting together qua persons-in-community. This power is aimed at the survival and flourishing of community and its individual members.

COMMUNITY, SOCIETY, AND THE STATE

I would like to take a short detour before discussing the role of the state vis-à-vis community—a detour that will set the framework for the discussion. Growing up, most of us were taught that part of the great American experiment involved freedom of religion. People arrived on U.S. shores, having left the religious violence and intolerance of Europe, so that they could practice their faith. Generally, this narrative is interpreted from an individualistic perspective. Individuals could not freely practice their religious faith in Europe, so they immigrated to America. This view overlooks the fact that individuals formed and were part of communities and that the difficulty in Europe was not simply the issue of individuals practicing their religious faith but communities. Communities that differed from state-sanctioned religion were considered a threat to the state, hence the state's role in the persecution and marginalization of minority religious views. I do not think European states, during that time, were concerned about lone individuals practicing their religious beliefs, but were instead concerned about the proliferation of religious communities that had customs, creeds, and practices that differed from the dominant state-sanctioned religion. An individual never threatens a state by him/herself. Rather, dissident groups, organizations, and communities evoke the state's ire. In part, Europe's struggle was understandable, because for centuries religious identity and the nation-state were closely allied. Could one still be English if one was Baptist? Of course, there were religious minorities (e.g., Jews) that had long existed in societies where, in this case, Catholicism and later Anglicanism dominated, but they were relegated to the fringes of society and the state. They were hardly a threat to national identity or state power, because they retained an Othered status. To return to the American experiment, one could offer the interpretation that the challenge was not simply the free exercise of religion by individuals in society, but also the mutual recognition and cooperation of diverse religious communities in a complex and pluralistic society. The state's role in this American experiment was not to advocate for one religion, at least ideally, but rather to safeguard the freedom to practice one's religious beliefs in community, as long as those practices did not harm others. In this way, American identity, ideally speaking, did not become linked to a single religious creed and practice.

The point I want to make here is that the protection of religious freedom cannot be understood simply as an individual right, because religious faith—at that time—was (and is) communal and social.[17] One could say that protecting an individual's right to practice his/her religious faith led to the secondary effect of the state protecting religious communities. Yet, we might also consider the state's role, not only with regard to not interfering in a community's religious practices, but also facilitating the community's survival and flourishing. While people might be rightly anxious about this latter view, I need only point out that the colonies and later the state, in subtle and overt ways, supported Christian faith communities, while, at times, discouraged others.[18] Of course, we can contrast this with the long history of the colonies and the state undermining, suppressing, and persecuting Native peoples and their religious customs and practices.

There is a little further to travel on this detour. Plato argued that politics was the art of caring for souls (in Appiah 2005, p. 155), which implies that the state has a role in caring for souls—cultivating citizens of the polis. We might imagine that Plato was concerned about the character and virtues of citizens and believed the city-state had a role in cultivating civic-religious virtues. In my view, Plato's focus on the cultivation of souls in the polis screens something he understandably took for granted—community and its deep symbols. Families and communities were the first and foundational caregivers of souls and, for Plato, the larger polis also had a role in cultivating souls. I suggest that communal life was taken for granted because it did not pose a problem for the polis. If we jump many millennia to the centuries after the Enlightenment, political philosophers who focused on the importance of individual rights (e.g., Hobbes, Locke, Mill), I believe, also took for granted the reality of community. Indeed, the anxiety regarding community vis-à-vis suppressing individual self-realization suggests that the reality of community was very much alive. If we skip to the 20th century, we find the emergence of communitarian philosophers (e.g., Charles Taylor, Alasdair McIntire, John Macmurray, Michael Sandel), which revealed something new in the history of the West, namely, the crumbling of communities—religious and otherwise. Sociologists like Robert Putnam (2001, 2015) and Jennifer Silva (2013) have documented the decline in communities during the last fifty years. This suggests to me that, unlike Plato and many other philosophers, we can no longer take for granted the reality of communities in the polis and, therefore, politics as care of souls/persons must now include care of communities—a view long held by pastoral theologians.

This detour has meant to highlight two points. First, an individual's exercise of freedom of religion during the early years of this nation was inextricably joined to his/her community of faith and its deep symbols. We therefore cannot ignore the government's role in recognizing these communities and the tacit or overt support of these communities (and the misrecognition and undermining of other religious faith communities). Second, the idea of politics as care of souls originally took for granted the existence of community as a part of the polis. Today, the demise of community, which I will say more about in chapter 5, raises questions about the role politics and the state have vis-à-vis community. More specifically, if politics involves the care of souls, then today it must also include care of communities. In saying this, I wish to stress I am not suggesting that this applies only to religious communities, but rather any community—religious or secular—that is concerned about the well-being of its members is respectful of other communities, and cooperates with other communities and groups toward the common good.

Let me say a bit more about this view. Above, I stated that the basic unit of communal life is family (cell of society) and the basic unit of the polis is community (organ of society). A good-enough polis is comprised of good-enough communities engaged in mutual recognition and cooperation toward the common good of all residents of society. If communities suffer or are in decline, the polis is ill. This necessarily raises questions about the state's role with regard to communities. We affirm that the state has a role in protecting individual rights, but what about the state's role vis-à-vis communities' practices and beliefs? What is the state's role in facilitating the survival and flourishing of communities? Are there communities that the state discourages or disciplines and, if so, by what criteria is this decision made?

Answers to these questions could take up quite a bit of ink and, of course, be contested. My modest aim is to propose that there are three guidelines with regard to the state's role in aiding communities. Before identifying and depicting these guidelines, it is helpful to recall from the introduction what is meant by the state and then indicate its relation to community. Leo Strauss and Joseph Cropsey (1987) indicate that modern people tend to view the state "in contradistinction to 'society'" (p. 6). This distinction is inconceivable, they argue, for classical political philosophers like Plato and Aristotle. Recall that Aristotle viewed the polis as "a kind of partnership, association, or community, that is, a group of persons who share or hold certain things in common" (Lord 1987, p. 134), which necessarily comprises governing structures. These governing structures, Macmurray (1991) argued, are human creations and, as such, can be altered or overthrown (p. 137). He also argued that "the State has no rights, no authority, for it is an instrument, not an agent; a network of organization, not a person" (conception of society, p. 106). As a created instrument, the state "exists to make society possible, to provide mechanisms through which the sharing of human experience may be achieved" (p. 106). Put another way, while the "state is merely a mechanism, and therefore a means to an end [having] no value in itself" (p. 106), its value as a mechanism is in its ability to facilitate the sharing of human experience, citizens speaking and acting together, and, of course, the survival and flourishing of its residents. The state, in short, functions to foster the polis' space of appearances, which means the state is created for the sake of the good life for individuals *and* for the communities that sustain society.

It is important to stress that the state, from Macmurray's perspective, is a socially constructed reality and, as such, it is secondary and subordinate to persons-in-community. Put another way, the "state must be kept morally subordinate to the community" (Kirkpatrick 2005, p. 83). The state, then, is created for the people, for the polis, for community. The people and community are not created for the state, though human beings often make the mistake of ranking the survival of the state ahead of the survival and flourishing of the people. I add that the state, as a created entity, not only secures individual rights vis-à-vis survival and self-realization; it also necessarily facilitates communities' survival and flourishing. The state as an organ of society has a vested interest in facilitating communities' survival and flourishing because families' and communities' thick relations are foundational units of faith and caring in society. Three tasks guide a state's role in facilitating communities' survival and flourishing.

The first task/guideline of the state is to recognize and facilitate the protection of diverse forms of life and faith—secular and religious—found in communities of the polis. I begin by offering a positive illustration. While we have the long-held principle of the separation of church and state, the state has constructed legislation that recognizes and enables many religious communities (and organizations) to survive and thrive. Religious communities that are recognized by the state are, in most instances, exempt from paying taxes, which is especially helpful to the survival of smaller religious communities. This indirect way of facilitating community also indirectly enables the community to care for its members, as well as to care for the people in the local community (e.g., various ministries helping the poor). More direct action is often seen in the government's help during times of disaster when national, state, and local governments marshal resources to help communities survive and rebuild after a natural disaster. After the devastation of Katrina and the initial inept response of the state and federal governments, assistance eventually helped the various communities of New Orleans to recover and, in so doing, to continue to practice their unique customs—forms of living.

There are also negative illustrations that nevertheless demonstrate the importance of this principle of governance. I have mentioned Plenty Coup and the Crow people. The state directly and indirectly undermined the Crow community by making it difficult for this community to retain its forms of life. Ethnic cleansings, denial of native customs, and forced education of children into white European mores and language were some of the government's actions vis-à-vis native peoples. Yet despite government interference, Plenty Coup led his people to labor hard to retain their unique customs and narratives (deep symbols)—exercise of mutual-personal power, of speaking and acting together, for the sake of the common good of the Crow people. While the Crow survived, they did not thrive because of the headwinds generated by government neglect and interference. Another example of the failure of the state is seen in the way African-American communities have been policed and punished by Jim Crow laws before the civil rights movement, and the new Jim Crow laws enacted and enforced after this movement (Alexander 2011). Harsh incarceration laws and policies have hit African Americans hard, undermining families and communities (Taylor 2015). Clearly, we can consider how these laws and practices impact negatively individuals and their families, but we need to also consider how past and present Jim Crow laws undermine communal life. The existence of societal oppression and marginalization of a group of people means that the state (with dominant group's support) is actively involved in undermining Othered communities. To be sure, these communities can survive and resist, but their ability to thrive (and the attainment of individual freedom and self-realization) is thwarted by the state and the larger society. Another negative example, which I address in greater detail in chapter 5, is the current neoliberal state's collusion with corporations vis-à-vis the market society's governance, resulting, in some cases, in the devastation of communities (Hedges and Sacco 2012) and the general undermining of communal life in society. A neoliberal state is created for the sake of corporations and individuals who are the economic-political elite and, therefore, bears no interest in cultivating either souls or communities. Its function is to create and discipline entrepreneurial subjects and organizations. In this sense, it is a failed state because the common good is overlooked and community (and residents/citizens, groups, etc.) is fostered chiefly for the sake of achieving the economic aims of the state and client corporations.

In chapter 1, I noted that philosopher Alex Honneth (2007) argues that in the polis mutual-personal recognition is a civil-moral act that regards the Other's needs and his/her self-realization (pp. 337–338). Moreover, personal recognition, which is foundational to the space of appearances and the civic power associated with people speaking and acting together in the polis, contributes to individuals' self-confidence, self-respect, and self-esteem (Honneth 1995, p. 129). The state, of course, plays an important role with regard to personal recognition in the political-public sphere, which we see clearly in negative examples such as the state's role in promulgating or turning a blind eye toward racism and other forms of misrecognition and nonrecognition. By focusing solely on individual recognition, we can overlook the need for communal recognition in the polis and the state's role in facilitating this recognition, which is the second task/principle of the state. Like individual recognition, communal recognition indicates that this community is an integral part of society and its space of appearances. As such, this community merits respect in its participation in public life and in its engagement in the political sphere or in choosing not to (e.g., Amish communities). This task includes the state's facilitating the mutual recognition among communities in a diverse society with the aim of cooperation toward the common good. It is not simply individuals who need to be recognized in the polis, communities require recognition as well.

To illustrate this principle, I begin with a negative example because it high-lights how critical recognition is for the polis. The rise of Jim Crow laws after the Civil War represents local, state, and national governments' codifying misrecognition of African Americans, not simply individuals but communities (and other forms of association). These laws and the willful avoidance of governments in prosecuting terrorism (e.g., lynching, rape, and beatings) initiated by white citizens (communities) and supported by white government officials revealed a systematic refusal to recognize African Americans as persons and citizens. Denying or restricting voting impacted individuals *and* communities. That is, in a racist society it is not simply that individuals are not permitted to participate in the polis' space of appearances; it is also the fact that African-American communities' voices are suppressed and margin-alized. Suppression and marginalization accompanies the mal-distribution of resources, making it more challenging for individual, families, and communi-ties to survive and thrive. Of course, the carelessness, injustice, and cruelty of the governments' (and white individuals') actions did not completely squelch individual African Americans or their organizations and communities (in particular, communities of faith) from speaking out and acting together to demand recognition and justice.

In cases such as these, the state not only promotes misrecognition and mal-distribution of resources, it undermines the very possibility of mutual recog-nition and cooperation between communities. The divide between white and black communities during Jim Crow was wide, seen physically in the segre-gation that took place in public spaces. This systematic forced misrecognition meant that the polis' space of appearances was primarily for white individuals and their communities, which concretely meant that the common good was for the sake of white communities.

One might respond by saying that since African Americans were speaking out and resisting, the state need not recognize those communities. This view fails to take into account the other side of the coin. While the state established laws, narratives, and practices of misrecognition vis-à-vis African Americans and their communities, it was at the same time providing privilege, power, and prestige to white individuals and their communities. Racism is not sim-ply about negative recognition; it is also about using that to undergird white self-esteem, privilege, and power (and resources). Moreover, the state's positive recognition of whites and their communities meant that the state facilitated whites speaking and acting together. There was not political par-ity with regard to speaking and acting together (power) in that racist society, and political disparity was established through the state's active (or, at times, "benign" neglect) participation in the cultivation of the institutions and prac-tices of misrecognition vis-à-vis African Americans and their communities. This systemic misrecognition had/has significant negative impacts on mutual recognition among African Americans and their care for each other. Writers like W. E. B Dubois, Zora Neale Hurston, James Baldwin, Robert Wright, Alice Walker, bell hooks, and Ta-Nehisi Coates inform readers about how racism infects the psyches of individuals, at times undermining mutual recognition and care among African Americans. At the same time, these writers and others (Malcolm X, Rosa Parks, and Martin Luther King Jr.) reveal the resiliency of African Americans, a resilience that arises and is supported by communities that provide positive recognition, mutual-personal faith and care, as well as a dynamic space of appearances in spite of state-sanctioned forms of misrecognition.

Previously, I noted that Alex Honneth argued that "material inequalities . . . must be interpretable as expressing the violation of well-founded claims to recognition" (Fraser and Honneth 2004, p. 134). The state's creation and support of institutions and practices of misrecognition vis-à-vis individuals and their communities are inextricably linked to material inequalities. Put another way, systemic misrecognition is always accompanied by the state's unjust distribution of resources, which points us toward the third related task. In a complex and diverse society, the state must work to facilitate equitable distribution of goods and services so that individuals, families, and communities can care for themselves and others. The existence of racism and classism in society is inextricably linked not only to systemic misrecognition, but also to unjust distribution of resources, which is enacted and supported by the state. Let me offer a few brief illustrations. The southwest part of the city in which I live in is comprised of working-class people who are mainly African American. Because of the tax codes, this part of the city has less money to spend on its infrastructure, public transportation, schools, police, and so on. Also, because this is a poorer section of the city, grocery store chains refuse to open stores, making it much more difficult for people to have access to food that is affordable and healthy. The "marts" that are open sell more expensive and unhealthy products. State and local ordinances make it extremely difficult for communities like this to thrive. There are simply too many obstacles. Local and state governments, then, are complicit in this situation in that they do not facilitate the distribution of resources so that citizens of the south end of the city can care for themselves, their families, and communities.

The other side of this picture is the distribution of resources to the more affluent neighborhoods and communities (mostly white) of the city. Someone might counter by saying that these neighborhoods and communities pay more in local, state, and federal taxes and thus should receive more resources. The implicit claims are that we should not have to "subsidize" the poor any more than we already are and the working poor do not merit these resources— we do because we pay more in taxes. It is not only the imbrication of class and race (misrecognition) that is evident here, but also a neoliberal mythic view of financial meritocracy. Moreover, the unjust distribution of resources reveals structural and ideological aspects of power and citizenship. That is, in terms of speaking and acting together in the society's space of appearances, poor people and people of color are not equal (not equal as persons and not equal in civic power), either in terms of recognition or parity of participation. One can safely assert that any society and state that enacts laws and produces institutions that mal-distribute resources such that certain communities and groups are denied resources, while other communities obtain them, can be assured of systemic-structural patterns of misrecognition.

Of course, the state's failure to distribute resources fairly so that the families and communities of the polis can care for their members and Others does not necessarily mean communities will die, though, in some cases, this can happen. Not all American Indian communities survived, though the Crow community was able to survive despite systemic misrecognition by the state (and non-state actors) and, correspondingly, the failure of the state to provide adequate resources so that the Crow community could continue its customs and practices—life forms. That communities survive deprivation arising from state-sanctioned misrecognition and attenuation of resources simply highlights that communities are necessarily resilient, though not invulnerable, with regard to protecting and nurturing their members.

A question may arise about whether the state should recognize and facilitate distribution of resources to all communities in the polis, which leads us to the final principle. Are there some communities and organizations the state should not recognize and thus deny them resources? Broadly, the state should not recognize and support communities and organizations that are involved in the political humiliation of individuals and communities. Philosopher Moshe Margalit (1996) argues that a "decent society is one that fights conditions which constitute a justification for its dependents to consider themselves humiliated" (p. 10). Political humiliation is, for Margalit, injury to persons' self-respect (p. 19), which accompanies "encroachment on the individual's sovereignty" (p. 13), which, in my view, can also be seen in terms of community. I would add and alter this slightly to suggest that political humiliation includes misrecognition or nonrecognition of individuals as persons and, correspondingly, attempts to deny or reduce individuals and communities from participating in the society's space of appearances. Moreover, political humiliation is a symptom of political carelessness and faithlessness. The pervasive humiliation of Crow individuals and community by the state and non-state actors reveals not simply systemic misrecognition of the Crow people, but a lack of care for them and an absence of social trust and fidelity toward them. This political humiliation and accompanying carelessness and faithlessness were not benign, because they were inseparable from the denial of appropriate resources needed for their flourishing.

As suggested, political humiliation can, of course, come from state institutions, but it can also arise from non-state organizations and communities. When the state is involved, the state and society cannot be decent, to use Margalit's term, because there is systemic misrecognition and the mal-distribution of resources. In this scenario, the state does not act alone. It enlists non-state actors and communities to humiliate select individuals and communities (e.g., Native peoples, African Americans and their communities). Assuming a decent state, there can still be organizations and communities that are actively involved in the political humiliation of Others. In these instances, the state should monitor, discipline, and deny these communities and organizations resources. Organizations and communities that are involved in the political humiliation of individuals, organizations, and communities do not contribute to the common good. They undermine social care, faith, civic power, and cooperation. They foster division and enmity. They are completely incapable of contributing to their own flourishing, let alone any other individual's flourishing, because the base of political humiliation is a profound unacknowledged insecurity and fear that are screened by the hatred of Others. Organizations like the KKK immediately come to mind as falling into this category. In saying this, I am not advocating that the state should humiliate and oppress these individuals and organizations, especially if they have not committed crimes. But the state can discourage these and other groups that promote hateful ideologies—ideologies that undermine political-social care, justice, and a diverse inclusion vis-à-vis the space of appearances.

To survive and achieve some level of self-realization, an individual needs a good-enough family and community. While political theorizing tends to focus on individual citizens and the state, I contend that the discussion must be expanded to communities and their relation to the state in a complex and diverse society. Indeed, I have suggested that there is past and present evidence demonstrating state involvement in misrecognition not only of individuals, but of communities. This misrecognition is accompanied by an attenuation of the space of appearances vis-à-vis these individuals and communities and the mal-distribution of resources needed for individuals and communities to care for themselves and Others. I proposed that a good-enough or decent state, which is a creation of society, must recognize and protect diverse communities, which includes facilitating mutual recognition and cooperation among society's communities, as well as facilitating just distribution of resources so that communities can care for their members and others.

CONCLUSION

In scripture we read that God freed the Israelites from bondage in Egypt, providing water and food during their sojourn in the desert. God eventually leads the chosen people to a land of milk and honey—a land where they could flourish rather than merely survive.[19] Care, faith, and freedom are not, in these stories, aimed simply at individual Jews, but at the community—or, more accurately, communities. God's recognition affirmed their sense of identity and this recognition accompanied care and fidelity, as well as the distribution of resources sufficient for the survival and flourishing of individuals, families, and the community. In these stories, we also note that the Jewish polis, if you will, comprised varying political organizations that, as the prophets tell us, had varying levels of success in following the covenant. While we often think of the covenant primarily in relation to God, it is clear that state leaders who broke the covenant also broke faith with the people, resulting in their suffering, instead of the flourishing of the community. There is, I believe, an existential truth in this religious tradition and that is the importance of community in the political realm. It is not merely individuals who are in need of recognition and care in the polis, but communities as well, for communities are necessary for the survival and flourishing of families and individuals. A good-enough polis, a decent polis, creates a state and institutions that recognize individuals as persons who live and have their being in particular families and communities. The decent society creates a state that fosters the space of appearances vis-à-vis individuals and their communities. In this space, communities work in concert with the state and in faithful cooperation with other communities toward the common good and the fair distribution of resources so that families and communities can care for their members and Others.

NOTES

1. The idea of thick relations refers to immediate, proximate, routine interactions of faith and care/knowledge. This would also suggest a strong shared identity, trust, and loyalty among members. The metaphor "thick" suggests levels of thickness. So, a close family and its extended members would have the thickest relations, while people attending religious services once a week would be less thick. Thin relations refer to social interactions that are more tenuous, distant, and infrequent.

2. Multiple Church documents dating back to Pope Leo XIII's (1891) *Rerum Novarum* have affirmed that the individual and family are prior to the existence of the state. The state is the creation of the people and thus, ideally, in service to them.

3. There are obvious limits to the use of any metaphor. One limit with the body metaphor in the Christian traditions is its use to support and legitimate patriarchal relations in families, communities, and societies.

4. This view is echoed by Timothy Baker (2009) who argues that "an understanding of community is central to any understanding of contemporary metaphysics, for community is perhaps best understood in relation to Being" (p. 129).

5. Attempting to identify criteria with regard to health and dysfunction vis-à-vis communities is beyond the scope of this chapter. Nevertheless, in the discussion

below, I do describe aspects of good-enough communities within the context of a viable polis.

6. Someone may contend that there have been attempts to do away with this institution (e.g., Maoist Revolution, slavery), yet what we see is the resilience in which this institution survives and revives. Community, as a social institution, may not have the same resilience, which I address below.

7. Axel Honneth (2007a) is a recent proponent of this view. He writes, "The freedom of self-realization depends upon the existence of communities in which individuals value one another in light of commonly shared goals" (p. 257). Honneth argues that John Dewey held this view regarding the relation between freedom and community (p. 233).

8. Except for the rare hermit who finds self-realization in his/her isolation from community and other social relations, most human beings live out their lives engaged in various relationships that entail obligations, responsibilities, and so on. Marital therapist David Schnarch (1999) observes, the relational obligations and struggles in married life *can* provide the crucible for individuals to create deep intimacy, meaning, freedom, and self-realization. Of course, as a therapist, he knows full well that some marriages are fraught with conflict and unhappiness, though this is a problem not of marriage as an institution, but of two poorly differentiated people.

9. In his book, *The Ethics of Identity*, Kwame Appiah (2005) notes the challenges of societies and communities in handling differences. Where does a community or society draw a line with regard to differences? Who draws the line and how is the line administered? What if, for instance, several members of the community believe that their self-realization will be found in active advocating for white supremacy? Does the community celebrate, tolerate, or discourage these different individuals? Or, what is the role of the state in recognizing and responding to white supremacist communities? While there are no simple answers, the discussion below will, I hope, provide some answers.

10. There are associations that claim that their work is for the betterment of society and this can be examined and debated. For instance, the American Legislative Exchange Council (ALEC) comprises individuals and companies that exercise power (coercion, intimidation) to effect legislation that advances the interests of the capitalist class. The organization may claim that it benefits society or the common good, but we would need to examine the evidence for this claim. When an association seeks to benefit its members at the expense of numerous citizens, then the exercise of power cannot be termed civil.

11. This is one reason why organizations based on the capitalistic symbol system may contribute to society, but not contribute to community. The relationships within these organizations are not based on liberty, equality, and fraternity, but on achieving economic aims. Thus, individuals within this organization must sacrifice some aspects of themselves to achieve the group's ends and purposes. Loyalty and trust within these groups are highly conditional and impersonal (only accidentally personal), fostering existential anxiety. Macmurray (1991–1961) warned against confusing social groups with personal life, because social groups cannot sustain personal life. In a society where capitalism is a dominant hermeneutic framework for

organizing social life, personal life will suffer (LaMothe 2012). I will address this in greater detail in chapter 5.

12. This view has numerous important implications for Macmurray's understanding of politics and the state, as well as views on justice, power, and freedom (Almond 2002; Kirkpatrick 2002). Very briefly, Macmurray (1991–1961), paralleling Levinas' view of the face vis-à-vis liberalism in France (see Caygill 2002), wrote, "the democratic slogan, 'liberty, equality, fraternity,' is an adequate definition of community—of the self-realization of persons in relation" (p. 158). The state or body of governing institutions and politics are assessed in terms of how they contribute to society as an organic unity of individuals cooperating together, but, more importantly, the state and politics are examined in terms of the ways they foster or detract from community. Communal life is not for the sake of the state or society. Society and politics exist for the sake of the person, for the communal. Put another way, the "state must be kept morally subordinate to the community" (Kirkpatrick 2005, p. 83). From this perspective, state-corporate capitalism would be considered a distortion of organic unity, because its primary aims are profit, wealth, and market expansion.

13. It is important to note Macmurray's point that in this community of persons there "is no fusion of selves, neither is it a functional unity of differences—neither an organic nor a mechanical unity—it is a unity of persons. Each remains a distinct individual; the other remains really Other. Each realizes himself in and through the other" (Macmurray 1991–1961, p. 158). Moreover, these "personal relationships override all the distinctions which differentiate people. . . . [This] does not mean that there are not immense differences between one person and another; it means that these differences have no bearing upon the possibility of personal relationships and have nothing to do with the structure or constitution of the personal life" (Macmurray 1992–1935, p. 60).

14. There are two important implications here. First, Macmurray would argue that the absence or lack of community gives rise to problems with the self. His starting point is community and not subjectivity or the self which is a claim echoed by Jean-Luc Nancy (1991). Cultural critics (e.g., Lasch 1979; Cushman 1995) point to materialism, individualism, capitalism, and the rise of bureaucratic "man" as sources of problems in subjectivity. Rarely do we see a critical analysis of how various sociocultural factors and ideologies impede the formation of community and, as a result, lead to problems in subjectivity. The work of Bellah, Madsen, Sullivan, Swidler, and Tipton (1985) is, at least, one exception.

15. It is important to stress that for Macmurray community included difference and diversity, not sameness. "Personal relationships," Macmurray (1999–1935) wrote, "override all the distinctions which differentiate people" (p. 60). Differences obviously exist in personal relationships, some of them huge, yet "these differences have no bearing upon the possibility of personal relationships and have nothing to do with the structure or the constitution of the personal life" (p. 60). This does not mean that differences are overlooked or unimportant. Indeed, these differences are part of the vitality and richness of community. These differences, in other words, "become the basis of the infinite variety of experience which can be shared in the life of personal relationships. . . . The greater the differences the more there is to share" (p. 60). Fellowship, then, is not contingent on similarity or likeness or sameness.

16. Emmanuel Levinas (1969) expressed this obligation using the metaphor of the face and our infinite (beyond ontology) ethical responsibility for the Other.

17. Bellah et al. (1985) recognized that in the 20th-century religious faith had become, in many instance, separated from tradition and community. In asking a woman (Sheila) what she believed in, she remarked, "Sheilaism." This is an extreme illustration of individualism gone wrong, wherein individual religious belief becomes separated from the deep symbols of community.

18. A commonly accepted way this is done today is by providing tax exempt status to religious communities and organizations, which clearly helps these communities survive. I hasten to add, the state has the power to recognize which religious communities and organizations qualify for these exemptions.

19. I need to point out that the Jewish people brutally took over this land from the communities that were living there. My point is about community and the state, but any religious-political sanctioning of actions that lead to the destruction of families and communities not only demonstrates a profound lack of care, but rank injustice.

Chapter 5

Political and Social Representations of Care, Faith, and Power in a Neoliberal Society

On the east side of the city, St. Matthew's Episcopal Church has, for many years, trained lay ministers to visit prisoners at the penitentiary and to help their families in concrete ways. Several blocks away, First Baptist Church participates with other congregations in supplying volunteers to help feed homeless persons, as well as to provide groceries for families struggling to feed their children. St. Steven's Catholic Church does not have any outreach programs, though they have training for lay people to visit community members who are homebound or in the hospital. Each of these Christian communities is informed by scripture and denominational tradition in terms of how they are to care and how they are to live out their faith in community and in relation to the wider society.[1] For instance, some members of First Baptist Church say that the parable of the Good Samaritan informs their ministry. The parable and other stories of Jesus' ministry comprise representations used to ground their faith, care, and power—speaking and acting together.

Similarly, other communities and groups take their cue about care, faith, and power from the social imaginaries[2] that shape and bind them. Erik Erikson (1952) explored the stories and practices of the Yurok and Sioux peoples, discovering that child-rearing practices were inextricably tied to founding myths that founded their respective community's vision of the common good (pp. 17–86). These myths or social imaginaries, which reflect forms of knowing related to the particular group's space of appearances, also reveal the group's faith, whether we understand this in terms of routine trust and loyalty among members of the community or in terms of the larger transcendent cosmos. Studying child-rearing literature, Alice Miller (1983) similarly identified underlying theological beliefs that supported secular views on childcare. The way children are conceptualized in society (Bunge 2001), whether that has religious roots or not, cannot be completely separated from

135

caring practices/knowledge and from the larger society's lived social-civil faith—representational systems.

All of this is to say that care, faith, and power, in their manifold expressions, are informed, supported, and legitimized by semiotic or representational systems, which, in turn, are reproduced and enforced by the group's justificatory and disciplinary regimes or institutions. Of course, this is further complicated by the fact that representational systems are neither pure nor singular. They are influenced by and intersect with other semiotic systems. We know, for instance, that Judeo-Christian scriptures were shaped by Babylonian, Hellenistic, Roman, and other cultural symbols systems. If we turn to the representational system or social imaginary of U.S. democracy, various (religious, economic, philosophical, Native American) semiotic systems have shaped the Constitution and Bill of Rights, which informs our social norms of care, faith, and speaking and acting together. In staying with the social imaginary of the Constitution and Bill of Rights, we note further that these documents are inextricably yoked to collectively held representations that support and legitimate patriarchy, racism, imperialism, and classism. To problematize this further, today we live in a complex and diverse society, possessing multiple language games that shape perceptions, identity, and behavior. Add to this the postmodern view that a person is comprised of multiple selves, though having the necessary illusion of a unitary self (Stern 1997). Each individual can find him/herself, in the span of a single day, making decisions and acting out of different semiotic systems that are only loosely connected. For instance, Sarah wakes up and begins her morning ritual of getting her children ready for school. Her sense of self as mother is informed by 1) her experiences of growing up in a Jewish American household, 2) the representational systems of the media, and 3) the democratic social imaginary of the United States. These representational systems shape how she cares for and works with her children. After dropping off her children at school, Sarah goes to the hospital, where she is a general surgeon. This physician-self is tied to the medical social imaginary, while in the background the economic social imaginary (e.g., insurance industry and capitalism) influences the context in which she works. After work, her physician-self recedes into the background, while her mom-self comes to the foreground when she picks up her children from soccer practice—sports is another social imaginary. Since it is Shabbat, the family goes to the synagogue where Sarah's religious-self is in the foreground. These different selves are not discrete or radically separate. They, like the semiotic systems that inform them, are entangled. If we were to ask Sarah whether her religious tradition and its understanding of faith and care shapes how she understands herself as a surgeon, she would likely say yes. Yet, as a surgeon, there is no visible sign that religious symbol system and religious-self are present. There are three points here. First, we live in a world of multiple, often competing and conflicting, representational systems, though one system may dominate others. Second, these representational systems are joined to different selves, shaping perception and behavior, and, more specifically, care, faith, and power. Third, specific representational systems are often associated with particular social contexts, which, in turn, evoke an individual's self-organization. Like water to a fish or air to a bird, the dominant representational systems we depend on are present and when, like a fish out of water, they are absent, we suddenly realize their importance—negatively, positively, or some mix of both.

The trope "fish in water" does not entirely fit here for two reasons. First, not all representational systems, dominant or otherwise, are life-giving or life-sustaining. We need only recall the centuries of slavery in the putative democratic United States and the representational systems used to justify it, as well as the violent, terroristic disciplinary regimes and practices that produced and reproduced it, crushing any hope of parity of participation in the society's space of appearances, to know that a dominant representational system is not life-affirming. Nazis and communist dictatorships emerged and survived for a time because of the representational systems that supported and legitimated them, all the while causing tremendous damage to their own peoples and Others. Thus, not all representational systems contribute to the common good. Second, citizens/residents unwittingly adopt the dominant representational system by internalizing it. This suggests that the justificatory and disciplinary regimes are often not readily apparent, largely because the dominant group benefits from the system. For those people who do not benefit from the dominant representational system, disciplinary and justificatory regimes will be more apparent and active to insure acceptance or, at a minimum, to force cooperation.[3] They are, if you will, forced to live in water that does not sustain them or allow them to flourish.

Identifying and exploring the representational system(s) that shape subjectivity vis-à-vis care, faith, and power is crucial because, to quote James Baldwin (2010), "Not everything that is faced can be changed; but nothing can be changed until it is faced" (p. 34). To face something means to become aware of it and how it impacts our lives in the polis. As examples, I am reminded of Edward Said's (1979, 1994) seminal works exposing how Western literature represented "Orientals," which shaped Western "knowledge" of and behavior toward Asians. Similarly, Stuart Hall's (1997, 2016) groundbreaking works in cultural studies examine representational systems and their formation of subjects, particularly with regard to colonized peoples. By turning our attention to dominant representational systems, we also become more aware of their positive and negative contributions to society. In this chapter, the concern is how a dominant societal representational system shapes care, faith, and power in the polis.

More particularly, in this chapter I argue that neoliberal culture/capitalism[4] is the dominant representational system that, through its justificatory and disciplinary regimes, produces and reproduces entrepreneurial-consumer selves in the United States. As Walter Mignolo (2011) notes, "Capitalism is not only a domain of economic transactions and exploitation of labor, but of control and management of knowledge and subjectivity" (p. 33). This said, a neoliberal capitalist social imaginary is also imbricated with other representational systems, such as racism, sexism, and religion, which I will address in the next chapter. For now, let me say that capitalism produces classes and class conflict (Sayer 2005), and these are joined with racist beliefs that are part of the disciplinary regimes of society (see Wacquant 2009; Soss, Fording, and Schram 2011). Another example of the neoliberal representational system's co-opting of other social imaginaries is the prosperity gospel movement, where neoliberal capitalistic values and expectations are intertwined with Christian theologies and church governance (Macdonald 2010). There are even apologists of capitalism who claim it is part of the divine plan (Novak 1982, 1987). Indeed, the entanglement of a neoliberal social imaginary with religious representational systems can, and often does, lead to churches serving as yet another disciplinary and justificatory regime in a neoliberal culture. As Harvey Cox (2016) notes, "The Market God . . . strongly prefers radical individualism and instant mobility. Since it needs to shift people to whatever production requires then, it becomes wrathful when they cluster or cling to local traditions and locations" (p. 21). This said, my main focus is to examine neoliberal culture/capitalism and its production of entrepreneurial-consumer selves in terms of care, faith, and power. In brief, I argue that neoliberal culture/capitalism promotes conditional relations and expressions of care and faith, while undermining mutual-personal relations of care and faith that are necessary for community and human flourishing. When communities are undermined, a society cannot flourish, though it may survive. I also argue that the presence of entrepreneurial-consumer selves reveals the distortion of civic power. Neoliberal power, which replaces civic power, involves individuals speaking and acting together to meet the imperatives and aims of a market society. Neoliberal power, then, is in the service of the good of the market and not the common good. Naturally, even a hegemonic system like neoliberal culture is faced with individuals and communities that resist and transgress it. I contend that it is important to identify different types of resistant or transgressive groups, because they hold out hope for the possibility of civic power and a recovery of the common good—the survival and flourishing of the residents of the polis. I begin by identifying and describing the representational system of neoliberal culture/capitalism and its attributes. This sets the stage for describing and critiquing this hegemonic representational system from the perspective of care, faith, and power. I end the chapter by briefly identifying different forms of resistance to this hegemonic culture.

Before beginning, I want to say a few words regarding my selection of this topic and its relation to pastoral theology and the polis and then offer a caveat. Millennia ago, Aristotle argued "that any polis which is truly so-called . . . must devote itself to the end of encouraging goodness . . . such as will make the members of a polis good and just" (Barker 1971, p. 119). When citizens become focused on "nothing further than matters of exchange and alliance, they would have failed to reach the stage of a polis" (p. 119). Aristotle recognized that privileging economic exchanges as a way of organizing social relations in the polis undermines human beings as political animals. Indeed, the very notion of *homo oeconomicus* was inimical to Aristotle's view of the polis, considering such a creature as unnatural (Brown 2015, p. 91). The underlying problem, he noted, was that "involvement with the exchange for profit can easily incite the desire for wealth for its own sake" (p. 90), which would conflict with and likely undermine notions of common good, the good life or weal (well-being), and justice. In short, privileging economic relations and economic wealth contradicts the aim of the polis, which is to cultivate virtues, not vices such as greed and acquisitiveness. Aristotle's insight into the problems associated with favoring economic exchanges vis-à-vis civic virtue and the health of the polis is also evident in the Judeo-Christian scriptures. In his survey of prophetic literature, scholar Richard Horsely (2009) notes the consistent condemnation of centralized economic power, because it undermined the "covenantal communitarian protection of people's rights to an adequate livelihood" (p. 67). In a similar vein, Martin Hengel argues that "Jesus attacks mammon with utmost severity where it has captured men's hearts, because this gives it demonic character by which it blinds men's eyes to God's will—in concrete terms, to their neighbor's needs" (in Capper 2009, p. 71). Bruce Longenecker and Kelly Liebengood (2009) likewise contend that a key theme in Christian scriptures is the warning that economic exchanges may end up promoting greed and neglecting the needs of the poor. Aristotle as well as Jewish and Christian writers, while using different social imaginaries, were, of course, not economists and lived long before the rise of capitalism, yet they shared an existential insight into the dangers of economic exchanges vis-à-vis organizing society and shaping subjectivity. It would have been impossible for them to imagine the extent to which the dominance of economic exchange has become a reality throughout the world today, and this reality demands the critical attention of residents.[5]

Naturally, it would be easy to dismiss these writers because they were not economists and they were writing long before capitalism emerged. Likewise, it would be easy to dismiss today those who are not economists or to assume that the hidden hand of the market can be divined only by the high priests and prelates (economists and very successful business leaders) of the market (see Cox 2015). More to the point, how can a pastoral theologian possess the temerity, let alone legitimacy, to critique such a complex system? I have a few responses to this question. First, pastoral theologians, like the prophets, seek to understand human suffering and its sources, as well as devise caring interventions to relieve suffering, when possible, whether through direct interventions vis-à-vis the sufferer or by resisting and transgressing the systems that cause suffering. When the sources of suffering are political and economic, political pastoral theologians stand in the long prophetic tradition of calling people and systems to account for the sake of liberating people from oppression and marginalization. Thus, capitalism has been of interest to some pastoral theologians, largely because of its relation to suffering, exploitation, and classism (Helsel 2015; LaMothe 2017, 2019; Poling 2002; Rogers-Vaughn 2014, 2016; Smith 1982). A second response is that my discussion of neoliberal culture/capitalism relies on the qualitative and quantitative analyses of philosophers, sociologists, and economists who have studied neoliberal culture/capitalism and who identified its failures in organizing society. Finally, like most citizens, I grew up unwittingly internalizing the neoliberal ethos and the beliefs and values associated with capitalism and I am one of the beneficiaries of the system. It took listening to working-class and poor persons in pastoral psychotherapy for me to begin to notice the limitations of focusing primarily on patients' unconscious and families of origin as *the* sources of their suffering. To be sure, these psychological models hold truth, but in some contexts they overlook significant sources of persons' suffering (Cushman 1995; Rogers-Vaughn 2014, 2016), namely neoliberal/capitalistic culture.

My final comment takes the form of a caveat. There have been numerous books and articles dealing with various types of capitalism and neoliberal capitalism in particular. In a single chapter, it is impossible to depict and analyze this complex representational system in depth. Instead, my intention is to highlight the main contours of capitalism/liberalism and neoliberal culture/capitalism, setting the stage for evaluating the latter representational system from the perspective of care, faith, and power.

MARKET SOCIETY: NEOLIBERAL CULTURE/ CAPITALISM AS THE DOMINANT REPRESENTATIONAL SYSTEM

It is, I think, a fair statement to say that, with the beginning of civilization, societies had markets where goods were bartered or sold. Markets, Woods (2017) explains, were a part of society, though subordinate to other representational systems that organized society.[6] Moreover, early and pre-capitalist markets were not, she contends, merely nascent capitalist markets, but rather complex representational systems based on numerous variables. It was during the 16th century in England that an early form of agrarian capitalism arose in England as a result of a particular intersection of property laws, the notion of improvement, the increasing unity of the state, and "a clearer separation between the political coercive powers of the state and the exploitative powers of the propertied classes" (p. 105). Eventually, the beliefs and practices of capitalism were instantiated in the liberal philosophies of John Locke, Adam Smith, David Ricardo (and others), codified into English law, and spread to other countries often through imperialistic practices (pp. 125–166).[7] As Woods notes, "in England, its economic logic became not just the driving force of the domestic economy but also an instrument of imperial domination beyond the boundaries of England" (p. 162).[8]

Fast forward to the present and the general consensus is that the *United States is a market society, rather than a society that has a market.* This particular market society is structured by a capitalistic economic system or social imaginary that "is not only a domain of economic transactions and exploitation of labor, but [one] of control and management of knowledge and subjectivities" (Mignolo 2011, p. 33). In short, in the United States, capitalism is the dominant semiotic system in organizing society, structuring relations and subjectivities.[9] Michael Sandel (2012) provides numerous illustrations of just how capitalistic beliefs and values have made inroads into areas previously deemed private and public[10]—the commodification of social life. For instance, some people have commodified their bodies (e.g., making one's body a billboard, p. 183; tradable procreation permits, pp. 70–71). Even life and death, Sandel notes, have become economized in this market society (pp. 131–162). The tenets of capitalism have even suborned ethical ideas of generosity and altruism, which is seen in the idea that "ethical behavior is a commodity that needs to be economized" (p. 126). Capitalistic beliefs and values have also made their way into churches (Macdonald 2010), shaped spirituality (Carrette and King 2005), and twisted theological beliefs (Novak 1982, 1987). Other scholars have described the unquestioned, unassailable, and ubiquitous nature of the market ethos as a kind of religion (Frank 2000; Nelson 2001) or akin to God—the market as God (Cox 2016), all of which points to the hegemony of capitalism in organizing social relations.

The evidence that we live in a market society is overwhelming and seemingly unquestionable, though we should not conclude that there are no pockets of resistance or types of transgressions vis-à-vis this hegemonic representational system, which I address below. For now, a question is raised regarding whether the United States has always been a market society or if this is, as Sandel argues, something new. If it is new, then, two other questions come to mind: what is different and how do we account for the changes? Scholars have addressed these questions with erudition and depth that I am not able to demonstrate here. However, for my purposes, there are two main responses. First, the end of World War II and the economic crises of the 1970s ushered in a shift from Keynesian-style economics, where protections were enacted to reduce the cycles and depths of economic booms and busts, to a neoliberal economy, where protections are removed for the sake of giving free rein to the market (Harvey 2005; Jones 2012; Mann 2013). Second, changes in the economy were and are accompanied and supported by neoliberal culture that, through various political and social disciplinary and justificatory regimes, extended, legitimated, and reproduced this particular type of capitalism (Centano and Cohen 2012).[11]

A society that moves from having a market to *being* a market represents a significant, if not revolutionary, transformation in human history, raising questions about the meanings of "market" and, by implication, the meanings, purposes, and aims of society. Recalling Aristotle's views above, I would take this further and suggest that a market society raises questions about its impact on human beings, on interhuman relations, on community. Philosopher Michael Polanyi was certainly not the first to observe the impact of the market society on human beings, but his observation remains true, even though his comments preceded the rise of neoliberal culture. Woods (2017) points out that Polanyi noticed a sharp "rupture between a market society and the non-market societies that preceded it" and that this had deleterious effects on the social relations and psyches of citizens (p. 23). Woods continues: "So disruptive was the system of self-regulating markets, Polanyi insists, not only to social relations but also to the human psyche, so awful were its effects on human lives, that the history of its implantation had to be at the same time the history of protection from its ravages" (p. 23). The rise of neoliberal culture/capitalism removed many of the protections that Polanyi hoped for and, as a result, opened the floodgates for the ravages that he feared. But before we can delve into the specifics of these ravages and how the market impacts social relations and subjectivities vis-à-vis care, faith, and power, it is necessary to provide a brief overview of capitalism and its connection to liberalism, since neoliberal capitalism emerges from and alters both. This sets the stage for identifying the specific features of neoliberal culture/capitalism and its production of entrepreneurial-consumer subjects. Once this is accomplished, I turn to the notions of care, faith, and power as hermeneutical lenses to critique this dominant social imaginary.

In general, capitalism is a complex semiotic system or social imaginary comprising ideas, beliefs, narratives/myths, treatises, rituals, and other practices for ordering relationships and institutions vis-à-vis financial exchange. In trying to arrive at a definition of capitalism one immediately confronts the fact that there are types of capitalism and, hence, no clear consensus on a definition, even within its various forms. There is classical capitalism (Adam Smith and David Ricardo; see Mann 2013), laissez-faire capitalism, supercapitalism (Reich 2007), neoliberal capitalism (Harvey 2005), state-corporate capitalism (Duménil and Lévy 2011), state-run capitalism (e.g., China), and democratic capitalism (Wolff and Resnick 2012). In each type, there are contestations. Given this complex reality, let me plunge ahead. Briefly, classical capitalism, which first developed in England during the 16th century (Woods 2017, pp. 125–146), is an intricate economic symbol system that outlines the principles, imperatives, dynamics, and ends of financial exchanges within and between societies. More particularly, this semiotic system is "organized . . . around the institution of property and the production of commodities" (Bell 1996, p. 14),[12] which is determined by a "rational"[13] calculus of cost and price—the commodification of goods and services—and the market law of supply and demand. The aims, values, and imperatives of capitalism are competition, productivity, and profit maximization or the accumulation of capital for reinvestment and market expansion (Woods 2017, p. 7). Profit, however, is the central value, imperative, motive, and *telos*. Profit is believed to be determined by "rational" decisions vis-à-vis expanding production, seeking larger market share through zero-sum competition, holding down wages and benefits, and so on. Labor and wages are inextricably linked to and "rationally" determined by material and immaterial production, services (Hardt and Negri 2005, 2009), supply and demand, and, naturally, the overarching aim of securing profit (Wolff and Resnick 2012). Surplus labor/value, which is "labor beyond that needed to produce goods and services the workers themselves consumed" (Wolff and Resnick 1987 p. 31), is integral to the overall profit that is kept by those who own the business—private owners (including corporations). Those who "own" surplus labor believe they are entitled to profits because they "legally"[14] own the means of production. It is a tenet of capitalism that workers, who do not own the means of production, sell their labor, the surplus of which is taken by the owner. The relation between owners and workers is conflictual, because owners are seeking to maximize profit by garnering as much surplus labor as possible, while workers seek to retain as much labor value as possible. Of course, this is not a fair match, because those who own the means of production have more economic and political power than workers (pp. 192–206). In terms of the relations between consumers and producers, there is Adam Smith's *belief* in the invisible or hidden hand of the market, whereby each individual "rationally" maximizes his/her self-interest in a milieu where supply will equal the demand, increasing the wealth of producers and shareholders.

The distinguishing characteristic, Woods (2017) notes, of the "capitalist market is not opportunity or choice, but, on the contrary, compulsion" (p. 7).

In a market society, then, "all individuals must in one way or another enter into market relations in order to gain access to the means of life" (p. 7). From her perspective, every resident of a market society is dependent on the dictates of the market, namely competition, accumulation, profit maximization, and increasing labor productivity. As Woods and others have pointed out, the capitalist market regulates "not only economic transactions but social relations" (p. 7).

As a semiotic system or social imaginary, capitalism emerged in conjunction with liberalism—a philosophy that in many ways provides the anthropological support for capitalism. The roots of liberalism are often associated with the philosophies of Hobbes and Locke, and these roots developed in concert with capitalism in England during the 17th and 18th centuries. In general, liberalism, as a representational system, entails "a contingent, malleable, and protean set of beliefs and practices about being human and being together; about relating to self, others, and world; about doing and not doing; about valuing and not valuing select things" (Brown 2006, p. 23). These beliefs include individual freedom, rational self-interest, moral autonomy, equal rights, secularism, and the rule of law (Brown 1995, p. 152). It is important to mention that not only is there no unanimity regarding the specific meanings of these beliefs, there is also the fact that these beliefs, or what Brown (2001) calls fictions, emerged in relation to and imbricated with other representational systems such as patriarchy, sexism, racism, and classism (p. 10). Consider, for instance, Hobbes' patriarchal (and sexist) view that citizens did not have an inherent "right to free speech, to free practice of whatever religion seems compelling to them, to the immunities against arbitrary arrest and ill-treatment" (Ryan 2012, pp. 444–445). Moreover, "governments are entitled to legislate on anything whatever" (p. 445). This sounds fairly draconian to modern ears, but the liberal twist is evident in Hobbes' belief that governments that legislate less have more contented citizens, precisely because they are able to speak freely and to choose their religious beliefs and communities. Other liberal philosophers would agree with the latter view, but not the former. Regardless of various differences, liberal philosophers, initially, considered questions regarding the subject and his/her rights and freedoms primarily in terms of the state and the exercise of political power and authority. That is, the citizen was understood to be a political subject in relation to the state. Secondary, though critically important, were issues of property rights, productivity, and exchange, which were key features, especially for Locke (Wolin 2016, pp. 287–289; Woods 2017, pp. 109–115). Let me stress here that liberal philosophy, including Hobbes' negative rights, constructed a citizen's subjectivity, freedom, and rights in light of the role of government in regulating society and the economy, which indicates that political power was distinct from, but related to, economic power (Woods, p.

105). I also wish to emphasize that in liberalism citizens are constructed as political subjects (*homo politicus*) who are self-sovereign through collective sovereignty (Rousseau in Brown 2015, p. 95) and who possess political freedoms and rights that are ideally protected by the government that the people create. It is a tenet of liberalism that citizens, having individual freedom and rights insured by the state, will ideally act rationally[15] on their self-interests that will result in benefiting the common good (Ryan 2012, p. 960), which is likewise understood in terms of relatively just distribution of resources. It is necessary to point out here that acting rationally on one's self-interests was not understood solely in terms of economic self-interests.

Liberalism, as a political philosophy, developed alongside the emergence of agrarian and later industrial capitalism in England (Woods 2017), but it was not constructed simply and solely as a support for or legitimation of capitalism. That said, its emphasis on individualism, rational self-interests, and individual freedom/sovereignty fit well with the tenets of capitalism. While liberal philosophy is distinct from capitalism, the philosophy of neoliberalism[16] is wedded to it. Neoliberalism took its starting point from liberalism, but significantly altered its core premises. The seeds of neoliberal capitalism, which emerged in relation to the growing "threat" of socialism in the West and the Russian revolution of 1917, blossomed shortly after World War II with political philosopher Friedrich von Hayek's creation of the Mont Pelerin Society (Harvey 2005, p. 20), which included famed economist Milton Friedman, whose Chicago School played a significant role in destabilizing various nations in the attempt to establish neoliberal states during the 1970s and 1980s (Klein 2007). The catalyst for the rise of neoliberal capitalists to positions of power and influence in the United States was the economic crisis of the 1970s.[17]

The core philosophical tenet of this social imaginary is that "market exchange [is the] guide to all human action" (Dean 2009, p. 51). This is a key point. Neoliberalism economizes political life and noneconomic spheres and activities (Brown 2015, p. 17). The term "neoliberal," then, aptly points to the appropriation and radical alteration of liberal beliefs. While it is difficult, in such a short space, to portray the significance of this revolution and its reframing of liberalism's ideas, I briefly highlight several significant interrelated changes that resulted from using market exchange as a dominant hermeneutical framework to reshape liberalism and social life. First, we note that the liberal concept of political freedom vis-à-vis self-sovereignty morphs into economic freedom. The idea in neoliberalism is that moral autonomy and "human freedom [are] best achieved through the operation of markets" (p. 51). David Harvey (2005) echoes this view, arguing that neoliberalism "proposes that human well-being can best be advanced by liberating individual entrepreneurial freedoms and skills within an institutional framework characterized by strong property rights, free markets, and free trade" (p. 2). The political subject in this neoliberal culture, then, exercises his/her freedom/agency and authority through entrepreneurial activities and by consuming goods and services. By contrast, a liberal state protects the individual's political sovereignty and rights vis-à-vis acting together toward the common good, while a neoliberal state makes laws and policies so that individuals can act "freely" on their rationally calculated economic self-interests. To be sure, liberalism would consider an individual's freedom in terms of economics as well, but what has changed is that economics (i.e., capitalism) has completely reframed the subject, making the market hermeneutic dominant, if not exclusive, in depicting the subject's sovereignty and freedom (see Hayek 2007). The shift is from *homo politicus* to *homo oeconomicus*.

There is another aspect of changes with regard to how freedom is understood. The liberal view of freedom was primarily political and secondarily economic. Hobbes and Locke recognized there would be conflicts vis-à-vis individuals acting on their individual freedom to rationally pursue their self-interests. This meant the state would be powerful enough to insure citizens achieved some level of cooperation in relation to the common good. In other words, liberal subjects do not have complete freedom to pursue their self-interests and the common good must be part of the mix in limiting freedom. To put it another way, political subjects live a life in common and, to exercise their freedom, they ideally take into account the needs and interests of others. Where there is conflict, the state has mechanisms to adjudicate differing interests. The neoliberal notion of freedom, on the other hand, is first and foremost economic. In this culture, the subject possesses the freedom and authority to pursue every possible need and desire that falls within the rules of the market (Rieger 2009, p. 104; Sung 2007). Freedom in this context is both freedom *from* the demands of others—unless their demands correlate with one's self-interests—and freedom to act on one's economic desires and needs. When there is conflict, *market rules* apply; the state is secondary and in a supportive role. As Silva (2013) notes, a neoliberal culture "has distorted liberal ideas of freedom into self-sufficiency in the market place" (p. 109) and, I argue, has made the state the handmaiden of the market. Instead of the state regulating the market in the service of society, the state and its citizens, who believe themselves to be free, serve the logic and grammar of the market (Streeck 2017, p. 20). Hayek (2007) was dead wrong: The road to serfdom lies in a neoliberal culture/capitalism that suborns the role of the state and provides the façade of democratic freedoms (Dugan 2003; Reich 2007; Stiglitz 2012).

The neoliberal idea of the individual's free pursuit in calculating and acting on his/her economic self-interests is accompanied by what Brown (2015) calls responsibilization, which is "forcing the subject to become a responsible self-investor and self-provider" (p. 84). Individual citizens, in other words, "are expected to cope with social risks and insecurities, to measure and calculate them, taking precautions for themselves and their families" (Lemke 2014, p. 65). Liberal philosophy also places emphasis on individual responsibility vis-à-vis acting on one's self-interests, but this is not defined solely in terms of economics and it is never entirely separated from the larger common good. Neoliberalism takes this to the extreme by indicating that the individual alone is responsible for the rational calculation of his/her economic self-interests and the resulting success or failure in his/her pursuits. The individual's economic success or failure in the market society, then, cannot be attributed to larger systemic forces and structures, unless the state has been implicated in failing to remove obstacles vis-à-vis the exercise of economic freedoms. As long as the state has done its role in making the free market possible, then the individual is completely responsible for his/her economic well-being. Of course, neoliberals will say they do believe in the common good, framed in terms of the economic well-being of entrepreneurial-consumer citizens who are rationally and responsibly pursuing their self-interests. But this is a specious perspective because it fetishizes individualism, responsibility, and the market, while ignoring the complexity of human desires, well-being, and shared responsibility with regard to living a life in common and the common well-being of a society's members. One consequence of this view of economic freedom and responsibility is that it sets the foundation for disciplining or punishing those who do not accept and live out neoliberal ideas of self-sufficiency and responsibilization (Wacquant 2009; Soss, Fording, and Schram 2011).

Let me summarize some of the main points. The rise and proliferation of a neoliberal culture ushers in a radical shift from liberalism's *homo politicus* to *homo oeconomicus* (Vatter 2014, p. 164), from a citizen as primarily a subject of the nation and its governing body to a citizen subject to the market. This change is inseparable from alterations in how the state is conceptualized and operates. In a liberal society, according to Locke, the state's use of political power involves the right of "making laws with penalties of death and, consequently, all less penalties for the regulating and preserving of property, and of employing the force of the community in the execution of such laws, and in the defense of the commonwealth from foreign injury, and all this only for the public good" (in Wolin 2016, p. 280). What is important here is that the state's use of power is for the sake of the public good.[18] Locke, while believing that private property is an essential aspect of a well-functioning society, did not make the public good identical to private property. In liberalism, the state, then, has a role in regulating the economy for the sake of the public weal. In a neoliberal culture/society, the state also functions primarily to ensure private property rights, but there were significant shifts when neoliberalism replaced liberalism. In a neoliberal culture, there is a belief that "market freedoms are natural and political restraints on markets are artificial" (Gray 1998, p. 17). This means the state is to refrain from instituting regulations or protections (of citizens/common good[19]) that might impede commodification. Put another way, the state not only tries to remove obstacles, but also works to increase the frequency and reach of market transactions that are deemed necessary for "market freedoms." This often appears as a negative power, but in reality the state in a neoliberal society is tasked to extend the market into previously private and public spaces (Vatter 2014, pp. 174–175). That is, where markets do not exist, the state and entrepreneurs/corporations work together to privatize and deregulate (e.g., privatization of public education, prisons, healthcare, military etc.). The state and its exercise of political power shift from seeking to serve the public good to serving the "needs" and demands of the market. This view is echoed in Wendy Brown's (2015) work, where she argues that the state is "subordinated to the market, govern(s) for the market, and gain(s) and lose(s) legitimacy according to the market's vicissitudes" (pp. 108–109). As a result, the citizen loses his/her "orientation to the public and toward values enshrined by, say, constitutions" (p. l09). She notes further, "No longer are citizens *most importantly* constituent elements of sovereignty, members of publics, or even bearers of rights. Rather, as human capital, they may contribute to or be a drag on economic growth; they may be invested in or divested from depending on their potential for GDP enhancement" (p. 110). The neoliberal state, then, does not reproduce citizens as political subjects who have civic obligations vis-à-vis each other, the public good, and the state, but rather works in concert with market institutions and forces in forming (LaMothe 2016a) entrepreneurial-consumer subjects fitted to serve the market—*homo oeconomicus* (Vatter 2014, p. 164). As Steve Fraser (2015) notes, "the world as reconstituted by flexible capitalism has given birth to the free-floating individual, so unmoored from all those ties of kin, home, locale, race, ethnicity, church, craft, and fixed moral order that her only home is the austere one of the marketplace furnished in unforgiving arithmetic. Her selfhood is that of the abstract, depersonalized fungible commodity, a homunculus of rationalizing self-interest" (p. 218). In brief, a market society with its neoliberal culture has revolutionized the state and, along with the state and other disciplinary regimes, reproduces economic subjects who heed the imperatives and compulsions of capitalism in order to obtain access to the means of life.

Erik Erikson said that all parents aim their children. What is also clear is that the dominant representational system of a culture forms (not determines) subjects. While there are myriad representational systems within Western societies, the dominant one has, for the last four or five decades, been neoliberalism, which is inextricably joined to capitalism. Its economic beliefs, values, imperatives, and practices have been promulgated by academic institutions, think tanks, lobbyists, corporations, business groups, media, and elected officials. In other words, there have been disciplinary and justificatory regimes that have reproduced a neoliberal culture that has insured both the emergence of a market society and the formation of entrepreneurial-consumer subjects needed to insure its longevity.

NEOLIBERAL CULTURE/CAPITALISM'S PRODUCTION OF ENTREPRENEURIAL-CONSUMER CITIZENS FROM THE PERSPECTIVE OF CARE, FAITH, AND POWER

This brief elaboration of neoliberal culture/capitalism as a complex representational system with its relation to the state and the production of entrepreneurial-consumer subjects is a necessary foundation for examining this type of subjectivity and its social relations from the perspectives of care, faith, and power. While I have focused primarily on subjectivity, it is equally important to note that subjectivity is inseparable from the relationships in which it is founded and maintained. Karl Marx recognized this in his analysis of capitalism and its origins. Woods (2017) argues that Marx offered an important shift in the analysis of capitalism. Instead of taking Adam Smith's view that the accumulation of wealth was the reason for the change from feudalism to capitalism, Marx contended "that capital was a specific *social relation*" (p. 36 emphasis mine). The "precondition of capitalism is a transformation of social property relations that generates capitalist 'laws of motion': the *imperatives* of competition and profits maximization, a *compulsion* to reinvest surpluses, and a systematic and relentless *need* to improve labour-productivity and develop the forces of production" (pp. 36–37). The entrepreneurial-consumer subject, in other words, is inseparable from the social relations in which s/he is produced and acts. Capitalism's production of these social relations, Wolfgang Streeck (2017) argues, undermines and "clashes with the logic of the social lifeworld" (p. lxiii). Or, as John Macmurray (1991/1961) wrote, "an economic efficiency, which is achieved at the expense of the personal life is self-condemned, and in the end self-frustrating" (p. 187).

To understand this further, I consider entrepreneurial-consumer subjects and their social relations from the perspectives of care, faith, and power.

Let me begin with care. In chapter 2, I claimed that the foundation of caring acts is the recognition of the Other as a person—unique, valued, inviolable, and agentic. Personal recognition, of course, includes personal knowing, which entails accurate knowledge/representations of the Other's needs and experiences. Personal knowing/recognition necessarily includes object knowing and, in caring acts, object recognition and its representations are subordinate to personal recognition. There are occasions of care, I argued, when personal knowing is subordinate to object knowing, but for these to fall within the category of care, they must be momentary and clearly aimed at benefiting the Other. Since human beings are fallible and miss the mark (theologically, sin), there is also the need for repair when care fails—when individuals are not recognized/known and treated as persons. I also argued that, in a society where some individuals and groups are misrecognized, one can be assured that they are deprived of resources needed to care for themselves and Others. In addition, I contended that a good-enough society, wherein people live a life in common, caring knowledge and relations predominate, which means that the distribution of resources are sufficient for people to care for themselves and Others. For this to occur, a good-enough society needs to have representational systems (e.g., narratives, rituals, etc.) and institutions that produce and reproduce caring political subjects and relations. What we find in a neoliberal culture/capitalism is something very different from this.

In general, neoliberal culture/capitalism fosters kinds of knowledge/representations that alter subjectivity and social relations. More particularly, neoliberal culture depends on and furthers instrumental-object knowing that is framed in terms of beliefs about property, the pursuit of self-interests, as well as imperatives of productivity, profit, and competition. Put differently, the entrepreneurial-consumer subject is focused primarily on the imperatives and compulsions of the market to access the means of life. In Dardot and Laval's (2013) view, citizens "accept the market situation . . . and incorporate the need to calculate their individual interest . . . . if they want to enhance their personal capital" (p. 170). The logic of the market ethos fosters and, in many ways, demands, at best, that personal knowing/recognition *be subordinate* to object knowing.

Neoliberal capitalism's object knowing can be further understood in two interrelated ways, namely, as instrumental reason, which involves both "rational" calculation in the pursuit of individual's economic self-interests and commodifying rationality. Object knowing as rational calculation has been called "technical reason (Marcuse), means-end rationality (Habermas), or instrumental rationality (Weber)" (Brown 1995, p. 33). As Brown (2015) later puts it, in a market society, calculative or instrumental rationality becomes the "governing rationality extending a specific formulation of economic values, practices, and metrics to every dimension of human life" (p. 30).[20] This rational calculation can be understood, in part, as a conscious and unconscious assessment of both how to achieve one's economic interests and how other individuals will aid in or obstruct one's path to achieving one's desires. In the competitive market society, then, entrepreneurial-consumer subjects compete, each "rationally" seeking to advance his/her self-interests, which means the social relation is contingent and conditional on whether one's self-interests are met. This rational calculation, at best, makes personal knowing secondary or subordinate to object knowing, which means care is possible, though secondary (or accidental) to meeting one's own desires. For instance, two businessmen work together toward mutually satisfactory economic ends and, in the process, become friends. *Their mutual care, however, is not the result of the neoliberal representational system.* Rather, their friendship manifests the presence of a different representational system—a system that reflects the ascendancy of a personal knowing/self that is decidedly different from an entrepreneurial-consumer knowing/self. I take this further and contend that *friendship and genuine care are inimical to neoliberal culture/capitalism's representational system*, because it undermines its core beliefs, practices, and imperatives such as competition, the attainment of self-interests, and the imperatives of profit. The two men, who become friends, if they are truly friends, will subordinate instrumental, calculative rationality and the imperatives of the market to personal knowing that undergirds the imperatives of care. The market and its rules will be secondary to their care for each other.

Of course, the neoliberal culture/capitalism is likely to lead to worse-case scenarios, wherein personal knowing is absent from the rational calculations of one's economic self-interests. Ironically, we see this played out in the yearly sacred neoliberal capitalist ritual of Black Friday, where millions of people compete to get the best deals for Christmas. At times, this competition devolves into acts of violence—a violence that deflects attention from the objectification that is at the root of this ritual. Someone might protest, saying these incidents are rare and that many people enjoy shopping with family members and friends. One might add that many people are in search of gifts for loved ones, indicating the presence of care in their actions. Human beings are complex creatures. An individual can be in search of a present for a loved one and be calculating and aggressive in the very act of seeking to advance one's interests that are connected to one's love for one's friend or family member. Also, an individual's instrumental-calculative reasoning may be mitigated by values and beliefs associated with personal knowing, as noted above. For instance, a Black Friday shopper can objectify the Other as an obstacle in his/her purchase of a toy, yet at the same time feel guilty that s/he grabbed the last toy. The guilt represents the presence of personal knowing—recognizing the Other as a person who is deprived of a desired object. Let's take this imaginary scenario a bit further. One possibility is the shopper/consumer will acknowledge his/her guilt, seeing the disappointment on the face of the other individual, and decide to keep the toy. Perhaps, s/he decides that meeting his/her child's needs is more important and that this is part of the game of shopping—winners and losers. Here market logic and instrumental reason or object knowing prevail. Another possibility is that s/he

will decide to let the other shopper have the toy. In this case, personal knowing is in ascendancy and neoliberal reasoning and associated representations
are secondary. Handing over the toy is an anti-neoliberal capitalist stance,
because it violates the imperatives of the market.

We do not have to rely on imaginary cases to reveal the impersonal and
cruel logic of neoliberal capitalism's object knowing and carelessness.
Indeed, Marx pointed out that a market society "has torn up all genuine bonds
between men and preplaced them with selfishness, selfish need, and dissolved
the world of men into a world of atomized individuals, hostile towards each
other" (in Eagleton 2011, p. 158). Marx's point is best illustrated in one of
the major evangelical figures of neoliberal capitalism, Friedrich von Hayek.
He believed that the concept of social justice "is simply a quasi-religious
superstition of the kind which we should respectfully leave in peace as long
as it merely makes those happy who hold it, but which we must fight when it
becomes a pretext for coercing other men. And the prevailing belief in 'social
justice' is at present probably the greatest threat to most other values of a free
civilization" (in Streeck 2017, p. 59). The very idea of social justice is based
on the recognition of individuals as person-in-community/society. Injustice
reveals realities wherein persons are being deprived of resources to care for
themselves and others. As a putative quasi-religious superstition practiced
only in some churches, synagogues, and mosques, neoliberal capitalists can
feel secure, because the belief in and practice of social justice will not harm
the market. But if this belief enters the body politic, it is a fundamental threat
to the neoliberal representational system, because it undermines cherished
beliefs as well as instrumental reason. Neoliberal capitalists, like von Hayek,
despise the notion of social justice because it threatens "market" laws and
imperatives, wherein individuals realize their "freedom" by pursuing their
rational economic self-interests. Put differently, social justice implies a kind
of personal knowing and care that takes into account the needs of Others,
which is the antithesis of the exploitative imperatives of the market. A paradigmatic, present-day example of Hayek's cruel reasoning is seen in the
decisions and attitude of entrepreneur Martin Shkreli. Shkreli "acquired the
anti-malarial and anti-parasitical drug Daraprim—used primarily to treat children and AIDS patients—and jacked up the price from $13.50 per pill to $750
per pill . . . a 5,500 percent increase" (Pitt 2015). Shkreli is not an anomaly in
a society where neoliberal capitalism holds sway and personal recognition is
secondary or absent from capitalistic logic; he is merely an icon or paradigmatic figure of the market. He is what a neoliberal capitalist society produces
and what sustains it. Like the fictional character Gordon Gekko, Shkreli and
his board are indifferent to the needs of people who are suffering, caring
instead about the "rational" pursuit of their self-interests, that is, profits.[21]
Shkreli, in short, is a paradigmatic example of an entrepreneurial subject who

operates out of an object knowing divorced from personal knowing, resulting in behaviors devoid of care.

Similar examples of the eclipse of personal knowing in neoliberal culture/ capitalism are seen at the highest levels of the government, examples that shock people who believe in a caring society. For instance, the U.S. House of Representatives and the Senate constructed healthcare legislation in the spring of 2017 (H.R. 1628, 2017). The CBO (Congressional Budget Office) scored both bills, indicating that around 23 million people would lose their health care, while the wealthy would receive a tax reduction. Both bills represent neoliberal ideology that views the individual able-bodied worker as responsible for entering the healthcare market and buying the appropriate product given his/her needs and income. Consider Representative Jason Chaffetz's comment:

> Well, we're getting rid of the individual mandate. We're getting rid of those things that people said that they don't want. And you know what? Americans have choices. And they've got to make a choice. And so maybe rather than getting that new iPhone that they just love and they want to go spend hundreds of dollars on that, maybe they should invest in their own health care. They've got to make those decisions themselves. (Nelson 2017)

While the willed ignorance reflected in this statement is both astounding and not surprising, it is important to note that what Chaffetz "cares" about are neoliberal ideas. This "care" is founded in instrumental objectifying reason and the adherence to the putative logic of the market, which lacks any vestige of personal knowing. Personal knowing is concrete and rather than abstract. Chaffetz's generalization regarding the poor is depersonalized. He objectifies "them," indicating "they" should make better decisions—decisions based on the rules of the market. Statements such as these signify not simply a kind of sociopathy, but the hegemony of neoliberal culture that promotes sociopathy.

Another related feature of the instrumental rationality of object knowing vis-à-vis market society is commodification, which has long been recognized as a source of social alienation[22] and, I argue, inimical to caring interpersonal relations.[23] Or, as Duménil and Lévy (2011) emphasize, "neoliberalism is indeed the bearer of a process of general commodification of social relations" (p. 9). To break this down, I begin by noting that, initially, commodification referred to the transformation of labor into an object of trade. Laborers sell their ability to work (Wolff and Resnick 1987, p. 138). Before extending this, let me take a moment to indicate how commodification vis-à-vis labor is alienating—subjectively and intersubjectively. Commodification is a type of objectification or reification, which in capitalism takes the form of instrumentally calculating activities and objects vis-à-vis capital. Georg Lukács

(1968) addressed this by writing, "Capital and with it every form in which the national economy objectifies itself is, according to Marx, 'not a thing but a social relation between persons mediated through things'" (p. 49).[24] Put another way, objectification or reification in commodification, Anita Chari (2015) notes, "refers to the very process of becoming material and 'thingly' in its etymology" (p. 5), which leads to interrelated types of alienation that eclipse care. To grasp this further, we can begin with Karl Marx's view of precapitalist relations. In a precapitalist society, a laborer's skills, work, and product are united. Let's imagine a carpenter who makes a table. The value of the table is inseparable from the skills, means of production, and labor needed to produce it. In capitalism, the laborer's skills and work are commodified. The worker sells not his/her product but his/her skills and labor to the owner, who also owns the means of production and calculates the cost of the worker's labor. The worker receives a wage that reflects his labor value, while the surplus labor/value goes to the owner. Owners, in other words, rationally calculate the costs associated with each worker in relation to the utmost aim of garnering profits, deciding that units of labor must be reduced to secure greater profits for the shareholders. As Marxist scholar Peter Hudis (2004) remarks, Adam Smith and David Ricardo viewed labor "as a *thing* or commodity that could be bought or sold, instead of as the expression of social relations that take on the form of things"—not persons (p. 155). The worker's labor, like the product, is measurable vis-à-vis capital. Her labor value can be calculated precisely. When commodification occurs alienation develops between the worker and his/her labor. To use Buber's (1958) term, there is an intrapsychic I-It relation between the subject and his/her commodified actions/skills.

Another related type of alienation due to commodification is between the worker and what s/he makes (Harman 2017, pp. 328–329). What a laborer produces is perceived merely as an object that possesses economic value that the invisible hand of the market determines and the surplus value the owner retains. In manufacturing, there are many individuals whose labor contributes to the production of an object. Each worker's labor is commodified in relation to the commodified object. That is, each worker's labor is calculated in relation to the final cost of the widget, which the owner intends to sell for a profit. Commodification, as the objectification of the worker's labor and product, is a form of object knowing or instrumental rationality based on capital valuation that alienates the worker from his/her labor and the object s/he produces.

The commodification of labor and products are only part of the story of alienation. In a neoliberal culture, where most people are pursuing their economic self-interests and commodifying their labor, time, products, ideas, etc., one can be sure there will be rampant competition and commodification of nearly all aspects of life—I-it alienation. This kind of alienation is also noted between workers who struggle to retain some surplus value and the capitalist class or producers who are working to keep as much surplus value as possible by reducing wages and benefits (Wolff and Resnick 2012, p. 181). People of different classes, Wolff and Resnick note, take part in this struggle. "A union of productive laborers," they write, "that presses for higher wages is a class struggle. Management pressing productive workers to accept compulsory overtime is a class struggle. The fight between two groups of representatives in Congress over a law that would raise the legal minimum wage is a class struggle" (p. 181). Class struggle represents social relations that are imbued with commodifying rationality (object knowing) and, while we may talk about these relations in terms of alienation, it is just as important to note that personal knowing and care are, at best, secondary and, at worse, absent from these social relations. Put another way, the imperatives and compulsions of a neoliberal culture depend on a commodifying rationality that lends itself to 1) unending conflict between producers or members of the capitalist class and workers and 2) a kind of sociopathic indifference or even cruelty that eclipses personal knowing and, of course, care.

I am tempted to say the market is inherently cruel and indifferent, but that would parallel Adam Smith's mystification of the market (invisible hand). The objectification associated with commodification is something human beings do, not the market. The market comprises a representational system that promotes and enforces object knowing, at the expense of personal knowing. That there are acts of personal knowing and care in a neoliberal culture/ capitalism is not evidence against what I am arguing. Instead, acts of care reveal the presence of other representational systems, which are at odds with the dominant ethos. In some cases, groups that advocate for social justice and/ care for residents of the society are countercultural, placing persons and the common good above the imperatives of the market society.

The subordination or eclipse of personal knowing vis-à-vis entrepreneur-ial-consumer subjects undermines not only care, but also mutual-personal faith relations, which are necessary for a flourishing family, community, and society. A half-century ago, Phillip Rieff (1987/1966) identified the emergence of "psychological man," which, he argued, accompanies post-communal faiths and depersonalization—the symptom of which is "fever-ish activity [we display] in order to demonstrate how alive" we are (p. 17). I would alter his view and suggest that "psychological man" is more aptly called an "entrepreneurial-consumer subject," and this subject is situated in post-communal faiths of a neoliberal culture. Communal faiths—religious and humanist—are formed and maintained by representational systems that promote personal knowing, care, and mutual-personal faith—trust, loyalty, and hope. These relations depend on the recognition and treatment of Others as persons, which accompanies the existential, unconditional obligation to care despite the person's failures. Naturally, communities also comprise conditional faith relations—conditioned by rules, expectations, etc. Conditional faith relations are, ideally, subordinate to the unconditional. By contrast, postcommunal faiths emerge out of a neoliberal capitalist representational system that produces conditional, impersonal (if not depersonalizing) trust, loyalty, and hope. If there is personal knowing/faith, it is secondary and accidental. I say accidental because, in a neoliberal culture, as I hope to make clear, personal recognition, care, and mutual-personal faith relations are inimical to neoliberal culture/capitalism.

Entrepreneurial-consumer subjects in a neoliberal culture use instrumental, calculative reasoning to identify their self-interests and to assess whether the Other will obstruct or facilitate meeting one's self-interests. The relational-faith question in a market society is "how will the Other advance or impede the achievement of my self-interests?" The Other is trusted to the extent s/he cooperates with my self-interests and, if not, s/he is deemed untrustworthy. Similarly, one's loyalty is conditioned by how satisfactorily one's self-interests are met. If the Other fails to advance my self-interests, I owe no loyalty toward him/her. And there is little hope that the relationship can recover or be repaired, unless the Other returns to furthering my self-interests. This relational faith is completely conditioned by the imperatives and rules of the market, wherein each is responsible for his/her own economic successes and failures.

I add here that the neoliberal representational system's conditional faith is not only, at its core, objectifying (commodifying/reifying) of persons and relations; it also tends toward exploitation, which is why many economists, like Maynard Keynes, and philosophers, like Michael Polanyi, believe capitalism needs to be highly regulated to ensure that people are protected. As noted above, the individual in a neoliberal culture/capitalism seeks to advance his/her self-interests and will conditionally trust and be loyal to other individuals who are seen to assist in this endeavor. The primary aim of advancing one's rational self-interests lends itself to greed, acquisitiveness, and the exploitation of others, but not necessarily in all cases. If there is parity and agreed-upon cooperation between two individuals, each believing their self-interests will be met, exploitation is absent. But a cursory examination of capitalism's long history of classism and neoliberal capitalism's reduction of protections/regulations reveals the reality of overt and subtle forms of exploitation (Sayer 2005). Those who possess the capital and the means of material and immaterial production enforce conditional faith on workers, while exploiting as much surplus value as possible—hardly the occasion to foster trust and loyalty. Workers are trusted to the extent they contribute to the imperatives of the market, in particular, profit. The capitalist class is obliged to provide a wage, but this obligation is conditioned by the demand to exploit as much surplus value/labor as possible from the workers, thus insuring greater profits. Laborers, who in a neoliberal culture are responsible for the pursuit of their own economic self-interests, are obliged, when possible, to retain as much surplus value as possible. Yet, workers and capitalists are not on the same level, especially in a neoliberal culture, where the capitalist class is also the elite political class. In short, then, faith relations in this culture are conditioned by the neoliberal representational system that leans toward objectification and exploitation.

Let's consider a general illustration. A business hires employees with the proviso that they work toward making the company profitable. All employees are expected to adhere to the imperatives and goals of the market. The value of the employee is determined largely by whether and to what degree s/he contributes to efficiency, market expansion, and profitability. Of course, this value is skewed, because owners and corporate leaders tend to value their contributions higher than those of the lowest worker, hence the exorbitant salaries of corporate leaders. Moreover, employers, adhering to the demands of market logic, seek to obtain as much of the workers' surplus value to increase profit, which is accomplished by keeping wages and benefits as low as possible. This system, then, produces a conditional faith determined by the expectations of the market. Any individual who is deemed a failure or falls short of his/her role in achieving profits for the company is owed no loyalty and is summarily fired. Or if there is a downturn in the market, executives may cut jobs to insure profitability. The company, this impersonal organization, and its leaders are loyal primarily to the rules of the market. The market is trusted. If need be, workers are sacrificed for the sake of profit to the market god (Cox 2016). Someone may argue that these practices insure a company's survival, which may be true in some cases. The point, however, is not whether a company should or should not survive. Rather, it is that trust, loyalty, and hope are thoroughly determined and conditioned by market rules, which means that relations are impersonally conditional.

This perspective seems a bit harsh, even cruel.[25] What about company executives who agonize over the fact that they have to let people go because of a downturn in the market? They may feel a sense of loyalty to their workers, which evokes distress, maybe even guilt, when they decide to fire them. First of all, the fact that company leaders are emotionally upset at having to let people go means they are not completely determined by the neoliberal representational system. A part of their subjectivity includes recognition of workers as persons, and this recognition necessarily involves (personal) knowing these workers will suffer. Their subjectivity, then, is influenced by a representational system that upholds an existential obligation for personal knowing and care. Second, the impersonal logic of the market nevertheless inevitably reigns. The company's survival and profitability are placed above the needs of workers. The executives who struggle are nevertheless captive to the logic of the market, though they may feel conflicted. There is no alternative, they believe. Sadly, workers must be sacrificed to save the company, to be more profitable—loyalty to the survival of the company and loyalty to the market. The bottom line, so to speak, is an impersonal, conditional faith that relies on the impersonal, commodifying logic of, in this case, neoliberal culture/capitalism.

Of course, it is true that organizations, including religious organizations, can sacrifice individuals for the sake of real or imagined survival of the organization or community. Conditional faith, in other words, is part of all human groups and relations and may take precedence, pushing mutual-personal faith to the background. For instance, a member of the community of faith is no longer trustworthy because she does not believe in the core tenets of the representational system that informs and sustains the community. The community or community leaders decide they owe no loyalty to this person and expel her. From a secular perspective, a citizen of the United States may be deemed disloyal because he does not believe in the democratic principles outlined in the Constitution. And there are instances in the United States when citizens are deemed to be untrustworthy and disloyal because they are not patriotic or because they are critical of patriotism. That conditional faiths[26] are evident throughout human life does not then give a pass to neoliberal culture's impersonal faith relations. The reason for this is that religious and humanist organizations and their accompanying representational systems include (and hold in tension) unconditional, mutual-personal faith relations, while the neoliberal culture undermines them. In the Judeo-Christian traditions, the metaphor of covenant points to this unconditional faith as part of the web of human relations—theologically understood. Scriptures are full of stories of human perfidy and God's loving fidelity to human beings and creation. Put another way, the Judeo-Christian representational system contains illustrations of both conditional and unconditional faith relations, which are often in tension. In my view, Jesus' forgiveness of his torturers is a paradigmatic example of this unconditional faith, which has often served as church's "bad conscience," (Boer 2014, p. 79) in that it reveals the failings when conditional faith operates to the exclusion of unconditional faith—when the organization is privileged above the person.

Neoliberal culture/capitalism does not have a bad conscience, because as a representational system it does not include unconditional, mutual-personal faith relations. Indeed, I suggest that this representational system is hostile toward unconditional faith relations, because these relations undermine the central imperatives of competition, productivity, and profit maximization. If there is "unconditional" faith in neoliberal culture/capitalism, it is the unquestioning and slavish devotion to the impersonal logic and goals of the market god (Cox 2016). I offer two brief examples. In a neoliberal market society, there is a drive to privatize public spaces and organizations. In the last few decades, we have seen the rise of for-profit prisons (Taylor 2015). These prison companies are motivated by profit and to insure this means that costly rehabilitative programs are reduced or excised, older or sick prisoners are transferred to government-run prisons, and prison pay (for work) is kept extremely low (Gabrielle 2015; Hedges 2014). Prisoners, then, are exploited not simply as workers, but as impersonal objects whose value is determined by the company's profit. The prisoners are trusted, not as persons, but as prisoners-objects who obey the rules of the prison company and, of course, they have little choice not to obey. This impersonal faith relation is even worse than that of workers in the larger culture, because these prisoners are completely commodified—mere units. It is not simply their labor, but who they are as objects in relation to the company's bottom line.[27] In other words, the products prison companies produce are prisoners. There is little incentive to reduce prison populations, either through rehabilitation programs or changes in laws. There is little incentive to treat prisoners as persons meriting care. In terms of faith relations, for-profit prison companies are obliged to provide some degree of minimal care for prisoners' survival and are, by law, obliged to provide a minimal amount of money for prisoners' labor. Without some protections, for-profit prisons would be the modern equivalent of slavery.

I have chosen this example not because it illustrates an extreme of neoliberal capitalism, but because it reveals the trajectory of neoliberal culture and its conditional, exploitative faith relations. Indeed, I hesitate to call these faith relations, because of the prevalence of depersonalization and exploitation. Yet, like the faith relations of slavery, where the master "trusted" the objectified slave to perform his/her duties and the slave could expect minimal care so that s/he could perform his/her duties, prisoners are similarly objectified and exploited.

Another, less draconian, illustration is taken from literature, which I discussed in chapter 2. In Arthur Miller's play, *Death of a Salesman*, Willy Loman is a ne'er-do-well salesman who is struggling to support his wife. After decades of working for the same company as a traveling salesman, Willy is weary. He sees himself as loyal to the company; after all, he has worked for them for many years. He holds the corresponding belief, more accurately, illusion, that the company is loyal to him, at least conditionally. This is evident in Willy's somewhat confident decision to go to his boss and ask him for a salaried position where he will no longer have to travel. Willy quickly finds out that his boss bears no loyalty to him, though Willy continues to plead that he be kept on, even at a reduced wage. The boss' logic is that Willy has not been contributing to the company's profit and, therefore, cannot be trusted. Moreover, the company owes no loyalty to Willy and, therefore, the boss is not obliged to keep him on.

The boss appears to see Willy's distress, but responds by saying that this is simply business, as if to say that it is out of his hands and that Willy shouldn't take it personally. And why would Willy or anyone take it "personally"? It is just business. It is just the way things are done in a market society. To say it is "just business" signifies a double faith. In one sense, the boss is revealing an "unconditional" faith in the market god and its rules. He must be loyal to and obey the system. Put differently, to continue to employ Willy defies market logic and its faith. Why would a businessman pay or help (or even care about) an employee who does not produce? Also, Willy is completely responsible for his predicament because he did not accede to the rules of the system. The other faith relation is between Willy and the boss. Willy's failure to contribute means he is no longer a trusted employee and therefore merits no loyalty. Willy's suicide, in my view, represents the objectification or reification inherent in the conditional faith relations in a market society. He commodifies himself, believing his death will provide necessary insurance money for his wife. Willy's wife will profit from his death. Willy's suicide is the ultimate faith response—hopelessness grounded in distrust and betrayal.

Conditional faith relations in a neoliberal culture are imbued with objectification and impersonalization that accompany various kinds of carelessness in society. In other words, I have been arguing that the neoliberal representational system undermines care and mutual-personal faith, which are necessary to communities and the flourishing of society. Indeed, I argued that personal knowing of mutual-personal faith relations is fundamentally at odds with the expectations and beliefs of neoliberal culture/capitalism. At best (when convenient), personal knowing and mutual-personal faith/care are secondary to the imperatives of the market, which means that the market prevails. At worse, care and mutual-personal faith are absent, leading to diverse forms of economic exploitation and deep economic inequalities. We see this in neoliberalism's attempt to unfetter capitalism from regulations/protections, which lays bare the truth that lies beneath the rhetoric of free markets—*capitalism is fundamentally impersonal and exploitative.* In the end, because neoliberal culture/capitalism as a representational system is essentially at odds with unconditional faith/care relations, we must acknowledge that it cannot produce or sustain community, which means a society cannot flourish. A neoliberal society can certainly survive, but it will be a Hobbesian society wherein society is grounded in the "primal act of recognition as enmity" (Wolin 2016, p. 418).

To understand this further, I turn to the notion of power. All societies have types of power that are coercive, violent, etc., which often exist alongside and even in support of civic power. For instance, police may exercise coercive or violent power to preserve the larger society's space of appearances and civic power. Of course, there are occasions when the exercise of power in this way preserves inequalities with regard to participation and distribution of resources. The disciplining of poor African American communities is an obvious example. This said, in chapter 3, I defined "civic power" as residents speaking and acting together toward the common good of society. There is, in this view, the idea that there must be sufficient shared knowledge (representational systems), a dynamic space of appearances, and mutual-personal faith for cooperative action toward a vision (often contested) of the common good. In general, all representational systems and associated social structures organize behavior, which means that representational systems are inextricably a part of all types of speaking and acting together (power). What I argue is that neoliberal culture/capitalism as a representational system undermines civic power, replacing it with what I call neoliberal power.

Above, I stated that the neoliberal representational system not only considers care and mutual-personal faith a threat, it undermines both. Generally speaking, in terms of power, this means that forms of power that emerge from personal knowing/care relations and mutual-personal faith are at odds with the neoliberal representational system and the form of power it promotes and produces. Put positively, power associated with personal knowing and mutual-personal faith counters and resists neoliberal culture. This said, in a neoliberal culture we find people cooperating—speaking and acting together—toward shared aims, even if some cooperation is coerced. And so, we could say that a market society produces entrepreneurial-consumer subjects who speak and act together—speaking and acting together to reproduce the imperatives of the market. Yet, this kind of "civic" power is fundamentally distorted in several ways. First, it is distorted because the neoliberal representational system produces entrepreneurial-consumer subjects, whose obligations and freedoms are framed in relation to the market, instead of citizens who have political obligations and freedoms vis-à-vis the common good. In other words, *homo politicus* becomes *homo oeconomicus* in a neoliberal culture. It is not citizens who engage toward shared political goals or visions, but individual entrepreneurs-consumers competing to advance their individual self-interests, while serving the market society. The altering of subjectivity, as I have argued above, alters relations, which is the second way to understand the distortion of civic power. When the neoliberal representational system becomes dominant, with its conditional faith relations, it pushes to the side or undermines mutual-personal faith relations, restricting the space of appearances to economic activity. What "appears" in this economic space is not persons *qua* citizens, but consumers-entrepreneurs. Third, civic power ideally involves some shared idea of the common good, even if contested, and citizens/residents can speak and act together in light of this vision. In a neoliberal culture, the common good is simply not a concern, because it conflicts with the imperative of pursuing self-interests. How can there be a notion of the common good when everyone is defining the good in terms of their individual desires and interests and speaking and acting together in terms of market imperatives? Of course, neoliberal politicians say that a market society has a notion of the common good, which means that the common good and well-being are reduced to economics. In other words, politicians and corporate leaders twist the notion of the common good without acknowledging the logical impossibility—each individual defining the common good in terms of his/her self-interests. At best, in this market society, "civic" power involves economic cooperation, but it is not speaking and acting together toward a common good, common well-being.

Given this general overview, let's consider power in terms of a small group of individual entrepreneurs who share self-interests and readily agree to speak and act together and use market knowledge and rules to form a corporation. Cooperation among them is not forced or coerced, in this instance, because they readily follow and trust in the dictates of the market. If this small group of individuals is of the capitalist class, then we also need to consider those who are enlisted to cooperate with them to achieve their ends—founding a company and becoming profitable. There may be various levels of coercion to get workers to cooperate to achieve the self-interests of the capitalist class. The most basic level of coercion is simply the pressure to have access to the means of life and, therefore, workers abide by the neoliberal capitalist terms such as submitting to the demands of the market in general and the capitalist class in particular. The coercion does not emanate from the small group itself, but from the disciplinary and justificatory regimes of society that produce and enforce market imperatives. The group that formed a corporation, in other words, relies on the state to recognize and legitimate the business, as well as to enforce rules and laws regarding property rights and profits. These business persons, because of the state, speak and act together (neoliberal power) and, in so doing, hire and fire employees, and determine wages, hours, and benefits, giving them enormous coercive leverage in getting employees to be productive vis-à-vis securing greater profits. If anyone has any doubt about this, consider three interrelated facts. Fact one: in the early 1960s the average pay for CEOs was twelve times greater than that of the lowest workers. By 2000, it was 531 times greater (Bauman 2017, pp. 107–108).[28] Fact two: net productivity of workers has risen 1.3 percent each year from 1974 to 2014, while wages have remained stagnant (Bivens and Mishel 2015). Fact three: the top 1 percent control over 40 percent of the wealth and the top 10 percent control 76 percent of the wealth (Stiglitz 2015, p. 88). These facts point to the disparity of neoliberal power between the capitalist class and the 90 percent. The capitalist class—business and political leaders—speak and act together to advance their economic-political self-interests, which are not oriented toward the common good. If we shift to speaking and acting together vis-à-vis employees, one could argue that they could speak and act together to secure better wages and benefits. Traditionally, these groups have been called unions, though unions, for a number of reasons, have been declining for the last four decades. Because capitalism founds class conflict, there will be a perennial adversarial exercise of power between the capitalist class and workers. Of course, the capitalist class has more economic and political leverage. As Warren Buffet notes, "Through the tax code, there has been class warfare waged, and my class has won" (Bradford 2011).

One notes the long history of conflict between the capitalist class and workers, and this conflict has been played out in the social-political arena, sometimes violently (Zinn 1998). Each side, in pursuing their collective self-interests, no doubt argues that they are focused on the common good, which suggests that this can be seen in terms of civic power, though with qualifications. If there is mutual-personal recognition between groups and some willingness to engage with each other, even in contentious ways, to find some level of cooperation and agreement, then I would consider this to be civic power. Yet, when one or both sides seek to achieve their ends through the co-opting of political institutions and violence, which deprives citizens of the means of survival and flourishing, then it is not civic power. In the history of the United States, the violence and coercion used by state and businesses toward workers who were agitating for living wages, reasonable work schedules, and other protections were not exercises of civic power, but rather tyrannical oligarchical expressions of power—power of the elite few speaking and acting together to secure their good at the expense of other citizens (Nichols 2011; Zinn 1998). Of course, unions have also been known to use violence to achieve their ends, but usually in response to resistance and violence by corporate and political leaders and institutions.[29]

This broad discussion has depicted the problems of power vis-à-vis capitalism, leaving open the question of how neoliberal culture/capitalism undermines civic power. To answer this question, I briefly turn to subjectivity, neoliberal relations, and the common good. Above, I indicated that the neoliberal representational system and accompanying disciplinary regimes (including the state) enforce market rules and imperatives, while producing entrepreneurial-consumer subjects who care about and seek to maximize their economic self-interests. Put another way, instead of the state and non-state organizations using representational systems to produce political subjects who speak and act together toward the common good, the state and non-state institutions (e.g., corporations, neoliberal think tanks) use neoliberal semiotic system to produce and discipline entrepreneurial-consumer subjects—*homo oeconomicus*—subjects of and for the market. In short, in a market society the state does not facilitate the exercise of civic power—people speaking and acting together for the common good. Rather, it facilitates neoliberal power whereby people use their "freedoms" to serve the market or what Harvey Cox (2016) calls the market god. This has several consequences with regard to power. First, the neoliberal production of *homo oeconomicus* lends itself, in part, to more isolated exercises of power (economic autonomy/freedom), at least as a fictional idea. That is, it is believed that the individual, in a market society, exercises his/her power by "freely" acting on his/her self-interests. The reality, however, is that individuals speak and act together to advance their economic interests over and against Others. The individual entrepreneur, then, is seen as having power, when, in fact, s/he has relied on 1) other capitalists to advance his/her interests, 2) the state to legitimate his/her profit-taking, and 3) using workers to advance his/her agenda. Bill Gates, Mark Zuckerberg, and Elon Musk are not self-made entrepreneurs. The neoliberal self-made entrepreneur is a fiction.

This fiction, however, accompanies and screens very real political realities vis-à-vis the exercise of neoliberal power. In a neoliberal culture, business leaders and political leaders speak and act together to create and maintain a market society, which undermines the civic power of workers in that there is little parity of participation. A second and related consequence is that the residents of society who cannot measure up to the demands of the market or who do not wish to play the game are constructed not only as "economic losers," but also as failed citizens—drags on the economy, leeches, dependents. These people are not seen as good citizens in a neoliberal culture—they are perceived to be failed entrepreneurial-consumer subjects because they have not exercised their freedom to advance their self-interests. There are entrepreneurial-consumer subjects who toil away, scratching out a life by participating in the market society, yet experience themselves as having no or little political or economic power (Silva 2013). The truth of this is evident in the fact above, where productivity has steadily increased, while wages have been stagnant. The lack of civic power among the poor and working-classes is due, in part, to the entrepreneurial individualization of a neoliberal culture, wherein workers struggle individually. That said, there are instances where the 90 percent speak and act together, like Occupy Wall Street, to resist, belying neoliberalism's distorted view of power. Occupy Wall Street, in particular, rejects neoliberal culture/capitalism and its production of *homo oeconomicus*, opting for the resident subject speaking and acting together for the common good—civic power.

Neoliberal culture's production of entrepreneurial-consumer subjects undermines and distorts the notion of civic selves speaking and acting together in yet another way. Thomas Piketty's (2014) exhaustive research demonstrates the steep rise of economic inequality, which has risen with the proliferation of neoliberalism. Accompanying rising economic inequality is what Michael Sandel (2012) points to as the "skyboxification of society." This means that members of the wealthier classes create numerous ways to segregate themselves from speaking and acting with people of the lower classes. "When I went to see the Minnesota Twins play in the mid-1960s," Sandel writes, "the difference in price between the most expensive seats and the cheapest ones was $2. . . . The advent of skybox suites high above the field of play has separated the affluent and the privileged from the common folks in the stands below" (p. 173). Sandel also highlights the rise of gated communities as another example of social separation in the market society. Skyboxification and subsequent separations between classes are inseparable from distortions of political power. It is, in other words, an expression of neo-liberal power that exacerbates social, political, and economic separations and distrust between classes. As noted above, Princeton researchers Martin Gilens and Benjamin Page (2014) found that, between 1981 and 200, the political "preferences of economic elites and the stands of organized interest groups" dominated the political process. Sadly, "the preferences of the average Amer-ican appear to have only a minuscule, near-zero, statistically non-significant impact on public policy" (p. 575). In my view this research confirms the presence of neoliberal power, wherein elites speak and act together over and against the lower classes, further securing their self-interests while neglect-ing, denying or overlooking the self-interests and needs of the lower classes. Economist Joseph Stiglitz (2012) echoes this. He warns that rising inequality is a threat to democracy or to what I would call a vibrant and inclusive civic space of appearances.

A third way to understand the rise of neoliberal power and its corruption of civic power is by noting how the notion of the common good has either dropped out of public discourse or, when it does appears, it is a pale shadow of its former meaning. While President Barack Obama used the notion of the common good in his second inaugural speech, it is a term that is almost never uttered by Republicans and rarely by Democrats. I suspect that this concept has fallen out of favor as neoliberalism and individualism have taken center stage in society. In some ways, this makes sense, since a neoliberal culture focuses on individual self-interests and not how those self-interests are part of or obstruct what is good for all. When the notion of the common good is brought into public discourse in a neoliberal culture, it is distorted. That is, the common good from a neoliberal perspective is warped to mean people acting on their individual self-interests and according to market impera-tives. We see this in the illusory beliefs in "a rising tide lifts all boats" and "trickle down" theory (Hendricks 2011; Rieger 2009). These neoliberal beliefs suggest that what is good for the market is good for all, which is false. Neoliberal culture further distorts the common good by narrowing the notion of well-being to economics. The survival and flourishing of human beings are too complex to be delimited by economics, which does not mean economics is not an important factor in well-being.

What does this have to do with power? The very notion of the common good suggests civic power, whereby people are speaking and acting together to articulate the vision of the common good, as well as speaking and acting together to try to enact this vision. In a neoliberal culture/capitalism, entrepreneurial-consumer subjects are produced and disciplined to speak and act together to attain the good of the market, which inevitably means that the political-economic elites are the prime beneficiaries. I add here that, in a market society, the state, which comprises individuals speaking and acting together, serves the good of the market (and by implication the economic-political elite) instead of the common good, neoliberal power ascends, class separation and distrust expands, and civic power recedes.

NODES OF RESISTANCE: HOPE FOR
A JUST AND CARING SOCIETY

The hegemony of a neoliberal representational system and its undermining of care, mutual-personal faith (community), and civic power are daunting. Indeed, given the overwhelming evidence of gross economic and political inequalities, one might edge toward the pit of despair. Yet, there are nodes of resistance—passive and active. I briefly identify several. First, there are women and men, who own small businesses, who are interested in making a living, but not preoccupied with expanding their business or maximizing profit. To be sure, they play by the rules of the capitalistic system, but they are not captive to neoliberal culture's imperatives of economic expansion and profit maximization. Several years ago, we had some work done on our house by a carpenter who owned his own business. He enjoyed his work and made a good-enough living. The two people he employed made a little less than he did and were considered coworkers. This gentleman asked for a fair price and paid fair wages. His ambition was not to grow his business so that he could make more money. In a neoliberal culture, he would not be considered a loser, but he would not be viewed as a success story either, at least according to neoliberal capitalist ideals. To be sure, people like this gentleman do not really question the system and, in some ways, help maintain it, but they also resist the pressures to exploit people (workers and buyers) for the sake of their own self-interests.

There are also companies that operate as cooperatives, wherein workers share in the profits, as well as in some business decisions that impact the company. In rarer cases, there are companies like Mondragon (Schweickert 2002, pp. 65–71). This Spanish-based corporation has around 75,000 employees. Instead of operating like a typical capitalist corporation, Mondragon bases its ethic on democratic capitalism where workers, speaking and acting together, have a voice in who their leaders are and how profits will be spent. Cooperatives and, in particular, democratic cooperatives resist the tenets of classical and neoliberal capitalism. To be sure, they are interested in expansion and profits, but not at the expense of workers. Moreover, a clear sign of difference from neoliberal capitalists is seen in their wage differentials. Recall that since the rise of neoliberal capitalism, executive salaries have grown exponentially, while workers' wages have remained stagnant. The salary differential in Mondragon is unbelievable, at least to a neoliberal capitalist. The CEO and other executives make only five times that of the lowest worker. Corporations such as Mondragon offer not only resistance, but an alternative to neoliberal culture's preoccupation with the imperatives of profit, market expansion, and productivity. These cooperatives recognize not only that the well-being of all workers needs to be taken into account, but that the company depends on workers speaking and acting together (civic power). This contrasts with the neoliberal power of typical corporations, which involves legitimating and furthering the economic and political power of the elites, while undermining the speaking and acting together of workers.

Some may remember Margaret Thatcher's campaign slogan, "There Is No Alternative." Many tout that capitalism has demonstrated its superiority to socialism and other economic projects. The corporate media, neoliberal politicians, and most business leaders echo this view, leaving many citizens to believe there really is no alternative to capitalism. There are some economists who see the problems of neoliberal capitalism and seek to save capitalism (Reich 2015), but they see no real viable alternative. At best, we can enact some protections/regulations. While Mondragon has demonstrated there are alternatives, scholars have for decades also argued that there are alternatives. While Marx did not offer a clear alternative, believing that workers would come up with something when capitalism failed, Peter Hudis (2015) contends that embedded in Marx's work is an alternative. Philosopher and mathematician David Schweickert (1993) argues not only against capitalism, but offers "an alternative that is not merely viable, but plainly superior" (p. ix). In a later book, Schweickert (2002) explicitly depicts an alternative economic system. Hahnel and Wright (2016), Buick (2013), Honneth (2017), and Sklair (2013) have also argued forcefully that there are alternatives to capitalism that seek "to generate knowledge to build communities in which life has priority over economic gains" (Mignolo 2011, p. 115). And there are other scholars who imagine a world after capitalism (Ferguson and Petro 2016). Resistance begins with a critical imagination and imagining alternatives.

Vigorous social and communal resistances to neoliberal capitalism have also taken shape over the last few decades. The Zapatistas in the Mexican State of Chiapas resisted the neoliberal project of NAFTA (North American Free Trade Act), as well as Western colonialism (Mignolo 2011, pp. 219–223). The decolonial project of Bolivian president Evo Morales and others (e.g., Ecuador) are attempts to resist and undermine neoliberal capitalism (pp. 309–315), which is inextricably yoked to Western imperialism (e.g., Klein 2007). These efforts include protecting and nurturing communities, which I understand as fostering care, faith, civic power, and a vital space of appearances in both communities and societies. There also have been expressions of resistance within Western countries. In Italy, there was a nationwide strike in opposition to the right-wing government's neoliberal austerity programs. A few years later, in 1999, activists from many nations gathered in Seattle to protest the WTO (World Trade Organization). And in 2011, after receiving little attention from the corporate media, the Occupy Wall Street protests came to national and world attention.

Finally, there are some political leaders who have resisted the trajectories of neoliberal capitalism. Perhaps the most well known are Senators Bernie Sanders and Elizabeth Warren. Less storied figures are Seattle's City Council-person Kshama Sawant, a socialist who successfully advocated for the raise in the minimum wage. While political leaders are important, resistance, resiliency, and alternatives need to emerge from people thinking, speaking, and acting together. Civic power resides not in a single person or office, but in the web of mutual-personal relations working, speaking, and acting together for the sake of the common good of persons and communities (not corporations). And civic power is a threat to neoliberal power—a power that heightens distrust, alienation, and attenuates the space of appearances for the sake of the few.

Resistance and resiliency can take many forms, each providing hope that alternatives to neoliberal culture/capitalism will promote instead of undermine the space of appearances, care, mutual-personal faith, and civic power in communities and societies. I add here that most forms of resistance and proposed alternatives to capitalism are not utopian. They do not seek some ideal world in the future, but rather a future of more humane relationships, a future where governments are focused on developing legislation that promotes the well-being of the country's residents, a future where civic power is protected and nurtured, a future where the economy serves the people, instead of the people serving the economy.

CONCLUSION

When political and economic elites begin to lose the argument in the wider society, they find ways to distract people from the real sources of their oppression. Keep the people distracted by fears of real and imagined enemies, domestically raise citizens' anxiety about immigration, exploit social issues such as race, abortion, etc. Add to this the constant drumbeat that there is no alternative to capitalism, the incessant disparagement of socialism, and the touting of capitalism's creation of wealth and we have a heady brew that stifles critique, imagination, dissent, and resistance. The real source of much suffering in the United States is neoliberal culture/capitalism. Its rise in the 1970s has undermined care, mutual-personal faith relations, and civic power. Our society may survive if it continues to embrace neoliberal culture/capitalism, but it will not thrive.

NOTES

1. Clebsch and Jaekle's (1994) classic book on the history of pastoral care demonstrates how scripture and tradition inform both the understanding and practices of pastoral care. To be sure, each age and each denomination identifies and addresses different needs and place different interpretive emphases vis-à-vis scripture, resulting in differences in methods and aims of care.

2. Charles Taylor (2007), echoing Cornelius Castoriadis (1997), broadly defines a social imaginary as the "way contemporaries imagine the societies they inhabit and sustain" (p. 6). More particularly, he notes that a social imaginary is "broader and deeper than intellectual schemes people may entertain when they think about social reality. . . . I am thinking, rather, of the ways people imagine their social existence, how they fit together with others, how things go on between them and their fellows, the expectations that are normally met, and the deeper normative notions and images that underlie these expectations" (p. 23). A group's social imaginary or representational system possesses forms of knowledge that "makes possible common practices and a widely shared sense of legitimacy" (p. 23). Social imaginaries, Taylor writes further, provide a sense of the moral order and is "more than just a grasp on the norms underlying our social practice. . . . There also must be a sense . . . of what makes these norms realizable" (p. 28). Put another way, social imaginaries possess a moral ethos that includes both the aims or goals and methods or sets of practices for achieving or realizing the group's ends. Finally, a social imaginary's moral ethos is embedded within and expressed in the group's narratives, rituals, and social practices.

3. James Baldwin (2010) provides an example of this. He writes that "The machinery of this country operates day in and day out, hour by hour, to keep the nigger in his place" (p. 115). Baldwin also wrote that "nigger" was a white illusory creation for the sake of exploitation.

4. Some authors argue that we live in a neoliberal culture or age, placing capital-ism in the background, while other authors focus on neoliberal capitalism, placing culture in the background. By pairing culture and capitalism, I am stating that they are inseparable. We live, in other words, in a market society where neoliberal culture is essential to the promotion and dominance of capitalism as a way of organizing society and social relations.

5. Readers should not jump to the conclusion that Aristotle and Judeo-Christian writers were addressing the early expressions of capitalism. Ellen Meiksins Woods (2017) identifies the faulty logic of economists and historians of capitalism who argue, in an apologetic attempt to lend support to capitalism, that early forms of capitalism can be seen in the economic exchanges of primitive civilizations. The eco-nomic exchanges that took place during the time of Aristotle or the Jewish prophets were not early examples of capitalism. Woods writes, "Where markets did exist in pre-market societies, even where they were extensive and important, they remained a subordinate feature of economic life" (p. 22). Moreover, capitalism, she argues, is a "specific social form with a distinctive social structure and distinctive social relations of production" (p. 31).

6. Meiksins Woods (2017) addresses and critiques the various theories regarding the origins of capitalism. Apologists for capitalism tend to think that every kind of exchange of goods represents the seeds of capitalism, which Woods undermines by demonstrating the differences between markets and why some precapitalist cities did not develop into capitalist economies, while other cities in Europe did. One of the values of her cogent work is recognizing there are alternatives to capitalism.

7. Two points are worth mentioning here. First, some philosophers were critical of capitalism. Rousseau, for instance, argued that capitalism "bound new fetters in the poor, and gave new powers to the rich . . . fixed forever the laws of property and inequality; converted clever usurpation into an inalienable right and for the sake of the few ambitious men, subjected all mankind to perpetual labour, servitude and misery" (in Eagleton 2011, p. 199). Karl Marx (1964), who was influenced by Hegel's cri-tique, wrote, "The lords of land and the lords of capital will always use their political privileges for the defense and perpetration of their economic monopolies." Second, even philosophers like Adam Smith (2003), the patron saint of capitalism, was con-cerned about its excesses.

8. See also Walter Mignolo (2011) for a discussion of the relation between West-ern capitalism and imperialism.

9. Adam Smith (2003) long ago recognized that in a commercial society every-one is a merchant, which is an early indicator of the claim that neoliberal society produces entrepreneurial-consumer subjects.

10. Here I mean areas of public life that previously were not structured by the capitalistic ethos.

11. Time does not permit me to address in depth the question regarding how neoliberal capitalism came to be the dominant social imaginary in this society. That said, scholars have discussed the origins and rise of neoliberal capitalism (Chibber 2013; Dardot and Laval 2013; Harvey 2005; Jones 2012; Mann 2013). These authors also point out that the rise of neoliberal culture/capitalism could not have taken place without the intersection and aid of academics (e.g., Friedman and Hayek), academic

institutions (e.g., University of Chicago), the proliferation of conservative think tanks (e.g., Heritage Foundation) and lobbyists, corporate media, pro-business, political organizations (e.g., ALEC), and, finally, Democrat and Republican elected officials. Moreover, some of the scholars, as well as academic and government institutions, interfered in other societies and cultures with the aim of spreading neoliberal capitalism for the sake of extending and maintaining United States' dominance in the world (Klein 2007).

12. There are two important points to highlight here. First, as Woods (2017) notes, capitalism first emerged not in the cities, but on the farms of England. Industrial capitalism and its production of commodities developed in the late 18th and early 19th centuries. Second, the decline of industrial capitalism in the United States did not mean that the foundational principles of capitalism changed. Today much of the economy is called the service economy and Hardt and Negri (2009) refer to this economy in terms of immaterial production versus material production (pp. 132–133).

13. I have placed "rational" in quotes because it is largely an illusion and it is often connected not to individuals but the system of capitalism itself. It is an illusion because it ignores the role of "irrational" and contradictory elements in human behavior.

14. "Legally" is in quotes because I wish to emphasize that the state creates laws that make it possible for people to control the means of production, retain the surplus value of workers. The notion of private property is a cultural creation—a belief—that is ensconced in law, institutions, etc. Private property, then, is not an existential, universal fact.

15. Liberalism, especially before the 20th century, tends to place high value on rationality. Freud undermined the apotheosis of reason, while philosopher John Macmurray (1935) considered reason to be imbued with emotion and emotion imbued with reason, which undermined Western philosophers' tendency to be suspicious of emotion. I have placed "rationality" in quotes because I find that there is a great deal of unreason in the rational calculation of one's desires and needs. Evidence of this is seen in any daily news outlet and especially politics.

16. Numerous authors distinguish between neoliberalism as a culture and its integral relation to capitalism (Helsel 2015; Johnson 2014; Rogers-Vaughn 2014, 2016). While they are distinct, they are inseparable. Just as it is difficult to imagine the rise of capitalism without the philosophy of liberalism, so too it is impossible to imagine the rise of neoliberal capitalism without the presence of a neoliberal culture.

17. Harvey (2005) argues that the power and influence of neoliberal ideas came to fruition in the 1970s/80s with the proliferation of conservative think tanks, as well as the elections of Margaret Thatcher and Ronald Reagan. See also Duménil and Lévy (2013) and Klein (2007) on the rise and influence of neoliberalism and the process of globalization through varied means of force and coercion by Western powers.

18. Wolfgang Streeck (2017) points out that previous to the rise of neoliberal culture, what he calls the tax state operated to secure taxes to address the needs of citizens and the larger public goods. Since the rise of neoliberalism, the state has become a consolidation state, reducing taxes and implementing austerity measures to insure a well-functioning market.

19. Neoliberals would disagree with this, because they view the common good as identical to the free market. In other words, social goods are maximized by expanding the reach and frequency of market transactions (Rieger 2009, p. 15). This is seen in the mythic statement that "a rising tide lifts all boats." Any cursory view of the economic realities of the last forty years, such as rising poverty, vast and growing income inequality, and stagnant wages, reveals that what is good for the "free" market is not necessarily good for the common good (see Marris 1996; Mander 2012; Piketty 2014).

20. Economist Gary Becker (1976) is an excellent example of neoliberal economization of everyday life. His book, *The Economic Approach to Human Behavior*, exemplifies the dominance of instrumental or calculative rationality and its purported utility in all spheres of life, including family and marriage. "I have come to the position," he writes, "that the economic approach is a comprehensive one that is applicable to human behavior" (p. 49).

21. Perhaps Mr. Shkreli believes that insurance companies and the government will pay the tab, calculating that individuals will still get the medication. First of all, insurance companies, according to market logic, will have to spread the costs by raising premiums. They have to make a profit as well. This means that individuals may not be able to afford insurance or will have to make other sacrifices to make ends meet. The government, while not making a profit, will have to deal with the rise in costs by raising taxes or cutting funding to other programs. In short, Mr. Shkreli's price gouging has nothing to do with concern for the common good and everything to do with his own "good."

22. See Lukács 1968; Marcuse 1964.

23. Marx's view of commodification and alienation is primarily aimed at labor, manufacturing, and material production, but in a neoliberal culture, alienation applies to service industry workers and what Hardt and Negri (2009, pp. 131–133) call immaterial production—for example, images, information, knowledge, social relationships. Commodification in a market society can include one's body and even emotions. Sandel (2012) identifies instances of individuals commodifying their bodies (pp. 180–187). Sociologist Arlie Hochschild's (2012) research into the airline industry shows how neoliberal capitalism has commodified feelings: "Feelings take on the properties of a resource. But it is not a resource to be used for the purposes of art, as in drama, or for the purposes of self-discovery, as in therapy. . . . It is a resource to be used to make money" (p. 55). Eva Illouz (2007) takes this further, arguing that emotional capitalism "is a culture in which emotional and economic discourses and practices mutually shape each other" (p. 5). The concept of emotional intelligence, she notes, is used to "classify productive and non-productive workers" (p. 65), which represents a troubling illustration of a kind of subjective and intersubjective alienation that Marx did not describe.

24. Axel Honneth (2008) attempts to recover Lukács understanding of reification, though he interlocutors (Judith Butler, Raymond Geuss, and Jonathan Lear) raised several key objections that could have been avoided if, in my view, Honneth had relied on Macmurray's notions of object and personal knowing.

25. While I am painting a negative picture of neoliberal culture/capitalism, I recognize there are companies that provide good wages and benefits for their employees.

Moreover, some companies operate as cooperatives or, like Mondragon, function as democratic capitalist organizations. While there may be individuals and companies that are not completely captive to the neoliberal representational system, that does not undermine my argument. These counterexamples simply indicate that individuals and companies can choose to operate out of a different representational system in organizing their company.

26. Not every conditional faith relation is a distortion vis-à-vis human relations. There are innumerable daily examples of conditional faith relations. I have an agreement with a person who will build a stone wall in my backyard for which I will pay an agreed-upon price. My trust and fidelity toward him (and his toward me) are conditioned by this mutual arrangement. This is in the foreground. Ideally, in the background is an unconditional faith, which is manifested in my unconditional recognition and treatment of him as a person. When this is absent, the relationship is purely impersonal, conditioned by the rules and expectations of the contract.

27. This is not to say that prisoners in government-run facilities are not exploited or treated badly at times.

28. There is some debate about how high CEO salaries have risen. One report indicates that in 2000 it was 381 times greater, then decreased during the recession and is not back to that level (Dill 2013). Even if we consider the lower percentages it is still egregious, especially when considering that neoliberal politicians and business leaders work mightily to make sure the minimum wage does not increase. Of course, the idea of limits on CEO salaries (a maximum wage scale) is anathema.

29. While there may need to be violence to achieve justice, this does not undermine the view that it is not civic power. In my view, the moment violence is used to achieve justice, we already know that civic power has been absent, precisely because people believe that they cannot cooperate together in the political space of appearances to have their needs and experiences recognized.

Chapter 6

Classism and Racism

Distortions of Care, Faith, and Power in the Polis

Racism, classism, and sexism[1] are part of the sinew of U.S. history. They are evident in our founding documents, which favored property rights for white men and declared black people to be less than fully human, thus legally exploitable and disposable. They were manifest when the Southern capitalist class established and expanded slave labor camps throughout the South, terrorizing black persons to increase profits (Baptist 2014).[2] They are seen today when political-economic elites—Democrats and Republicans alike—slash social programs, remove protections, and increase harsh sentencing, which together disproportionally impact persons of color—devastating and undermining their families and communities. They are revealed in the fact that the wealth gap between whites and blacks has nearly tripled in the last twenty-five years (Shinn 2015) and the income gap between whites and blacks is nearly double (Vega 2016). They are seen in black unemployment figures, which is nearly twice that of whites (Macrotrends 2018), and in the fact that black persons are three times more likely to be in poverty than whites. Income and wealth inequalities are also joined to lack of access to quality education, healthcare, healthy and reasonably priced food, affordable and safe housing, and habitable community infrastructure. Racism and classism intersect and are also evident when "Southern managers are . . . more apt to use race to divide union support" (Urbina 2017, p. 69). "When unions arrive, the very first thing many Southern bosses do is tell white workers to get ready for a black manager" (Stewart Acuff in Urbina 2017, p. 69). This strategy furthers racial divisions, while insuring that the capitalist class's power is unchecked by unions. Stated differently, many of those in the capitalist class are willing to use racism to insure they retain economic and political power and privilege.

Both racism and classism are supported by distinct, yet intersecting, representational systems and accompanying disciplinary and justificatory institutions and practices that produce and maintain them. And when we consider the long history of classism and racism in the United States, we note that a society can survive and, by some measures, thrive. However, as Martin Luther King Jr. recognized, racism and classism are like cancers in the body politic, sapping spiritual and psychosocial vitality. From a different angle, a classist and white racist society can be wealthy and possess great military power, but it cannot be a decent society (Margalit 1996), because its wealth depends on exploitation and humiliation. Or, as I will argue, racism and classism undermine social care, mutual-personal faith, civic power, and the space of appearances, all of which are essential components of a decent society and a decent world.

While racism and classism are distinct phenomena, they often intersect and reinforce each other, in part, because they share several properties—properties that are inimical to a decent society—a society wherein residents, living a life in common, speak and act together toward the common good. To develop this point of view, I briefly define classism and racism, which provides a foundation for identifying those properties and the dynamics that they share. This serves as a starting point for analyzing both from the perspective of care, faith, and civic power. In so doing, I am not arguing that racism and classism destabilize a society, for it is pretty clear that the United States (and other countries) has been stable, for the most part, despite racism and classism. That said, both understandably breed discontent, which appears periodically in social unrest that is often contained through the disciplinary and justificatory regimes of state and non-state actors.[3] I also contend that racism and classism are inherently contradictory with regard to society, because in the very process of organizing social relations in privileged groups, they undermine social care, mutual-personal faith, and civic power. Add to this a pastoral theological perspective wherein racism and classism are not only existentially contradictory, but fundamentally inimical to the notions of *imago dei* and kingdom of God.[4] More to the point, they represent ontological falsehoods.

I would like to add a few words before beginning. First, one reason for addressing racism and classism is that the rise of neoliberal culture/capitalism has resulted in a steep rise in wealth and income inequalities, not just in the United States, but in other countries as well (Organization for Economic Cooperation and Development: OECD 2015). Esteemed economists such as Joseph Stiglitz (2012), Robert Reich (2007), and other scholars (e.g., Brown 2015; Dugan 2003; Frank 2000) have warned that rising inequality and class divisions undermine democracy, replacing democracy with plutocracy or worse, an inverted totalitarian system that has the façade of democracy (Wolin 2008). Second, while capitalism, which I will say more about below, inevitably depends on and produces class divisions, Keynesian capitalism, with its protections and tax structure, helped reduce class divisions. More positively, before the rise of neoliberal capitalism, there was less economic inequality vis-à-vis wealth and income, and more social interactions between classes (Putnam 2015; Sandel 2012), though racism was virulent in producing divisions. Steep disparities in income and wealth demand analysis and critique, but equally important is that classism cannot be separated from racism in the United States, especially given the reality that income and wealth disparities are even greater when one factors in race. That said, classism does not necessarily lead to racism,[5] but racism is always connected to class. It is possible, in other words, to have a classist society that does not have racism or very little of it. Consider that in many northern towns, where there were few if any black people, privileged whites exploited lower-class whites. A racist society, however, is necessarily classist with one privileged group disciplining, oppressing, and exploiting another group of color. As bell hooks (2000) writes, "It is impossible to talk meaningfully about ending racism without talking about class" (p. 7).

Third, Chris Harman (2017) argues that class has been a part of every society since the dawn of civilization, raising the question of whether any society can be classless. Perhaps we should simply accept class and classism as a matter of fact in human life. While I will say more about this below, let me offer two quick responses. Harman also points out that when class divisions are deep a society's stability is undermined, which points to the fundamental contradiction regarding class: organizing a society based on class actually destabilizes it in the long run. The greater the class division, the more repressive the state becomes to maintain stability, causing instability. A vicious cycle ensues. This suggests that a society that endeavors to reduce inequalities will be a more stable and content society (e.g., Sweden, Norway, and Finland). Second, one can find throughout history glimpses of movements that sought to eradicate class divisions. The early Christian community in Acts and the rise of communes and communism in the 19th century are other examples. These were not utopian movements, in the sense that they were seeking to develop perfect or Eden-like societies. The early Christian community was not trying to *be* the kingdom of God on earth, but to live out the principles of love and equality—a community where all are heirs to God's promise (Gal. 3:2–9) and where all are created in the image and likeness of God. We may not ever succeed in achieving a classless society, but I see no reason to cease critiquing class and classism and I see no reason not to develop social structures and programs that reduce, if not eradicate, income and wealth inequalities.

The final point regards the theological premises that will make their way into the analysis below. First, consider the theological notion of *imago dei*. As noted in chapter 1, to be created in the image and likeness of God implies that each human being is unique, invaluable, and inviolable. Forms of depersonalization, oppression, marginalization, and exploitation not only reflect failures in care and mutual-personal faith, but are fundamentally contrary to this theological principle. Relatedly, representational systems, such as racism and classism, which claim that one group of human beings are inferior while the privileged group is superior, are rejections of this theological principle, even though people of Christian faith may claim that they are living out the gospel. The second theological metaphor is the kingdom of God. This political metaphor points obviously to the reign of God, distinct from earthly kingdoms. The kingdom of God is organized by love, where residents are heirs, which suggests that there are no classes or racial divisions.

For those who remark that the kingdom of God is otherworldly, recall the gospel refrain that the kingdom of God is among you. Wolfart Pannenberg (1969) uses the term "prolepsis" to refer to the partial in-breaking of the kingdom of God in the present, the signs of which are mutual-personal recognition, love, and care. Put another way, the in-breaking of the kingdom of God is seen and experienced in the absence of class and racial divisions. In brief, there is no theological justification for classism or racism, though people find many ways to use scripture to justify and legitimate both.

I add here that the notion of the kingdom of God does not necessarily refer simply to a society with geographical borders. In other words, one can consider the in-breaking of the kingdom of God in U.S. society to the degree that there are examples of people resisting classism and racism. The Civil Rights Movement and the Poor Peoples Campaign are illustrations. But, like Martin Luther King Jr., we must not confine ourselves to one society. Rather, we must recognize that while we have many societies, we have one world. Moreover, the proliferation of neoliberal capitalism means that class and classism is global, which means that hundreds of millions of people experience various degrees of oppression—often intertwined with forms of racism. This will only deepen with the realities of climate change and if capitalism is not confronted and resisted. Furthermore, those societies imbued with racism, of which there are many, class and classism exacerbates and further cements racial divisions. This means one can expect that those deemed to be inferior will suffer the most as global warming leads to natural disasters. The kingdom of God refers, then, not to one society, but to one world and this propels us to examine critically all societies, though in this chapter I focus on U.S. society. Perhaps, if we can face the negative effects of racism and classism, we might better be able to consider how we can live a life in common with other communities and other societies.

CLASSISM AND RACISM:
DEFINITIONS AND INTERSECTIONS

In this section, I briefly define and describe the properties of classism and racism. I also argue that neoliberal culture/capitalism has exacerbated inequalities, resulting in a more classist society, wherein some political-economic elites use racism to distract and divide. In addition, it is important to point out that greater class divisions or income and wealth inequalities impact African Americans and Hispanics more than whites, which is not to say there are not poor white Americans.[6] When class divisions are steep, race relations will not improve, not simply because some white people will inflame racism to further their economic and political privileges, but also because oppressed groups have fewer economic and political resources to resist (less civic power). Of course, it is important to note that even during periods when economic inequality and class divisions were less dramatic, racism was still pronounced. So, while race and class intersect, they are not necessarily correlated.

I begin with class and classism, because class is "an overlooked, undertheorized, and often repressed dimension of modern capitalist society" (Wolff and Resnick 1987, p. 25)—especially in the United States. It is rarely addressed in the media and, more particularly, in pastoral theology, unlike the topic of racism. Also, the prevalence of class and classism can accompany the idea that it is an inevitable reality of civilization. Harman (2017), for instance, argues that class and class divisions in society emerged with the dawn of civilization, and grew with changes in technology and production that gave rise to surplus and accumulation (pp. 24–25).[7] As Harman notes, a group's leaders "could begin to turn into 'rulers', into people who came to see their control over resources as in the interests of society as a whole. . . . In short, they would move from acting in a certain way in the interests of the wider society to acting as if their own sectional interests were invariably those of society as a whole" (p. 25). In this Marxian view of history, the ruling classes "were able, through their collective control of the state machine, to exploit entire peasant communities which farmed the land jointly without private ownership" (p. 27).[8] Whether one examines history through a Marxian lens, the point is that class was present long before capitalism and perhaps preceded racism as well (p. 252). That said, understanding class/classism is important because of its history, but also to note that it is not an omnipresent reality.

Of course, when we talk about class today, we necessarily consider the economic system that produces and maintains class. Indeed, the various iterations of capitalism depend on and produce class, as Marx noted. As discussed in the previous chapter, Ellen Woods (2017) argues that the origins of capitalism lay in the agricultural system of England during the 16th century.

It's important to point out that capitalism's emergence took place in a society that was already structured by class relations—feudalism—that had its own laws about property and an ethos regarding social relations between the ruling-propertied classes and peasants (Chibber 2013). This early form of capitalism involved the propertied classes extracting the surplus from farmers,[9] while encouraging competition to obtain greater surplus/profit for the property owners. Farmers who could not produce were removed and replacements were found who could produce more. As capitalism extended to other sectors of the society, class became increasingly constructed in terms of what Adam Smith called masters (capitalists) and workers. Indeed, long before Karl Marx, Adam Smith recognized that these two groups were pitted against each other, though the workers held the short end of the stick.

> What are the common wages of labor, depends everywhere upon the contract usually made between those two parties, whose interests are by no means the same. The workmen desire to get as much as possible, the masters to give as little as possible. The former are disposed to combine in order to raise, the latter in order to lower the wages of labor. It is not difficult to foresee which of the two parties must, upon all ordinary occasions, have the advantage in the dispute, and force the other into compliance with their terms. The masters, being fewer in number, can combine much more easily; and the law, besides, authorizes or at least does not prohibit their combinations, while it prohibits those of the workmen. . . . Masters are always and everywhere in a sort of tacit, but constant and uniform combination, not to raise the wages of labor. (Smith 2003, pp. 94–95)

Little has changed since Adam Smith penned those words. Today the capitalist class, which comprises those who directly (and indirectly—e.g., shareholders) own and manage (managerial classes) the means of production, legally owning the workers' surplus labor. Legal ownership of the means of production, surplus labor, and profit means that workers have no rights or legal claims to these, though they have legal claims to the wages they are given—wages that the capitalist class, as Adam Smith recognized, works hard to keep down, while their own salaries and wealth rise. As noted in the previous chapter, there is then the perennial tendency of the capitalist class to secure as much surplus labor as possible to maximize profits, while workers struggle to hold onto their wages (and benefits, if they have any). Of course, this was, as Smith noted, never a fair contest, because those who hold political and economic power speak and act together in constructing the rules of the game—rules that benefit the upper classes (see Harrington 2016). Moreover, any cursory reading of the proliferation of capitalism in the United States shows how the capitalist class and political elites have, time and again, used force, violence, and legislation to undermine workers' protections (see

Fraser 2015). Today in neoliberal culture/capitalism, the state sides with the capitalist class, enacting legislation that reduces worker protections, undermines unions, sells off public spaces, and shrinks or eliminates benefits.[10] The point here is that capitalism, which emerged in a society already rife with class, produces and depends on class wherein lower classes have less economic and political power. It is, in other words, impossible to think about capitalism without including class.

It is important to stress here that the control, extraction, and distribution of surplus resources are not simply an economic reality; they are a political reality. Hardt and Negri (2005, p. 104) rightly claim that class (and class struggle[11]) is a political concept. Put another way, while capitalism reproduces class (and class conflict), capitalism and class are also deeply embedded in and dependent on the political realm. Legislatures enact property laws and other laws that affect the creation of corporations and financial products. Laws, not nature, legitimate capitalist possession of surplus labor and the distribution of resources. As Eagleton (1999) notes "The state is ultimately the instrument of the governing, a way of securing hegemony over other classes" (p. 54). The privatization of health care, prisons, and education are all dependent on legislatures that create laws and policies legitimating the control of surplus labor by the capitalist class. From another angle, the decline of labor unions, which has occurred for a number of reasons, is due in part to legislation that seeks to undermine them, revealing class struggle in the realm of politics and a furthering of political control over economic resources. There is no "invisible hand" or, more accurately, invisible fist of the market. The "invisible hand" depends on the arm of the government for its very existence and for its reach into public sectors in a neoliberal society. Moreover, the political realm is suffused with members of the capitalist class, who possess tremendous financial resources and hence political power vested in nongovernmental organizations (e.g., think tanks and lobby groups). This means that people in laboring classes, especially with the decline of unions, are significantly disadvantaged not only in the realm of economics, but of politics.

Since the rise of civilizations, then, class has meant that a group(s) of people construct and use representational systems[12] to legitimate their ability to control the distribution of resources and to own surplus for the sake of accumulating wealth at the expense of members of the lower classes. Control of the distribution of resources means that the ruling class also has control over the distribution of economic and political power (Rieger 2009, p. 47). Put another way, the ruling class speaks and acts together such that it determines the distribution of resources to further their wealth and power. The distribution of resources and power may have always been connected to class, but with the rise of capitalism and, in particular, neoliberal capitalism, the state is in service to the capitalist and managerial classes and, in many cases, the ruling elites are of the capitalist class. The representational system of neoliberal capitalism functions, then, to legitimate, mystify, and extend (privatization of public domains) the distribution of resources and power. There is, however, a difference between class associated with neoliberal capitalism and precapitalistic civilizations. In precapitalistic civilizations the "ruling classes looked to enforce conservatism to bolster their rule" (Harman 2017, p. 331) and were distinct from merchants, artisans, and farmers—people who would be considered of the lower classes. In a neoliberal culture, the ruling class and the capitalist class are nearly indistinguishable. If those in the ruling class—political elites—are not of the capitalist class, they certainly are in service to the capitalist class—at least most political elites. In brief, in neoliberal culture/capitalism, elected officials enact legislation and programs that distribute resources and power to the capitalist class, legitimating and exacerbating income and wealth inequalities. Wall Street and the White House are occupied by members of the same class.

Of course, someone will point out that the state has almost always been on the side of the capitalist class, which is mostly true. In the 19th century, the state of Illinois and the city of Chicago, in cahoots with businesses, violently quelled workers' protests, which became known as the 1886 Haymarket Massacre (Hendricks 2011, p. 105). In 1913, the Colorado governor called out the National Guard, whose wages were paid by the Rockefellers, to crush a miners' strike. The miners continued to resist and, in the spring of 1914, the National Guard machine-gunned the miners' encampment (Zinn 1998, pp. 354–356). The federal government also pursued and harassed socialist leaders, like Eugene Debs and Emma Goldman, largely because they and other socialists were deemed to be threats to the capitalist class (pp. 339–357). The election of Franklin Roosevelt marked a period where the government provided more protections for workers, which infuriated the capitalist classes (Stone and Kuznick 2102, pp. 47–86). The rise of neoliberal capitalism in the 1970s ushered in a period of the removal of those protections, though not necessarily a return to the overtly violent tactics of earlier periods. Conservative political-economic elites did not and do not need to use the National Guard to quash resistance today, because they cleverly gut unions by enacting legislation under the guise of workers' rights (Right to Work Laws). Indeed, the American Legislative Exchange Council (ALEC) is a paradigmatic example of how the capitalist class devises legislation that political elites pass. There is also the presidential tactic of simply firing workers on strike, as Reagan did to the air traffic controllers who sought better wages and protections (Moberg 2017, pp. 59–61). While the state has, more often than not, sided with the capitalist class, the rise of neoliberal capitalism marks an important shift in this cooperation.

Let's consider some more evidence. President Reagan, who was in my view the first neoliberal president, was able to enact a 60 percent reduction of the top tax rate for the richest Americans. Hendricks (2011) writes, "Between 1981 and 1990 the poorest 20 percent of Americans saw their after-tax family incomes drop by 12 percent. The wealthiest 1 percent, however, saw their incomes increase by 136 percent" (p157). Rieger (2009) points out that "between 1979 and 2000, the top percent gained 201 percent in after-tax household income, while the top 20 percent gained 68 percent. The bottom 20 percent gained 9 percent, and the next-highest 20 percent gained 13 percent" (p. 41). In addition, "the top 5 percent of the population owns 67.5 percent of the nation's wealth, and the top 20 percent owns 91.3 percent of the nation's wealth" (p. 41).[13] As indicated in the previous chapter, CEO salaries have increased exponentially during the last 40 years, while working-class wages have been stagnant and the minimum wage has decreased. This reality is inextricably related to income and wealth inequalities. "According to the World Bank's GINI index," Mander (2012) writes, "(where 0 equals the highest degree of equality and 100 equals the worst level of inequality) the United States' rank was 99. Canada (83), Netherlands (82), and Switzerland (79) came next" (pp. 23–231). If we move to the political elite, from 2004 to 2011 the average worth of Congress grew from a little over $6 million to nearly $8 million (BallotPedia 2012). Jennifer Calfas (2016) reports that Trump's Cabinet has a combined net worth of more than a third of American households. Put another way, the combined wealth of Trump's Cabinet is estimated to be over $14 billion, fifty times greater than George W. Bush's Cabinet (Jackson 2016). Do we need more proof that the capitalist class is also the political class?

When we talk about class in a market society, it is typical to note inequalities in wealth and income, but this screens a more insidious reality. Andrew Sayer (2005) points out that class is not simply about measuring wealth or income, because class "affects our access to things, relationships, experiences and practices which we have reason to value, and hence our chances of living a fulfilling life" (p. 1). He goes on to say that class "struggles are not merely for power and status but about how we live" (p. 3). For instance, a person from a poor working-class background will have less access to good education and healthcare: she will not have the benefit of social relationships that will help her advance in her profession and income/wealth. This is even worse for people of color (hooks 2000). As Terry Eagleton (2011) states, "In a class-society, the free self-development of the few is bought at the cost of the shackling of the many" (p. 105).

Of course, one can always point to the exception, like Ben Carson, a 2016 African American presidential candidate who rose from a poor background to become a neurosurgeon. Exceptions, however, merely prove the rule about how rare and difficult it is to have the resources, relationships, and access to move from lower-class to upper-class status in the United States. A child, for instance, born to a poor family has less than a 9 percent chance of making it into the upper classes—a rate less than many European countries (Greenstone, Looney, Patashnik, and Yu 2013). Those who use the exceptional case to laud the possibility of moving from a lower to an upper class are like magicians who use sleight of hand to distract the audience from what is taking place. "Look at this exception and not at the larger systemic exploitative reality of capitalism that continues to produce inequalities."

To be sure, class can be understood in terms of wealth, power, distribution of surplus labor, and access to resources and social privileges. Yet, class has also been understood in terms of group ethos and what people share in common. Terry Eagleton (2011) argues that classes "are also social formations. . . . They have customs, traditions, social institutions, sets of values and habits of thought (p. 120). Paul Fussell (1983) illustrates this in his depiction of the idioms, habits, and styles of working, middle, and upper-class people (see also Isenberg 2016). In other words, people tend to sort themselves into groups of people who share similar social, political, and economic beliefs and values, which in turn often means possessing similar socioeconomic status and mores. For instance, Rauschenbusch considered class as "a body of men who are similar in their work, their duties and privileges, their manner of life and enjoyment, that a common interest, common conception of life, and common moral ideals are developed and connect individuals" (in Estey 2013, p. 131). Roland Boer (2015) calls this the subjective dimensions of class consciousness that include a "complex web of cultural assumptions, modes of speech, social codes, world outlook and religion" (p. 98). Today, however, class as a group that shares an ethos is less clear than perhaps it was during the heyday of labor unions. This said, the waning of "class solidarity and the absence of mobilization in no way imply class (or class struggle) is disappearing" (Sayer 2005, p. 80) or that there are no differences vis-à-vis shared values and expectations within the classes. Indeed, in their work, Hardt and Negri (2005), recognizing steep economic and political inequalities and the fading of clear class distinctions, argue for the notion of the multitude—those who are exploited by the 1 percent. The multitude includes those who are excluded from wage labor—people who are unemployed, poor, homeless, and so on (p. 129). The multitude comprises "innumerable elements that remain different, one from the other, and yet communicate, collaborate, and act in common" (p. 140), indicating that there are some shared values and expectations even though class distinctions are not as clear. A recent past example of the action of the multitude vis-à-vis class and class struggle is the protest against Wall Street—Occupy Wall Street—that comprised individuals from various laboring classes.

Class, then, is the sorting out of social relations through income, wealth, status, privilege, and commonly shared beliefs, expectations, and values. This sorting out depends on the use of representational systems and disciplinary regimes to justify, legitimate, and enforce the distribution of surplus resources and privileges toward the economic-political elite. While class, as Harman (2017) argues, has been around since the beginning of civilization, the rise of neoliberal capitalism has exacerbated economic, social, and political inequalities, ushering in yet another gilded age of seemingly unchecked decline in worker protections and distribution of wealth to the top tier of society (Fraser 2015).

In any discussion of class, it is necessary to address the reality of classism. Classism is distinct from, but dependent on class. Sayer (2005) notes that "'classism' is not necessary for the production of class" (p. 94). In other words, classism does not produce class (capitalism does), but it may accompany class. The key attribute of classism is the belief in one's superiority because of income and wealth, which is reinforced by its economic, political, and social privileges. People of the lower classes are deemed to be inferior. While there is no moral (or theological) justification for these widely held illusions (p. 4), individuals of the upper classes rely on representational systems and disciplinary regimes to provide evidence for these beliefs. *Another way of saying this is that because belief in one's superiority is a fiction the upper classes must create and enforce a reality that provides them with "experiences" of being superior.* The trappings of wealth are seen to legitimate entitlement and serve as "incontrovertible proof" of one's superiority. Gated communities, privileged access to public venues (e.g., sports), people hired to serve the needs and desires of the wealthy, and so on can create not only a sense of entitlement, but also the "experience" of being superior.[14] Of course, the other side of this coin is that people of lower classes are constructed as inferior by the representational system and the use of disciplinary regimes to debase people in the lower classes (Desmond 2016; Isenberg 2016). For instance, the creation of a "poor door" is not simply a statement about class (Navarro 2014); it is classism wherein the poor are made to feel inferior, while the elite feel superior—keeping the unwashed from mixing with their betters. Poor persons are made to feel inferior and humiliated by forcing them to beg for the scraps from the table (welfare) in order to care for themselves and their children. For instance, classism (and racism) is seen in Malcolm X's (Haley 1964) autobiography when he recalls how his mother and siblings were humiliated by the welfare and juridical systems. Experiences similar to Malcolm X's are evident today. Sociologists (Wacquant 2009; Soss, Fording, and Sanford 2011) provide numerous examples and data of how the poor are disciplined and humiliated by the policies, programs, and bureaucracies that are in place to "help" them. These structures and strategies of humiliation are inextricably joined to the upper class' belief in their superiority, their entitlement, and their economic, political, and social privileges.

When wealthy people erect poor doors to avoid contact with people of the lower classes, when political-economic elites take the best seats, ensconced in luxury sport boxes, when wealthy communities construct gated areas, one can be confident that classism is rife. When poor people are policed (Soss, Fording, and Schram 2011) and forced to live in areas with fewer resources and poor housing, when political policies are enacted to shame people who are in need (Wacquant 2009), we can be sure that classism is present—a classism that aims to communicate to people in the lower classes their inferiority. Classism is evident in the media, where rich and famous people are portrayed in glamorous ways, while, as bell hooks (2000) observes, poor people, in the media, are depicted as "self-centered, corrupt, and dysfunctional" (p. 72). In these instances, representations accompany valuation and recognition that are linked to beliefs in superiority and inferiority. Poor people are constructed as inferior, not simply because they are not "educated," but because they are economic failures.

Classism, with its illusions of superiority and inferiority, intersects with and reinforces racism in the U.S. market society. Where classism and racism join hands is around the beliefs/illusions of superiority and inferiority, as well as the disciplinary regimes that justify and enforce these beliefs. To be sure, classism and racism are distinct, because, as indicated above, one could live in a classist society that was free of racism, yet, in a society imbued with racism, there is always classism.

Chris Harman (2017) argues that people tend to think that racism has always existed and that slavery was/is "a byproduct of racism" (p. 252). However, he points out that racism "developed from an apology for African slavery into a full-blown system of belief" (p. 253), long after class and classism had been established. Citing the works of various scholars, Harman continues by noting that the economic system used racism to justify the exploitation (and disposability) of blacks (pp. 254–256). Edward Baptist's (2014) research adds to this view. He portrays how in the South capitalism and racism combined to produce huge profits through horrific, brutal exploitation of slaves before the Civil War, reflecting the intersection of racism and classism. After the Civil War, black persons continued to be horribly exploited by upper-class white people. Fast forward to the present, David Goldberg (2009) argues persuasively that neoliberal capitalism, which is responsible for the current huge wealth and income disparities (class), has exacerbated racism. He writes:

> In diluting, if not erasing, race in all public affairs of the state, neoliberal proponents nevertheless seek to privatize racism alongside most everything else. They seek . . . to protect preference determination and expression behind the wall of

privacy, untouchable by state intervention, the outcome of which is to privatize race-based exclusions. . . . Devoid of race in the public sphere, racism--as a mode of racially driven subjection and exclusion, debilitation and humiliation— is freed up to circulate as robustly as individuals or non-government institutions should choose in private. (p. 395)

What Steve Fraser calls death zones and Chris Hedges and Joseph Sacco (2012) call sacrifice zones reveal how capitalism, classism, and racism become intertwined, exploiting and harming people and communities of color. Another example of this intersection is environmental racism. To be sure, poor whites are also exploited, humiliated, and disposable in a neoliberal society. However, the main point here is that racism and classism intersect, reinforcing and, in many ways, mystifying each other.

Before addressing how racism and class undermine care, mutual-personal faith, and civic power, it is important to linger for a moment and identify some of the features of racism. Farhad Dalal (2006) writes that "whatever racism is, it is essentially a dehumanizing process through which an other is transformed into The Other, from one of us into one of them. The racialized and dehumanized other is positioned outside the moral universe, with all its attendant requirements and obligations to fellow human beings" (p. 158). From Dalal's perspective, the black Other is depersonalized and estranged by white individuals who construct and treat black people as inferior and themselves as superior. That is, this process of depersonalization or dehumanization (misrecognitions and nonrecognition) is contingent on the forceful use of representations wherein whiteness signifies superiority and blackness inferiority (Aralepo 2003).[15] These representations are embedded in everyday social narratives and rituals, as well as in government policies, laws, and programs (Alexander 2010; Frederickson 1981; West 2001), which function to "create" experiences of black inferiority and white superiority. When white superiority is challenged by black persons' economic and political successes, there is the inevitable backlash of white rage—a rage that points to fear vis-à-vis the loss of white privilege and belief in white "superiority" (Anderson 2016). Even in the putatively post-racial culture in which we now live (Wise 2010), representations of inferiority are hidden in laws, legal procedures, and housing practices that marginalize large numbers of African Americans (Alexander 2010). Put another way, like classism, racism is supported by disciplinary regimes that enforce the illusion of inferiority vis-à-vis black persons.

White racism, in brief, is a social construction involving the social-political-economic use of negative representations to communicate and enforce inferiority, marginalizing, alienating, suppressing, and oppressing black persons (e.g., lynching, Jim Crow laws, laws that result in high rates of incarceration, exclusion from job opportunities and equal pay, housing discrimination). This social construction and the corresponding use of negative representations are inseparable from the white racist's use of positive or idealized self-representations (superiority) to secure social and economic privilege, prestige, power, and position.

I wish to stress here that the illusions of black inferiority and white superiority must continually be produced and enforced, precisely because they are illusions, though with very real consequences. Like classism, which has no moral justification, racism also has no moral justification not simply because it has no theological justification, but because it has no basis existentially. There is nothing in human existence or nature that lends proof to these beliefs and, as a result, these beliefs must be continually manufactured to be felt as if they are real.

White racism can be defined, then, as the social construction and the corresponding social-political-economic use of disciplinary regimes to inculcate and impose inferiority onto black persons, while fostering the illusion and experience of superiority among white persons. Racism also manifests a psychological dependency on the putative inferior black people for whites' illusory beliefs in and experiences of superiority. This dependency is seen in classism too, wherein the felt superiority of the upper class depends on the felt inferiority of the lower classes. I suspect this unconscious dependency is part of the resentment white racists and upper-class people feel in relation to blacks and poorer peoples. At some level, those who believe themselves to be superior unconsciously know that they are dependent on demeaned Others for a sense of their own superiority. If this ever came to consciousness, people would deny both their dependency and that they manufacture inferiority and superiority, which, it seems to me, is further evidence that both classism and racism are based on existential falsehoods.

To sum up, racism and classism intersect in the following ways: Both are reliant on the illusions of superiority and interiority. Both develop representational systems and concomitant policies, programs, and institutions to legitimate and enforce these illusions. The disciplinary regimes associated with classism and racism distribute social, political, and economic resources and privileges toward the "superior" group, while depriving "inferior" Others. Both tend toward denying and mystifying the dependency of "superior" people in manufacturing "inferior" people.

CLASS, CLASSISM, AND RACISM: CARE, MUTUAL-PERSONAL FAITH, AND CIVIC POWER

Classism and racism depend on representational systems that have at their core beliefs in superiority and inferiority, which are reproduced and enforced by disciplinary and justificatory regimes. These representational systems may be said to comprise types of knowledge, which shape perception, recognition, expectations, and behavior. The knowledge produced by classism and racism is fundamentally corrupt and corrupting, because it is based on two existential/ontological falsehoods—the belief in one's superiority and the belief in the inferiority of the Other. This is one reason why there is no epistemological and moral justification for racism or classism, even if both are deemed to be legal in a society. "Knowledge" may lack moral and epistemological justification, but when it is allied to political and economic power, when it is continually produced, justified, and enforced by state and non-state institutions and individuals, it takes on the aura of reality by inscribing pain on those deemed to be lesser and assigning privilege to those deemed superior. With regard to the polis and the common good, racism and classism corrupt not only knowledge, but also care, faith, power, and the space of appearances.

Recall that in chapter 1, I argued that the knowledge associated with care is based on the recognition of the Other as person—a unique, valued, inviolable, and responsive subject. In recognizing the Other as a person, I identify with him/her as a person and simultaneously disidentify with him/her so that s/he may assert her/himself and appear in the relational space—space of appearances. In racism and classism, inferior Others are not recognized or treated as persons, but as inferior objects—objects that are necessary for the dominant group's belief in and experience of superiority. At best, care is grudgingly given and meted out in trickles to insure "those people" retain their inferior status. I will say more about this below, but for now I simply return to Malcolm X's (Haley 1964) experience as a child as an illustration. The grinding poverty and the humiliating "help" and surveillance of government bureaucracies functioned to ensure that Malcolm and his family experienced themselves as inferior, both in terms of class and race. They received minimal care—care for a bare life, as Agamben (1998) describes. At worse, the presence of classism and racism eclipses care wherein individuals, constructed as inferior, live a bare life or become disposable. This may take the form of direct violence legitimated by the state (slavery, see Baptist 2014) or tacitly accepted (e.g., lynching). As Martin Luther King Jr. (1998) noted "Any law that degrades human personality is unjust. All segregation statutes are unjust because segregation distorts the soul and damages the personality. It gives the segregator a *false sense of superiority and the segregated a false sense of inferiority*. Segregation substitutes . . . an "I-Thou" relationship for an "I-It" relationship and ends up relegating persons to the status of things" (p. 193; emphasis mine). "Inferior" people become usable and disposable when the state and society overlook, ignore, deny, and rationalize forms of depersonalization (e.g., Native Americans; Hedges and Sacco 2012), leaving the possibility of care an illusion. Put another way, the knowledge of the inferior Other distorts perceptions and behaviors, which means that genuine care, which is based on personal knowing, cannot be said to take place.

I suspect some may push back and note that African Americans, Native Americans, and Hispanics who are poor receive aid from the government and, for this reason, one could argue that care vis-à-vis the larger society is present, though admittedly lacking in vigor. Perhaps, one could try to argue that this minimal aid is "care" in that people are provided sufficient resources to survive—a bare life. It's better than nothing, one might say. I reject the notion that this is care. First, it is not clear that care can be effective if one's recognition of the Other is infused with the belief in his/her inferiority (e.g., Isenberg 2016), which corrupts any accurate knowledge of the Other as person. Corralling native peoples onto reservations and forcing their children to go to government schools, thus undermining their culture, are hardly caring acts. White representations of native peoples were distortions, which led to diverse forms of violence, marginalization, and oppression. Put differently, white representations of native peoples involved a consistent misrecognition and mistreatment of them, undermining native peoples' cultural-personal traditions, as well as their self-confidence, self-respect, and self-esteem as a people (see Honneth 1995, p. 129). The long history of racism toward African Americans similarly reveals highly distorted representations/knowledge of individuals and communities and, concomitantly, the absence of caring actions. This past week, I heard a person say that a deacon in the Catholic Church told her that black people are lazy. This is not a benign representation. Moreover, it is linked to beliefs in black inferiority—an intersection of classism and racism. It may be true that this white man is not directly involved in actions that are harmful to individual African Americans, but he is part of a larger culture of white privilege that is captive to distorted representations/ beliefs that cannot support caring actions vis-à-vis the black Other.

If these false beliefs lead to distorted knowledge and the eclipse of care, then what could be the motivation to "care" for or provide aid to an inferior Other? This leads to a second and related reason why care is absent in classism and racism. "Care," meted out to "inferior" people, has nothing to do with generosity or charity and everything to do with insuring "these people" remain inferior. I am not talking about people who genuinely help people who are poor, recognizing and treating them as persons and seeking to assist them to survive and flourish. Instead, I am addressing systems that are supported by individuals of the "superior" class and race, that police and punish the "inferior" classes/races, while allotting meager resources for their bare survival (Wacquant 2009; Soss, Fording, and Schram 2011). For the "inferior" others to be given what they are *due* vis-à-vis survival and flourishing would undermine the "knowledge" of "superior" individuals. Put differently, to genuinely care for "inferior" Others would require providing them with the resources and means to care for themselves and others—to flourish. This would contradict the dominant group's belief in their superiority, which is why people who believe in their superiority cannot actually care for or about "inferior" Others. Genuine care would involve accurate knowledge/recognition that would undermine beliefs in inferiority and superiority. Aid or "care" from superior individuals, in short, is fundamentally distorted because, at its core, the unconscious or unstated motivation is to keep inferior Others "inferior." Carol Anderson (2016) documents this well when she highlights numerous examples of white rage whenever African Americans are successful in the social, economic, and political realms. While Anderson does not say this, I contend that part of white rage is due to the undermining of "knowledge" (and power) and subjectivity/identity linked to and dependent on the illusion of white superiority. Successful black people are a threat to the "knowledge" of white superiority.

Perhaps this is too stark. What about the servant who cares for the master and the master who cares for the servant? I am willing to concede that there are situations of care in asymmetrical relations, but as long as any servant is constructed and "known" as inferior, then care is absent. Pity or sentimentality may be present, but not care, because the servant is not known and treated as a person. I add here that the servant who sees himself as inferior and the master as superior cannot care as well. Care cannot be based on the existential/ontological falsehoods that distort knowledge, recognition, and treatment of others. We have to come up with some other term to label those situations when "inferior" Others are given meager resources to survive, but not thrive.

There is another possibility for the meager aid given to inferior Others. It may be inconceivable for those who believe themselves to be superior to see "inferior" Others starve and die, so they have the government provide some of the basic needs for poor people. This sentiment attests to their humanity, one might suggest, but it is a distorted humanity because it is motivated not by genuine knowledge about and concern for the experiences and needs of "inferior" Others, but out of a wish to retain a superior moral sense of themselves, while avoiding guilt for the resources and privileges derived at the expense of Others. There are numerous examples of upper-class people in every city who give to charities and who are self-congratulatory, confirming their superiority in terms of their generous giving to causes that help the poor. I stress here that I am not talking about wealthy persons who do not see themselves as superior or blacks and poor persons as inferior. Instead, I am arguing that wealthy patrons who believe themselves superior give, not out of generosity and accurate personal knowledge of poor persons, but out of their desire to demonstrate their superiority by maintaining self-confidence, self-esteem, and self-respect through the illusion of their superiority. Charity, in other words, is not corrupt in itself, but it is corrupted when it is linked to and dependent on the beliefs about inferiority vis-à-vis class and race—beliefs that corrupt knowledge and motivation. Moreover, charity is corrupt when it functions to maintain class (and race) divisions.

Let me state this in summary form. As long as the representational systems (and attending practices) associated with classism and racism are predominant in culture, as they are in the United States, recognition/knowledge about poor people and people of color will be corrupted, which, in turn, will lead to corrupt and corrupting forms of care. Indeed, "care" that is linked to classism and racism is, as I have argued, aims at reinforcing and reproducing inferiority. Put another way, the aid offered to people who are poor by the government functions as a disciplinary regime, producing experiences of humiliation by creating a dependency for basic survival needs. Consider this in terms of welfare programs. Conservatives and center-right Democrats are partially correct when they say that welfare fosters dependence, and they take this to mean that welfare should be available for a limited period of time in one's life. What they refuse to see and acknowledge is that 1) neoliberal capitalism depends on a reserve army of out-of-work people (putative economic failures), 2) capitalism unjustly distributes resources to the wealthy (legal exploitation), and 3) most importantly, welfare itself does not function to enable people to flourish, but instead to maintain an "inferior" class. The crazy logic of neoliberal politicians is that they would like to eliminate welfare—minimal aid—to enable poor people (whites and people of color) to be self-sufficient, though, at the same time, they refuse to acknowledge that poor persons live in communities that are bereft of resources necessary for flourishing—infrastructure, affordable housing, affordable healthy food, good education, etc.—all those things available to the upper classes. Of course, it is not really "crazy" or contradictory logic/knowing, because the flourishing of poor people and people of color would undermine the "superior" person's belief in the Other's inferiority.

Implicit in this discussion of knowledge and care is the issue of power. In chapter 3, I quoted Francis Bacon and Michel Foucault. Bacon wrote that "knowledge and human power do really meet in one" (in Wolin 2016, p. 395). Centuries later, Foucault (1979) echoed this view stating, "there is no power relation without the correlative constitution of a field of knowledge, nor any knowledge that does not presuppose and contribute at the same time to power relations" (p. 27). When it comes to class-based society, knowledge, as Terry Eagleton (2016) notes regarding Marx, "is largely in the service of power" (p. 98). More particularly, the corrupt knowledge of classism and racism distorts care, which is accompanied by a distortion of political and economic power. That is, the representational systems associated with classism and racism are inextricably linked to and dependent on people acting and speaking together to create formal and informal social, political, and economic practices, programs, laws, policies, and institutions to produce and enforce the beliefs in inferiority and superiority. In so doing, the illusion of superiority obtains a sense of feeling real, as if there are people who are superior, while others are inferior. Power/knowledge vis-à-vis classism and racism must be continually exercised, because the beliefs are existentially and theologically false.

Chris Harman's (2017) history of class struggle demonstrates, in part, that whenever and wherever we see a society structured by class and classism (and racism), there are inevitable societal conflicts between the superior and inferior classes. In reading Harman's work, one notes a pattern. The power/knowledge used to justify and promote class privileges (and inferiority) is eventually challenged by the lower classes, leading to more concerted efforts (e.g., violence, coercion) by the ruling classes to maintain their privileges and sense of superiority. These efforts may stabilize the society for a time, but eventually those who exercise power/knowledge are overthrown—only to reappear later. One could argue that this pattern is due to members of the lower classes becoming angry and weary of being exploited. They band together—speaking and acting together—to resist, revolt, and so on, with the aims of securing civic recognition (e.g., self-esteem, self-respect, and self-confidence) and exercise of civic agency/power (parity of participation in the society's space of appearances). This resistance is also a rejection of the knowledge/experience of putative inferiority, as well as a rejection of power/knowledge based on class or racial superiority. For instance, Martin Luther King Jr.'s Poor People's Campaign was not simply about racist and classist exploitation; it was also about the inherent dignity of poor persons—affirming their self-confidence, self-respect, and self-esteem, while claiming their voices and power. In speaking and acting together, in exerting their power/knowledge, they rejected the false beliefs of their inferiority and the superiority of whites and the wealthy.

Let me move to the other side of the political divide. People claim they live in a representative democracy in the United States, but we need to ask who represents the demos. A 2011 study indicated that, for the first time in history, the majority of the members of Congress is comprised of millionaires (BallotPedia 2012). These representatives speak and act together ostensibly for the common good of all citizens, but this is mostly myth when we consider the state is the handmaiden of neoliberal capitalism. As Eagleton (2011) remarks, "parliament or the state represents not so much the common people as the interests of private property" (p. 192). Evidence of political inequities is seen in the arrival of another gilded age where income and wealth disparities are significant (Fraser 2015). The exercise of political-economic power is in the hands of the upper classes, and it is clear that the upper classes are speaking and acting together not to address the survival and flourishing needs of the lower classes.[16] In this current gilded age, knowledge/power is corrupt, which necessarily means that not only care is undermined, so too is parity of participation in the public-political spaces of appearance.

It is not simply personal knowledge/power and care that are corrupted by classism and racism; it is also mutual-personal faith. James Baldwin (2010) wrote, "It is the American Republic—repeat, the American Republic—which created something which they called a 'nigger.' They created it out of necessities of their own. The nature of the crisis is that I am not a 'nigger'—I never was. I am a man" (p. 49). This creation is an abject, inferior Other, who is not to be trusted and to whom no loyalty is owed. Any cursory reading of U.S. history shows how whites often feared and distrusted slaves, ostensibly because of the possibility of slave uprisings. Of course, whites failed to acknowledge that the representational system and tools necessary to enslave people are sure to breed resistance and insurrection. That is, white slave owners and supporters did not acknowledge that their distrust, fear, and hatred were of their own making—black resistance was and is inevitable in situations of vicious, relentless depersonalization and perfidy. Once legalized slavery ended, white distrust, fear, and hatred continued unabated as Jim Crow laws and the extra-judicial terrorizing of blacks were aimed at keeping blacks from experiencing themselves as equals (speaking and acting together—power) in the political-economic-social realm (JanMohamed 2005). Even as Jim Crow laws were being dismantled during the 1960s, new Jim Crow laws were being created, leading to mass incarceration of blacks (Alexander 2010). Jim Crow laws and the new Jim Crow laws reflect not only white distrust of blacks vis-à-vis parity of participation, but also ongoing attempts to insure the belief/illusion in white superiority, while trying to insure blacks experience themselves as inferior (Anderson 2016; Goldberg 2009). As inferior Others, black persons are not due any personal loyalty by whites. "The machinery of this country," James Baldwin (2010) writes, "operates day in and day out, hour by hour, to keep the nigger in his place" (p. 115). "In his place" means to be inferior and to be denied trust and loyalty, which, of course, means the absence of care. This happens from the earliest years of a child's life. Baldwin (1984) observes that "long before the Negro child perceives this difference [white superiority], and even longer before he understands it, he has begun to react to it, he has begun to be controlled by it" (p. 26).

Baldwin (1990) had firsthand experience of the terrible toll illusions of superiority and inferiority had on a person's psyche. Talking about his father, Baldwin writes "He was defeated long before he died because, at the bottom of his heart, he really believed what white people said about him" (p. 4). Another way of saying this is that James Baldwin's father came to believe in and trust the illusion of "inferiority" and, in so doing, succumbed to the daily humiliations of a racist society where white perfidy rules.

Understandably, many African Americans, in the past and present, struggle to trust white people. However, there can be no mutual-personal faith, and thus no mutual-personal cooperation, when beliefs in inferiority and superiority are present and dominant. Ta-Nehisi Coates' (2015) recent book illustrates in numerous ways how a young black man must navigate a social realm where whites believe themselves to be superior (and blacks inferior). How can he trust whites, when whites, wittingly or unwittingly, have not demonstrated any personal loyalty to him and other African Americans? This is not to say that Coates and other African Americans do not have friendships of deep trust and fidelity with white men and women. That said, I think it would be fair to say that, in a society imbued with racism, African Americans are more likely to be initially wary of whites, wondering if they are indeed trustworthy. It is doubtful that friendship, trust, and fidelity would emerge if an African American person discovered that a white individual believed himself to be superior because he was white. Of course, many white people are wary or distrustful of black people, which may involve both classism and racism.

As noted in chapter 2, the absence of mutual-personal faith does not mean there is an absence of faith. In situations dominated by the illusions of inferiority and superiority, trust and loyalty are contingent upon living up to and out of these beliefs. So, whites who believe themselves to be superior can form groups, living a life in common. Indeed, they can engage in mutual-personal faith and cooperation with other whites. But when it comes to engaging black people, trust and loyalty depend on their submission to white people and their representational systems that affirm the illusion of white superiority. As long as black persons do not contradict (e.g., become successful), undermine, resist, deny, or attack these existential illusions, they are to be trusted. To return to the illustration of the black servant and white master, the master's affection, trust, and fidelity to his servant is contingent on the poor black servant accepting his inferior status—racism and classism—and cooperating with the master and the representational and disciplinary systems that produce masters and slaves. The master may entertain the illusion that he is personally trustworthy and loyal. I say illusion because this kind of faith relation depends on existential lies lived out in concrete everyday situations. It would be more accurate to depict the master's faith as contractual-functional—the black Other is to perform his/her duties as an inferior Other. If the servant (or poor person) begins to assert himself or rejects and resists this oppressive system, s/he is breaking this contractual-functional faith and thus opens him/herself up to discipline or being disposed of. The "inferior" Other is never constructed as a person and therefore the faith relation that exists is a depersonalized contractual-functional form of faith wherein the "inferior" Other is trusted to the degree that s/he accepts, submits, confirms, and cooperates with the system that enforces publicly his/her inferiority and the master's superiority.

While slave-master faith relations are outlawed today, this does not mean the contractual-functional forms of faith inherent in classism and racism are not alive and well. Consider two current examples, namely the Black Lives Matter movement and protests by NFL players who knelt during the national anthem. While white individuals have supported both, there has been a significant, mainly white, backlash against both forms of protest, which is not at all surprising. A quick Google search of white protests reveals numerous stories from across the country where whites have countered Black Lives Matter. Moreover, Kenneth Arthur (2017) cited a Reuters' poll that said 72 percent of Americans oppose NFL players' protests during the national anthem. Rachel Leah (2017) reports that a recent poll indicates "that black voters approve of the demonstrations 79 to 18 percent, while white voters disapprove 60 to 37 percent." These polls reveal other divisions in the population, but the central issue is one of race and, more particularly, the issue of racism in this society, despite being couched in terms of patriotism. These racial divisions can be understood as a lack of mutual-personal faith and the presence of a type of faith that is rife with illusions and contractual expectations of inferiority and superiority.

Let me shift from racism to classism and class. Fraser (2015) writes that "flexible capitalism . . . undermines trust and stability" (p. 316). "Flexible capitalism" ushers in a "new regime of voluntary servitude" (p. 324) wherein citizens are constructed as independent entrepreneurs—free agents, associates, temps, or contractors in a gig economy. Companies like FedEx, Microsoft, Walmart, Uber, Lyft, and many others "redefine workers as independent contractors" and thus are able to "circumvent both labor laws and obligations to provide fringe benefits, from healthcare and retirement to vacations and overtime" (p. 328). A gig economy is neoliberal capitalism on steroids, leaving lower-class individuals to fend for themselves, while the capitalist class reaps huge profits and privileges, creating vast inequalities vis-à-vis income and wealth. Fraser cites an academic who said, "People have come to accept that they're on their own. . . . We simply have to accept that there is no corporation or institution that will take care of us—that we are truly on our own" (p. 331).

The euphemistic term "flexible" economy is more aptly called a market society, wherein political and economic elites are given greater flexibility in exercising power to exploit workers. In a market society, contractual-functional forms of faith dominate social relations—everything is for sale and everyone is an entrepreneur. This is not quite a Hobbesian society where enmity is the first social relation, but one where the dictum "Use others as they would use you" prevails (Fraser 2015, p. 333). Of course, in this gig society, those who have nothing to sell, whether that involves labor, skill, one's body, or something else, are seen as disposable or of no use/value to the society. One's social value, in other words, is not based in being a person, but in being a successful entrepreneur—an individual who can be trusted because s/he has adopted and lives out of neoliberal capitalist ideas, beliefs, values, and expectations. Being a successful entrepreneur is, more often than not, linked to beliefs in inferiority and superiority. Successful entrepreneurs are deemed to be trustworthy and socially valuable in a so-called flexible economy, as long as one participates in, supports, and contributes to the market god (Cox 2016). An individual is considered an entrepreneur even if one is driving a car for Lyft. People who fail to produce, who are unwilling and unable to be entrepreneurs, have not only broken faith with the market society; they are deemed inferior—failures—and not to be trusted. They are either disposable or merit minimal social loyalty/care (e.g., welfare programs) and, in either case, are humiliated by various disciplinary regimes, including, at times, churches (MacDonald 2010).

This kind of social-market faith vis-à-vis classism is also seen in the prevalence of wage theft by the capitalist class. Fraser (2015) cites a study that "revealed the severe extent of wage theft among low-wage workers, especially women and the foreign-born. No labor law was left inviolate: overtime, minimum wage, illegal deductions, miscalculations to elude coverage under the Fair Labor Standards Act or to escape unemployment and disability insurance legal commitments" (p. 329). To systematically steal from persons who have minimal power, resources, and privileges reveals not simply sociopathic entitlement to exploit whenever possible, but pernicious beliefs in superiority and entitlement, as well betrayal. Members of the capitalist class who exploit workers do not recognize "workers" as persons, but rather as functional cogs in the neoliberal machine who are used and then discarded when no longer useful (or the cogs resist, confront, protest, revolt). These cogs, like Willy Loman, merit contractual loyalty at best, but in the case of wage theft, this "loyalty" is more aptly betrayal. To steal from people who are already struggling to survive demonstrates a profound kind of human perfidy that is rationalized by the logic of superiority-inferiority—a logic that is intertwined with neoliberal capitalism.

In chapter 2, I argued that mutual-personal faith is necessary for the existence and vitality of community and, while a society can survive by relying on contractual-functional forms of faith, it cannot thrive in the absence of mutual-personal faith. This is especially true when prevalent contractual-functional faith relations are based on exploitation and illusions of inferiority and superiority. That is, the faith relations associated with classism (and racism) undermine the possibility of a decent society, not only because both racism and classism negate personal knowing and care, but also because they diminish and corrupt civic power/cooperation and the space of appearances. Civic power/cooperation in a democracy is measured by exercising the right to vote, to speak out, and to run for office—parity of personal recognition and participation in the polis. When we first consider the reality of classism, we note that nearly 58 percent of poor people do not vote, which makes sense when one considers that politicians, as noted above, by and large represent the capitalist class and not the poor (Kavoussi 2013). It is not simply that persons of the lower classes fail to vote because they believe the game is rigged (genuine distrust of the system/state); it is also the challenges of getting time from work to engage in the political process. This reduction in participation and the society's space of appearances accompanies a kind of economic-social apartheid where people of the poorer classes are relegated to under-resourced areas of cities and states, where they can be policed (Soss, Fording, and Schram 2011). Put another way, an indecent society humiliates people of the lower classes and works to undermine parity of participation in the political field, further reducing their political power and agency. The upper classes are content with this arrangement, because it insures their social, economic, and political privileges. The class divide in an indecent society is marred by distrust and lack of fidelity between classes (and races). An indecent society, then, cannot be said to flourish, when the flourishing of the economic and political elites depends on exploiting the vast majority of the country's population. Put another way, in a society marred by exploitative contractual-functional forms of faith, enmity, distrust, and betrayal become increasingly prevalent, eventually undermining social cooperation and social stability.

In an indecent society, the presence of classism's exploitative faith relations does not exclude expressions of mutual-personal faith relations, a vibrant space of appearances, parity of participation, and shared exercise of power. Consider the early Christian communities in Acts. Christians gathered together living lives in common, wherein mutual-personal faith relations predominated—faith relations that expressed personal knowledge and behavior that supported distribution of resources so community members could care for themselves and each other. In other words, this community's space of appearances involved members speaking and acting together aimed to meet common needs for survival and flourishing. All of this took place against the backdrop of the Roman Empire (and its client actors) with its practices of terror (e.g., crucifixions), exploitation, and classism, all of which produced distrust, perfidy, and despair. The early Christian community was an *alterpolis*—one that lived out knowledge, faith, life, and power free from the twin false beliefs of superiority and inferiority. The deaths of Ananias and Sapphira can be understood metaphorically. By holding back resources, they took resources from the community, which represented a fundamental threat to the community's way of being. Deceptively holding onto to their wealth, while pledging to share resources, they signaled their belief in their own privilege, if not superiority.

Jumping forward to the 20th and 21st centuries, we can discover communities and groups where mutual-personal faith relations existed and exist within an indecent society marred by classism and racism. Many vibrant African American churches have served as enclaves of mutual-personal faith/ knowledge, wherein members can express their agency and experience self-esteem, self-confidence, and self-respect.[17] These communities and groups (e.g., NAACP) not only have helped members survive the perfidy of a racist society, but in many cases, despite numerous obstacles, have enabled members to flourish in terms of education, business, and the arts.

Mutual-personal faith is also evident in groups that form associations to protest and resist economic, social, and political marginalization and oppression. Wall Street protests, Black Lives Matter, the current Poor Peoples Campaign, and other groups/movements are examples of people speaking and acting together (power/mutual-personal faith) to resist and undermine political and economic institutions and practices that 1) reproduce types of impersonal and depersonalizing knowledge, 2) restrict persons' participation in public space of appearances, 3) breed exploitative faith relations, and 4) use coercive and depersonalizing forms of power to maintain the privileges and prestige of dominant groups. An indecent society can thus have groups and communities that resist the perfidy and exploitation of classism and racism.

Given this, I rush to note that a cursory glance at history shows that any group of people seen and treated as inferior face many obstacles in their efforts to obtain justice, civic care, and civic power. Traditionally, dominant groups use coercion and violence/terror to subvert people who are gathering to resist. Crucifixion, for instance, was used to terrorize the poor people of Israel into accepting Roman rule, which included Jewish leaders of the upper classes who collaborated with imperial Rome. William Cavanaugh (1998) points out that a state's use of torture or other terror-inducing actions, while harming individuals, is aimed at disrupting and destroying what he calls social bodies—groups, communities that can mount resistance. The various illustrations above, where the state and non-state actors used coercion, violence, and terror to insure that "inferior" Others experience themselves as inferior, and hence submissive, corroborate Cavanaugh's view. Torture and other forms of oppression are examples of distorted knowledge, an absence of care, the corruption of power, and the eclipse of mutual-personal faith.

Let me add that, in the absence of torture and obvious forms of oppression, an additional insidious obstacle faces "inferior" Others today and their ability to form social bodies to resist. Sociologists Robert Bellah, et.al. (1985) and Robert Putnam (2000, 2015) have noted that the rise of individualism in the United States has accompanied a loss of what Putnam calls social capital.

This increasing atomization has been furthered by the emergence of neoliberal capitalism with its emphasis on individual responsibility for economic success or failure (Brown 2015; Silva 2013). Citizens, in other words, have internalized neoliberal beliefs, making it more difficult to join social bodies of resistance. The state, then, does not have to resort to violence or torture to undermine social bodies of resistance and mutual-personal faith. Although groups have formed to resist racism and classism, Steven Fraser (2015) documents in depressing detail, social bodies of resistance, for a variety of reasons, are fewer and more anemic compared to the late 19th and early 20 centuries.

In sum, when dominant groups develop and maintain narratives and concomitant institutions that profess and enforce illusions of inferiority and superiority, as seen in classism and racism, one can be assured that the society is an indecent one. Indecent societies, Margalit (1996) argues, humiliate citizens, but not all citizens, and this humiliation involves enforcing inferiority. As I have argued, indecent societies, which are rife with the racist and classist illusions of superiority and inferiority, undermine personal knowing necessary for caring actions aimed at the survival and flourishing of all citizens. Put another way, false beliefs lead to the corruption of knowledge and care, whereby the resources necessary to care for oneself and others are diminished (in some cases nonexistent) vis-à-vis members of the lower classes and persons of color. Corrupt knowledge accompanies corrupt and corrupting forms and expressions of power—coercion and violence used to make the illusions a reality—and a corresponding attenuation or loss of the space of appearances or parity of participation vis-à-vis blacks and poor persons. All of this attends the undermining of mutual-personal faith relations between those deemed to be superior and those constructed as inferior.

CONCLUSION

In the Bible story of the wealthy man who lived lavishly while Lazarus suffered outside his gates, we read that after their deaths the rich man, from his perch in hell, sees Lazarus at Abraham's side. In terrible agony, the rich man pleads for Abraham to let Lazarus cross the divide to dip his finger in water to cool the rich man's tongue (Lk 16:24). Abraham tells him that the chasm cannot be crossed by anyone on either side. The rich man then begs Abraham to send Lazarus from the dead to warn his brothers. Abraham replies, saying that they have Moses and the prophets. To which the rich man replies, "No, father Abraham; but if someone goes to them from the dead, they will repent" (Lk. 16:30). Abraham responds, "If they do not listen to Moses and the prophets, neither will they be convinced even if someone rises from the dead" (v.31).

In my view this is not a story of class comeuppance or necessarily a cautionary tale to challenge the wealthier classes to be more charitable. Evidence for the latter claim is seen in reading that even a man rising from the dead will not be taken seriously. Moses, the prophets, and Jesus are not enough to persuade the wealthy to recognize and respond to poor persons. The unbridgeable chasm in the afterlife parallels the seemingly unbridgeable class divide in life. Note that the rich man recognizes Lazarus, which means that he knew him in life. The rich man, who interestingly has no name, had separated himself from the plaints of Lazarus by keeping the "disgusting" man outside of his gates. The unbridgeable divide in life is not created by the physical gates. The gates are only a symptom of a deeper reality, which is a blindness that comes from the corruption of knowledge by the illusions of superiority and inferiority. Distorted knowing is reflected in the lack of personal recognition and care and the eclipse of mutual-personal faith vis-à-vis Lazarus. So distorted is the rich man's knowing that Moses and the prophets cannot awaken him to his responsibility to care. As if to put an exclamation point on this parable, perhaps presaging a future reality of wealthy Christians, even a man rising from the dead will not prick the conscience of his brothers. To add to this, Lazarus, in being outside the gates, is kept from speaking and acting with others. He is isolated from human beings. Outside the gates, Lazarus has no power, no voice that will be recognized and responded to. Like the poor, he is denied not only the bare necessities of life, but also any hope of civic participation or civic power.

It is easy to think of this parable simply in terms of class, but Lazarus could be black or Hispanic. The distortion of knowledge and the resulting chasms we construct vis-à-vis class and race are, as I have argued, rooted in the malignant beliefs in superiority and inferiority that are concretized by way of political-public and economic institutions and cultural practices. As valuing creatures, we assess and judge what is good or bad, positive or negative, of worth or not. Valuation, which is inextricably related to knowledge and behavior, often accompanies the proclivity to assign worth to our group. It is, in other words, a short step from valuing my group to holding onto the illusion of the superiority of my group and, naturally, the inferiority of those outside our gates. These valuations and beliefs are accompanied by elaborate narratives, rules, laws, practices, and institutions that justify, legitimate, and enforce these illusions, giving them the seemingly impregnable air of not simply reality, but truth. And yet, to hold onto these illusions reveals an underlying existential insecurity, which is handled by the constant attempt to create and enforce existential or ontological lies.

This parable and my comments about the illusions of classism and racism are not a counsel of despair. While Abraham said the chasm cannot be crossed, this does not mean we cannot work to remove bricks from the divisive walls of racism and classism. The early Christian community in Acts was an attempt to live lives free from the grammar of superiority and inferiority, thus freeing people to care for each other as persons. During the civil rights movement, many black churches resisted racism and classism (e.g., Poor People's Campaign). Today some Christian communities eschew class and fight against racism, hoping to live out a knowledge that supports care, mutual-personal faith, parity of participation in the public space of appearances, or what I have called civic power. In short, some people, some Judeo Christian communities, not only heed Moses and the prophets, but also the risen Christ.

I add here that if residents are unwilling to confront the illusions of inferiority and superiority, we cannot call this a decent society, because our home is racked with alienation and carelessness. To begin to confront and dismantle representational systems and institutions that support, enforce, and embody these illusions means recognizing that we share a common home. If we can work toward this in our society, perhaps we can similarly recognize that persons from other societies share our common home, the earth. If we cannot learn to live in our local homes, there is little hope we can live together in this one world. The adage a house divided cannot stand no longer refers to nation-states, but to the world as our collective home.

NOTES

1. Sexism continues to be a critical issue today. Even after hundred years of gaining the right to vote, women today in the United States are under-represented in political offices, business leadership, and science. And as seen in the media of late, women and girls are often objects of sexual harassment. That said, every writer makes judgments about what to focus on given limited space. In this chapter I have decided to focus on racism and classism, though readers will, I hope, see the parallels and intersections of these topics with sexism.

2. "Racism," Fraser (2015) writes, "was the cancerous phobia present at the creation [of the United States]. . . . Racial rancor became the medium of a class consciousness that dared not speak its name" (p. 220).

3. Chris Harman (2017) offers numerous examples from history that classism breeds resentment and, when inequalities deepen, this often leads to social unrest and revolutions.

4. Many pastoral theologians have addressed issues of racism in myriad ways (e.g., Ashby 1996, 2003; Lee 2015; Poling 2012; Ramsay 2012; Wimberly 2003; 2006), though the issue of classism has received far less attention (LaMothe 2017; Mercer 2012; Rumscheidt 1998). My approach is different, because I interrogate racism and classism from the interrelated perspectives of political notions of care, faith, and power.

5. Someone might argue that economically privileged people may not be racist, as if to suggest that race and class are not imbricated. Indeed, one might point to a progressive who contributes to various programs that deal with racism and other injustices. One could also point out that people of the lowest economic class can be racist, while others are not. All of this does not mean that race and class do not intersect. Moreover, using individuals as counterexamples vis-à-vis race and class does not disprove the reality of the representational systems in society that give rise to both.

6. For a discussion of class vis-à-vis poor white people in the United States, see Isenberg (2016), *White Trash*.

7. Marx, Eagleton (1999) notes, argued that "social classes exist in a state of mutual antagonism on account of conflicting material interest" (p. 35). In the *Communist Manifesto* Marx wrote, "The history of all hitherto existing society is the history of class struggles (in Eagleton, p. 35). Harmon (2017) takes up Marx's view of history and social class.

8. Marx was not the only person to be concerned about the exploitation of the working class. Eagleton (2011) writes that "Voltaire believed that the rich grew bloated on the blood of the poor, and that property lay at the heart of social conflict. Jean-Jacques Rousseau . . . argued much the same" (p. 32). He contended "that property brings war, exploitation and class conflict in its wake" (p. 117). Later Eagleton points out that "What is unique about his (Marx) thought is that he locks these two ideas—class struggle and more of production—together, to provide a historical scenario which is indeed genuinely new" (p. 36).

9. Marx conceptualized class, then, not in terms of "wealth and power distribution but rather to processes of producing and distributing surpluses in society" (Wolff and Resnick 2012, p. 154). That is, people are sorted by class "according to their participation in the production and/or distribution of surplus labor" (Wolff and Resnick 1987, p. 45). Wolff and Resnick (2012) contend that "Marx's focus on class in surplus terms sharply differentiates him from the neoclassical economists who are generally disinterested in class, deny that a surplus exists, and place emphasis on individuals and market interactions" (p. 29). Marx focused on and "developed a class theory because class and class struggle in his time was—as it largely remains today—an overlooked, undertheorized, and often repressed dimension of modern capitalist society" (p. 29).

10. This may become even worse in the so-called gig economy where people cobble together part-time jobs to make a living—jobs that do not offer protections or benefits.

11. For Marx, "class struggle is essentially a struggle over the surplus, and as such is likely to continue as long as there is not a sufficiency for all. Class comes about whenever material production is so organized as to compel some individuals to transfer their surplus labour to others in order to survive" (Eagleton 2011, p. 43). Today, as Hardt and Negri (2005) point out class and class struggle are not simply associated with material production, such as manufacturing. It is also seen in service industry. The same Marxian principles apply, however.

12. Another way to talk about representational systems is ideologies. Dominant representational systems in a society are promulgated by and instantiated in

governing classes. That is, the ruling ideology is produced and enforced by the ruling classes, which Marx and Engels noted.

13. Compare this with Sweden where the top 5 percent have less than 20 percent of the overall wealth (Chartbook of Economic Inequality, 2015).

14. Experience is in quotes to emphasize that the experience of one's superiority is dependent on the illusion in one's superiority. The political-economic elite expect to be treated as special, as royalty, which gives rise to experiences associated with the belief/illusion in one's superiority. On the other side of the equation is the experience in one's inferiority, which feels real precisely because people have treated a person in demeaning and depersonalizing ways. This experience of being demeaned is real, but the belief that one is inferior is existentially and ontologically false.

15. George Fredrickson (1981) examines the development of racial logic in the United States and South Africa. He argues that the notion of white superiority developed later to justify the enslavement of blacks.

16. The marriage of political and economic elites is addressed by Jacques Ranciére who said "Marx's once scandalous thesis that governments are simple business agents for international capital is today an obvious fact one which 'liberals' and 'socialists' agree. The absolute identification of politics with the management of capital is no longer the shameful secret hidden behind 'forms' of democracy; it is the openly declared truth by which our governments acquire legitimacy" (in Eagleton 2011, p. 198).

17. I note here that the prevalence of capitalism and class impacted some African American communities. In Malcolm X's (Haley 1964) autobiography, Malcolm notes the classism prevalent in Boston, where his aunt lived.

Chapter 7

The World Is Our Home

Care, Faith, Power, and International Relations

If we turn to scripture for guidance on international relations, we find rampant tribalism, enslavement of one group by another, slaughter, torture, terror, and oppression all sprinkled with the occasional welcoming of strangers. Yahweh and the Chosen People are hardly exemplars of promoting peace and cooperation between and among nations. Indeed, they typically appear bent toward conquest and control. Shifting to Jesus and his disciples, we find that they seemed more concerned about the kingdom of God than realpolitik of national and international relations. Of course, this changed with Constantine's calculating embrace of Christianity and the accompanying exercise of state power by Church leaders. Then Christian history became tainted by internecine warfare, devious political machinations within and between countries, lust and greed for empire, and rationalized violent and exploitative evangelization of conquered peoples. Any quick survey of history, Christian or otherwise, reveals that international relations seem to be founded on Hobbesian relations of shared enmity and guided by lex talionis, rather than the prophet Isaiah's (2:4) vision of nations beating their swords into plowshares and their spears into pruning hooks.

While lex talionis and conquest may dominate international relations throughout history, we note important shifts in the 20th century. After the devastation and horrors of World War I, President Woodrow Wilson took up British foreign secretary Edward Grey's idea of a League of Nations where countries could establish procedures for addressing and working through conflicts, as well as create rules for cooperation for the welfare of their peoples. The United States, because of Republican opposition, did not take part in the League of Nations, which was in existence from 1920 to 1946. It would take the unprecedented destruction and terrors of World War II before the United States got behind the idea and joined the United Nations. The establishment of the Charter of the United Nations and the International Court of Justice (1945), the Charter on Human Rights (1948), and the various organizations created to carry out peace and aid operations marked something new in history. There was growing recognition of the interconnected nature of the world, as well as the need to work together to reduce conflicts and provide aid for countries and their peoples. Naturally, wars, human rights abuses, and economic coercion and disparities continued. Nevertheless, the United Nations made real the idea that countries could gather to work through their conflicts, to find ways to cooperate for the betterment of people in their own and other countries, and to establish a system of justice to guide all countries.[1]

In the realm of organized Christianity, there were also significant historical changes in the 19th and 20th centuries. In 1891, Pope Leo XIII issued the encyclical *Rerum Novarum* (*The Workers Charter*), which addressed global capitalism and the resulting suffering of workers throughout the world. This document was followed by many others (e.g., Pius XI's *Quadragesimo Anno* in 1931; John XXIII's *Mater et Magister* in 1961; and *Populorum Progressio*, 1967), all of them dealing with global issues and appealing for countries to work together to promote peace and the welfare of all peoples. More recently, Pope Francis argued that "relations between states must be respectful of each other's sovereignty, but must also lay down mutually agreed means of averting regional disasters which would eventually affect everyone. Global regulatory norms are needed to impose obligations and prevent unacceptable actions, for example, when powerful companies dump contaminated waste or offshore polluting industries in other countries" (*Laudato Si*, 2015, Para. 173). He stressed in *Evangelii Gaudium* that human beings have a common home and that all nations need to cooperate so that poorer nations receive the aid needed to care for their peoples and the environment. Moreover, Francis is critical of wealthy nations and capitalism not only for exploiting the poor and poorer nations, but also for ignoring the environmental damage done in so-called Third World countries. Similarly, the World Council of Churches (established 1937–38; First Assembly 1948) has not only worked to promote interreligious cooperation, but has taken on global political and economic issues with the aim of encouraging international collaboration for the common good of all peoples. In 2002 the WCC published a document on international sustainability:

Our hopes for the outcome of the WSSD (World Summit on Sustainable Development) process are linked to our commitment to building just and sustainable communities. This notion embodies the vision of an economic system based on equitable sharing of resources; a decent quality of life for all in a healthy environment; people's empowerment to participate at every level in decisions affecting their lives; accountability by public and private institutions for the social and environmental consequences of their operations; and a harmonious and just relationship between humans and the rest of the natural world. From this standpoint, we insist that an ethical approach to the WSSD process requires the integration of social justice and ecological sustainability.

The various papal encyclicals and the World Council of Churches represent steps toward ecumenism and internationalism, which are grounded in the revelation that human beings, with all of their diversity, are children of God and that we have and share a common home. This revelation, which is both religious and existential, accompanies responsibility for the well-being of all peoples and for our shared habitat—the earth. As Terry Eagleton (2011) notes, "The earth is the first condition of our existence" (p. 228).

The horrors of two world wars, the specter of nuclear war, and the proliferation of capitalism led some political leaders of various countries and religious organizations to realize the absolute necessity of international cooperation if peace and security were to be possible. Indeed, as Ellen Meikens Woods writes, "The two great threats to human survival that confront us are military and environmental" (in Eagleton 2011, p. 236). She explains further that the "expansionary, competitive and exploitive logic of capitalist accumulation in the context of the nation-state system must, in the longer or shorter term, be destabilizing, and that capitalism . . . is and will for the foreseeable future remain the greatest threat to world peace" (p. 236). Capitalism, Wood comments, "may be able to accommodate some degree of ecological care, especially when the technology of environmental protection is itself profitably marketable. But the essential irrationality of the drive for capital accumulation, which subordinates everything to the requirements of the self-expansion of capital and so-called growth, is unavoidably hostile to ecological balance" (p. 237). Global capitalism and war are not contributors to global peace, security, and the common good.

In the history of humanity, then, the 20th century saw greater international cooperation, which was and is a significant historic change, even though war, nuclear proliferation, and environmental destruction continue to threaten the planet and its inhabitants. I add here that during the last two decades the realities of global warming have sparked even greater urgency for international agreements and cooperation. Perhaps we are slowly learning that we need to care for each other and the earth if we are to survive, though it is an open question of whether we have learned in time (see Kolbert 2015).

In this chapter, I discuss international relations from the perspective of care, faith, and power. My aim is not an exhaustive excursus on international relations, but rather some thoughts about how we, as citizens/residents of the world, can think, converse, and work together toward the common well-being of all peoples with all of their attending particularities, which includes caring about their habitats and the overall habitat of the earth. I begin by addressing the notion of care and its implications for international relations. Here I stress that care is applicable to state and global institutions to the degree that these institutions facilitate the conditions through which individuals, families, and communities can care for their (and others') survival and flourishing needs. This is followed by a section regarding faith, in particular, functional-contractual faith aimed at global and regional cooperation vis-à-vis preserving and repairing the earth, as well as addressing the particular needs of the earth's inhabitants.[2] The final section deals with the notion of power and the challenges of exercising power in a world that cannot survive by continuing to employ power in Machiavellian-Hobbesian ways or power based on global capitalism and militarism.

There are a number of points to address before beginning. First, liberal contractarian ideas of justice, fairness, reciprocity, and noninterference are central features of discussions regarding international ethics. My focus on care and faith is not meant to supplant or replace these, but rather to add to them as a lens for understanding and evaluating international relations, as well as standards or aims through which countries can operate. Second, any discussion regarding international relations immediately confronts the issue of universality and particularity. Understandably, scholars and activists have rightly pointed out that powerful countries have employed the notion of "universal" at the expense of the particular needs of other peoples. In other words, more powerful countries assume that their view of being human is universal (Hall 1997; Said 1979), while ignoring or dismissing the particular needs and customs of other peoples (Easterly 2013). This suspicion regarding universal claims has often led academics to reject anything that has a whiff of the universal. While I appreciate the suspicion and its sources, I can't help but wonder if denial of the universal means we cannot agree that all human beings have bodies and senses. We all breathe, eat, and defecate, though we have different customs about the latter two. Moreover, rejecting the idea of the universal tends to lead to a paralysis regarding making moral and political value judgments—a universal relativism, if you will. So, if a country endorses the marriage of twelve-year-old girls, we should simply say that this is particular to their culture, instead of condemning the practice. Do we simply look askance at China's excessive use of coal, polluting the air of major cities, arguing that this is merely their practice of spurring economic development? Do we overlook the United States' militarism and its negative effects globally and environmentally simply because of the peculiar and particular culture of U.S. exceptionalism and imperialism? This said, I opt for Seyla Benhabib's (1992) view of interactive universalism. She writes:

> Interactive universalism acknowledges the plurality of modes of being human, and differences among humans, without endorsing all the pluralities and

differences as morally or politically valid. . . . Interactive universalism regards difference as a starting point for reflection and action. In this sense, "universality" is a regulative ideal that does not deny embodied and embedded identity, but aims at developing moral attitudes and encouraging political transformation that can yield a point of view acceptable to all. (p. 153)

Benhabib is careful to note that interactive universalism "is not the ideal of consensus of fictitiously defined selves, but a concrete *process* in politics and morals of the struggle of concrete, embodied selves" (p. 153). Given the realities of global warming, we must embrace a universalism, while respecting particularities and promoting collaboration among all peoples.

Naturally, this is easier said than done. It requires developing national and international institutions that facilitate dialogue and cooperation among diverse peoples. We do not, as Benhabib suggests, need to create a clear global identity and story, but it is also not outside the realm of possibility to have an overarching global story and identity as human beings sharing a common world, along with institutions that promote cooperation.[3] Consider that in the United States there is, in general, a shared national story and identity, which are embraced by Americans who are African, Asian, Pakistani, Indian, Russian, and so on. Moreover, individuals who see themselves as American can also embrace and hold dear their identities as Michiganders, Hoosiers, Texans, and so forth. They can possess identities as Bostonians, New Yorkers, Angelinos, and so on. These are all political identities, but we can also include other identities in the mix—Jews, Muslims, Baptists, Catholics, Wiccans, and so forth. Is it possible, with the help of national and international institutions, to have a local identity and a global one? Can we be American citizens and citizens of the world, just as I am a citizen of Kentucky and of the United States? I think this is possible because I have seen and heard people think (and identify) locally and globally. Type "citizens of the world" in your search engine and thousands of sites appear. We have and share one home and we are all human beings, even given our diversity and particular habitats.

Another clarification involves institutions—national and international. International relations are conducted by nation-state institutions (e.g., State Department), extra-state institutions (e.g., United Nations, G8 or G7), and nongovernmental organizations (e.g., CARE International, UNICEF). These institutions are human creations, though, more often than not, they take on a life of their own, sometimes distorting the very aims they were created to address. William James (1956) recognized this, writing:

It is a matter unfortunately too often seen in history to call for much remark, that when a living want of mankind has got itself officially protected and organized in an institution, one of the things which the institution most surely tends to do is stand in the way of the natural gratification of the want itself. . . . Too often do the place-holders of such institutions frustrate the spiritual purpose to which they were appointed to minister. (p. 1)

Add to this the problem that some institutions are granted the status of being persons and, thus, having rights (e.g., Citizens United), which simply confirms that ostensibly very intelligent human beings can concretize illusions.

There are two implications here. First, the fact that institutions are human creations ideally indicates that they are created to benefit human beings and, when they do not, they can be dismantled or changed, though often they are not. They take on a life of their own. When considering the topic of international relations, this means that institutions associated with states are human creations that can be evaluated in terms of what specific human needs are being met. Who benefits? Who is harmed? In terms of international relations and international institutions, the question becomes how do these institutions benefit all human beings? The common good, in other words, does not simply and solely refer to people in a specific society, but all residents of the earth. Second, institutions are not persons. They do not have agency. They do not perceive, desire, love, or hate. They do not feel pain and do not suffer. They are neither moral nor immoral, though they can promote either. Institutions do not care in the sense of recognizing and treating individuals as persons, though they can facilitate these attitudes and behaviors. Institutions cannot engage in mutual-personal faith relations, but they can develop guidelines and practices that support cooperative forms of faith. Institutions do not exercise power in the sense of individual agents speaking and acting together, though individuals ensconced in various institutions can speak and act together with representatives of other institutions, thus exercising tremendous power through persuasion, coercion, or violence. For instance, ALEC (American Legislative Exchange Council) does not exercise power. Rather, individuals who identify with, support, and represent this institution speak and act together to create legislation that furthers their aims. Finally, an institution is not accountable, but each member qua person is. From a religious perspective, Dante's hell is comprised of individuals, not institutions. This is an important point to stress. Imagine the extinction of the human race as a result of global warming. Of course, all national and international institutions will become extinct as well, but these institutions will not struggle to breathe in a CO_2-saturated atmosphere, will not experience hunger from lack of food, and will not feel the relentless heat—only human beings will.

There is another factor regarding institutions vis-à-vis nations and international relations. National institutions are manifold and complex. They organize a society and reflect dominant or core values, beliefs, and expectations. In a letter to a friend, Karl Polanyi wrote that "the heart of a feudal nation was privilege; the heart of a bourgeois nation was property" (in Brie 2017, p. 7).[4] We could add that the heart of a neoliberal capitalist society is profit. The "heart" of a society is a metaphor for the institutions that support, promulgate, and enforce core values and practices. So, for instance, in a bourgeois and neoliberal capitalist society, political, judicial, and economic institutions enact, promote, and enforce beliefs, rules, and values associated with property and profit. As seen in chapter 5, it is fairly obvious who the primary beneficiaries are of these institutions. If we move to international institutions and relations, one can consider what values, beliefs, and practices these institutions represent, as well as raise the question of who benefits. For instance, before the end of World War II, the United States organized a financial conference (Bretton Woods) that was instrumental in creating international financial institutions (e.g., World Bank, International Monetary Fund). These institutions were created to stabilize the international markets, which, in turn, would insure the supremacy of capitalism and largely benefit the United States and its European client-states (see Jones 2012). International institutions are also created to promote justice, like the International Court. It is important to consider what values and practices are central to various national and international institutions, as well as what human needs, if any[5], these institutions were created to address.

Many institutions are created to meet some need(s), but it is important to note that they also "shape our inner experience" (Eagleton 2011, p. 95) and behavior.[6] That is, institutions are not merely instrumental. Millennia ago, Aristotle recognized this when he argued that the institutions of the polis should promote virtues necessary for citizenship. As this view suggests, institutions can promote virtues or vices. The questions are: what kind of subjects do institutions produce and to what ends? The various institutions associated with neoliberal capitalism shape persons wherein they become entrepreneurial-consumer subjects preoccupied with unlimited desire, accumulation, and profit. Democratic institutions shape subjectivity such that individuals believe they have a voice, a right to vote—political agency. When we reflect on the institutions in which we participate, we can ask ourselves how they shape us, for good or ill. When we turn to national and international institutions, we investigate how they shape subjectivity and, given the threats of militarism, capitalism, and global warming, consider whether the subjectivities formed promote cooperation toward the common good of all human beings.

My third comment has to do with qualifications. One of the hats I wear is that of pastoral theologian, which would indicate my lack of qualifications vis-à-vis discussing international relations and institutions. To be sure, numerous people are more qualified because of their education and expertise in this arena. I, of course, will rely on a number of them. That said, while I depend on care ethicists who have explored this topic, I believe as an individual inhabitant of the earth and a pastoral theologian concerned about alleviating, whenever possible, human suffering, I should enter this conversation, as other pastoral theologians have (Rumscheidt 1998). We all have a stake in and responsibility for the future of our children (and children of other peoples) and our children's children. We all have a stake in our home, our world.

Finally, I would like to say that the dire realities of global warming or what Kolbert (2014) calls the Anthropocene Era, reveal that we can no longer, though many do, hold the illusion that our actions are confined to my little tract of land, the air I breathe in my city, the water I drink in my town. We can no longer assess local, state, and national institutions in terms of our part of the globe. For instance, our political and military institutions may provide security for most American citizens, yet these institutions create insecurity and harm for other peoples, including poor persons and people of color in the United States. Certainly, we can continue to operate as myopic creatures preoccupied by our specific habitats and local politics (city, state, nation), but doing so will insure the destruction of the habitat. Politics may be local, but local politics is also international. We have only one world, one habitat. There are no other worlds to escape to. This is why national and international relations becomes critical in any conversation about political philosophy and political theology.

CARE AND INTERNATIONAL RELATIONS

Let me state again that national and international institutions cannot care, though they can foster the conditions that facilitate individuals to recognize and treat Others as persons. Put another way, institutions can shape subjectivity such that citizens have the motivation, knowledge, skills, and resources to care for themselves and others. The Red Cross, FEMA (Federal Emergency Management Agency), and the UN's Office for the Coordination of Humanitarian Affairs are just a few national and/or international institutions that respond to needs of individuals, families, and communities that have suffered from natural and human-made disasters. They establish procedures, rules, and expectations their members follow to provide aid for those in need. In other words, these *institutions* do not recognize and respond to the needs of particular people. Rather, the individual members of these organizations care for those they are charged to aid.

Of course, individuals within these organizations may deliberately or inadvertently interfere with the institution's aim of helping people. An institution may not have clear or relevant policies and procedures to guide members. Members may have inadequate knowledge, skills, and motivations to provide resources to people in need. Leaders may be inept. Recall state and national governments' responses to Hurricane Katrina. There were examples of multiple failures of leadership, resulting in insufficient responses to the needs of victims of the disaster, especially poor and black residents of New Orleans. It was not simply a failure of leaders in various institutions. The failures demonstrated how racism and class can undermine individual and institutional responses to disasters. Moreover, what Katrina and other disasters demonstrate is that the institutions of daily life can fail to provide or strengthen the infrastructure needed to withstand the worst of the storms, which was seen in the failure to distribute funds over the years to strengthen the levees. There are four points here. First, while institutions possess the aims and resources to aid people, they can have members who are not skilled or lack necessary knowledge to help victims care for themselves and others. Second, aid institutions, like FEMA, can confront organizations that have contributed to the disaster or have taken advantage of the disaster to advance their agendas (Klein 2007). Third, institutions that are created to facilitate persons working together to provide resources for affected individuals, families, and communities to care for themselves and others often fall short because of inadequate policies and procedures. This is not a reason to despair, but rather a reason to assess rigorously institutions vis-à-vis how they actually aid the common good. Fourth, disasters often reveal the underlying failures of institutions of daily life to provide resources for people to care for themselves and others. For instance, class and race are frequent factors, not simply with regard to disaster response, but in how poor communities, families, and individuals fare before the disaster.

Given this beginning, let me turn to discussing ways we can understand the notion of care vis-à-vis international institutions and relations. First of all, when considering international relations and institutions, one must have a framework of principles and values that can be used to assess practices and results. Fiona Robinson (1999) argues,

> An ethics of care is not about the application of a universal principle ("We must care about all others.") nor is it about a sentimental ideal ("A more caring world is a better world."). Rather, it is a starting point for transforming the values and practices of international society; thus, it requires an examination of the contexts in which caring does or does not take place and a commitment to the creation of more humanly responsive institutions. (pp. 47–48)

Robinson is not dismissing the importance or necessity of universal principles or ideals. Instead, she contends that the starting point must be a critical analysis of particular contexts and the international institutions created to address the material and psychosocial needs of persons, families, and communities.

Of course, engaging in international relations and the creation of international institutions would require, it seems to me, working toward some agreement about the norms, values, and criteria for evaluating international relations and institutions. For example, the UN Charter on Human Rights outlines principles and values that have to do with the recognition of the rights of persons, which could be understood in terms of a universal principle of care—recognizing and treating individuals as persons. Nations (and their institutions) that signed the Charter and the UN's institutions can be evaluated in terms of how they abide by these principles, given particular national and international contexts and relations. Organizations such as Human Rights Watch and Amnesty International critically assess national and international contexts largely based on universal principles and rights.

It is a mistake, in my view, to see an international agreement such as the UN's Universal Declaration of Human Rights simply in terms of "rights." This document provides a hermeneutical lens for evaluating national and international contexts and institutions in terms of care. Consider that Article 6 states, "Everyone has the right to recognition everywhere as a person before the law." The law and all legal institutions must establish and support the view that all human beings are persons, regardless of the country in which they reside (Article 2). As noted in chapter 1, this is the basis not simply of rights, but of acts of care. Granted, this can raise all sorts of legal, philosophical, and theological disputes about what exactly a person is. Moreover, we know that there are violations of this principle even in so-called established democratic nations that have signed the Charter and have agreed to abide by it. Nevertheless, this basic principle is established and can be used to assess whether national and international institutions are actually living this out.

While recognition of individuals as persons is a basic principle and ideal of this Charter, there are more specific statements regarding what this entails. Article 22 reads: Everyone, as a member of society, has the *right to social security* and is entitled to realization, through national effort and international cooperation and in accordance with the organization and resources of each State, of the economic, social and cultural rights indispensable for his dignity and the free *development of his personality* (emphasis mine). My interpretation of this article is that states and their institutions need to provide a level of social, cultural, and economic stability so that individuals can survive and, more importantly, flourish. Add to this the recognition of the importance of leisure for the well-being of individuals in Article 24, which requires limiting the number of work hours and insuring paid holidays. Moving to Article 25, we read that all human beings have a right to a standard of living necessary for physical health and well-being for him/herself and his/her family. Article 26 upholds the right to education and Article 27 states that individuals have a right to share in the public goods of society. These articles clearly demonstrate the necessity of national and international organizations to care for those who are residents (not just citizens) of their respective territories. Put another way, the document establishes universal principles for the survival and flourishing of human beings and these principles can be used as a critical hermeneutic for evaluating national and international organizations in terms of both rights and care.

Let me take a little detour to elaborate on a critical hermeneutic vis-à-vis institutions and international relations regarding care. Consider the United States and its Constitution. The three branches of government were created to establish and enforce the principles and rights embedded in the Constitution. Moreover, local and state governments as well as nongovernment institutions are to follow these as well. Put another way, government institutions are positive creations in the ideal sense because they are to insure these rights are lived out. Other institutions, like corporations, can pursue other principles, like profit, though they are not to violate constitutional rights. Corporations fulfill the principles of the Constitution negatively in that they need not actively promote these rights, but they must not violate them. I add here that local, state, and national governments operate (ideally) in light of the principles of democracy. Other institutions, like most corporations,[7] are not democratic and, therefore, do not contribute to living out democratic principles and values. Of course, these negative institutions are ideally not to undermine the democratic principles of the larger society, though, of course, in a neoliberal capitalist society, the institutions of business are allied with state and national governments, which clearly undermines democracy (Reich 2007; Stiglitz 2012, 2015). The point of this detour is to indicate that the principles and rights of the Constitution, if they are to have concrete effects, must permeate society at the local, state, and national levels, whether positively or negatively. It is, therefore, not sufficient simply to have a hermeneutic framework to critique institutions. The Constitution will have little meaning if its principles and rights are not promoted, lived out, and enforced by government and nongovernment institutions, from towns to national government. In short, any critical hermeneutic emerges out of and in relation to institutions that embody and promote principles of care.

Let's return to the UN Charter. When we consider the Charter on Human Rights, we find that while many nations have signed it, they do not necessarily have national and local institutions that positively or negatively abide and enforce these principles. One might point out that there is an International Court of Justice, but it has little authority and effect on nation-states or locales. The challenge is not simply to get countries to sign the Charter, but to create national and international institutions that will work to achieve the values and principles the Charter enshrines. More specifically, the Charter would be a more realistic evaluative hermeneutical framework for assessing intuitions and practices on whether they contribute to caring activities (and justice) if the Charter's principles were embedded in local and state institutions of the countries that signed the Charter.

Focusing on the UN Charter is meant to suggest that there can be near universal agreements regarding rights and care or well-being. Naturally, the Charter need not be the only international agreement that can serve as a critical hermeneutic vis-à-vis care. There are, for instance, global agreements regarding climate change, which can be understood as concern for the earth and its residents. I add here one principle to this discussion of a critical hermeneutic and that is the least of these. John Paul Sartre, an existential philosopher, asked, "why not decide every situation by asking how it looks to 'the eyes of the least favored', or to 'those treated the most unjustly?'" (in Bakewell 2016, p. 271). Similarly, Simone Weil (1952) believed that "patriotism inspired by compassion gives the poorest part of the population a privileged moral position" (p. 173). If poor people are provided the resources to survive and thrive, then we can be assured that people who are better off will be doing well. If individuals who are unjustly treated are then treated justly, we can expect that those who previously were treated justly would continue to be given what they are due. Care and justice are not zero-sum games.

Naturally, there will be contestations as to what "the least of these" means and to whom it applies. That said, I am confident that the task is not too difficult. The least of these are people who are homeless, people who experience food insecurity (or worse), people underemployed, people living in unsafe neighborhoods and unsafe housing, people who do not have access to a good education, people who have little or no access to health care, people who have no voice in the echelons of government and business. If we consider these individuals, we can work to insure that they have a voice about the necessary resources to care for themselves and their families.

This principle can be used at local, state, and national levels. Decent cities, states, and societies provide resources for persons who are on the lower rungs of the economic order. We can also include this principle at the level of international relations. The Global North has for centuries exploited the Global South. International relations were/are guided by those with power to extract resources from weaker nations. The metropoles of Europe and the United States grew wealthy at the expense of other nations. Of course, we can continue these kinds of international relations, but the cost to the planet and to billions of people from poorer or less well-developed nations are and will be enormous.[8] Lest one think that this is merely an issue of justice, I would point out that it is of global interest that poorer countries obtain resources such that they participate in addressing global climate change and its consequences. It is a matter of care.

There are numerous obstacles to creating local, state, and international institutions that address care and rights. Perhaps the biggest obstacles are nation-states. The rise of nation-states has been attributed to the treaties of Westphalia (1648) and this rise has accompanied the idea of national sovereignty and national identity. Most nations do not want to cede sovereignty to international organizations like the World Court, let alone any hint of international organizations that would involve enforcement. For powerful nations, like the United States, sovereignty is generally seen as a zero-sum game, which it is not. The thinking is that one either has or does not have sovereignty, which is why the United States has repeatedly refused to adhere to the International Court whenever the ruling has gone against the United States. One memorable example is the International Court of Justice's (ICJ) decision against the United States regarding its involvement in human rights abuses in Nicaragua in the 1980s. The United States rejected the Court's rulings, citing the sacrosanct sovereignty of the United States. This was not a decision simply about not taking responsibility and refusing to pay billions in reparations. It was primarily about the United States retaining the sovereign power associated with being an imperial nation. It is important also to point out that the United States' rejection of the ICJ accompanied the support of U.S. citizens who also resist ceding any sovereignty because they believe it undermines their sense of identity as Americans. So, even though the UN Charter possesses principles and values that parallel those embodied in the U.S. Constitution, there is neither effort to create local, state, and national institutions that will seek to live these out, nor a willingness to cede a little sovereignty to international institutions.

Ironically, we can also take a page from the United States to show that ceding some sovereignty can be beneficial for citizens. The fifty states all have some degree of sovereignty in conducting their affairs. They have their own police forces, National Guard, judicial institutions, democratic institutions (local and state elections), and budgets. Many states also conduct trade relations with other nations. The citizens of these states pay both state and federal taxes, which ideally are aimed at the common good of all citizens. Naturally, there are tensions and conflicts between states and the federal government, which can be understood as arising from the issue of sovereignty. These are often decided by the courts, but they can also be decided at the ballot box or by constitutional amendments. A similar arrangement is found in the European Union wherein members cede some sovereignty for the sake of cooperation. It is not inconceivable to extend this to the world where all nations cede some sovereignty for the greater good, but also for their own good. A century ago, this idea might have been simply a thought experiment, if not a naïve hope. But the dangers of global warming are collective. They are local and universal. This means that the common good is no longer a concept reserved simply and solely for locales and states. It is universal. If nations do not hand over some of their sovereignty, I am confident that humanity will have a diminished chance of survival. Put another way, if care is to have any real meaning and force in international relations, nations will have to cede some sovereignty to international bodies—organizations created to facilitate the distribution of resources so that individuals, families, and communities are able to obtain the necessary goods to survive and thrive.

Of course, there is another significant obstacle to the possibility of creating global institutions that live out, promote, and enforce principles and practices of care. Global capitalism comprises numerous local, state, national, and international institutions that live out the principles of capitalism (e.g., profit and market expansions). These institutions engage in and enforce the rules of the game, while also shaping subjectivity. As discussed in chapter 5, the institutions of neoliberal capitalism, which include state institutions, form subjects into entrepreneurial-consumer subjects. For those who believe that there cannot be a universal story and identity, they need only consider the hegemonic grasp capitalism has on countries throughout the world. To be sure, capitalism takes many forms (e.g., China's dictatorship, Europe's mix of social concerns, and the United States' apotheosis of neoliberalism), which does not negate the diversity of cultures. However, capitalism is supported and enforced by local, state, national, and international organizations, shaping subjectivity, perceptions, and behaviors. As I argued previously, the institutions of capitalism undermine care. Indeed, when care takes place, it occurs despite capitalism and its institutions.

This is not to suggest that international relations do not have institutions that clearly support care, but that global capitalism serves as a significant impediment to global and local care, because it slavishly focuses on market principles. Consider corporations as institutions at the local and national levels. Corporations play by market values and rules and are not interested in the distribution of resources to enable persons to care for themselves and others. Certainly, corporations are interested in distribution, but this has nothing to do with care and everything to do with profit, productivity, market expansion, and so on. Distribution is not guided by the needs of persons, but by the desires and the demands of the market. One can point to corporations that are involved in helping their local communities, as well as national and international issues related to care. First of all, these are the exception and not the rule. Second, there is nothing in capitalism that would motivate corporations to act in this way, except that 1) it is good for publicity and profit and/ or 2) the leaders are operating out of another symbol system and its mores. International organizations and relations that operate out of principles associated with care and justice are dwarfed by the institutions of global capitalism. International relations, in brief, are largely about and for business.

Someone might say that this is realpolitik and that it is naïve to consider international relations in terms of care. Moreover, nations need to be concerned about international business relations if they are to care for their own people. I have two responses. First, if we continue to conduct business as usual, and by this I mean international relations relentlessly promoting global capitalism and its institutions, then there is little hope that international relations will be able to handle climate change and its effects. It is analogous to people on the Titanic selling their wares, competing for market share, and obtaining profit while the ship is sinking. Perhaps, if asked, a Titanic entrepreneur might say, "Well, it is going down anyway, so why not make some money?" Naturally, if this were true, we would see the tragedy and sheer madness of this way of being, but many people cannot see how capitalism and its institutions are contributing to the sinking of our world. Second, it is true that capitalism has enriched some nations, which enables its better-off citizens to care for their survival and flourishing needs. As discussed in chapters 5 and 6, this is at the expense of poorer citizens and countries. Capitalism is not very effective at distributing resources (or promoting the common good and care of others) so that most, if not all, citizens can care for themselves and others.

There are alternatives to capitalism and capitalistic organizations—alternatives that involve institutions that would abide by principles that involve care and the common good. I have pointed to these briefly in earlier chapters. There are also countries in Europe that mitigate some of the effects of capitalism through protections and social policies that help citizens care for themselves and others. Previous to the neoliberal takeover of the U.S. government, Keynesian-style capitalism provided some relief to poor and working-class persons by instituting financial protections, support for unions, and some degree of redistribution money. These situations are not alternatives to capitalism, but they are examples of nations trying to tame the sociopathic and irrational tendencies of capitalism. Global capitalism is incredibly destructive to the environment and to poor persons and, therefore, it must be strictly regulated and replaced by alternatives if care and the common good for poor and working-class people throughout the world are to be even partially realized.

A related obstacle to nations working together vis-à-vis care is the militarism of powerful nations. Militarism is closely connected to capitalism in the sense of extending markets through military and paramilitary means (Butler 1935; Zinn 1998). The United States, for example, is the largest supplier of military hardware and training in the world. Its imperial reach spans the globe and has been used to expand its economic power (LaMothe 2007, 2013). China and Russia are also significant military powers that respond to the military power of the United States. Martin Luther King Jr. (1998) remarked in his Riverside speech that the Vietnam "war is the enemy of the poor" (p. 337). It is not just war itself; it also involves preparations for war. Trillions of dollars have gone into the machinery of war and other national security industries. As Major General Smedley Butler (1935) recognized later in his career, war and the preparation for war are great for big business, but do little in the way of aiding the poor. Put another way, the militarism of the United States and other powerful nations does not and cannot contribute to the common good of all persons, let alone the common good of their respective citizens. This last clause is only partly true. The militarism of the United States has gone a long way toward enriching the country, from slavery to taking land from native peoples to its numerous wars and military interventions to advance its economic power. Like all imperial powers in history, most of the benefits go to the elites of the metropole, though one could argue people on the lower classes benefit as well. But, to finance armies, resources must be taken from the populace and these resources cannot be used to help people who are poor care for themselves and others. In short, the institutions of militarism and capitalism not only overlook the needs of the least of these, whether "these" are individuals, groups, or nations, but also contribute to the suffering of less affluent and less powerful folk.

Narrow preoccupation with national sovereignty, militarism, and capitalism undermine care and the common good, especially when we consider international relations. Together they make finding adequate solutions to poverty untenable, they increase poverty globally. Moreover, as we consider the realities of climate change, both militarism and capitalism, if they are not diminished,[9] will undermine hope for humanity's survival.

In terms of international relations, while it is an uphill battle to address the ills created by the institutions of capitalism and militarism, there are institutions, like the United Nations, that are guided by principles that promote care and justice for all human beings. To be sure, it is a steep challenge to establish local, state, and national institutions that will, positively and negatively, work to live out, or at least not undermine, these values. Institutions that are created to live out and enforce rights associated with justice and care will more likely shape the subjectivity of citizens in positive ways, which will not eradicate the influences of greed, envy, and other vices that undermine care and justice. Nevertheless, as noted above, institutions are not merely instrumental, they also shape subjectivity, which enables them to carry out their functions and live out their principles.

International relations comprise an intricate web of institutions representing diverse national interests. Most nations have signed the UN Charter on Human Rights, which illustrates the possibility of having universal principles serve as ideals vis-à-vis care (and justice). While there are numerous challenges to living up to ideals that promote care and the universal common good, it should not deter persons from creating institutions and practices that are aimed at providing resources (e.g., healthcare, adequate food and water, education, infrastructure, and arts) for individuals, families, and communities to care for their and others' survival and flourishing needs. This is not a utopian view, because failure to work toward local and universal care (and justice) for human beings and the earth will almost certainly result in the extinction of humanity.

FAITH AND INTERNATIONAL RELATIONS

An interesting passage in William James' work, *The Will to Believe*, points to the intersection of cooperation and faith. James (1984) writes:

> A social organism of any sort whatever, large or small, is what it is because each member proceeds to his own duty with a trust that the other members will simultaneously do theirs. Wherever a desired result is achieved by the co-operation of many independent persons, its existence as a fact is a pure consequence of the precursive faith on one another of those immediately concerned. A government, an army, a commercial system, a ship, a college athletic team, all exist on this condition, without which not only is nothing achieved, but nothing is even attempted. . . . There are, then, cases where a fact cannot come at all unless a preliminary faith exists in its coming. (p. 322)

This preliminary faith founds cooperation toward shared aims, purposes, and functions, whether we are talking about local, state, national, or international organizations. In this section, I take up the issue of faith as it refers to international relations and the idea of care.

I have argued that care is founded on recognizing and treating Others as persons. In situations of direct relations, this is usually associated with mutual-personal faith relations. When we consider something as complex as international relations and their institutions, we find that mutual-personal faith cannot exist between national institutions conducting international relations. Institutions are not persons. Yes, particular individuals representing their respective nations may embody mutual-personal faith, but this is the exception and not the rule. Moreover, representatives are more likely to manifest strong trust in and loyalty to their respective institutions and nations.

If we cannot expect international relations to reflect mutual-personal faith, then what kind of faith relation is manifested? Consider international relations in terms of countries joining regional organizations (e.g., Organization of American States [OAS], South East Asia Treaty Organization [SEATO]) and global organizations (e.g., United Nations, Group of Eight [G7]). These international treaties and organizations establish agreed-upon principles and rules by which they operate, as well as rules to resolve specific disputes when they arise. Each organization facilitates cooperation and a contractual-functional faith. This contractual-functional faith is conditional, wherein trust and loyalty exist as long as the participants abide by the treaties. "Trust but verify," to recall Ronald Reagan's comment about a nuclear arms treaty with the Soviet Union. There is, then, a kind of international faith and cooperation when nations abide by agreed-upon rules.

Regional and international forms of cooperation are usually evaluated in terms of their aims, functions, and effects that are particular to the treaty. The North Atlantic Treaty Organization (NATO), for instance, aims and functions to provide security for European nations and the United States. This is mostly accurate in that NATO has been a significant factor in maintaining security in Europe. By "mostly," I am suggesting the reality is a bit more complicated. The functional-contractual faith manifested in NATO also is connected to the deep distrust between NATO countries and the Soviet Bloc. Indeed, NATO was a player in the arms race. Moreover, with the demise of the Soviet Union, NATO has expanded into Eastern European countries, which has heightened Russia's concern and led, in part, to further militarization of the region, as well as military conflict. Security is provided, but the international institution, in one sense, fosters insecurity. There are also international organizations like the G7 (or G8), which function to assess and promote international economic relations and agreements. This it does, but the benefits tend to accrue for countries of the G7 and not poorer nations. The Paris Climate Treaty is aimed at reducing pollution that contributes to global warming, which ideally will result in a habitable earth. Many signatories are working toward providing clean energy, with some countries doing so more effectively than others. The long-term effects of these actions are not clearly known, but if no cooperation occurs, we can be sure that millions, if not billions of persons, will not have the resources of habitat to survive. All of this is to say that various international relations represent contractual-functional faith that is often ambiguous in its effects, even when it appears to succeed in its function and aims.

While nations have cooperated with other nations, manifesting a kind of contractual-functional faith between national and international institutions, they can also be evaluated in terms of how and whether they contribute to care of persons regionally and globally. An objection may arise regarding international (and regional) relations and agreements regarding trade. Someone might argue that these treaties need to be evaluated solely in terms of economic benefits, because the treaties are contractually and functionally economic. I have no qualms about this, as long as economics (or security) is not the sole criterion of efficacy. International economic agreements and cooperation need to be evaluated in terms of care and contribution to the common good. *Cui bono?* Agreements by the G7 benefit those member countries who have found ways to cooperate to further their economic ends. If we consider who benefits within those countries, it is the capitalist class. Poorer nations and people (the least of these) of the individual countries in the G7 do not benefit when the wealthy and corporations get richer. These economic international agreements and their resulting contractual-functional faiths can be evaluated in terms of economic criteria, but to do so is to enter into a willed state of ignorance or naiveté, at best, and a deliberate sociopathic cruelty, at worse.

This is not to say that international economic cooperation is all bad. Wealth is produced and millions of people benefit, but we must also point out that billions of people do not. While this suggests ambiguity vis-à-vis many international economic agreements, this does not mean we should simply shrug our shoulders and carry on. In my view, we should evaluate the various international economic agreements and their contractual-functional forms of faith in terms of whether they are effectively attending to the common good and providing resources for people to care for their survival and flourishing needs, while also caring for others.

Let's move from international economic relations to consider the level of contractual-functional cooperation among numerous nations providing relief during national and regional disasters. In 2004 an earthquake unleashed a series of deadly tsunamis in the Indian Ocean, killing over 230,000 people and devastating coastal cities, towns, and villages. Numerous nations and international organizations responded immediately to provide aid to the survivors, as well as clean up. Once the emergency was over, donor nations gathered to help countries rebuild. International institutions, representing many nations, cooperated to attend to the diverse needs of people impacted by the tsunami. There were some failures and miscommunications, but the overall aim and function of these international responses were to provide resources so that people could survive and eventually thrive. It is wonderful when we see this level of international cooperation, though unfortunate it takes a terrible tragedy to ignite an international contractual-functional faith that is focused primarily on care of individuals, families, and communities.

Of course, it is easy, if not obvious, to use the criteria of care when considering international institutions that cooperate to provide resources during times of natural and human-made disasters. A friendly critic, then, may simply say the criteria of care with regard to contractual-functional faith are not applicable to international relations vis-à-vis other contexts (such as economic treaties and arms treaties), because they operate out of very different functional-contractual faiths. Consider the complex international engagement involving Israel and Palestine. The impasse between these two countries has existed for decades, and nations have taken sides, contributing to deep distrust. Despite some agreements, the overall relation between these two peoples is best characterized as enmity. It seems that these two peoples and their respective advocates are a long way from developing a functional-contractual faith. The Israelis, because of their concern about security, have enacted numerous measures that make life difficult for most Palestinians. Of course, Israel is a tremendously more powerful state than Palestine and can impose its will, which it does frequently and violently. After decades of being treated poorly, to say the least, after repeated violations of international agreements regarding building in disputed territories, and bearing much more devastation than Israel, it is not surprising that Palestinians do not trust Israel. It is a vicious cycle of violence and distrust, resulting in the near absence of functional-contractual faith and cooperation. The first step toward any semblance of trust will be, I believe, functional-contractual agreements where the more powerful party (Israel) will agree to recognize the needs of the Palestinian people and provide or enable resources for them to care for themselves and Others. Israel resists these small steps because of security concerns, citing Hamas' doublespeak about Israel's existence. That said, the very fact of Israel's overwhelming strength should provide some confidence that it exists and will continue to exist. This confidence based on an obvious reality could motivate them to take small steps in providing or facilitating the movement of resources for Palestinians to thrive. Any beneficial functional-contractual faith between these two peoples cannot take place or grow if there is not some small demonstration of care, which in my view is the responsibility of the more powerful nation.

My point here is that international relations involve diverse kinds of functional-contractual faiths; while they are typically evaluated in terms of agreed-upon aims and functions, they can also be assessed in terms of care. How do these treaties or agreements enhance cooperation and attend to the needs of the people of the nations involved? To what degree do international agreements facilitate or hinder the common good of their respective nations and the common good of all peoples? When nations cooperate in such a way that all their citizens benefit, the trust between nations deepens. The functional-contractual faith between the United States and Canada, for instance, reflects a deep and abiding trust, wherein numerous institutions are engaged in cooperative relations locally, nationally, and internationally. In general, citizens of both countries possess some level of care about and trust in the other country's citizens. When the common good and the needs of the other country's citizens are taken into account, international relations vis-à-vis functional-contractual faith deepen.

Contractual-functional faiths between and among nations and their respective institutions can be tied to principles that support and advance international cooperation, as well as mutual-personal faith, care, and the common good. What is necessary as well is the development of institutions that are able to handle conflicts and disruptions in contractual-functional faith. Disruptions and conflicts are inevitable in mutual-personal relations and in international relations. The challenge is how institutions are created to deal with this. In simple terms, disruptions in contractual-functional faiths between nations require mending so that cooperation can be restored. This necessitates some ceding of sovereignty. Nations must be willing to abide by not only shared principles that guide international cooperation, but also adjudications handed down by international institutions that are constructed to attend to disputes between nations. What has previously occurred in history and continues mostly today is the rule of more powerful nations and their institutions over smaller, weaker nations. "Might makes right" has been the rule of the day, meaning that disputes have been handled by and in favor of more powerful nations. To be sure, this is a kind of enforced contractual-functional relationship, not unlike Hobbes' Leviathan at the international level. But in this scenario, the settlement of conflicts and disputes does not foster greater trust, but only more wariness of the powerful nation(s). The Leviathan connotes power, but a power that supports discord.

INTERNATIONAL RELATIONS AND POWER

I suspect that when people think about nations and international relations with regard to power two ideas spring to mind. The first is that power is exercised by a strong man/woman. We frequently hear or read that the president of the United States is the most powerful man in the world. A tyrant like Stalin is seen as nearly all-powerful. The second common idea is that power resides in and is exercised by particular political, economic, and military institutions, using coercion, force, and violence to achieve their aims. These beliefs take on an air of reality, of unquestionable fact, yet they are, in part, mistaken beliefs.

To explain how these beliefs are illusions, recall that in chapter 3 I used Hannah Arendt's definition of power vis-à-vis the polis as people speaking and acting together. President Trump is the most powerful man in the world because 1) of the Constitution and other legal documents, which were constructed by people speaking and acting together and 2) citizens speaking and acting together who believe in and support him. We know this is true because if a president's approval rating falls to 10percent, then his "power" is greatly diminished. A positive example is President Franklin Roosevelt's first year in office where he enjoyed a great deal of popular support and, as a result, was able to push through New Deal legislation. Tyrants, who are not popular, require sufficient numbers of people speaking and acting together so that he can retain power through coercion and terror. Power does not reside in the tyrant alone, but in those who speak and act together to extend his rule.

One may agree with this, yet say that the United States is the most powerful country in the world. Or perhaps a similar claim is that the United States possesses the most powerful military in the world. On the one hand, this is true, but only partially true. The military is comprised of a number of different institutions (e.g., Army, Navy, and Air Force) and these organizations are comprised of people speaking and acting together to carry out the aims of the institution—aims that are grounded in the Constitution and other legal edicts. Add to this the fact that military institutions are dependent on political institutions not only for their legitimacy, but also for the funding needed to fulfill their mission. Other economic institutions are necessary as well. The military and national security industrial complexes are comprised of civilian and paramilitary organizations that directly support the military's mission. And then there are economic institutions, like corporations that, as Major General Butler (1935) pointed out, support the use of the military to advance the economic aims of the corporations. All of these institutions comprise people speaking and acting together, all of which lend support to the military. Finally, citizens who speak and act together support the military, which is necessary for the military's legitimacy and for the resources it needs to carry out their missions. All of this is to say that power does not reside simply and solely in the institution.

The focus so far has been on national leaders and institutions. Let's move to an international institution, like the International Monetary Fund (IMF), which is considered to be a powerful institution, especially by nation-states that are poor and dependent on international assistance (Harvey 2005; Jones 2012). The United States and its client-states cooperated to create this international institution, ostensibly to stabilize markets and to assist economic development in Third World nations.[10] The IMF, which comprises numerous individuals speaking and acting together to achieve the aims of the organization, is powerful precisely because it is supported by powerful and wealthy nations and their banking institutions. As a result, the IMF can use economic coercion to force poor countries to accept and implement economic policies and programs that the IMF deems to be beneficial. Other international organizations demonstrate a lack of power. For instance, the United Nations' International Court of Justice (ICJ) is an institution created to adjudicate disputes between UN members and to prosecute war criminals. Like any institution, the ICJ employs workers who speak and act together to carry out its aims. However, this international body has very little power, because the Court is not connected to national or international institutions that enforce its rulings. Nations, like the United States, can easily ignore the Court's rulings. There are two points here. First, national and international institutions comprise persons speaking and acting together to achieve its purposes. If an institution has difficulty finding members or is comprised of individuals lacking skill and motivation, then it will not be effective in achieving its aims. Its "power" will be diminished. Second, national and international institutions are powerful to the extent that they are connected to and supported by other organizations that assist in achieving the institution's mission.

A concern may be raised about individuals and groups of people who experience significant oppression within their country and around the world. Am I saying that they are not victims—persons lacking agency and power? Are these groups capable of exercising power—nationally and internationally? Let's consider the suffering of Jews in Germany and in other European nations before and during World War II. Enough Germans created Nazi institutions that sought to capture, exploit, and annihilate Jews. These institutions could not have achieved their aims without other institutions cooperating and without the overt or tacit support of German citizens.[11] It is important to mention the complicity of Allied institutions. Given all of this, one recognizes that Jews speaking and acting together (as a people and its institutions) faced incredible odds and many found ways to resist. I add here that while it is important to put on trial individuals responsible for participating in the Holocaust (e.g., Eichmann), institutions like the SS comprised people speaking and acting together to support, directly or indirectly, the state's policies of extermination. Moreover, many German citizens, who had absolutely no direct role in the Holocaust, spoke and acted together to support the state. In this, they exercised power that helped facilitate the state's use of violence toward Jews. International institutions were complicit in the sense of having persons in these institutions who had knowledge of what was taking place and yet did not speak and act together to confront the Nazis and to liberate Jews. This said, there were organizations and individuals (e.g., Raoul Wallenberg) working within national institutions to save Jews.

This discussion is meant to clarify the notion of power in terms of international relations. As indicated above, international relations are conducted through institutions, whether they are related to individual states or created by nations to facilitate economic, political, juridical, and/or military cooperation. Nations may cooperate (exhibiting contractual-functional faith) to create institutions that coerce or force other nations to adopt economic rules. As noted above, a group of nations can create institutions that provide military security (e.g., NATO). More positive examples of exercising power vis-à-vis international relations are joint scientific ventures (e.g., Russia and NASA), relief efforts (e.g., Haiti earthquake), and educational exchanges.

The exercise of power in international relations has tended to be justified and evaluated according to the needs and desires of individual nations or groups of allied nations (e.g., collective security), yet it is not always clear that the exercise of power, whether that is unilateral or by a group of nations, is guided by the common good of the individual nation using its power unilaterally or cooperating with other nations. Let's ponder a brief illustration of unilateral exercise of power. In the 19th century, the United States fabricated the notions of Manifest Destiny and the Monroe Doctrine to justify the use of economic, political, and military power to expand its territory and influence in this hemisphere. The exercise of U.S. power was supported by state and business institutions, as well as by the majority of the citizenry. Moreover, some national governments, which had close business and military ties to the United States, exercised power locally in support of U.S. aims (e.g., Cuban dictator Fulgencio Batista, Nicaraguan dictator Anastasio Somoza). While all nations and their institutions tend to provide "good" reasons for the exercise of power, more often than not, the exercise of power befits the more powerful state institutions and certain persons and nongovernmental organizations. In other words, the unilateral actions of the United States in the 19th century with regard to countries in this hemisphere were not conducted for the common good of U.S. citizens and clearly not for the common good of citizens in those nations that were the recipients of U.S. involvement. For example, the United States acquired Cuba and the Philippines after the Spanish American War, shattering the hopes of liberation and freedom harbored by Cubans and Filipinos who were fighting their previous colonial master (Zinn 2005). The United States, through military and political force, garnered lands and resources. They did this by forcing the Cuban government to adopt the Platt Amendment, whereby the United States was able to "purchase" over "1,900,000 acres of land for about 20 cents an acre," and by 1909, U.S. companies, like Bethlehem Steel, controlled "at least 80 percent of the export of Cuba's minerals" (p. 310). In terms of international relations, the United States unilaterally used military, economic, political, and social institutions to exert power, which benefited, first, corporations and, second, some American citizens. This exercise of power was not for the common good of U.S. citizens and most certainly not for Cuban citizens.

There are many occasions when nations cooperate in contractual-functional ways in the exercise of shared power, the effects of which are often ambiguous with regard to the common good. I mentioned above the creation of NATO after World War II as an example of international relations wherein select countries agreed to cooperate for common security. NATO exhibits a shared contractual-functional form of faith that benefits (measured in terms of security and economic ties) the common good of multiple nations and their peoples. Since the fall of the Soviet Union, NATO has expanded into states that previously were part of the Warsaw Pact. This over-reach heightened Russia's concerns, leading, in part, to military interventions in Georgia, Crimea, and the Ukraine. Here we see an international organization (NATO) exercising power on the international stage that has positive benefits for its peoples, but does not benefit Russians.

Someone might say that the aims of NATO have nothing to do with the common good of Russia and its citizens. Therefore, we must evaluate the success of NATO in terms of the aims of the treaty, as mentioned above. I am arguing that this is only half the story. The cooperative exercise of power may be beneficial to some nations, while detrimental to others. The expansion of NATO destabilized the region by ignoring Russian concerns and warnings and, in the process, undermined the very aims of NATO in the sense of being a defensive organization aimed at providing collective security. The point here is that nations that cooperate in the exercise of power need to consider the concerns and needs of nations and their peoples excluded from the treaty. If the world is our home, we need to consider how the exercise of power impacts all of us.

Let me return to the example of nations agreeing to cooperate around economic treaties. The G8 or G7 is comprised of the most powerful economic nations. From the perspective of trade, these nations have found ways to exercise economic power that, in general, is said to benefit the citizens of their respective countries. To some degree this is true, if we measure success in overall economic terms. Yet, if we consider the economic realities of the most powerful G7 member, the United States, we discover that the distribution of income and wealth is skewed to the top 5 percent (Piketty 2014).[12] These economic arrangements are not for the common good and cannot be because the distribution of resources and wealth is profoundly distorted. Put another way, millions of people do not have access to sufficient resources to care for themselves and others; I add here that it is not entirely clear that regional or global cooperation vis-à-vis neoliberal capitalism benefits the majority of citizens of the countries entering into treaties or those of nations who are not signatories. NAFTA (North American Free Trade Agreement) and the TPP (Trans-Pacific Partnership) are neither constructed in terms of the common good of the respective signatories nor the common good of the other countries, which is not to say that some people (and many corporations) from these signatory nations have not benefited.

In the 20th century, as noted above, nations spoke and acted together to create the United Nations. Even though the most powerful nations had (and have) a greater voice in its creation, other nations agreed to participate and to sign the UN Charter. During the last twenty-six years, most nations have gathered to create and sign global treaties on climate change (e.g., United Nations Framework Convention on Climate Change, Kyoto Protocol, Paris Climate Agreement). While there continue to be many problems with these treaties, overall they signify nations and other institutions speaking and acting together for security, stability, and the preservation of earth's habitat.

Ideally, one could argue that the UN Charter and climate treaties are aimed at the common good of all human beings, though in practice all countries fall short in varying degrees. This fact is not a reason to despair. Instead, we have evidence of the real possibility of nations trying to speak and act together to aid in the survival and flourishing of all people. That there are obstacles, shortcomings, and failures, should, I believe, not dissuade us from working toward creating national and international institutions where power focuses on the common good of all peoples.

This said, it is important to identify some of the obstacles and to figure out ways to remove or reduce them. To do this would require another book. My aim here is to identify a few challenges and discuss principles designed to limit these obstacles. Perhaps the biggest obstacle to international cooperation and constructive expressions of power is militarism or the exercise of military power (threat, coercion, or violence), which includes and is fostered by the manufacture and sale of weapons. While it is true that some smaller countries use the military to support ruling factions, the most egregious use of military power is conducted by superpowers, in particular, the United States (and Russia), which is the world's largest arms dealer (CNN 2017). Add to this the United States' exercise of military power, which is supported by the military and national security industrial complexes—corporations that are entwined with government institutions and the military. These complexes are not motivated solely by security and peace, but by profit, market expansion, and maintaining dominance or superpower status.

Superpowers, like the United States, do not exercise power alone. The United States' militarism is supported by the imperium's client-states (e.g., Britain and Germany). Client-states are not always traditional allies. Client-states can also be countries that use the military to maintain control over its citizens (e.g., Egypt) or to harm, control, and oppress a group of people (e.g., Israel's oppression of Palestinians). This means that the militarism of superpowers is supported by other nations that calculate militarism's benefits for themselves.

While there are usually benefits in engaging in militarism, it is almost never for the common good, whether we understand this in terms of a particular country or the common good of all peoples.[13] For instance, the distribution of a nation's resources to support a large military and its ancillary institutions (e.g., spy and surveillance organizations) means that resources needed for survival and flourishing are denied other residents. Of course, war and the prospect of war, as Major General Smedley Butler (1935) noted, is good for business and for imperialists, but not for the populace. Yes, a superpower (modern term for imperium) can provide stability for the metropole, but the vast amount of resources needed for the aims and exercise of military power makes the lives of many people difficult. What good is stability if one lives in a food desert? How much stability is needed if one is unable to get health-care? How is the notion of stability understood if one is under the constant threat of eviction? I agree with Martin Luther King Jr.'s comment that war (and I would say militarism) is the enemy of the poor—poor persons of the United States, as well as residents of countries that purchase and use U.S. weapons (or the citizens of countries we engage militarily).

Included here is that militarism is deeply destructive environmentally. Any cursory glance at military interventions will note the destruction not sim-ply to people, but habitats. For instance, many people in Vietnam continue to suffer from the environmental effects of the U.S. war on Vietnam.[14] Even military exercises are environmentally destructive (EPA 2017). Wars and militarism are inherently destructive and, while there may be occasions when a war results in more good than not, the proliferation of weapons leads to greater instability—by way of coercion and force—and destruction. In short, militarism is a major obstacle to greater cooperation among all nations for the good of all of the planet's residents.

Militarism, especially in the United States, is inextricably tied to capital-ism, which, of course, is global. Global capitalism is another major obstacle to developing international institutions and relations that manifest a construc-tive exercise of power focused on the common good, not only of individual nations, but of all peoples. There are, of course, international and regional institutions that are aimed at fostering economic and political cooperation. The IMF, World Bank, and G7 are examples of international cooperation to extend and secure capitalism. As I argued in chapter 5, capitalism is funda-mentally based on exploitative relations, leads to the proliferation of zero-sum competition, undermines community, and fosters significant problems in income and wealth inequalities. Capitalist institutions, whether we are talking about corporations or national and international organizations that support them, are also nondemocratic and preoccupied with profit and market expansion. All of this means that capitalism and its institutions are obstacles to creating and promoting institutions that are unwilling to exercise power to insure the fair distribution of resources so that all residents can care for the survival and flourishing needs of themselves and Others. Even within a nation, the exercise of political-economic power vis-à-vis institutions nega-tively impacts those with less power. This is evident in individual capitalist nations, like the United States, where there are huge disparities in wealth and income, which means that poorer persons have restricted access to the goods and services necessary for their flourishing. Moreover, the poor have less power vis-à-vis speaking and acting together because they are locked out of political and economic institutions. But this reality is not limited to the United States. A tiny fraction of wealthy individuals possesses most of the world's wealth (Piketty 2014), which means that capitalism entails institutions (and individuals) that exercise power to distribute unjustly resources away from the least of these. Put differently, national and international institutions comprise people speaking and acting together in ways that negatively impact millions of people—people who are kept from speaking and acting together within these institutions lack civic power.

It is important to point out that there are businesses (a fraction) that function as cooperatives. They tend to be more democratic in how they function, more egalitarian in pay and benefits to workers, and more socially and environmentally conscious. Corporations like Mondragon, for instance, are concerned about profits as only one variable in the mix of how the corporation operates and cares for its workers. Moreover, the wealth and income gaps in companies like Mondragon are very small, which means the lowest-paid workers have greater access to the resources needed for their flourishing and a greater voice vis-à-vis the company. Unfortunately, these kinds of businesses are not encouraged or supported by national and international institutions, which means that for the foreseeable future traditional capitalistic organizations will continue to dominate national and international politics and economics. As long as they do, global capitalism will continue to thwart the kinds of international institutions that foster cooperation and constructive power aimed at the common good.

The last obstacle vis-à-vis power is corruption. Zephyr Teachout's (2014) book, *Corruption in America*, discusses how the founders of the United States had a very deep appreciation for the proclivity of human beings toward corruption in the political realm. Corruption is evident "when private interests trump public ones in the exercise of public power, and a person is corrupt when they use public power for their own ends, disregarding others" (p. 9). She writes further that John Adams argued that "patriotism and corruption were opposites" (p. 19). "A corrupt courier is one who puts his own interests in his care when in public service" (p. 19). This was why the nation's early leaders enacted strict rules and laws to prevent political corruption in the exercise of power. The laws and rules about corruption, Teachout notes, have changed in dramatic ways since the early years of the nation. These changes, she argues, have narrowed the understanding of what corruption means and, not surprisingly, increased the instances of political and economic leaders seeking their interests instead of the public's.

At the local and national levels, corruption undermines public trust, which is necessary for cooperation or civic power with regard to achieving the common good. Corruption undermines institutions that are created to address particular needs of citizens. I mentioned earlier the Princeton study that showed how Congress voted, more often than not, for legislation that benefited lobbyists and their patrons. This is a form of legal corruption that clearly undermines trust in political institutions—institutions that are created to serve the people and not the particular interests of the economic and political elites. Corruption in this context means not only that individuals are unethical, but also the system itself (e.g., lobbyists, campaign financing) has been corrupted. Is it any wonder why there is so little public trust when it comes to the Senate or the House? Not surprisingly, there is corruption in the economic realm—legal and illegal. Displays of rampant corruption by companies like Enron and Wells Fargo undermine public confidence. Of course, some of what these companies did was illegal. But legal corruption also exists in the sense that national and international companies are able to make profits while paying workers minimum wages and no benefits. This is legalized wage theft. As I argued in an earlier chapter, neoliberal capitalism is a corrupt and corrupting system in that it puts private interests ahead of public interests. My point here is that corruption, as Teachout discusses, can be legal in some cases and not legal in others, yet it has the same effect—the undermining of public trust and the decline of cooperation toward the common good.

Militarism and global capitalism are licit forms of corruption because they are systems that highlight and promote the self-interests of the group and individuals. I am not suggesting that everyone in the military or business is corrupt. There are many virtuous people in both. Nor am I saying that military and business institutions are corrupt in themselves. My point is that militarism and capitalism promote a kind of myopia, where self-interest is associated with one's group or oneself and this corrupts international forms of functional-contractual faith whereby nations and their institutions speak and act together toward the common good of all peoples. The militarism of the imperium corrupts the world public, because the imperium is focused on achieving its self-interests at the expense of others. Let me return to Major General Smedley Butler. He was an honorable and courageous soldier, though Butler knew he worked for an institution that exploited people for the sake of big business. He wrote that, during his thirty-three years in the Marine Corps, "I spent most of my time as a high-class muscle-man for big business, for Wall Street and for bankers. . . . I helped in the raping of half dozen Central American republics for the benefit of Wall Street" (in Zinn 2004, p. 252). Capitalist corporations (national and international) are public institutions that are focused on gaining profit for their shareholders, but they are part of a corrupting system in that capitalism only accidentally contributes to the common good. When a system distributes resources so egregiously in the direction of a tiny fraction of the population, when a system gives rise to political-economic power wherein the elite speak and act together to meet their desires while neglecting the needs of the many, it is fundamentally corrupt and corrupting.

Militarism, global capitalism, and corruption intersect and are major obstacles to creating national and international institutions that aim to address the survival and flourishing needs of all people. These obstacles eschew the notion that the world is for all people, and instead operate out of *the idea the world is my own to control and exploit.* I am not sanguine about how and whether we can overcome these obstacles, though I am not hopeless because there is some evidence of nations cooperating for the benefit of all peoples. Militarism can be addressed nationally by removing the profit motive of corporations that manufacture weapons. Nations can work to control the manufacture and sale of weapons and define and ban all offensive weapons. Countries that deal in the export of weapons can be sanctioned. There can be cooperative efforts to rid the world of nuclear weapons. Nations can create legislation that fosters the creation and establishment of business cooperatives that are democratic, socially and environmentally conscious and active, and function to distribute income and wealth justly. International organizations can be created to do the same thing. Individual nations and nations together can begin to speak and act together to develop rules, regulations, and laws that reduce corruption and protect residents of the world. All institutions can be publicly evaluated by the principles of care and cooperation. That is, to what degree is this institution contributing to the welfare of local, national, and international residents? How are public and private institutions contributing to the common good of their communities, the larger society, and the world? Power—speaking and acting together—needs to be understood in terms of persons and national and international institutions working toward the common good of all people. This is the hope for a world that is our collective home and where the fate of all persons is tied together in the Anthropocene Era.

CONCLUSION

Historians often point to important shifts in world history. Some argue that the treaties associated with the Peace of Westphalia (1648) marked the beginning of the rise of modern nation-states. The American and French revolutions ushered in the decline of monarchies and the rise of democracies. It appears that particular exigencies of an era give rise to changes at the international level. While not a historian, I wonder if we are not at another period in history where the exigencies of climate change will foster international changes—changes that lead to the creation of national and international institutions that facilitate the distribution of resources so that individuals, families, and communities can care for themselves and Others, changes where national and international institutions engage in greater cooperation regarding the common good of all people, precisely because we have and share one habitat, one world.

NOTES

1. Examples of peacekeeping operations, as well as coordinating aid for countries unable to meet the needs of their people, reflect an important change in how countries operate for the benefit of others, despite the fact that lex talionis and enmity continue to exist, especially among powerful nations.

2. We are accustomed to presume that "inhabitants" means human beings, but I include animals. Seeking to maintain the habitats for animals is not simply for the pleasure of seeing such diversity; it is also necessary for human life. A complex and diverse ecosystem is necessary for human well-being.

3. As in any story, we need to be cautious about who are left out of the story and how the story functions. Poor people, people of color, and women have often been left out of dominant stories, which lead to forms of marginalization and oppression. We must guard against particular and global stories and identities that exclude the voices and needs of other human beings.

4. It is necessary to note that Polanyi believed that the "essential connotation [of 'nation'] is always about the communion of humans." He continued to comment that the "heart of the socialist nation is the people, where collective existence is the enjoyment of a community culture. I myself have never lived in such a society" (in Brie 2017, p. 7). A socialist society possesses democratic institutions as well as institutions that promote communities and the common good. The values of profit and accumulation are secondary and subordinate to democracy, community, and the common good.

5. This may seem odd. Aren't all human institutions created to address and meet some human need(s)? The simple and unqualified answer is no. Some institutions are created to promote desire. Max Weber (1992) described the rise of capitalism and its relation to the spirit of acquisitiveness. Another way of saying this is that the institutions associated with the rise of capitalism promoted the vice of greed, which has nothing to do with human needs. Another example is the creation of institutions associated with the U.S. military and intelligence organizations, which ostensibly meet the security needs of the American people. This is only slightly true. Any cursory reading of history reveals they serve not needs for security, but the desire for economic expansion and profit.

6. Each individual is formed by a variety of institutions and their associated forms of knowledge, which points to the complexity of the intersection of subjectivity and institutions. Add to this the fact that institutions do not determine us. As history repeatedly shows, even ostensibly good institutions can include people who behave despicably.

7. There are exceptions to this. The Spanish company, Mondragon, and other similarly run cooperatives are organized around democratic principles.

8. Someone may point out that many poorer nations are plagued with corruption. This is often pointed out when people discuss providing aid to these countries. This is a legitimate concern, but participants need to examine their legal forms of corruption such as the IMF and the World Bank. Moreover, there are ways to ensure that resources and assistance get to people in these countries.

9. I suspect most readers are familiar with President Eisenhower's comments about the dangers of the military industrial complex, to which we could add the national security industrial complex. To reduce the danger of these complexes would necessarily involve a transformation at the national and international levels. Nationally, we would have to give up our arrogance and lust for power. We would also have to reduce the attractiveness of making military weapons, such as taxing corporations that are involved in military and security matters. These companies would be taxed so they could not obtain any profits and these taxed profits would be used for peacemaking. Internationally, there would need to be agreements regionally and globally regarding the elimination of nuclear weapons and any other weapons of mass destruction. An international body would need to be created to handle disputes. These are not utopian ideas. Certain weapons have been outlawed. International rules have been adopted regarding conflicts. We simply need to do more to reduce and eventually eliminate weapons of war and companies that profit from the sale of these weapons.

10. It is ironic that the IMF was created just prior to colonies rebelling against their colonial masters. While the major colonial powers lost their hold, they nevertheless retained economic mastery during the postcolonial era. The IMF and World Bank are institutions created by the United States and other colonial powers, which, not surprisingly, have largely benefited the previous colonial powers.

11. Citizens who choose not to speak and act with regard to government atrocities are tacitly supporting the government. In other words, "not speaking and acting" is a kind of agency that supports the status quo.

12. Income and wealth inequalities are mitigated by legislation in some European countries that are more socially minded (e.g., Sweden, Germany, and France). Nevertheless, G8 nations and other countries that have embraced neoliberal capitalism have seen growing income and wealth inequalities, which by definition mean that the common good is being ignored.

13. Some wars are fought mainly for defensive purposes and, while destructive, have positive effects. For instance, The Korean War led to stability and eventually democracy in South Korea. It should be pointed out that the United States' engagement in this war was not for altruistic reasons. There was also the motivation to maintain hegemony in Asia and to thwart communism.

14. Our seminary often has priests and students from Vietnam. I recall one conversation where a priest said that there is a high incidence of various cancers in the village where he lives. He said that he does not drink the water, because the area is still contaminated from defoliating agents used by the United States during the war.

References

Agamben, G. (1998). *Homo sacer: Sovereign power and bare life*, D. Heller-Roazen (Trans.). Stanford: Stanford University Press.

Alder, N. and Newman, K. (2002). Socioeconomic disparities in health: Pathways and policies. *Health Affairs*, http://content.healthaffairs.org/content/21/2/60.full, accessed April 28, 2017.

Alexander, M. (2010). *The new Jim Crow*. New York: The New Press.

Almond, B. (2002). Macmurray and the role of ethics in political life. In D. Fergusson and N. Dower (Eds.), *John Macmurray: Critical perspectives*, 15–72. New York: Peter Lang.

Amery, J. (1995). Torture. In L. Langer (Ed.), *Art from the Ashes*, 121–136. Oxford: Oxford University Press.

Anderson, B. (1983). *Imagined communities*. New York: Verso.

Anderson, C. (2016). *White rage*. New York: Bloomsbury.

Appiah, K. (2005). *The ethics of identity*. Princeton: Princeton University Press.

Aralepo, O. (2003). The white male therapist/helper as (m)other to the black male patient/client. *Free Associations*, 10, 382–398.

Arendt, H. (1958). *The human condition*. Chicago: University of Chicago Press.

Arendt, H. (2005). *The promise of politics*. New York: Schocken Books.

Arthur, K. (2017). Why fan reactions to NFL national anthem protests is about racism, not patriotism. *RollingStone*, September 26, https://www.rollingstone.com/culture/culture-sports/why-fan-reaction-to-nfl-national-anthem-protests-is-about-racism-not-patriotism-201838/, accessed December 10, 2017.

Ashby, H. (1996). Is it time for a black pastoral theology? *Journal of Pastoral Theology*, 6(1), 1–15.

Ashby, H. (2000). Pastoral theology as public theology: Participating in the healing of damaged and damaging institutions. *Journal of Pastoral Theology*, 1, 18–27.

Ashby, H. (2003). *Our home is over Jordan: A black pastoral theology*. St. Louis, MO: Chalice Press.

Baker, T. (2009). *George Mackey Brown and the philosophy of community*. Edinburgh: Edinburgh University Press.

Bakewell, S. (2016). *At the existentialist café: Freedom, being, and apricot cocktails.* New York: Other Press.

Baldwin, J. (1984). *Notes of a native son.* Boston, MA: Beacon.

Baldwin, J. (1990). *The fire next time.* New York, NY: The Dial Press.

Baldwin, J. (2010). *The cross of redemption: Uncollected writings.* New York: Pantheon.

Balko, R. (2014). How municipalities in St. Louis Count, MO, profit from poverty. *Washington Post,* https://www.washingtonpost.com/news/the-watch/wp/2014/0 9/03/how-st-louis-county-missouri-profits-from-poverty/?utm_term=.f4a09e891 645, accessed February 7, 2017.

BallotPedia. (2012). *Net worth of United States Senators and Representatives.* https: //ballotpedia.org/Net_worth_of_United_States_Senators_and_Representatives, accessed November 20, 2017.

Baptist, E. (2014). *The half has never been told: Slavery and the making of American capitalism.* New York: Basic Books.

Barker, E. (1971). *The politics of Aristotle.* Oxford University Press.

Bauman, Z. (2017). *A chronicle of crisis 2011–2016.* London: Social Europe Edition.

Becker, G. (1976). *The economic approach to human behavior.* Chicago: Chicago University Press.

Beebe, B., Lachmann, F., and Jaffe, J. (1997). Mother-infant interactions: Structures and presymbolic self and object representations. *Psychoanalytic Dialogues,* 7(2), 133–182.

Bell, D. (1996). *The cultural contradictions of capitalism.* New York: Basic Books.

Bellah, R., Madsen, R., Sullivan, W., Swidler, A., and Tipton, S. (1985). *Habits of the heart.* New York: Harper and Row.

Benhabib, S. (1992). *Situating the self.* New York: Routledge Press.

Benjamin, J. (1995). Sameness and difference: Toward an "over-inclusive" model of gender development. *Psychoanalytic Inquiry,* 15, 125–142.

Berman, M. (2017). North Carolina's bathroom bill cost the state at least $3.7 billion, new analysis finds. *Washington Post,* https://www.washingtonpost.com/news/post -nation/wp/2017/03/27/north-carolinas-bathroom-bill-cost-the-state-at-least-3-7- billion-new-analysis-finds/?noredirect=onandutm_term=.f956d916f34e, accessed April 4, 2017.

Bivens, J. and Mishel, L. (2015). Understanding the historical divergence between productivity and a typical worker's pay. *Economic Policy Institute,* http://www.epi. org/publication/understanding-the-historic-divergence-between-productivity-and-a -typical-workers-pay-why-it-matters-and-why-its-real/, accessed August 2, 2017.

Boer, R. (2014). *In the vale of tears: On Marxism and theology.* Chicago: Haymarket Books.

Boer, R. (2105). *Marxist criticism of the Hebrew Bible.* New York: Bloomsbury.

Boff, L. (2008). *Essential care: An ethics of human nature.* Waco, TX: Baylor University Press.

Bosman, J., Davey, M., and Smith, M. (2016). As water problems grew, officials belittled complaints from Flint. *New York Times,* http://www.nytimes.com/2016/01 /21/us/flint-michigan-lead-water-crisis.html?_r=0, accessed November 21, 2016.

Bradford, H. (2011). Warren Buffett: "My class has won and it's been a rout." *Huffington Post*, November 15, 2011, http://www.huffingtonpost.com/2011/11/15/warr en-buffett-tax-code-l_n_1095833.html.accessed, accessed August 16, 2017.

Brie, M. (2017). *Karl Polanyi in dialogue: A socialist thinker for our time*. Montreal: Black Rose Books.

Brown, W. (1995). *States of injury: Power and freedom in late modernity*. Princeton: Princeton University Press.

Brown, W. (2001). *Politics out of history*. Princeton, NJ: Princeton University Press.

Brown, W. (2006). *Regulating aversion*. Princeton, NJ: Princeton University Press.

Brown, W. (2014). *Walled states, waning sovereignty*. New York: Zone Books.

Brown, W. (2015). *Undoing the demos*. New York: Zone Books.

Bubeck, D. (1995). *Care, gender, and justice*. Oxford: Clarendon Press.

Buber, M. (1958). *I and thou*. New York: Charles Scribner.

Buick, A. and Crump, J. (2013). *The alternative to capitalism*. UK: Theory and Practice.

Bullard, R. (2004). Poverty, pollution and environmental racism: Strategies for building healthy and sustainable communities. http://www.ejrc.cau.edu/PovpolEj.html, accessed August 18, 2014.

Bunge, M. (2001). *The child in Christian thought*. Grand Rapids, MI: Eerdmanns.

Bureau of Justice Statistics. (2016). Key statistic: Total correctional population. https ://www.bjs.gov/index.cfm?ty=kfdetailandiid=487, accessed June 26, 2018.

Butler, S. (1935). *War is a racket*. Port Townsend, WA: Feral house.

Calfas, J. (2016). Trump's cabinet picks have more wealth than third American household. *The Hill*, http://thehill.com/blogs/blog-briefing-room/news/3 10566-trumps-cabinet-picks-have-more-money-than-third-of-american, accessed November 20, 2017.

Capper, B. (2009). Jesus, virtuoso religion, and the community goods. In B. Longenecker and K. Liebengood (Eds.), *Engaging economics: New testament scenarios and early Christian reception*, 60–80. Grand Rapids, MI: Eerdmanns Publishing Company.

Carlin, N. (2014). *Religious mourning: Reversals and restorations in psychological portraits of religious leaders*. Eugene, OR: Wipf and Stock.

Carrette, J. and King, R. (2005). *Selling spirituality: The silent takeover of religion*. New York: Routledge.

Castoriadis, C. (1997). *World in fragments*, D. Ames Curtis (Trans and Ed.). Stanford, CA: Stanford University Press.

Cavanaugh, W. (1998). *Torture and Eucharist*. London: Blackwell Publishing.

Caygill, H. (2002). *Levinas and the political*. New York: Routledge.

Centano, M. and Cohen, J. (2012). The arc of neoliberalism. *Annual Review of Sociology*, 38, 317–340.

Center for Media and Democracy. (2018). *Workers' rights and consumer rights*. http://www.alecexposed.org/wiki/Worker_Rights_and_Consumer_Rights, accessed March 21, 2017.

Chari, A. (2015). *A political economy of the senses: Neoliberalism, reification, critique*. New York: Columbia University Press.

Chartbook of Economic Inequality. (2015). *Economic inequality in Sweden.* https://www.chartbookofeconomicinequality.com/inequality-by-country/Sweden/, accessed November 17, 2017.

Chibber, V. (2013). *Postcolonial theory and the specter of capital.* London: Verso Press.

Chinula, D. (1997). *Building King's beloved community: Foundations for pastoral care and counseling with the oppressed.* Eugene, OR: Wipf and Stock.

Clebsch, W. and Jaekle, C. (1994). *Pastoral care in historical perspective.* Northvale: Jason Aronson.

CNN. (2017). And the world's biggest arms dealer is. . . *CNN,* 2 February, https://money.cnn.com/video/news/2017/02/20/global-arms-trade-explainer.cnnmoney/index.html, accessed January 30, 2018.

Coates, T. (2015). *Between the world and me.* New York, NY: Spiegel and Grau.

Cone, J. (2011). *The cross and the lynching tree.* New York: Orbis Books.

Congressional Budget Office. (2017). H. R. Bill 1628, American Health Care Act 2017, https://www.cbo.gov/publication/52752, accessed August 20, 2017.

Corradi-Fuimara, G. (1990). *The other side of language: A philosophy of listening.* London: Routledge Press.

Cox, H. (2016). *The market as God.* New Haven, CT: Harvard University Press.

Crossan, J. (1995). *Jesus: A revolutionary biography.* New York: HarperOne.

Crossan, J. (2007). *God and empire.* San Francisco: HarperSanFrancisco.

Cushman, P. (1995). *Constructing the self, constructing America.* New York: Addison Wesley.

Dalal, F. (2002). *Race, color and the process of racialization: New perspectives from group analysis, psychoanalysis, and sociology.* New York, NY: Brunner-Routledge.

Dardot, P. and Laval, C. (2013). *The new way of the world: On neoliberal society.* New York: Verso.

Dean, J. (2009). *Democracy and other neoliberal fantasies.* Durham, NC: Duke University Press.

D'Entreves, M. (1994). *The political philosophy of Hannah Arendt.* London: Routledge Press.

Desmond, M. (2016). *Evicted.* New York: Crown Publishers.

De Wilde, M. (2006). Violence in the state of exception: Reflection on theological-political motifs in Benjamin and Schmitt. In H. de Vries and L. Sullivan (Eds.), *Political theologies,* 188–200. New York: Fordham University Press.

Dill, K. (2013). CEO pay has risen more than twice as much as the stock market. *Forbes,* June 27, https://www.forbes.com/sites/kathryndill/2013/06/27/ceo-pay-has-risen-more-than-twice-as-much-as-the-stock-market/#bc4a41c1258d, accessed July 9, 2018.

Dillen, A. (2014). *Soft shepherd or almighty pastor: Power and pastoral care.* Eugene, OR: Wipf and Stock.

Doehring, C. (2012). Teaching an intercultural approach to spiritual care. *Journal of Pastoral Theology,* 22, 1–24.

Doehring, C. (2015). *The practice of pastoral care.* Louisville, KY: Westminster John Knox Press.

Dufour, D. (2008). *The art of shrinking heads: On the new servitude of the liberated in the age of total capitalism.* Cambridge: Polity Press.

Dugan, L. (2003). *The twilight of equality: Neoliberalism, cultural politics, and the attack on democracy.* Boston: Beacon Press.

Duménil, G. and Lévy, D. (2011). *The crisis of neoliberalism.* Cambridge: Harvard University Press.

Dykstra, R. (2005). *Images of pastoral care: Classic readings.* St. Louis, MO: Chalice Press.

Eagleton, T. (1996). *Postmodernism.* Oxford: Blackwell Publishing.

Eagleton, T. (1999). *Marx.* London: Routledge.

Eagleton, T. (2011). *Why Marx was right.* New Haven, CT: Yale University Press.

Eagleton, T. (2016). *Materialism.* New Haven: Yale University Press.

Easterly, W. (2013). *The tyranny of experts: Economics, dictators, and the forgotten rights of the poor.* New York: Basic Books.

Ehrenreich, B. (2011). On turning poverty into an American crime. *Truthout*, 9 August, http://www.truth-out.org/opinion/item/2579:barbara-ehrenreich-on-turning-poverty-into-an-american-crime, accessed October 29, 2017.

Engster, D. (2007). *The heart of justice: Care ethics and political theory.* Oxford: Oxford University Press.

Environmental Protection Agency. (2017). The environmental challenge of military munitions and federal facilities. *EPA*, https://www.epa.gov/enforcement/environmental-challenge-military-munitions-and-federal-facilities, accessed February 1, 2019.

Erikson, E. (1952). *Childhood and society.* New York: W. W. Norton.

Estey, K. (2013). Protesting classes through Protestant glasses: Class, labor, and the social Gospel in the United States. In J. Rieger (Ed.), *Religion, Class, and Theology*, 121–142. New York: Palgrave Macmillan.

Farley, E. (1996). *Deep symbols: Their postmodern effacement and reclamation.* Valley Forge, PA: Trinity Press International.

Ferguson, K. and Petro, P. (2016). *After capitalism.* New Brunswick, NJ: Rutgers University Press.

Flannery, A. (1980). *Vatican II.* Collegeville, MN: Liturgical Press.

Flesberg, E. (2008). *The switching hour: Kids of divorce say good-bye again.* Nashville, TN: Abingdon Press.

Foucault, M. (1979). *Discipline and punish: The birth of prisons.* New York: Vintage Books.

Foucault, M. (1980). *Power/Knowledge.* New York: Pantheon.

Foucault, M. (2005). *The hermeneutics of the subject: Lectures at the College de France, 1981–1982.* New York: Picador.

Francis. (2013). Evangelii Gaudium, http://w2.vatican.va/content/francesco/en/apost_exhortations/documents/papa-francesco_esortazione-ap_20131124_evangelii-gaudium.html, accessed 11 July 2018.

Francis. (2015). *Laudato Si,* http://w2.vatican.va/content/francesco/en/encyclicals/documents/papa-francesco_20150524_enciclica-laudato-si.html, accessed 11 July 2018.

Francis. (2016). *Amoris Letitia,* https://w2.vatican.va/content/dam/francesco/pdf/ap ost_exhortations/documents/papa-francesco_esortazione-ap_20160319_amoris-la etitia_en.pdf, accessed June 20, 2018.

Frank, T. (2000). *One market under God: Extreme capitalism, market populism, and the end of economic democracy.* New York: Anchor Books.

Fraser, N. and Honneth, A. (2003). *Redistribution or recognition?* New York: Verso Books.

Fraser, S. (2015). *The age of acquiescence.* New York: Basic Books.

Fredrickson, D. (1981). *White supremacy: A comparative study in American and South African history.* Oxford: Oxford University Press.

Freeberg, E. (2008). *Democracy's prisoner: Eugene Debs, the Great War, and the right to dissent.* Cambridge: Harvard University Press.

Freeman, J. (2013). *American Empire: The rise of a global power and the democratic revolution at home.* New York: Penguin Books.

Freis, H. (1984). Faith and knowledge. In Rahner (Ed.), *The encyclopedia of theology: The concise sacramentum mundi.* New York: Crossroad.

Fussell, P. (1983). *Class.* New York: Ballantine.

Gabrielle, C. (2015). Here's the latest evidence on how private prisons are exploiting inmates for profits. *Mother Jones,* June 17,http://www.motherjones.com/mojo/2015/06/private-prisons-profit, accessed August 20, 2017.

Gallup. (2011). Congressional job approval percent15. *Politics,* September 12, https://news.gallup.com/poll/149399/Congressional-Job-Approval.aspx, accessed June 26, 2018.

Gerkin, C. (1997). *An introduction to pastoral care.* Nashville, TN: Abingdon.

Gilens, M. and Page, B. (2014). Testing theories of American politics: Elites, interest groups and average citizens. *American Political Science Association,* September 12(3), 564–581.

Gilligan, C. (1982). *In a different voice: Psychological theory and women's development.* Cambridge: Harvard University Press.

Gilligan, J. (2011). *Why some politicians are more dangerous than others.* Cambridge: Polity Press.

Giroux, H. (2012). *Zombie politics and culture in the age of casino capitalism.* New York: Peter Lang.

Giroux, H. (2012a). *Disposable youth: Racialized memories and the culture of cruelty.* London: Routledge Press.

Goldberg, T. (2009). *The threat of race: Reflections on racial neoliberalism.* Malden, MA: Wiley-Blackwell.

Graham, E. (2002). *Transforming practice: Pastoral theology in an age of uncertainty.* Eugene, OR: Wipf and Stock.

Graham, L. (1992). *Care of persons, care of worlds: A psychosystems approach to pastoral care and counseling.* Nashville: Abingdon Press.

Gray, J. (1998). *False dawn.* New York: New Press.

Greenstone, M., Looney, A., Patashnik, J., and Yu, M. (2013). Thirteen economic facts about social mobility and the role of education. *Brookings,* June 26, https://www.brookings.edu/research/thirteen-economic-facts-about-social-mobility-and-the-role-of-education/, accessed July 9, 2018.

Grinberg, E. (2016). Racial bias pervasive among Baltimore police, DOJ says. *CNN*, https://www.cnn.com/2016/08/09/us/baltimore-justice-department-report/index .html, accessed April 4, 2017.

Hahnel, R. and Wright, E. (2016). *Alternatives to capitalism: Proposals for a democratic economy.* New York: Verso.

Haley, A. (1964). *The autobiography of Malcolm X.* New York: Ballantine Books.

Hall, S. (1997). *Representation: Cultural representations and signifying practices.* New York: Sage.

Hall, S. (2016). *Cultural studies 1983.* Durham, NC: Duke University Press.

Hamilton, J. (2013). *Security: Politics, humanity, and the philology of care.* Princeton, NJ: Princeton University Press.

Hamington, M. (2004). *Embodied care.* Urbana: University of Illinois.

Hardt, M. and Negri, A. (2000). *Empire.* Cambridge, MA: Harvard University Press.

Hardt, M. and Negri, A. (2005). *Multitude.* New York: Penguin Books.

Hardt, M. and Negri, A. (2009). *Commonwealth.* Cambridge, MA: Belknap Press, 2009.

Harman, C. (2017). *A people's history of the world.* New York: Verso.

Harrington, B. (2016). *Capital without borders: Wealth managers and the one percent.* Cambridge, MA: Harvard University Press.

Harris, J. (1991). *Pastoral theology: A Black church perspective.* Minneapolis, MN: Augsburg.

Harvey, D. (2005). *A brief history of neoliberalism.* Oxford, United Kingdom: Oxford University Press.

Hayek, F. A. (2007). *Road to serfdom.* Chicago: University of Chicago Press.

Hedges, C. (2014). The prison state of America. *Truthdig*, December 28, http://www .truthdig.com/report/page2/the_prison_state_of_america_20141228, accessed August 20, 2017.

Hedges, C. and Sacco, J. (2012). *Days of destruction, days of revolt.* New York: Nations Books.

Held, V. (2006). *The ethics of care: Personal, political, and global.* Oxford: Oxford University Press.

Helsel, P. (2015). *Pastoral power beyond psychology's imagination.* New York: Palgrave.

Hendricks, O. (2011). *The universe bends toward justice.* New York: Orbis.

Hochschild, A. R. (2012). *The managed heart: Commercialization of human feeling.* Berkeley, CA: University of California Press.

Hollerich, M. (2007). Carl Schmitt. In P. Scott and W. Cavanaugh (Eds.), *The Blackwell companion to political theology*, 107–122. London: Blackwell Publishing.

Holton, J. (2011). *Building the resilient community.* Eugene, OR: Cascade Books.

Honneth, A. (1991). *Critique of power: Reflective stages in a critical social theory.* Cambridge, MA: MIT Press.

Honneth, A. (1995). *The struggle for recognition.* Cambridge, MA: MIT Press.

Honneth, A. (2007a). *Disrespect: The normative foundations of critical theory.* New York: Polity Press.

Honneth, A. (2007). Recognition as ideology. In B. Van den Blink and D. Owens (Eds.), *Recognition and power*, 323–347. Cambridge: Cambridge University Press.

Honneth, A. (2008). *Reification: A new look at an old idea*. Oxford: Oxford University Press.

Honneth, A. (2014). *Freedom's right: The social foundations of democratic life*. New York: Columbia University Press.

Honneth, A. (2017). *The idea of socialism*. New York: Polity Press.

Honneth, A. and Ranciére, J. (2016). *Recognition or disagreement: A critical encounter on the politics of freedom, equality, and identity*. New York: Columbia University Press.

Hooks, B. (2000). *Where we stand: Class matters*. New York: Routledge Press.

Horsley, R. (2003). *Jesus and empire*. Minneapolis, MN: Fortress Press.

Horsley, R. (2009). *Covenant economics: A biblical vision of justice for all*. Louisville, KY: Westminster John Knox Press.

Horsley, R. (2011). *Jesus and the power: Conflict, covenant, and the hope of the poor*. Minneapolis, MN: Fortress Press.

Howard, J. (2012). Appalachia Turns on Itself. *New York Times*, July 8, http://www.nytimes.com/2012/07/09/opinion/appalachia-turns-on-itself.html?_r=1and>, accessed July 14, 2018.

Hudis, P. (2015). *Marx's concept of the alternative to capitalism*. Chicago: Haymarket Books.

Hudis, P. and Anderson, K. (Eds.) (2004). *The Rosa Luxemburg reader*. New York: The Monthly Review Press.

Illouz, E. (2007). *Cold intimacies: The making of emotional capitalism*. Cambridge: Polity Press.

Illouz, E. (2008). *Saving the modern soul: Therapy, emotions, and the culture of self-help*. Berkeley: University of California Press.

Isenberg, N. (2016). *White trash: The four-hundred-year untold story of class in America*. New York: Viking Press.

Jackson, L. (2016). President-elect Trump's $14 billon cabinet. *CBS MoneyWatch*, https://www.cbsnews.com/pictures/donald-trumps-14-billion-cabinet/, accessed November 20, 2017.

James, W. (1956). *The will to believe and other essays in popular philosophy*. New York: Dover Books.

James, W. (1984). *William James: The essential writings*, B. Wilshire (Ed.). Albany, NY: SUNY Press.

Jamison, F. (2016). *An American utopia: Dual power and the universal army*, S. Žižek (Ed.). New York: Verso.

JanMohamed, A. (2004). *The death-bound subject: Richard Wright's archaeology of death*. Durham, NC: Duke University Press.

John XIII. (1961). *Mater et Magister*, http://w2.vatican.va/content/john-xxiii/en/en cyclicals/documents/hf_j-xxiii_enc_15051961_mater.html, accessed July 11, 2018.

John Paul II. (1981). *Familiaris Consortio*, http://w2.vatican.va/content/john-paul-i i/en/apost_exhortations/documents/hf_jp-ii_exh_19811122_familiaris-consorti o.html, accessed June 20, 2018.

Johnson, C. (2016). *Race, resilience, and resistance in a neoliberal age*. New York: Palgrave.

Jones, S. (2012). *Masters of the universe: Hayek, Friedman, and the birth of neoliberal politics*. Princeton: Princeton University Press.

Kavoussi, B. (2013). Rich American are nearly twice as likely to vote as the poor. *Huffpost*, https://www.huffingtonpost.com/2013/03/01/voter-turnout-income_n_2790755.html, 1 March, accessed December 15, 2017.

Kegley, A. (1980). Josiah Royce on self and community. *Rice University Studies*, 66(4), 33–53.

Kelley, M. (2010). *Grief: Contemporary theory and the practice of ministry*. Minneapolis, MN: Fortress Press.

King, M. L. (1998). *The autobiography of Martin Luther King*, C. Carson (Ed.). New York, NY: Grand Central Publishing.

Kirkpatrick, F. (1986). *Community: A trinity of models*. Washington, DC: Georgetown University Press.

Kirkpatrick, F. (2002). Public and private: The search for a political philosophy that does justice to both without excluding love. In D. Fergusson and N. Dower (Eds.), *John Macmurray: Critical perspectives*, 189–208. New York: Peter Lang.

Kirkpatrick, F. (2005). *Macmurray: Community beyond political philosophy*. New York: Rowman and Littlefield.

Klein, N. (2007). *Shock doctrine: The rise of disaster capitalism*. New York: Henry Holt and Company.

Klein, N. (2014). *This changes everything: Capitalism vs. the climate*. New York: Simon and Schuster.

Kolbert, E. (2014). *The sixth extinction: An unnatural history*. New York: Henry Holt.

Lakoff, G. (2008). *The political brain*. New York: Penguin Group.

LaMothe, R. (2007). Pastoral care and the American Empire. *Journal of Pastoral Psychology*, 55(3), 339–351.

LaMothe, R. (2010). The transition from object faith to personal faith: Transitional subjects. *Journal of Pastoral Psychology*, 59, 617–630.

LaMothe, R. (2012). State-corporate capitalism, political polarization, and a culture of unquiet desperation: Pastoral analysis and responses. *Journal of Pastoral Psychology*, 61(1), 15–29.

LaMothe, R. (2013). U. S. Empire, systemic violence, and the refusal to mourn. *Journal of Pastoral Theology*, 23, 1–16.

LaMothe, R. (2014a). Pastoral counseling in the 21st century: The centrality of community. *Journal of Pastoral Care*, 68(2), 1–17.

LaMothe, R. (2014). Winnicott and Arendt: Bridging potential and political spaces. *Psychoanalytic Review*, 101(2), 289–318.

LaMothe, R. (2016). Madness and method: A pastoral theological reflection. *Journal of Pastoral Theology*, 65(6), 787–802.

LaMothe, R. (2016a). The colonizing realities of neoliberal capitalism. *Journal of Pastoral Psychology*, 65(1), 23–40.

LaMothe, R. (2017). *Care of souls, care of polis: Toward a political pastoral theology*. Eugene, OR: Wipf and Stock.

LaMothe, R. (forthcoming 2019). The least of these: Political-Economic dimensions of Roman Catholic pastoral theology. *Journal of Pastoral Theology,* (1).

Langer, S. (1979). *Philosophy in a new key*. Cambridge, MA: Harvard University Press.

Lartey, E. (2013). *Pastoral theology in an intercultural world*. Eugene, OR: Wipf and Stock.

Lasch, C. (1979). *The culture of narcissism*. New York: W.W. Norton and Company.

Leah, R. (2017). New poll says anger over NFL protests isn't just a race thing, it's an age thing. *Salon*, October 12, https://www.salon.com/2017/10/12/new-poll-says-anger-over-nfl-protests-isnt-just-a-race-thing-its-an-age-thing/, accessed December 10, 2017.

Lear, J. (2006). *Radical hope*. Cambridge, MA: Harvard University Press.

Lee, S. (2015). Engaging difference in pastoral theology: Race and ethnicity. *Journal of Pastoral Theology*, 19(2), 1–20.

Lee, S., McGarrah Sharp, M., and Shepherd, P. (2017). Empowering activist pedagogies in pastoral theology: Accountabilities and transformative possibilities. *Journal of Pastoral Theology*, 27(3), 131–133.

Leeb, R. and Rejskind, F. (2004). Here's looking at you, kid! A longitudinal study of perceived gender differences in mutual gaze behavior in young infants. *Sex Roles*, 50, 1–14.

Lemke, T. (2014). The risks of security: Liberalism, biopolitics, and fear. In V. Lemm and M. Vatter (Eds.), *The government of life: Foucault, biopolitics, and neoliberalism*, 59–76. New York: Fordham University Press.

Lemm, V. and Vatter, M. (Eds.) (2015). The government of life: Foucault, biopolitics, and neoliberalism. New York: Fordham University Press.

Leo XIII. (1891). Rerum Novarum. *Vatican Documents*, http://w2.vatican.va/content/leo-xiii/en/encyclicals/documents/hf_l-xiii_enc_15051891_rerum-novarum.html, accessed November 12, 2017.

Lester, A. (1985). *Pastoral care with children in crisis*. Philadelphia: Westminster Press.

Levin, F. and Trevarthen, C. (2000). Subtle is the Lord: The relationship between consciousness, the unconscious, and the executive control network (ECN) of the Brain. *Annual of Psychoanalysis*, 28, 105–125.

Levinas, E. (1969). *Totality and infinity*. Pittsburgh, PA: Duquesne University Press.

Levinas, E. (1981). *Otherwise than being*. Pittsburgh, PA: Duquesne University Press.

Longenecker, B. and Liebengood, K. (Eds.) (2009). *Engaging economics: New testament scenarios and early Christian reception*. Grand Rapids, MI: Eerdmanns Publishing Company.

Lord, C. (1987). Aristotle. In Leo Strauss and Joseph Cropsey (Eds.), *History of political philosophy 3rd Edition*, 118–154. Chicago: University of Chicago Press.

Lukács, G. (1968). *History and class consciousness*. Cambridge, MA: MIT Press.

MacDonald, J. (2010). *Thieves in the temple: The Christian church and the selling of the American soul*. New York: Basic Books.

Macmurray, J. (1935). *Reason and emotion*. New York: Humanity Books.

Macmurray, J. (1991a/1957). *The self as agent*. London: Humanities Press International.

Macmurray, J. (1991/1961). *Person in relation*. London: Humanities Press International.

Macmurray, J. (2004/1941). The Conception of Society. In E. McIntosh (Ed.), *John Macmurray: Selected philosophical writings*. Exeter: Imprint Academic.

Macrotrends. (2018). *Unemployment rate by race*. http://www.macrotrends.net/2508/unemployment-rate-by-race, accessed July 10, 2018.

McDermott, J. (1980). The Promethean self and community in the philosophy of William James. *Rice University Studies*, 66(4), 87–102.

McGuire, D. (2011). *At the dark end of the street: Black women, rape, and resistance*. New York: Random House.

McWilliams, N. (1994). *Psychoanalytic diagnosis*. London: Guilford Press.

Mander, J. (2012). *The capitalism papers: Fatal flaws in an obsolete system*. Berkeley, CA: Counterpoint Press.

Mann. G. (2013). *Disassembly required: A field guide to actually existing capitalism*. Edinburgh: AK Press.

Marcuse, H. (1964). *One-dimensional man: Studies in the ideology of advanced industrial society*. Boston: Beacon Press.

Margalit, A. (1996). *The decent society*. Cambridge, MA: Harvard University Press.

Marris, P. (1996). *The politics of uncertainty*. London: Routledge Press.

Marshall, J. (1997). *Counseling lesbian partners*. Louisville, KY: Westminster John Knox.

Marx, K. (1964). Inaugural address of the working men's association. *Marxists Internet Archive*, http://marxengels.public-archive.net/en/ME1400en.html, accessed August 29, 2017.

Mayeroff, M. (1971). *On caring*. New York: HarperPerennial.

Meisner, J., Sweeney, A., Hinkel, D., and Gorner, J. (2017). Justice report rips Chicago police for excessive force, lax discipline, bad training. *Chicago Tribune*, http://www.chicagotribune.com/news/local/breaking/ct-chicago-police-justice-department-report-20170113-story.html, accessed April 4, 2017.

Mercer, J. (2012). Economics, class, and classism. In B. Miller-McLemore (Ed.), *The Wiley-blackwell companion to practical theology*, 432–442. Maiden, MA: Wiley-Blackwell.

Merriam-Webster Dictionary. *Power*. https://www.merriam-webster.com/dictionary/power, accessed March 7, 2017.

Mignolo, W. (2011). *The darker side of western modernity: Global futures, decolonial options*. Durham, NC: Duke University Press.

Miller, A. (1983). *For your own good: The hidden cruelty in child-rearing and the roots of violence*. New York: Farrar. Straus, Giroux.

Miller-McLemore, B. (1995). *Also a mother: Work and family as a theological dilemma*. Nashville: Abingdon Press.

Miller-McLemore, B. (2006). Children and religion in the public square: "Too dangerous and too safe, too difficult and too silly." *The Journal of Religion*, 86(3), 385–401.

Moberg, D. (2017). As PATCO goes, so do the unions. In J. Gantz (Ed.), *The age of inequality*, 59–61. New York: Verso.

Moritz, T. and Moritz, A. (2001). *The world's most dangerous woman: A new biography of Emma Goldman*. Vancouver, TO: Subway Books.

Mounier, E. (1952). *Personalism*. London: Routledge and Kagan Paul Ltd.

Nancy, J. (1991). *The inoperative community*. Minneapolis, MN: University of Minnesota Press.

Navarro, M. (2014). 'Poor door' in a New York tower opens a fight over affordable housing. *New York Times*, August 26, https://www.nytimes.com/2014/08/27/nyreg ion/separate-entryways-for-new-york-condo-buyers-and-renters-create-an-affo rdable-housing-dilemma.html, accessed November 20, 2017.

Nealon, J. (1998). *Alterity politics*. Durham, NC: Duke University Press.

Nelson, L. (2017). Chaffetz: Americans should forego new iPhone to afford healthcare. *Politico*, 3 March, http://www.politico.com/story/2017/03/jason-chaffetz-ne w-gop-health-care-plan-235762, accessed July 11, 2017.

Nelson, R. (2001). *Economics as religion*. University Park: University of Pennsylvania Press.

Nichols, J. (2011). *The "S" word: A short history of an American tradition. . .socialism*. New York: Verso.

Niebuhr, H. (1942). War as the judgment of God. *Christian Century*, 59, 630–633.

Niebuhr, H. (1943). War as crucifixion. *Christian Century*, 60, 512–515.

Niebuhr, H. R. (1963). *The responsible self*. New York: Harper and Row.

Niebuhr, H. R. (1989). *Faith on earth*. New Haven, CT: Yale University Press.

Noddings, N. (1984). *Caring: A feminine approach to ethics and moral education*. Berkeley, CA: University of California Press.

Novak, M. (1982). *The spirit of democratic capitalism*. New York: Simon and Schuster.

Novak, M. (1987). *Toward a theology of the corporation*. Washington, DC: AEI Press.

O'Brien, D. and Shannon, T. (Eds.) (1977). *Renewing the earth: Catholic documents on peace, justice, and liberation*. New York: Image Books.

OECD. (2015). In it together: Why less inequality benefits all. *OECDpublishing*, https://read.oecd-ilibrary.org/employment/in-it-together-why-less-inequality-ben efits-all_9789264235120-en#page4, accessed November 19, 2017.

Ortega y Gasset, J. (1957). *Man and people*. New York: W. W. Norton.

Pannenberg, W. (1969). *Theology and the kingdom of God*. Philadelphia: Westminster Press.

Parenti, C. (2011). *Tropic of chaos: Climate change and the new geography of violence*. New York: Nation Books.

Patton, J. (1993). *Pastoral care in context: An introduction to pastoral care*. Louisville, KY: Westminster John Knox.

Paul VI. (1967). *Populorum Progressio*. https://www.cctwincities.org/wp-content/ uploads/2015/10/Populorum-Progressio.pdf, accessed July 11, 2018.

Piketty, T. (2014). *Capital in the 21st century*. Cambridge: Belknap Press.

Pitt, W. (2015). A corrupt CEO busted? Well, Merry Christmas. *Truthout*, 20 December, http://www.truth-out.org/opinion/item/34110-a-corrupt-ceo-busted-well-merry-christmas. accessed August 20, 2017.

Pius XI. (1931). *Quadragesimo Anno.* http://w2.vatican.va/content/pius-xi/en/encyc licals/documents/hf_p-xi_enc_19310515_quadragesimo-anno.html, accessed July 12, 2018.

Poling J. (2002). *Render unto God: Economic vulnerability, family violence, and pastoral theology.* Eugene, OR: Wipf and Stock.

Pomerleau, A., Bolduc, D., Gérard Malcuit, G., and Cossette, L. (1990). Pink or blue: Environmental gender stereotypes in the first two years of life. *Sex Roles: A Journal of Research*, 22(5), 359–367.

Putnam, R. (2000). *Bowling alone: The collapse and revival of American community.* New York: Simon and Schuster.

Putnam, R. (2015). *Our kids: The American dream in crisis.* New York: Simon and Schuster.

Rahner, K. (1984). A way to faith. In Rahner (Ed.), *The encyclopedia of theology: The concise sacramentum mundi.* New York: Crossroad.

Ramsay, N. (2002). Navigating racial difference as a white pastoral theologian. *Journal of Pastoral Theology*, 12(2), 11–27.

Ramsay, N. (2004). *Pastoral care and counseling: Redefining the paradigms.* Nashville, TN: Abingdon.

Ramsay, N. (2017). Resisting asymmetries of power: Intersectionality as a resource for practices of care. *Journal of Pastoral Theology*, 27(2), 83–97.

Ramsay, N. (2018). *Pastoral theology and care: Critical trajectories in theory and practice.* Oxford: John Wiley and Sons.

Ransom, J. (1997). *Foucault's discipline: The politics of subjectivity.* Durham, NC: Duke University Press.

Raz, J. (2001). *Value, respect, and attachment.* Cambridge: Cambridge University Press.

Reich, R. (2007). *Supercapitalism: The transformation of business, democracy, and everyday life.* New York: Vintage Books.

Reich, R. (2015). *Saving capitalism: For the many, not the few.* New York: Random House.

Rieff, P. (1987/1966). *Triumph of the therapeutic: Uses of faith after Freud.* New York: Harper and Row.

Reno, R. (2007). Stanley Hauerwas. In P. Scott and W. Cavanaugh (Eds.), *The Blackwell companion to political theology*, 302–316. Oxford: Blackwell Publishing.

Rice University. (2015, March 9). Eviction can result in depression, poorer health and higher stress. *ScienceDaily*, www.sciencedaily.com/releases/2015/03/1503091 74831.htm, accessed June 21, 2018.

Rieger, J. (2009). *No rising tide: Theology, economics, and the future.* Minneapolis: Fortress Press.

Ritterman, J. (2014). The beloved community: Martin Luther King's prescription for a healthy society. *Huffington Post*, March 21, http://www.huffingtonpost.com/ jeffrey-ritterman/the-beloved-community-dr-_b_4583249.html, accessed February 10, 2017.

Rizzuto, A. M. (1979). *The birth of the living God.* Chicago: University of Chicago Press.

Robinson, F. (1999). *Globalizing care: Ethics, feminist theory, and international relations*. Boulder, CO: Westview Press.

Robinson, F. (2011). *The ethics of care: A feminist approach to human security*. Philadelphia: Temple University Press.

Rogers-Vaughn, B. (2014). Blessed are those who mourn: Depression as political resistance. *Journal of Pastoral Psychology*, 63(4), 489–502.

Rogers-Vaughn, B. (2016). *Caring for souls in a neoliberal age*. New York: Palgrave.

Rucker, D. (1980). Selves into persons: Another legacy from John Dewey. *Rice University Studies*, 66(4), 103–118.

Rumscheidt, B. (1998). *No room for grace: Pastoral theology and the dehumanization in the global economy*. Eugene, OR: Wipf and Stock.

Ryan, A. (2012). *On politics: A history of political thought*. New York: Liveright Publishing.

Said, E. (1979). *Orientalism*. New York: Vintage Books.

Said, E. (1994). *Culture and imperialism*. New York: Vintage Books.

Sandel, M. (2012). *What money can't buy: The moral limits of markets*. New York: Farrar, Straus and Giroux.

Sanders, C. (2017). *A brief guide to ministry with LGBTQIA youth*. Louisville, KY: Westminster John Knox.

Sassen, S. (2014). *Expulsions: Brutality and complexity in the global economy*. Cambridge, MA: Belknap Press.

Sayer, A. (2005). *The moral significance of class*. Cambridge: Cambridge University Press.

Schafer, R. (1990). *Aspects of internalization*. Madison, CT. International Universities Press.

Scheib, K. (2004). *Challenging invisibility: Practices of care with older women*. St. Louis: Chalice Press.

Scheib, K. (2016). *Pastoral care: Telling the stories of our lives*. Nashville, TN: Abingdon Press.

Schore, A. (2003). *Affect regulation and the repair of the self*. New York: W. W. Norton.

Schmidt. (2016). Japanese leader offers condolences in visit to Pearl Harbor. *New York Times*, http://www.nytimes.com/2016/12/27/us/politics/pearl-harbor-abe-obama-visit.html?_r=0, accessed June 25, 2018.

Schnarch, D. (1997). *Passionate marriage: Love, sex, and intimacy in emotionally committed relationships*. New York: W. W. Norton and Company.

Schweickert, D. (1993). *Against capitalism*. Boulder, CO: Westview.

Schweickert, D. (2002). *After capitalism*. New York: Rowman and Littlefield.

Sevenhuijsen, S. (1998). *Citizenship and the ethics of care*. London: Routledge Press.

Shepherd, K. (2012). 19 Percent of Congress is women: Why not half. *Mother Jones*, 20 November, http://www.motherjones.com/politics/2012/11/19-percent-congress-women-why-not-half, accessed November 27, 2016.

Shinn, L. (2015). The racial wealth gap. https://www.forbes.com/sites/laurashin/2015/03/26/the-racial-wealth-gap-why-a-typical-white-household-has-16-times-the-wealth-of-a-black-one/#792c0e51f45e, accessed July 10, 2018.

Silva, J. (2013). *Coming up short: Working class adulthood in the age of uncertainty.* Oxford: Oxford University Press.

Skelton, R. and Miller, V. (March 17, 2016). The environmental justice movement. *Natural Resources Defense Council,* https://www.nrdc.org/stories/environment al-justice-movement, accessed June 21, 2018.

Sklair, L. (2013). *Globalization: Capitalism and its alternatives.* Oxford: Oxford University Press.

Smiley, T. and Ritz, D. (2014). *Death of a King.* New York, NY: Little, Brown, and Company.

Smith, A. (1982). *The relational self: Ethics and therapy from a Black church perspective.* Nashville: Abingdon Press.

Smith, A. (2003). *The wealth of nations.* New York: Bantam Books.

Soss, J., Fording, R., and Sanford, S. (2011). *Disciplining the poor: Neoliberal paternalism and the persistent power of race.* Chicago: University of Chicago Press.

Sroufe, A. (1995). *Emotional development.* Cambridge: Cambridge University Press.

Steeves, P. (1996). Constituting the transcendent community: Some phenomenological implications of Husserl's social ontology. In L. Langsdorf and S. Watson (Eds.), *Phenomenology, interpretation and community.* Albany, NY: SUNY Press.

Stern, D. N. (1985). *The interpersonal world of the infant.* New York: Basic Books.

Stern, D. B. (1997). *Unformulated experience: From dissociation to imagination in psychoanalysis.* Hillsdale, NJ: Analytic Press.

Stiglitz, J. (2012). *The price of inequality.* New York: W. W. Norton.

Stiglitz, J. (2015). *The great divide: Unequal societies and what we can do about them.* New York: W. W. Norton.

Stone, O. and Kuznick, P. (2012). *The untold history of the United States.* New York: Gallery Books.

Strauss, L. and Cropsey, J. (1987). *History of political philosophy 3rd Edition,* Leo Strauss and Joseph Cropsey (Eds.). Chicago: University of Chicago Press.

Streeck, W. (2017). *Buying time: The delayed crisis of democratic capitalism.* New York: Verso.

Sung, J. (2007). *Desire, market, and religion.* London: SCM Press.

Taylor, C. (1989). *Sources of the self.* Cambridge, MA: Harvard University Press.

Taylor, C. (2007). *Modern social imaginaries.* Durham, NC: Duke University Press.

Taylor, M. (2015). *The executed God: The way of the cross in lockdown America.* Minneapolis, MN: Fortress Press.

Teachout, Z. (2014). *Corruption in America.* Cambridge, MA: Harvard University Press.

Tillich, P. (1952). *Courage to be.* New Haven, CT: Yale University Press.

Tillich, P. (1957). *Dynamics of faith.* New York: Harper and Row.

Tillich, P. (1963). *Systematic theology, vol.3.* Chicago, IL: University of Chicago Press.

Trevarthen, C. (1993). *Playing into reality: Conversations with the infant communicator.* Winnicott Studies, 7, Spring. London: Karnac Books.

Trevarthen, C. (1998). The concept and foundations of infant intersubjectivity. In S. Bräten (Ed.), *Intersubjective communication and emotions in early ontogeny,* 15–46. Cambridge: Cambridge University Press.

Tronick, E. and Gianino, A. (1986). Interactive mismatch and repair: Challenges to the coping infant. *Zero to three bulletin of the national center clinical infant program*, 5, 1–6.

Tronick, E. and Cohn, J. (1989). Infant-mother face-to-face interaction: Age and gender differences in coordination and the occurrence of miscoordination. *Child Development*, 60, 85–92.

Tronto, J. (1993). *Moral boundaries: A political argument for an ethic of care*. New York: Routledge Press.

Tutu, D. (1999). *No Future without Forgiveness*. New York: Doubleday.

United Nations Declaration of Human Rights, https://www.ohchr.org/EN/UDHR/Documents/UDHR_Translations/eng.pdf, accessed January 4, 2018.

United States Census Bureau. (2018). Income and poverty data. http://www.census.go v/topics/income-poverty/data/tables.html, accessed June 21, 2018.

United States Department of Justice Civil Rights Division. (2015). *Investigation of the Fergusson Police Department*. https://www.justice.gov/sites/default/files/o pa/press-releases/attachments/2015/03/04/ferguson_police_department_report.pdf, accessed April 4, 2017.

Urbina, I. (2017). Southern bellwether. In J. Gantz (Ed.), *The age of inequality*, 69–70. New York: Verso.

van den Brink, B. (2007). Damaged life: Recognition and power. In B. Van den Brink and D. Owen (Eds.), *Recognition and power*, 79–99. Cambridge: Cambridge University Press.

van Deusen Hunsinger, D. (2015). *Bearing the unbearable: Trauma, gospel, and pastoral care*. Grand Rapids, MI: William B. Eerdmans Publishing Company.

Vatter, M. (2015). Foucault and Hayek: Republican law and liberal civil society. In V. Lemm and M. Vatter (Eds.), *The government of life: Foucault, biopolitics, and neoliberalism*, 163–186. New York: Fordham University Press.

Vega, T. (2016). Blacks still far behind whites in wealth and income. *CNN Money*, June 27, http://money.cnn.com/2016/06/27/news/economy/racial-wealth-gap-bl acks-whites/index.html, accessed July 14, 2018.

Wacquant, L. (2009). *Punishing the poor: The neoliberal government of social insecurity*. Durham, NC: Duke University Press.

Walzer, M. (2012). *In God's shadow: Politics and the Hebrew Bible*. New Haven: Yale University Press.

Weber, M. (1992). *The protestant ethic and the spirit of capitalism*. London: Routledge Press.

Weeks, D. (2016). *Democracy in poverty: A view from below*. Boston, MA: Edmond J. Safra Center for Ethics.

Weil, S. (1952). *The need for roots: Prelude to a declaration of duties towards mankind*. London: Routledge.

West, C. (2001). *Race matters*. Boston, MA: Beacon Press.

White, E. (1998). *Saying good-bye: A time for growth for congregations and pastors*. An Alban Institute Publication.

Wimberly, E. (2003). *Reclaiming God, reclaiming dignity: African American pastoral care*. Nashville, TN: Abingdon Press.

Wimberly, E. (2006). *African American pastoral care and counseling: The politics of oppression and empowerment.* Nashville, TN: Abingdon Press.

Winnicott, D. (1960). The theory of the parent-infant relationship. *International Journal of Psycho-Analysis*, 41, 585–595.

Wise, T. (2010). *Color-Blind: The rise of post-racial politics and the retreat from racial equality.* San Francisco: City Lights Books.

Witt, S. (Summer, 1997). Parental influence on children's socialization to gender roles. *Adolescence*, 32(126), 253–259.

Wolff, R. (2012). *Occupy the economy: Challenging capitalism.* San Francisco: City Light Books.

Wolff, R. and Resnick, S. (1987). *Economics: Marxian versus neoclassical.* Baltimore: Johns Hopkins University Press.

Wolff, R. and Resnick, S. (2012). *Contending economic theories.* Cambridge: MIT Press.

Wolin, S. (2008). *Democracy incorporated.* Princeton: Princeton University Press.

Wolin. S. (2016). *Politics and vision.* Princeton, NJ: Princeton University Press.

Wolin. S. (2016a). *Fugitive democracy.* Princeton, NJ: Princeton University Press.

Woods, E. (2017). *The origins of capitalism.* New York: Verso.

World Council of Churches. (2002). *Justice the heart of sustainability*, https://www.oikoumene.org/en/resources/documents/wcc-programmes/public-witness-addressing-power-affirming-peace/poverty-wealth-and-ecology/neoliberal-paradigm/justice-the-heart-of-sustainability?searchterm=international+relations+environment, accessed December 27, 2017.

Young, I. M. (1990). *Justice and the politics of difference.* Princeton, NJ: Princeton University Press.

Zinn, H. (1998). *A people's history of the United States.* New York: HarperPerennial.

Zinn, H. (2004). *Voices of a people's history of the United States.* New York: Seven Stories Press.

Zizioulas, J. (1985). *Being as communion.* Crestwood, NY: St. Vladimir's Seminary Press.

Zizioulas, J. (2006). *Communion as otherness.* New York: T and T Clark.

Index

absolute dependence, 76
Adams, John, 232
ALEC. *See* American Legislative
    Exchange Council
Alexander, Michelle, 24, 59
alterpolis, 198
American Legislative Exchange Council
    (ALEC), 82, 84, 86, 182
Amery, Jean, 43
Amnesty International, 214
Anderson, Carol, 191
Appiah, Kwame, 132
Arendt, Hannah, 24, 69, 72
Aristotle, 101
Arthur, Kenneth, 196
associations:
    atomistic/contractual, 110–13;
    communities, 109–15;
    economic, 110;
    mutual/personal, 110–11, 113–15;
    organic/functional, 110–13
atomistic/contractual associations,
    110–13
attributes of care, 12–28. *See also* care
    dispositions, 12, 22–24;
    equal regard, 12, 24–27;
    knowledge, 12–22

Bacon, Francis, 76

Baker, Timothy, 131
Baldwin, James, 137, 169, 194
Baptist, Edward, 186
Becker, Gary, 172
belief, 38
Bellah, Robert, 199
Benhabib, Seyla, 29, 208
Bethlehem Steel, 228
Bill of Rights, 136
biological needs, 9
biopower. *See* governmentality
Black Friday, 151
Black Lives Matter Movement, 23, 93
Boer, Roland, 184
Boff, Leonardo, 3
Brown, Wendy, 70, 73, 95, 148
Bubeck, Diemut, 4
Buber, Martin, 51
Buffet, Warren, 163
Butler, Smedley, 230

capitalism, 52, 64, 65, 87, 138–40;
    agrarian, 141;
    classical, 143;
    and classism, 179–82;
    definition of, 142–43;
    flexible, 196;
    global, 218, 219;
    international relations and, 218–19;

About the Author

Ryan LaMothe is Professor of pastoral care and counseling at Saint Meinrad Seminary and School of Theology. He has written numerous articles and books in the areas of pastoral counseling, psychoanalysis, psychology of religion, and political pastoral theology. In 2017 he received a Springer Publishing Award: Transforming the World One Article at a Time.

Lightning Source UK Ltd.
Milton Keynes UK
UKHW041459241121
394461UK00020B/10